OUTSIDE THE MAGIC CIRCLE

The Autobiography of Virginia Foster Durr

Edited by Hollinger F. Barnard

With a Foreword by Studs Terkel

A TOUCHSTONE BOOK
Published by Simon & Schuster, Inc.
New York

First Touchstone Edition, 1987

Published by Simon & Schuster, Inc.
Simon & Schuster Building
Rockefeller Center
1230 Avenue of the Americas
New York, New York 10020

TOUCHSTONE and colophon are registered trademarks of
Simon & Schuster, Inc.

Manufactured in the United States of America

10 9 8 7 6 5 4 3 2 1 Pbk.

Library of Congress Cataloging in Publication Data

Durr, Virginia Foster.
    Outside the magic circle.

    (A Touchstone book)
    Includes index.
    1. Durr, Virginia Foster.   2. Durr, Clifford.
3. Civil rights workers—United States—Biography.
4. Lawyers' wives—United States—Biography.
5. New Deal, 1933–1939.   6. Afro-Americans—Civil
rights—History—20th century.   7. Afro-Americans—
Civil rights—Alabama—History—20th century.
I. Barnard, Hollinger F., 1943-   II. Title.
CT275.D8848A3   1987   973.91′092′4 [B]   87-9777

ISBN 0-671-63855-6 Pbk.

Virginia Durr said it: there were three ways
for a well-brought-up young Southern
white woman to go.

She could be the actress, playing out
the stereotype of the Southern belle.
Gracious to "the colored help," flirtatious to
her powerful father-in-law, and offering a
sweet, winning smile to the world. In short,
going with the wind.

If she had a spark of independence or
worse, creativity, she could go crazy—on
the dark, shadowy street traveled by more
than one stunning Southern belle.

Or she could be the rebel. She could
step outside the magic circle, abandon
privilege, and challenge this way of life.
Ostracism, bruises of all sorts, and
defamation would be her lot. Her reward
would be a truly examined life. And a world
she would otherwise never have known.

—STUDS TERKEL

CONTENTS

ILLUSTRATIONS

FOREWORD

VIRGINIA DURR said it: there were three ways for a well-brought-up young Southern white woman to go.

She could be the actress, playing out the stereotype of the Southern belle. Gracious to "the colored help," flirtatious to her powerful father-in-law, and offering a sweet, winning smile to the world. In short, going with the wind.

If she had a spark of independence or worse, creativity, she could go crazy—on the dark, shadowy street traveled by more than one stunning Southern belle.

Or she could be the rebel. She could step outside the magic circle, abandon privilege, and challenge this way of life. Ostracism, bruises of all sorts, and defamation would be her lot. Her reward would be a truly examined life. And a world she would otherwise never have known.

It is the third road Virginia Durr traveled. In this remarkable memoir, we are witness to the flowering of a unique "personality." Her original title for her book was "The Emancipation of Pure White Southern Womanhood." In a sense, this work is Virginia's own Emancipation Proclamation.

The depression of the thirties was her first revelatory moment. "Up to this time, I had been a conformist, a Southern snob. I actually thought the only people who amounted to anything were the very small group I belonged to. I valued the idea of being well-born." After all, she was vice-president of the Junior League. "What I learned during the Depression changed all that. I saw a blinding light like Saul on the road to Damascus." Even now, I hear her laugh as she recalled those times. It is a laugh of astonishment; not so much a shock of recognition as a recognition of shock. "It was the first time I had seen the other side of the tracks. The rickets, the pellagra—it shook me up. I saw the world as it really was."

From that moment on, she was dynamite. And has been so ever since. I first met her in 1939–or was it 1940? She and Mary McLeod Bethune were on a speaking tour, battling the poll tax. It was an exhilarating experience for me in the audience at Chicago's Orchestra Hall. I've a hunch it was so for the other 4,000 Northerners in the house. Of course, the celebrated black spokeswoman impressed us all. But it was the tall, large-boned, "well brought up" Southern white woman who knocked us out. She set our hearts on fire.

As I went backstage to meet her, she immediately handed me a stack of leaflets. Of course. There were things to be done. I was a member of her battalion before I knew what hit me. Saying no to Virginia Durr was as meaningless as Canute holding back the waves.

It was inevitable that this troublemaker get in trouble. All sorts of trouble. There were early intimations during World War II. She lived in Washington, where her husband, Clifford (an equally remarkable being), worked for the New Deal of FDR. She had taken into her already overcrowded household a Japanese couple and their young child and Jessica Mitford and her young child. "We were under eternal vigilance. By that time, I took it casually. The children would cry out: 'Mother, milkman's here.' 'Mother, laundryman's here.' 'Mother, FBI's here.' " Again, she laughs. Her humor, in face of adversity, has always been her safety valve. And did she need it in the days ahead! With the cold war coming on fast and witch-hunting in vogue, "our surveillance had begun. Two years ago," says Virginia, turning eighty, "they were still watching me." The woman would not behave. She was simply nonadjustable to the fashion of the day. The blinding light was to affect her for the rest of her life.

Who can ever forget her appearance before the Eastland Committee? It has become part of folklore. Remember the climate. McCarthy was riding high. So was the Massa of Sunflower County. Groveling and self-flagellation were in high fashion. Or low, depending on how you look at it. Informers had become the darlings of the Respectables.

This woman, though, was obstinate and perverse. In fact, she was downright unfriendly. In her well-brought-up way, she told Senator Jim Eastland to go to hell. Recently, I reminded her of a photograph I had come across: Virginia Durr powdering her nose as the senator fumed. It had appeared on the front pages of many newspapers. "Well, I just said, 'I stand in total and utter contempt of this committee and I won't have anything to do with it.' I'm still a Southern snob, I guess. I thought Eastland was as common as pig tracks. I had total contempt for him as a person and as a senator. Instead of getting frightened, I got mad."

Her intransigence, as well as Cliff's, cost them quite a bit. Hard times were upon them. During the Korean War, with anti-red hysteria mounting, Virginia did it again. She signed a petition opposing the war's extension. The *Denver Post*'s headline: "Wife of Counsel of Farmers' Union Signs Red Petition." Cliff's job was up for grabs unless he could persuade his wife to retract. "They wanted me to sign a statement that I was a poor, weak woman who was duped by vicious reds." Boy, were they barking up the wrong tree!

One of the most moving passages in this impassioned work is her remembrance of the moment. "I happened to look out the window and there he [Cliff] was, hobbling up the walk on his crutches." He had just undergone painful back surgery. " 'What in the world are you doing home?' I asked. 'I've been fired. They called me into the office and showed me this letter they wanted you to sign and said that you wouldn't sign it. They said you would have to sign it or I would be fired. . . . I told them I would never allow you to sign a letter like that.' "

Back home in Montgomery, Cliff and Virginia, bruised and broke, were still at it. Something big was about to happen and they were in the middle of it. Of course. One day, Rosa Parks—a gentle, educated black tailor's assistant at the Montgomery Fair department store who had sewed for the Durrs on occasion and had become a friend—left work one day very tired. She sat in the bus, up front, and was arrested. Clifford Durr went down to the jail that night. The rest is history.

Virginia, up in years—she's slowed a step or two—is still at it: getting the next thing done.

STUDS TERKEL

EDITOR'S NOTE

THE EASIEST WAY to introduce Virginia Foster Durr is by saying that she is Dr. Sterling Foster's daughter, Clifford Durr's wife, and Justice Hugo Black's sister-in-law. But the easy introduction will not suffice. The family relationships are interesting—and Virginia is quite interested in those relationships—but she is an important person in her own right, and her autobiography is much more than a family history.

Virginia was born and reared in the South, in Birmingham, Alabama, shortly after the turn of the century. In 1933 she and her husband Cliff and their first daughter, Ann, moved to Washington, D.C., where they lived throughout the New Deal years. Cliff and Virginia and their three younger daughters, Lucy, Tilla, and Lulah, moved back to Alabama, to Montgomery, in 1951 on the eve of the civil rights struggle.

In each of these times and places Virginia befriended interesting and "important" people and turned her considerable energy to work that she considered important. As a young woman in Birmingham in the early thirties, she conceived and organized two major projects to relieve depression-era suffering: she talked local dairies into donating milk for distribution to the poor instead of pouring the unsold milk down gutters, and she planned free concerts in the city auditorium featuring the local firemen's and policemen's bands. When she and Cliff moved to Washington, Virginia became active in the movement to abolish the poll tax and later led that effort as vice-chairman of the National Committee to Abolish the Poll Tax. After a series of personal calamities forced the family to return to Alabama in 1951, Virginia helped bolster their waning fortunes by working as her husband's legal secretary, but she also found time to provide room, board, and moral support for many of the young civil rights workers who traveled to and through Montgomery. Through these various projects—and Virginia's own

gregariousness—she came to know Eleanor Roosevelt, Mary McLeod Bethune, John L. Lewis, Rosa Parks, Coretta and Martin Luther King, Jr.,
and many others whose names and accomplishments are familiar.

Virginia's autobiography is the story of these times, places, and people.
Because Virginia has an uncanny memory for detail, the story is remarkably
accurate. But the importance of this work lies not in accurate presentation
of historical events; professional historians are trained to make those pre-
sentations. The importance of Virginia's story is her personal perception of
the times, places, and people that she has known.

The possibility of a Virginia Durr autobiography first began to take
shape in the mid-1970s. Virginia's friends had for some time been urging
her to write such a work, but Studs Terkel suggested that she tell her story
instead. It was a task she was well suited to do from having told the stories
so often to friends and to the many reporters, students, and historians who
came to interview her.

The first effort to tape Virginia's life history occurred in 1974. James
Sargent had interviewed Cliff Durr for Columbia University's Oral History
Collection in April of 1974. When Columbia shortly thereafter asked to
produce a similar oral memoir of Virginia, her only request was that she
select the interviewer so that she would not be telling her life story to a
stranger. That series of interviews was conducted in the fall and winter of
that same year by historian William D. Barnard.

In the spring of 1975, Jacquelyn Hall, director of the Southern Oral
History Program at The University of North Carolina at Chapel Hill, made
arrangements to tape a series of interviews with Virginia for the Program's
study of Southern women after suffrage. That study, funded in part by the
Rockefeller Foundation, was designed to produce a collection of oral memoirs of Southern women who were active in public life between 1920, when
women won the right to vote, and the 1960s, when a new feminist movement emerged. The Virginia Durr interviews for that study were conducted
by Jacquelyn Hall and by Sue Thrasher, who was at that time co-director
of the Institute for Southern Studies.

The Virginia Durr memoir that was taped in 1975 was one of the first
in the SOHP study of Southern women after suffrage. And it proved to be
one of the most exciting. In the words of the interviewers, Virginia's memoir "is filled with vivid and irreverent vignettes and with the observations
of a seasoned political veteran. The interview's chief theme was Virginia's
attempt to come to terms with the social and psychological forces that made
her who she is. She approached our conversation with painful honesty; the
interview at times became an exhausting emotional and intellectual engagement with the past. Virginia is a consummate storyteller. Each character in the drama of her life was fully realized in the telling; each theme
was interwoven in a complex pattern of significance. She was what every

practitioner of oral history hopes for: a source of vivid historical detail and a master of historical interpretation."

Those spring 1975 interviews were so rich and the collaboration so promising that Sue Thrasher remained with Virginia for another year and recorded more than thirty additional hours of reminiscences to provide the material to complete the autobiography that Virginia had already begun. Sue's affection and admiration for Virginia made it possible for Virginia to talk freely. And her love of laughter prompted Virginia—who also loves to laugh—to remember even the painful times with good humor.

About the time the Thrasher interviews were completed, in March 1976, Wilbur H. Hinton, manager of the public television station in Montgomery, began a series of video tapings of interviews with Virginia. Those interviews continued into 1977 and were conducted by Mr. Hinton, public television reporter Marie Antoon, and William D. Barnard.

A number of other sets of interviews of Virginia Durr are in existence, but this book is based upon the following interviews:

the transcripts of the oral history memoirs of Clifford and Virginia Durr in the Columbia Oral History Collection, which are copyrighted by The Trustees of Columbia University in The City of New York, 1976, and are used by permission;

the transcripts of the interviews of Virginia Durr conducted for the Southern Oral History Program of The University of North Carolina at Chapel Hill by Jacquelyn Hall and Sue Thrasher in 1975; these interviews are on deposit in the Southern Historical Collection, Library of The University of North Carolina at Chapel Hill (Interview of Virginia F. Durr in the Southern Oral History Program Collection, #4007), and are used by permission of the Southern Oral History Program;

the transcripts of the interviews of Virginia Durr conducted by Sue Thrasher in 1975 and 1976; these interviews are on deposit in the Southern Historical Collection, Library of The University of North Carolina at Chapel Hill, and are used by permission of Ms. Thrasher;

the transcripts of the interviews of Virginia Durr conducted for Alabama Public Television by Wilbur H. Hinton, Marie Antoon, and William D. Barnard in 1976 and 1977 and used by permission of Mr. Hinton.

The Southern Oral History Program interviews and the Sue Thrasher interviews, all on deposit in the Southern Historical Collection at The University of North Carolina at Chapel Hill, constitute the most complete oral memoir of Virginia Durr—more than 1,000 pages of transcription altogether. Those interviews are the primary source for this book. The Columbia and Alabama Public Television interviews are used interstitially, to tell a story that does not appear in the primary interviews or to augment a story that does appear there. Because the several interviews are now interwoven, the text itself does not include citations to the different sources. Only the portions of the Columbia memoir of Clifford Durr that appear in Virginia's autobiography are identified by source.

The book is Virginia's own telling, with two exceptions. Parts of Cliff Durr's Columbia memoir appear in chapter 14, "Cliff," and in chapter 21, "White Southerners." And the story of the Eastland hearing is told partly by Cliff. The Eastland hearing interviews were taped in the winter before Cliff's death. Cliff was a rather quiet and gentle-mannered man. That he would interrupt Virginia's interviews to relate portions of that story himself is a clue to the anger he still felt about those hearings.

I have pieced the various interview materials together into a whole that is, by and large, chronological; some of the chapters on the Washington years are more thematic than chronological. I have deleted interviewer questions and comments, reduced twice- and thrice-told tales to the one best telling, culled most of the rhetorical traces of casual speech, and added phrases when necessary to tie paragraphs together or to identify someone Virginia has mentioned. Virginia has worked closely in this effort, especially in correcting names and adding details.

As in any work of this sort, a number of people provided personal and professional assistance. John Rosenberg first introduced me to the Durrs and made clear to me their importance. Howell Raines encouraged the editing of this work, both by example in his own oral history, *My Soul Is Rested,* and by practical suggestions. Wythe Holt gave legal assistance with a generosity that is his hallmark. Culpepper Clark, Alan Heldman, and Jim Barton gave good advice. Nancy Zeilig gave up more than one lunch hour to search for the *Denver Post* article that appears in chapter 16. Helen Delpar, Bob Mitchell, and Virginia Hamilton read the manuscript for historical accuracy, but responded with suggestions that included that and more. Virginia's daughters—Ann, Lucy, Tilla, and Lulah—contributed photographs and recollections and moral support.

Studs Terkel has graciously contributed the foreword to Virginia's autobiography. Mr. Terkel is a pioneer in oral history, with works such as *Hard Times, Working,* and his most recent book, *"The Good War": An Oral History of World War II.* As a personal friend of Virginia, and the person who first suggested that she tell her story instead of writing it, his role as author of the foreword is special, and he has set a fine tone for the book.

Before I became involved in the production of this book, I often wondered why authors invariably acknowledged their gratitude to editors, copyeditors, and the like. Now I understand. Malcolm MacDonald, Director of The University of Alabama Press, has remained enthusiastic about Virginia's book for a longer period of time than anyone had a right to expect. The staff of the University Press has answered my numerous telephone calls with patience and good cheer even though, as often as not, my reason for calling was to announce a new problem. Joanne Ainsworth of the Guilford Group, copyeditor for this book, combined professional skill with personal interest in the work to make Virginia's book accurate, clear, and a joy to read.

Ruth Kibbey and Kitty Sassaman typed the final manuscript. They did so with characteristic skill and care, but it was their enthusiasm for the story itself that was most gratifying. They became so interested in Virginia's life story that they swapped copy each evening so that they could each read what the other had typed that day.

Several friends have contributed to this book even though none of them read a word of it before publication. Linda Albritton, Corella Johnson, Caroline Powell, David Myers, Sam Pointer, Jr., and Paul Toppins all shared their time and themselves with me in a number of ways that helped to move the manuscript from beginning to end.

My parents, Margaret Pace Farmer and Curren Adams Farmer, read most of the interviews over my shoulder as I transcribed them and said, "Yes, that's what the depression was like. That's how it was in the South. I remember seeing children who looked the way Virginia describes them." My children, Will, Meg, and Josh, proofread the galleys aloud and almost never complained.

When husband and wife share the work on a manuscript, it is often difficult to determine whose name should appear on the title page. Bill Barnard suggested that I transcribe the Durr tapes, that I edit the transcriptions, and that I submit the edited work for publication. He also propped me up while I accepted all these suggestions. In addition, he interviewed Virginia for the Columbia University series, and he had a substantial hand in the final editing of this book for publication. When I look at the Virginia Durr book, I will always see Bill's name on it, too—just as I, with much less justification, see my name on Bill's book, *Dixiecrats and Democrats*.

It is Virginia herself, of course, who has contributed most to this book, both in living the life and in telling the story. She is her own best biographer. I only hope that we have not edited out the twinkle in her eye and the hearty chuckle freely given. The reader who fails to see the twinkle and hear the chuckle will miss too much.

HOLLINGER F. BARNARD

PART ONE

BIRMINGHAM

1903–1933

I

Family, Nursie, the Church

My father's family came from Union Springs, Alabama, which is right in the heart of the black belt, and my mother's family came from Memphis, Tennessee. Before I was born my father went to Birmingham as the preacher for South Highland Presbyterian Church, which is on the corner of Highland Avenue and Twenty-first Street. I was born in the parsonage. My mother said that from the beginning I was an extremely greedy and red-faced yelling baby. I was considered the bad child of the family. I was the youngest and evidently was demanding from the beginning.

As far as I know, my father's family was English, and the name Foster comes from "forester," the king's forester. Probably they were woodchoppers, and they arrived in this country way back, about 1700. The story was that one brother settled in Massachusetts and one brother settled in Virginia around South Boston, where there are still a lot of Fosters. Dr. Luther Foster, who is president of Tuskegee Institute, came from that area. Dr. Foster is black, and he and I can't claim kin, but a lot of black and white Fosters live in that area.

My great-grandfather came south with General Greene's army in the Revolutionary War and fought at Cowpens and Kings Mountain. After the war was over, the state of Georgia gave General Greene a land grant to settle his soldiers on. It's called Greene County.

My great-grandfather married a girl named Hannah Johnson. I was told that because of the Indian wars, they met in a stockade. Of course, the white settlers were taking the land away from the Indians. But Great-grandfather and Hannah were married and had thirteen children—twelve sons and one daughter. My grandfather was one of them. They prospered and did very well. My grandfather was sent to Jefferson Medical School in Philadelphia and became a doctor. Then he came back to Georgia, and about the 1840s he met my grandmother. She was a Heard and her mother was a MacGruder. They were Scottish Presbyterians. She was only fifteen when they married and went to Alabama. They settled in Union Springs, and evidently they brought some slaves with them.

Union Springs at that time was a very rich part of the country. People settled there as part of the migration from the old worn-out lands in the East to the West—to Alabama, Mississippi, and Louisiana and finally to Texas. They didn't know how to conserve the land and fertilize it in those days, so they had to get fresh land. Union Springs has quite a history because there was a terrible competition among the slave traders. One man poisoned the big spring and killed all the slaves the other trader was selling. Horrible things like that come out of the past and chill your blood. Whatever glamour the society had, it was based on this terrible slave system.

My grandfather acquired a lot of land in Union Springs. Outside the town is a ridge they call Chunnenuggee Ridge. It is above the lowlands where the slaves worked and cotton was grown. My family settled on that because the high land was thought to be outside the malaria belt. All plantation owners lived up on the ridge. Of course, no one really knew what caused malaria. They thought it was the miasma of the swamps. They didn't know it was mosquitoes.

My grandmother had fifteen children, but a lot of them died. The Foster graveyard down in Union Springs is just full of little graves: "Such-and-such child that died of summer complaint at the age of nine months." Out of the fifteen children, only four lived to be old. Two of the boys, I was told, were killed in the Civil War.

My grandfather opposed the Civil War. He was a Whig and by that time he had become quite prosperous. He thought the nation should settle the slavery issue the way England did, by the government buying up the slaves and recompensing the owners. He hated William Lowndes Yancey. He thought Yancey was a firebrand and was plunging the South into war. Since Grandfather was opposed to the war, he bought a substitute to fight for him. So Grandfather didn't go to war, which was a great disgrace in those days. I never heard about it until I was older.

Not only did my grandfather not go to the war, but he also didn't buy Confederate bonds. In those days, the cotton growers shipped their cotton through Mobile to Liverpool, and the factors in Liverpool made the settlements. Grandfather told the factors in Liverpool to keep his money for him. When the war was over, he was one of the few men in Alabama who had any money, any gold. The Confederate money was worthless by then, of course. So Grandfather prospered considerably after the Civil War. The family lived in great style, and Grandfather bought up all the lands of these poor fellows who had invested in Confederate bonds. When I first remember the plantation, it covered about 35,000 acres of land—which was a lot of land.

My grandfather had slaves, of course. I was always told that the slaves were so loyal that "Ole Mose" hid the family silver and took the horses into the swamp during the war to protect them from marauding Yankees. They all loved Grandfather dearly. I was brought up, you see, on the romantic tradition of the benevolent slave system.

I never knew my grandfather, because he died before I was born, but my grandmother died when I was about eight and I remember her very well. I was named for her, Virginia Heard Foster. I had reddish hair and she had reddish hair. Very red, in fact. She was the most delightful person. She was like a queen bee. She had always been surrounded by servants or slaves. She never had to do anything in her life but be charming. Everybody loved her dearly and called her "Miss Ginny." Her husband adored her. He would go down to New Orleans and send fine dresses back to her. She was like Dora in *David Copperfield*: she was childlike. But she was full of laughter and everybody loved her.

The person I remember best from the plantation in Union Springs is old Easter. She was a black woman who had been a slave. I was told as a child that after Reconstruction the slaves would not leave or they would leave and then come back. And when I was a child, the backyard in Union Springs was still full of slave cabins filled with old men and old women who had been slaves and still lived on the plantation. They were scared of freedom maybe. I don't imagine they had any money either. They may have gotten a little bit, but they stayed on the plantation and were fed. I remember sitting in their laps.

Easter was probably one of the smartest women I ever knew. I think this is one reason it was hard for me to swallow the prevailing theory that blacks were inferior. Easter was a short black woman who wore white aprons and dresses and a white starched bandanna on her head, and she ran the plantation. She wore the keys. You couldn't get a cookie unless you asked Easter. She put the food out for every meal, and I'm sure she even planned the meals. She may have asked my grandmother about some things, but Easter was in charge of everything. She was always in charge of us children. We did exactly what she told us to do. She had a very great dignity.

I remember that Easter never laughed. I think a sense of humor is very hard on a dictator, because Easter was always dignified and autocratic. She couldn't punish us—not physically—but she could punish us by saying, "You're not going to get your morning cookie." Easter was absolutely the law and there was no appeal—not to your mother or your grandmother or whoever else you complained to about Easter. They always thought Easter knew best. And she really did. She was a very wise woman, and she really was a woman of tremendous achievement, because she ran that whole place.

I don't know how many people there were on the plantation. They raised their own sheep and cattle and chickens and had eggs and milk and clabber and butter. There was an enormous orchard and a tremendous scuppernong arbor. Almost everything came off the place except sugar, salt, coffee, and flour.

We lived in Birmingham, but we went down to Union Springs every Christmas and every summer. At Christmas we would stay about a week, but in the summer we would stay weeks and weeks at a time. To me the plantation was absolutely the Garden of Eden. Every meal was a delight. I always have liked to eat, unfortunately, and the meals were delicious and abundant. For breakfast we would begin with a baked apple. In those days, they couldn't get oranges and grapefruit. Then we would have oatmeal, and there would be broiled chicken and fried sweet potatoes and steak sometimes and batty-cakes and waffles and grits. You never saw such a huge breakfast. For dinner we would have lamb or beef or fried chicken. In the winter there would be great platters of birds, quail, just drowned in butter. Everything was drowned in butter, which was churned every morning. Ice cream was a great treat and was made once a week. The meals had endless vegetables and all kinds of fruit. The fruit was picked just when it was ripe, so we would have delicious figs just bursting with juice, and peaches. I thought it was the most perfect place in the world. I never saw anything wrong with it at all.

My nurse would go to Union Springs with me from Birmingham. She would bring her little girl and we would all play in the backyard. It was absolute, sheer, unadulterated joy, as far as I was concerned. I can remember the smell of it now. Everything smelled so fresh and good. And I remember waking to the sound of cowbells in the morning, with the cows going to pasture.

My grandmother, since she had no work to do at all, would play with us. She would play flinch with us, which was a card game, and she would always cheat. When she could cheat and get by with it, she would laugh. She thought that was so much fun. All my aunts ever did was sit on the front porch and rock and do fancy work. I had one aunt who didn't do anything. She never even did fancy work. She just rocked. She never even talked. She just ate and rocked and slept and had some children.

Sometimes my grandmother would take us to the little town of Union Springs. I got the idea at that time that she owned the town. She had two carriages besides two or three buggies. One carriage was an open carriage, a Victoria, and she had matched bay horses. She had a coachman named Washington who wore a high silk hat. Grandmother Foster was the biggest, richest person in town. She wouldn't even go into the stores. The people who ran the stores would come out to the buggy or the carriage and ask her what she wanted and bring out the things. She would buy us the most beautiful material, real linen and lace.

All of our underwear was made of linen and lace by Miss Paulk, who

Grandmother Foster's home in Union Springs, Alabama. Grandfather Foster, who was both a physician and a planter, built the house in 1852–1856. (Courtesy of Mrs. Grady Brown)

lived next door. The Paulks had fallen on hard times. I suppose they had gone to the war and lost their lands. They had a big beautiful house, but they had lost all their money, so Miss Katie Paulk sewed for my grandmother. Our dresses were hand embroidered with a lot of scallops. To me, this was bliss. Just lavish bliss. I adored it. I was absolutely entranced by it.

In the winter Granny Foster would go to church in her carriage, which was lined with red satin. She would wear a little bonnet and a little fur cape. When I went to the church with her, Wash would get out and open the door and then Granny Foster would make her royal progress into the church. I just knew that she owned that church. I'm sure she provided most of the upkeep. The preacher was named Dr. Bell, and I was aware that Dr. Bell was obligated to my grandmother.

As a child, I knew that Grandmother owned the church and she owned the town and she owned the great big house with white pillars and she owned the plantation. She was the queen bee. And when I was little, that was what I wanted to be. I wanted to be like my grandmother and have everybody love me and everybody obligated to me.

Christmases were marvelous. There would be a great big tree, and in the morning, the family would gather with presents. Then in the afternoon Granny Foster would have the black children in first, and they would get their presents. Then she would have the Sunday school children in. She didn't have them together; they came at different times. But I do remember that one little black child got a tiny toy piano, and one of us white children wanted it and tried to snatch it away. My grandmother wouldn't allow that. She was very fair-minded about things like that.

My father was raised in this atmosphere of wealth and abundance and servants. He had two brothers and a sister—Uncle Hugh and Uncle Robert and Aunt May. There were only these four when I grew up. My uncle Hugh lived across the street from my grandmother, and my uncle Robert lived in St. Louis. Aunt May, who was so fashionable and so unpleasant, lived in New York. Uncle Robert was destined for the bar and became a lawyer. My father was destined for the church and became a Presbyterian preacher. Uncle Hugh was destined for business, so he went into the bank. And Aunt May was destined to be a great Southern belle, which I suppose she was. Later she was the cause of the downfall of the whole Garden of Eden for me.

Nothing had changed since my father's childhood. The black people on the plantation were free, but they were still there. And there was still that old abundance. Everybody was welcome for dinner. No matter how many people you had, you could have more.

My father went off to school and then went to Southwestern, which was a Presbyterian college. It's in Memphis now, but it was in Clarksville, Tennessee, when my father went. He also went to Hampden-Sydney in Virginia, which was another Presbyterian school, then to Princeton Theological Seminary. And since his family was well off, he also went to Edinburgh.

When I was grown up I went to see the big Presbyterian seminary in Edinburgh. It looked like a great fortress on the side of a hill, very dark and stark. I found my father's registration and his records there. From Edinburgh he went to Germany and studied at Heidelberg and the University of Berlin. That was his undoing later; that was where he got the new theology—the idea that not every word in the Bible was literal truth, that a lot of it was myth.

For a long time, we had Daddy's theological library, but it got to be too heavy to carry around. Nobody ever wanted those old books. They were just so out of date and foolish, it seems. But my father had an excellent education and he read a great deal. He had a passion for books. He loved sets of books, beautiful sets of books.

Daddy was brought up to do absolutely nothing for himself. He always had somebody to wait on him. He would ride up on a horse and throw the reins and yell, "Jim" or "Joe," and somebody would come and take his horse. His clothes were washed and laid out for him, and the fires were built and food prepared. Daddy just thought all that came about by magic. He never did one single thing in his life. He never washed a dish or cooked a meal or washed his clothes or curried a horse. He could hardly learn to drive an automobile, because he was so used to somebody doing everything for him. He was an honorable man, but he was brought up to think that he was the Lord of Creation. Everybody else was inferior. He was very kind about it, but black people were just so far down the scale that you never thought of them except as somebody to wait on you. He thought Easter was a fine woman, and he treated all the servants with great respect, but Daddy was a child of his time.

When my grandmother died, the system at the plantation was just the same as before the slaves were freed except that they were paid a little something. Granny Foster still had the same number of servants, and they still lived in the backyard. She still had Easter, who slept at the foot of her bed. Easter would bathe Granny every morning. And when my father went off, he had a body servant who went to school with him for a while—a Negro boy who had waited on him when he was on the plantation.

When Daddy returned from Europe and a trip to the Holy Land, his first church was in Tennessee at Mount Pleasant. After that he became pastor of the Idlewild Presbyterian Church in Memphis, where he met my mother.

My mother's mother was Josephine Rice. Her family lived in the Tennessee Valley at a place in Alabama called Somerville. I was brought up on the tale about a huge brick house in the Tennessee Valley and a huge plantation, all luxury and wealth. Theirs was the first brick house built in the Tennessee Valley, I was told. My great-grandfather was named Green Pryor Rice. He had been a Presbyterian preacher himself, but he was also in the Legislature of Alabama. He was in the Alabama Senate for a long time. In one of the early histories of Alabama, the author goes on about his distinguished appearance and great oratorical ability and brilliant mind. Then the author ends by saying, "Mr. Rice had all the attributes of a great man, and no doubt he would have achieved far more fame than he did except for his unfortunate weakness for the bottle." I was always told that he was a great planter from Kentucky with hundreds of slaves.

A cousin of mine has studied the Rice family. He has gone back to England to study the records, and he has discovered that like a lot of families, ours came over here because they couldn't get on in England. They were poor. Everybody wants to pretend they came from some great noble family, but it is a matter of fact that most of America's settlers came over because they were poor. If they had done well in their native country, they would have stayed there. The people in Virginia are like that. If you tell Virginians that your people were from Virginia, they always look at you peculiarly—nobody who was doing well would have left Virginia, because, of course, Virginia is paradise. We in Alabama felt the same way about the people who went to Texas. I used to tease Lyndon Johnson about his family's going from Alabama to Texas. We felt that anybody who went to Texas had the sheriff after him.

In any case, I was told that when my grandmother Rice married, the slaves were lined up in two ranks from the house to the gate and her father gave her fifteen slaves as a wedding gift. When my father and I went up to the Tennessee Valley for the dedication of Wheeler Dam, which is not far from Somerville, we decided to go and see this great plantation and great big house that I'd always heard about. We turned onto a country road and found Somerville, which is an old decaying village. It was built around a square like old New England towns, and before the Civil War it must have been charming. We asked about the Rice place and we went out to see it. Sure enough, there was a brick house. It consisted of two rooms with a dogtrot in between, a loft above, and a kitchen in the back. It was brick all right, but that's all there was. There had never been a great plantation at all.

A young man here in Montgomery was doing his doctoral dissertation on the effect of slave ownership on the votes in the legislature before the war, and I asked him if he would look up my grandfather, who, I had heard, had had hundreds of slaves. He looked him up and found that he had had twelve slaves. My great-grandfather Rice had been fairly well off. He was in the legislature, and he and his family probably lived very comfortably. But the great plantation and the great brick mansion and the hundreds of slaves were just a myth.

My grandfather Patterson, Josiah Patterson, came down to the Tennessee Valley as a poor boy out of the mountains. He married my grandmother, Josephine Rice, when he was just a poor young schoolteacher. It was not thought to be a great marriage on her part. Her sister, Miss Molly Rice, married a Weakley, who was supposed to be a great catch. He was very rich and had a lot of land, but unfortunately, I was always told, he died in the gutter as a drunkard. I remember I used to look in the gutters all the time. I had heard so often that he died in the gutter, and that seemed to be the fate of a great many people—they died in the gutter, drunkards. I was always looking in the gutters thinking I would find somebody lying there.

When the war broke out, my grandfather Patterson was a captain in the Twentieth Alabama Cavalry. He fought under Nathan Bedford Forrest, and I was told he was a dashing cavalryman and a very attractive man. When the war was almost over, he was captured in the battle of Selma. He had promised some young ladies, the Wilkinsons, that he would come back for Sunday dinner, but of course, he and the rest of the army were being marched to Montgomery. When dark came, Grandfather Patterson fell in a ditch by the wayside that had a lot of water in it and lay there for hours with his nose above the water while the columns marched by, all the captured soldiers. Then he went back to Selma and the Misses Wilkinsons dried him out and cleaned up his clothes and he was there for Sunday dinner. He died before I was born, but the image I had of him was of this dashing young man. He was the one we always thought was such a great Confederate soldier. We were brought up to think he was just the grandest thing in the world. *He* didn't send any substitute to the war.

After the Civil War, my grandfather Patterson moved to Memphis to be near Nathan Bedford Forrest. Forrest was a slave trader before the war. He wasn't an aristocrat at all. I don't know what happened to him after the war, but I know he had a lot of power in that section of Tennessee. He was the leader of the Ku Klux Klan.

My grandfather became a lawyer and was elected to Congress. He was in Congress a long time and was a very conservative man. C. Vann Woodward, one of the great Southern historians, talks about him in *Origins of the New South*. My grandfather was a gold bug, a conservative man who believed in the gold standard and fought William Jennings Bryan. He was finally defeated for reelection when Bryan came to Memphis and campaigned against him, nailed him to the cross of gold, as they said. But then Grandfather Patterson became custodian of Shiloh, the great Confederate park. He was an old Confederate soldier and this was just a sinecure. He had little to do but ride around the park a couple of times a year and look it over. But he was honored because he had been a Confederate soldier.

I used to think it was funny that my husband Cliff and I were later accused of trying to overthrow the government by force and violence just because we were trying to get voting rights for people. Here was my grandfather, who spent four years trying to overthrow the government by force, who fought in the Confederate cavalry, and yet he was elected to Congress and became a very honored man and was head of the Shiloh Cemetery. I've often thought how strange it was that those who actually did try to overthrow the government by force and violence became great honored figures in the South, whereas we, their grandchildren, were reviled because we were trying to get the vote. The South is a peculiar place.

My grandfather Josiah Patterson was a very honored man and did well in his law practice. His son Malcolm Patterson also went to Congress and later became governor of Tennessee. That was my mother's brother. He was a great orator, and he had three wives. He was also accused, fairly or unfairly, of being too fond of the bottle. But in any case, a tragic thing happened to him that ruined his career.

Uncle Malcolm's first wife committed suicide, the second wife died, and he had married for the third time when he was governor of Tennessee. One of his political enemies was Edward Carmack. Carmack was editor of the *Nashville Tennessean* and had run a series of bitter editorials against my uncle. Uncle Malcolm's third wife told me they were sitting at breakfast shortly after their marriage when the Coopers came by. The Coopers, both son and father, were great supporters of my uncle, and they told him they were going to kill Carmack because he had been so vicious in his attacks. Uncle Malcolm remonstrated with them, but the Coopers were determined to kill Carmack. After they left, my uncle said to my aunt, "Do you suppose they could possibly kill Carmack?" He got up to go after them, and she said, "Oh, Malcolm, don't go. You would be involved in it and they might kill you." She threw her arms around him and held him. He broke away and went out, but the Coopers had already killed Carmack. He was lying in a pool of blood in the center of Nashville. The two Coopers were convicted of murder and were to be hanged. As governor, Uncle Malcolm pardoned them. In his later life he was a judge in Memphis, but he knew that his political career had been ruined by the Carmack affair. He told my mother, "Annie, of course I will never be elected to political office again, but I cannot let my friends hang. I know they did it for me, as unwise as it was, and I can't let them hang." Now, whether that was noble or silly depends on your point of view.

After he left office, Uncle Malcolm practiced law in Memphis and became a great advocate of prohibition. He was a wonderful orator and attracted thousands of people to the cause. Prohibition was a great political issue in the South for years, and I remember Uncle Malcolm's coming to our house in Birmingham and speaking on prohibition at a meeting in the city auditorium. I never knew Uncle Malcolm well at all. Even my mother never got on too well with him. She always said Malcolm was a very self-absorbed man, and he was. He was a man who led his own life and his own career, a brilliant man but very self-absorbed.

All the Pattersons went to the Idlewild Presbyterian Church in Memphis, and that's where my mother met my father. My father was minister of the church, which was a Southern Presbyterian Church. The Southern Presbyterian Church had withdrawn from the United Presbyterian Church in the United States of America during the Civil War. After my father and mother married, they left Memphis for Birmingham, for my father to become pastor of the South Highland Presbyterian Church. We lived in a parsonage on Rose Avenue, which is several blocks from the church. I also look on that period of my life as sheer, unequaled bliss.

I was born in a house nearer the church, a parsonage just off Highland Avenue. Mother said when I was born I was red-faced and hungry all the time. She nursed me for months and if she was fifteen minutes late, I'd scream so loudly that the whole neighborhood would be upset. I always wanted what I wanted, and I always wanted something to eat. Evidently, I was a lusty, loudmouthed child.

I was a terrible disappointment because I wasn't a son. My parents had already picked out a boy's name. They had named my brother for Daddy's father, Sterling Johnson Foster, and they were going to name another boy for Mother's father, Josiah Patterson Foster. Then, I came along instead. I used to spend hours trying to kiss my elbow because they told me if I kissed my elbow, I'd turn into a boy. Daddy used to say that if I broke my arm I could kiss my elbow, but I never was able to do it. I grew up feeling that I had disappointed my father by not being a boy.

My mother was my champion in the family. I always felt my father hadn't been exactly delighted when I came along. My sister was his great favorite. I was too much like my father. He talked a lot and I talked a lot. He had a lot of curiosity and I had a lot of curiosity. He lost his temper and I lost my temper. And I defied him. I was scared of him in a way, because he would spank us children with folded newspapers, which didn't hurt a bit, but it frightened us because it was so noisy and he was so noisy. He had a very powerful personality.

Father used to give us Pluto Water. He thought he could cure anything with Pluto Water and castor oil. Pluto Water came from French Lick Springs in Indiana, and the bottle had a red devil on it. When we got sick, whatever we had, Daddy would put us in the tub and give us orange juice laced with castor oil, the most horrible combination I can think of. Then, to get rid of the castor oil, we would have to drink a big glass of Pluto Water. Well, we would usually throw it up. That's why he put us in the tub, you see. He kept up this routine until we finally kept it all down. Of course, the next day we were purged of everything in us. Maybe it did cure us, but it was a drastic means, I must say.

Being the preacher's family, we had to go to Sunday school and church, and then in the afternoon, we had to go to Christian Endeavor, the young people's group. Then we had to go to night service. On Wednesday, we had to go to prayer meeting. Of course, Mother had to go to ladies' meetings, too. And Daddy had meetings with the Session. The church absorbed our life. We would also have prayers in the morning before breakfast.

At that time we had two servants, my nurse, Alice—we called her Nursie—and a cook named Sally. Sally used to cook wonderful breakfasts, with grits and gravy and broiled chicken and sweet potatoes. She never came to the prayer service, because she was cooking breakfast. We would kneel down and pray and Daddy would pray and read the Bible. Of course, we were always in agony with impatience to get to the table and eat breakfast. We always thought breakfast was God's reward to us for the prayer effort.

My sister was four years older than I was, and Sterling, my brother, was about five or six years older. He was a very handsome boy. He adored my mother, but was scared of Daddy. Daddy expected him to be brilliant, and he wasn't. My poor brother was always being fussed at because he wasn't brilliant in school.

I'm sure that Daddy was fond of us all, but the love of his life was my sister, Josephine. She could do no wrong, and he excused her from everything. She was an unusually sweet, beautiful child, and everyone adored her. Even though Josephine was the angel of the family and I was supposed to be the devil, I adored her, too.

I was the bad child, and Josephine was the good child. I was the ugly child, and she was the pretty child. I was the mean child and had a high temper. She was the sweet child. Now, I know this is all exaggeration, because I was loved by my mother and I remember I was told by her that I was a sweet, beautiful child—that is, I could be if I wanted to and didn't lose my temper.

My nurse was devoted to me anyway, and really, my early life was joyful. Whenever I went to bed either my mother or my nurse would lie by me and pat me to sleep. I was a very privileged child, brought up in a little cocoon of love and devotion and care. I even liked going to church. Mother would let me put my head in her lap and go to sleep. And I loved Sunday school. I thought that was lots of fun. We'd sing "Brighten the Corner Where You Are" and get little presents and pictures of Jesus.

Nursie was a second mother to me, as black nurses were to many Southern white children. I was devoted to Nursie. She was as much a symbol of safety to me as my mother was. She took care of me completely—even bathed and dressed me. Nursie put me to bed at night, and her little girl, Sarah, who was just my age, slept with me quite often. Nursie didn't live at our house. She had a husband or a beau who would come and get her every night. I forget his name. We just called him Nursie's beau. He was a tall yellow man, and he would come every night and take her home. My mother resented this because she wanted Nursie to stay on the place—so that she would get up with us in the night, I suppose. Sarah wasn't the daughter of Nursie's beau; she was the daughter of Nursie's first husband. I actually lived in two worlds until I was seven years old. I lived in a white world and a black world, and I was accepted in both.

My aunt May came to Union Springs the summer I was about six. She had married a great friend of my father's from Memphis, a Mr. Johnston, and she had divorced him, which was almost unheard of in those days. She then married another man, who was Irish, and she lived in New York and was very fashionable. She dressed in great style and went abroad a lot. Her daughter, Elizabeth, who was with her that summer, later married very rich men. The last one was Count von Furstenberg, a German nobleman. They had a daughter named Betsy von Furstenberg who is now an actress in New

Aunt May, Daddy's sister, who caused Nursie to leave.

York. Aunt May was determined to live well. She would be known as a jet setter now. Her lifestyle was supported, of course, by money from the plantation.

Aunt May's second husband, Mr. Leary, was a rather poor man, and the family looked down on him because he was Catholic and Irish and didn't have any money. I think he had a lot of charm, but he didn't know how to hunt or shoot, and the family always thought Aunt May had made a very serious mistake to marry him. I'm sure this must have irritated her very much, because her brothers were not very kind about Mr. Leary. Poor Mr. Leary had a pretty hard time. When he came down to Union Springs at Christmas time, all the men went hunting and he was left behind. Sometimes he was taken along and made fun of because he couldn't shoot. The family all thought Mr. Leary had married Aunt May for her money and that she was getting more than her share out of Grandmother. I was aware of a great deal of friction about that.

During the summer of Aunt May's visit, she heard the little black children in the backyard calling my sister "Sis." My brother called her Sis, and I called her Sister. Well, Aunt May sent Grandmother's house servant, Easter, out to tell the little black children they couldn't call Josephine Sis. They had to call her Miss Josephine. We were astonished and hurt and didn't know what this was about. Here Sister, who had been playing with the black children all her life, had to be called Miss Josephine all of a sudden. But Sister solved the problem by telling them, "Now, you don't have to call me Miss Josephine; you just call me Miss Sis." So after that all the children, white and black, called her Miss Sis. She solved the problem by not hurting anybody's feelings. She spent her life doing that.

That incident was a warning that our idyllic days were over, but the great trauma of my early life came with my seventh birthday. I had always celebrated my birthday in Union Springs because it was in August. We would have a barbecue in the backyard with the black children. We would dig a pit in the backyard, which was sandy, and place a grill over the hole and build a fire. Then the cook would give us chickens, which we were allowed to baste and turn. Of course, by the time we got through, the chickens were full of sand, but to me this was a great event. Here I was presiding over the chickens! But on my seventh birthday my mother and grandmother and aunts all said I had to have my birthday in the front yard and have just white children. No black children could come to the party. Well, I got very angry about that. Mostly, I wanted the barbecue. I was thinking of food, as usual.

I had been planning the party for months. I'd had typhoid fever and had spent the whole time that I was ill planning my birthday party. I was going to have a pink cake and pink slippers and pink socks and a pink dress and a pink sash and a pink bow in my hair and a pink cake and strawberry ice cream. When August arrived, I had a pink dress, the pink socks, the pink everything, except the strawberries, which weren't available in August, but I was told none of the black children could come to the party. Only white children—perfect strangers they had picked up in Union Springs. So I had a temper fit early that morning and they finally agreed that I could have the barbecue in the morning and the party in the afternoon. The barbecue would be in the backyard with the black children, and the party would be in the front yard with the white children.

Elizabeth, Aunt May's daughter, was there. Aunt May had brought a French maid with her to Union Springs, too, if you can imagine. Aunt May really put on airs. Elizabeth was always dressed up in beautiful dresses with sashes and everything matching and her hair curled. She was a little older than I was, about my sister's age.

We had the birthday barbecue and everything was going fine. One of the little black girls was tearing up the chicken, and she offered a piece to Elizabeth. Elizabeth, who must have felt like an outcast in this group, all of a sudden said, "Don't you give me any chicken out of that black hand of yours. I'm not going to eat any chicken that your black hand has touched, you little nigger." I told Elizabeth to go to hell. I was just furious. You see, the black girl was Nursie's little girl, Sarah. She and I played together all the time. I was raised with her. The grown-ups put me to bed and said *I* was going to hell for being so bad.

When the afternoon came, I went to the birthday party with all these strange white children. I had another temper fit and screamed and yelled. I bashed the cake in and was put to bed again. By that time, the seventh birthday was pretty well shot, cake and all. That night at the supper table, my aunt said I was the worst child she had ever known. She told my mother, "I really think you have got to do something about her because she's so high-tempered, such a bad child." I was sitting right there listening to her, so I took a knife and threw it at her. Well, I was really a disgrace then, so they sent me away from the table. I went out to the back porch and sat in Nursie's lap. We could hear Aunt May through the window saying, "Annie, the trouble with Virginia is that nurse. She spoils her to death. And besides, I think it's terrible that you let her sit in her lap and sleep with her and kiss her and hug her. You know all those black women are diseased."

My mother defended me, but she didn't try to defend her nurse, and neither did my grandmother. Nursie had been spending the summer in Union Springs all my life. She had been with our family for seven years, caring for me and my brother and my sister. They knew how kind she had been to us and what a faithful servant she was. Yet they did not defend her from Aunt May's charges. Of course, it was venereal disease that Aunt May was talking about, but I didn't know that at the time.

Nursie was a dignified woman and she was, I am sure, highly insulted. She put me to bed that night and the next morning she was gone. She took her child and left and never came back. She got a job somewhere in the neighborhood in Birmingham, and I would go and cry and beg her to come back, but she never would. She never forgave the insult. That was a terrible trauma in my life.

But a curious, almost unbelievable, thing happened years and years later. I was in Washington working to abolish the poll tax, and I was working with a very light-skinned black woman from Birmingham named Mrs.

Spraggs. We would kid each other about being from Birmingham. She was a handsome woman, and very smart. She had worked in the National Youth Administration with Aubrey Williams, and then she became a correspondent with the *Chicago Defender,* which was a big Negro newspaper. She was supporting the anti–poll tax fight, and we became quite friendly.

One day Mrs. Spraggs came up to me and said, "Mrs. Durr, my mother-in-law is visiting from Birmingham. She wants to see you."

"Who is that?" I asked.

"Her name is Mrs. Spraggs." She added, "She knows you." I didn't know who in the world that could be. I had never heard of another Mrs. Spraggs.

"I'm sorry," I said, "but I don't have the least recollection in my entire life of knowing anybody named Mrs. Spraggs." So I didn't see her.

About a year later she came up to me again. "Mrs. Durr, my mother-in-law is visiting with me and she wants to see you. Her name is Mrs. Spraggs."

"Mrs. Spraggs? I have no recollection of her at all, but I would like to see her. Bring her down to the office." For some reason, though, I didn't meet her mother-in-law that time either.

Well, the third year, she came to me and said, "Mrs. Durr, my sister-in-law would like to see you. She's visiting me and she knew you as a little girl."

"What is her name?"

"Sarah Spraggs." All of a sudden, I realized who she was—Nursie's daughter. I had never known the last name of Nursie, the love of my life, who had raised me from a baby for all those seven years. It just shows how completely backward I was.

Sarah came to the office, and she was a handsome woman then. We were both in our thirties. I had suggested that we all have lunch together. The problem was where in the name of God two black women could have lunch with a white. At that time, the only place that was integrated in Washington was the YWCA, but I called a Chinese restaurant right near the office and asked if they would take us. We went there and they put us in a private room.

Sarah and I had a wonderful time talking about our childhood. Nursie by that time had died. I had missed seeing her because I didn't know her name. The thing that Sarah remembered about me was when I told my cousin to go to hell because she called Sarah a little nigger and wouldn't eat the chicken out of her hand. She had remembered that all her life, and I remembered it, too. We tried to stay in touch with each other, but she finally went to Chicago and I can't find her. I think she became a teacher.

A great many Southern white children in those days had the experience of giving their first love to a black woman or a black man and then being taught little by little that it was a relationship they couldn't have. I was just as intimate with Sarah and Nursie and the tall yellow man as if they were members of my family. Yet I literally never knew their names. After that summer in Union Springs when I turned seven, I went to school where there were only white children. We had a succession of cooks and servants in the house, but I never got on such intimate terms with any of them. I was taught by the environment and by my mother that you can't call a black woman a lady. You can't say, "A lady's here"; you have to say, "A woman's here." Mother was very kind, and my father was always helping black people get out of jail and helping them in other ways. But little by little, I was taught that they were not like us.

Actually, I never met an educated Negro in my life until I went off to Wellesley College. But between Nursie and Easter, I had a mighty hard time believing in the natural inferiority of the black race. I was accustomed to being looked after by blacks. They were my refuge in times of trouble. That was really the basis of my relationship with Mary McLeod Bethune some years later. Mrs. Bethune translated into the black woman who looked after me and became my protector.

The great trauma of my seventh birthday party was followed soon after by a second one—my father was thrown out of the church. The leading members of the church were my mother's two first cousins, Sam Weakley and John Weakley, who were Aunt Molly's sons. Aunt Molly was my grandmother's sister. She married the rich Mr. Weakley who died, they said, in the gutter from drink. My grandfather Patterson had taken these two boys and brought them to Memphis to live with his family. My mother looked on them as brothers more than first cousins because they had been raised in the house with her. Sam and John Weakley were very devoted, and later they both were taken into my grandfather's office and became lawyers, very good lawyers. Eventually they returned to Birmingham and became quite successful. Cousin Sam was a great prohibitionist. John was not as conservative as Sam, but they were both strict fundamentalist Presbyterians.

The church was full of fine, upstanding, moneyed citizens. It was one of the leading churches in the city, and very fundamentalist. Some of the members worked convicts in the mines, but they were considered to be the leading citizens of Birmingham. In most Southern towns, the Episcopal church is the most fashionable, the Presbyterian church is next, and then come the Methodists and the Baptists and the evangelical groups. The Catholics at that time were hardly considered, because there were so few of them. There was always a rank so that being a Presbyterian meant something. It was the same thing as Jacob's ladder—there was always somebody above you and somebody beneath you. The Presbyterian church was highly thought of, but I knew that St. Mary's, the Episcopal church which was not far from us, was the most fashionable church. That was something I learned by osmosis. Nobody told me; I just knew it.

Anyway, the church people—particularly Cousin John and Cousin Sam—
began to suspect that my father was heretical. Daddy was called up several
times because they noticed things that showed he didn't believe in a literal
interpretation of the Bible. Finally, they called him in and asked if he realized
the sermons he was giving were heretical. They asked him to declare on
oath before the Session that he believed the whale swallowed Jonah and
Jonah stayed in the whale's belly for three days and was spewed up alive.
He had to swear to that as the literal truth, God given. They gave him a
week to make up his mind, and they told him if he didn't agree to do it, he
would be denounced as a heretic.

Now, this was done by my mother's two cousins. Cousin Sam lived
right near us in a great big red house. I was devoted to his daughter and to
Cousin Sam. They were part of the family, and they created a terrible breach
in it. Daddy just walked up and down that whole week. I can hear him now,
walking up and down in his study upstairs. We were all just terrified, Sister
and Brother and I. Mother was crying, and the servants were upset. Mother
kept taking Daddy some coffee or buttermilk and trying to get him to eat.
He was up all night. He would say, "Oh, God. Oh, God." And it wasn't
blasphemy; he was really praying.

At the end of the week, he went back and told them that he didn't
believe the story of Jonah and the whale. He was dismissed from the church
and brought before the Presbytery and the Synod as a heretic. He never got
another church.

I was just starting school, I remember, and these two shattering experiences had happened all within the same year or the same few months.
Of course, I didn't understand what all the theology was about, but I did
know that Daddy had a nervous breakdown afterward. He couldn't sleep
or eat or anything. He was a very high-strung man. He went off to French
Lick Springs, where Pluto Water came from, and Mother was left with the
three children. I don't know what we lived on. I suppose my grandmother
helped us out. She was prosperous at the time. I remember going to Cousin
Sam's for Sunday dinner and Mother crying and having an argument with
him. She cried, and oh, how distressed I was!

About that time, I began to get some ideas about the Devil. I had been
hearing about the Devil, you see. At that time, hell wasn't something remote; it was right down there underneath you, and you burned eternally.
The Devil took you and turned you over on the hot coals and let you fry
and sizzle. Well, one day I did something that I knew was wrong—I stole
a piece of pie out of the icebox or something. I always had a passion for
food and for lemon pie especially. I remember being terrified that the Devil
was going to get me and fry me forever. I was sitting on the stairs crying.
Mother sat by me and put her arm around me and said, "What in the world
is the matter?" I was almost hysterical. I said the Devil was going to send

me to hell and fry me forever because I had stolen the pie. She said, "Oh, don't believe a word of that. I don't care what you hear in Sunday school or church, just don't believe a word of that. It is the silliest thing in the wide world. There's not a word of truth in it. God is your father, and you know your father does spank you sometimes with a folded newspaper, but that is as much as God would ever do. You know that your father is a very good, kind man, so God is a good, kind man." I said, "But, Mother, I hear it every Sunday." She said, "Well, just don't believe it. I'm telling you there is not a word of truth in it." Mother just banished the Devil and hell out of my life right then and there. She got rid of them. I might have been a better woman if she hadn't!

We moved to Memphis then. Mother's sister, Aunt Louise, had married Edward Lemaster, a real estate man. We lived in a little cottage he owned in back of his home on Union Avenue, and we went to Idlewild Presbyterian Church. I remember how delighted I was because we had snow in Memphis, and I never had seen snow before. My aunt, whom we called Oo-Oo, was a very cheerful, laughing person. She had a great big house and a lot of daughters, and everybody there was laughing and cheerful. She made waffles for breakfast every morning, and I would stop by for some after my own breakfast.

The Lemasters were prominent in the church. Uncle Edward had done well and had a successful real estate business. They are still a prominent family there. They were just as sweet to us as they could be, but it was hard on Mother. Her husband had been thrown out of the church as a heretic and he was having a nervous breakdown. I remember that my father came home for Christmas and then went back to French Lick Springs.

When spring came, Daddy got better and in some way—and I don't quite know how this happened—we went back to the parsonage on Rose Avenue. I think my grandmother bought it for us, because we went back to that same place. Daddy went to work for a Mr. Orr, who had been in the church and had a big insurance company that sold insurance to black people.

Mr. Orr was a lovely person and so was his wife, the daughter of John T. Milner, who founded Birmingham. They had a lot of children and were very kind to all of us. I think Daddy felt rather disgraced selling insurance to black people, though. He never was much of a businessman, but after he left the ministry, he worked for a number of insurance companies. My grandmother died shortly after that, and Daddy inherited quite a lot of money.

2

Growing Up:
Beaus, New York, Sister and Hugo

WHEN GRANNY FOSTER died, Daddy inherited part of the plantation, between 9,000 and 10,000 acres. The boll weevil hadn't come yet, and the tenants were still on the land. The bank handled the estate, and we got an annual income from it. Grandmother left some money, too. Shortly after she died, we sold the house on Rose Avenue and built a big brick house on Niazuma Avenue, right at the edge of Red Mountain. We bought a Packard automobile, and we joined the country club.

My mother began to lead a much more fashionable life. She never learned to play bridge, but she went to a lot of luncheons and teas. I can see her now, all dressed up. My grandmother had given her a set of furs, and Mother would pin violets on them and wear a great big hat with plumes. She smelled like violet cologne, Richard Hudnutt's Violet Toilet Water. I thought she was the most beautiful creature in the world. She had two very fashionable friends, Mrs. Maben and Mrs. Cabaniss.

Mother also joined a literary club, the Cadmean Circle, to which all the leading ladies belonged. The Cadmean Circle was a great institution in Birmingham and was just the ultimate for all the proper ladies. The members had to give papers, so they couldn't just be fashionable and frivolous ladies; the club was both social and literary. Miss Willie Allen, who had a private school, was the leader. Cadmus is from Greek mythology, as I recall. He sowed teeth and warriors sprang up. The Cadmean Circle met every Friday afternoon, and when it was their turn to have the meeting my mother and the other ladies had every window and every bit of woodwork washed, upstairs and down. Every floor was polished. The china was washed and the silver polished. The delicate little sandwiches, the mints, the nuts, the coffee, and the tea—everything was perfect. And the flowers, too—because this was the day that your contemporaries came and judged you. If there

Mother, Anne Patterson Foster.

was dust underneath the rug or anything was dirty, you were slipping. I loved meeting days because the ladies always served salted almonds and mints. Mother would bring them to me in the corner of her handkerchief. I was always looking out for something to eat.

We must have had more money than we had later. I went to public school, but I was beginning to be conscious of social distinctions. I had had a lot of friends around Rose Avenue, but I made new friends in our more fashionable neighborhood. Pauline Maben and I became great friends. Pauline was a timid child and was always terrified of dogs. My mother said if we would bend down and look at the dogs through our legs, they would run away. So we would, and you know, they would run away! In those days, there was an answer for everything, whether right or wrong. Nothing was left undecided.

One of my Weakley cousins married a lady from Minnesota, a Yankee. Their daughter was about my age, and I remember going to her birthday party. We played drop-the-handkerchief and had ice cream and cake. Both she and her mother were pale and had blue eyes. One day, my cousin just disappeared. Nobody ever knew what happened to him. He just disappeared. At that time, husbands often just disappeared. Rather than get a divorce or kill their wives, they just disappeared. One of them here in our county started out for the depot in a hack one day and vanished before it got there. For thirty years nobody heard of him and then he finally showed up again, and his wife took him back.

When Mr. Weakley disappeared I was very much puzzled because he had been at the birthday party. There was lots of talk about it—where he was and how they couldn't find him. So I said to my father, "Why in the world did he leave?" And Daddy said in a patronizing way, "Well, darling, that Yankee wife of his never fed him anything but cold store-bought light bread. That is enough to make a man leave a woman, to feed him cold, store-bought light bread." I just took it for the truth, and after I was married I always tried to make homemade bread for Cliff. Commercial bread, you have to admit, is pretty bad. I couldn't make biscuits and cornbread at every meal, so I started making bread. Cliff never had a slice of store-bought bread when he lived with his mother. With me, he would sometimes eat Pepperidge Farm bread, but whenever I served him other kinds of commercial bread he just refused to eat it, absolutely refused. He said that it tasted like it was made out of blotting paper.

I believed what the grown-ups told me. On the plantation I used to ask my father why the black people were such different colors—almost white, cream, tan, brown, and black. It puzzled me, because they were all called black, but they weren't black. I used to ask Daddy; I was always a curious child. Daddy got tired of my constant questions, so finally one day he said to me, "Dear, that was all due to the Union Army." Well, I just accepted it. I didn't know what it meant, but I took it for granted that the Union Army caused them to be different colors. There were answers to everything even though the answers didn't always make sense.

The structure of society was changing all around us, but I was completely protected from the changes. Birmingham was a new town and people were coming in from all over. There were strikes and labor violence and racial troubles, but it was as though I had never even broken the shell: I lived on the Southside, far from all the troubled areas.

Birmingham was founded after the Civil War. It began as just a little village called Elyton, but it became a great commercial center after the

L & N and the Southern railroads arrived. Then when iron ore and coal and limestone were discovered in the valley, the city became a great center of coal and pig iron. All the big iron and steel companies—United States Steel; Tennessee Coal, Iron and Railroad Company; Republic Steel; the Woodward Iron Company—established plants in Birmingham. When I was growing up, people didn't think about pollution. The air was so full of dirt that you couldn't go out without having your nose and throat stop up and your white gloves get dirty. It meant that Birmingham was prosperous.

Still, the industrial side of Birmingham was distant from my life, which consisted entirely of downtown Birmingham, Highland Avenue, and the Southside. What lay beyond was a foreign country, and the people who lived there might as well not have existed. My whole life was securely concentrated in my social group and my neighborhood.

We did have a big break within the Presbyterian church, though. We had continued to go to my father's church even after he was removed from the pulpit. As a matter of pride my father wasn't going to let people think he had been run out of the church or that they had hurt him. They didn't take away his membership. They just made it impossible for him to get a church. One of the preachers who came after my father was a young man named Henry Edmonds. He had been pastor of the First Presbyterian Church in Wetumpka and then in Montgomery. He was a very fine preacher, but some of the congregation began to question him about the literal interpretation of the Bible. By his responses, Dr. Edmonds broke the church in two. My father went with Dr. Edmonds across the street to the Jewish temple, the Temple Emanu-El. Jewish services were on Saturday, and we used the Temple Emanu-El on Sunday. The Weakleys, of course, all stayed in the old church.

At that time, I was going to the Lakeview School, and my best friends were a group of Jewish boys. I must say in all modesty that the reason we got to be such good friends was because we were the smartest ones there. We made the best grades, and we were interested in school. Often on Saturdays some of the Jewish boys would ask me to go to the temple with them. I remember thinking that the Jewish religion was very interesting. But I never could get them to go to church with me on Sunday. We were devoted friends, and as long as we were just playing outdoors it was fine with the grown-ups. We could have our Jewish friends just as we used to play with the black children in the backyard. But when I was about thirteen or fourteen and we started dating and going to parties, the axe fell. Their mamas didn't want them to date us, and our mamas didn't want us to date them. These were the boys that I would naturally have started going out with, and it was a very sad thing for me that we were completely divided. They went to a country club called the Standard Club, and we went to the Birmingham Country Club.

I had been to South Highland Public School when I was little. Then when we moved, I went to the Lakeview Public School. I always found school an absolute joy. I loved to read. I was curious and I wanted to know about the world. Nobody seems to have such wonderful teachers any more. In my first grade, I had a Miss Taylor, who made the world come alive. All through my career at public schools, I had marvelous teachers. Learning was a joy.

Up until this point, sex had never been discussed, and as far as we knew it didn't exist. The only thing I knew was that something happened in the basement, because Mother was always worried about the cooks having men in the basement. The cook always lived in the servants' rooms in the basement of the house on Niazuma so that she could rise early to cook breakfast. The servants were paid five or six dollars a week with room and board. We had a succession of cooks, and I remember the terrific anxiety about the men in the basement. I didn't know what they did in the basement, but if Mother or Daddy knew there was a man in the basement, there was always a big row and sometimes the cook would leave. The men would creep out early in the morning, and Mother would say, "I see a man going down the alley. I bet he spent the night here." I realized there was something going on in the basement that was just terrible, but I didn't know what it was.

You cannot imagine the ideas that built up in us about sex. It really was something that black people did in the basement. No one ever told me about the menstrual period. When I had my first one, I was absolutely terrified. It happened in school, and I thought I was dying. I called home and Mother came for me. She said, "Well, that's just something that women have to do." She never told me why or what it was about. I said, "Mother, do black women do this, too?" She said, "Yes, all women do. It is the curse of women." Of course, I always had terrible cramps after that. I matured very early; I was a full-grown woman when I was about twelve, and I began to feel these pangs about young boys, thinking they were so attractive. I always felt guilty about it. I thought I must be some sort of fiend.

Every summer we went to Mentone, which is up in the mountains of northern Alabama. When I was thirteen or fourteen, I met a young boy up there named Carlton Wright who was just about my age. He came from Rome, Georgia. Well, we fell in love, and nobody objected to our kissing and hugging. It was very pleasant indeed. He was not regarded as a sexual threat, and of course he wasn't. He just kissed me goodnight. That was my first intimation of any real kind of sexual feeling. I didn't know what went on except that it was nice, and I enjoyed kissing and hugging with Carlton.

We were all brought up that way. Nobody discussed sex. Maybe some of the girls did, but as far as I know, it was a completely verboten subject. We began to say that some girls were "fast," because they kissed all the boys goodnight. But we noticed that they were more popular than we were!

Kissing Carlton was about as far as I went until I was sixteen or seventeen. I wasn't fast. Oh, no, indeed—I was one of the nicest girls in Birmingham! If a strange boy had tried to kiss me, I would have been terrified. Because Mother did not take Carlton seriously, I did have a period of young love which was totally without sin attached to it. So I knew there was such a thing as warm loving feelings without sin or guilt.

By about this time, my sister was going to Sweet Briar College in Virginia. At fifteen I was still going to public schools in Birmingham and had started dancing school. I began to date and have boyfriends come to see me. I had begun to be aware of all the social distinctions—you couldn't go with the Jews, and you couldn't go with the Negroes, and the steel mill workers, who lived in the outlying districts, just didn't exist. Even on the Southside, there were social distinctions—the people who belonged to the country club and the people who didn't, people who were Baptists and Methodists and others who were Presbyterians and Episcopalians.

I had some Methodist friends, and I went to a Bob Jones revival in a Methodist church. Rev. Jones asked that anyone stand up who was on the side of the Lord. Well, of course, my father having been a Presbyterian preacher, I just assumed that not only was I on the side of the Lord, I was one of the chosen. So I stood up. In no time at all, I was down on the mourners' bench and they were all praying over me and singing that I had come through and was saved. It embarrassed me very much. I thought, "This is just like those Methodists. They're not like us Presbyterians or Episcopalians. All of this is common."

"Common" was a great word. If anything was common, it was just terrible. Mother used that word often. She would say, "Well, dear, I think that it is extremely common." That meant it was just vulgar. You felt guilty if you did anything that was common. If you ate too much, if your mouth was full, if you didn't use the right fork, whatever you did that wasn't right, was common.

I escaped from the Methodist church as quickly as possible, but all my friends were so envious of the attention I had gotten that they went down and got saved all week long. I didn't tell my parents what I had done, because I knew they wouldn't approve. They would think it was common— to be sung over and prayed over. Revivals were considered common. It was just ordinary, common people who did that kind of thing. There was a great distinction between what "proper" people did and what "common" people did.

One of the proper people in my life was a woman in New York whom we called Aunt Mamie. She had been married to my father's best friend, Mr. Patterson, who had been the pastor of a church in Montgomery. Aunt Mamie had come from Tennessee and Daddy had known her when he lived at Mount Pleasant. She had been brought up by her sister after her mother

Me at fifteen.

had died, and her sister was very well off. Aunt Mamie was used to champagne and four-in-hand coaches. She lived on Pike Road in Nashville, a seat
of fashion, and Aunt Mamie was very fashionable. She wore the biggest
hats. She even rouged, which was supposed to be rather fast. When her
husband died she was left with a son and a daughter but without very much
money. Then she did something that was considered awful: she married a
shoe clerk named Mr. W——. That was considered to be absolutely beyond
the pale. "Who was Mr. W——?" Nobody could place Mr. W——. He was
like Mr. Leary, Aunt May's husband; he just didn't exist. He had no roots
at all. People would say, "Well, I never heard of anybody that knew Mr.
W——." It was very important to be placed. They would say, "Now is he
kin to the Smiths who lived in Eufaula? Is he related to the W——s who
lived in this place?" You had to place people to be sure they were respectable
and your kind of folks. And Mr. W—— never got placed.

Aunt Mamie took Mr. W—— to New York, and she began to take in
Southern girls. This was something that Southern ladies did to make a liv-
ing. The girls would go to the opera and to the theater and take music or
French. Aunt Mamie would get them introduced to boys and invited to
Annapolis or to West Point. The girls would get "polished."

Daddy was guardian of Aunt Mamie's children in some way. She would
come to visit us for long periods of time, and Daddy would always give her
handsome presents. In those days, ladies used to wear French puffs. They
were big sausage rolls that were worn on top of their hair, which was always
pinned up. They were very expensive, and Mother got furious at Daddy for
buying those French puffs for Aunt Mamie. Aunt Mamie had a way of getting things out of people. She was a very pretty woman and very sexy, with
a great big bosom and a tiny little waist and swelling hips. She was not a
bad woman in any way. She was very virtuous. I'm sure she would not have
married Mr. W—— if she hadn't been. He was an extremely handsome man.

After my sister had been to Sweet Briar, Aunt Mamie wanted Daddy
to send her to New York. Aunt Mamie's daughter, Ella Vaughn Patterson,
had visited us a great deal, and she and Sister were friends. Ella was one of
the most beautiful creatures I have ever seen. She put every other Southern
belle I have ever known in the shade. She had curly red-gold hair and big
blue eyes and a marvelous complexion, just beautiful. Girls didn't use much
make-up in those days, but she was gorgeous without it. She wore the prettiest dresses you have ever seen, satin slippers and chiffon and georgette
crepe. I can't remember anybody in my life who was prettier than Ella Vaughn
Patterson.

Aunt Mamie, of course, was very anxious for Ella Vaughn to marry a
rich man. I can't tell you how many beaus Ella had. When she came to visit
us, the telephone would ring and the doorbell would ring and five-pound

boxes of Nunallys' chocolates would arrive and great long boxes of American Beauty roses and little square boxes of violets and gardenias. She would have an early date to go out for dinner at six or seven o'clock and then have another date at nine o'clock and a late date at eleven o'clock. She could only stay with each caller for a little while. All day long, the men were calling up.

These great Southern belles became an institution. A man was proud to be seen with them. It gave him status. Their cities were proud of them. Zelda Sayre, who later married F. Scott Fitzgerald, was a belle, but of course she was younger. Willie Gayle and Margaret Thorington from Montgomery and Mary Allen Northington were all authentic Southern belles, as were Blanche Divine and Sarah Orme from Atlanta. I remember a lot of them. When they came to town, there was a lot of excitement. They were almost like visiting movie stars. They were not on the stage, but they were playing a part all the time. They were the epitome of success, and oh, I wanted to be like them so badly. But I knew that I wasn't. That was the ideal that was held up to me, to be a belle.

My sister was extremely popular, too. Crowds of boys, eight or ten at a time, would come on Sunday afternoon. As each new crowd arrived, the one that came before would have to leave. Sister would sometimes have as many as fifty or sixty callers in one Sunday afternoon. Sister was never an institution like Ella Vaughn Patterson or Blanche Divine, but she was very pretty and the boys were crazy about her.

Aunt Mamie finally persuaded Daddy to send Sister to New York. During the two years she was there, she took a business course, of all things, and became a secretary. When the war broke out in 1917, Sister was still in New York, and she and Ella Vaughn Patterson joined the Navy as yeomanettes. You should have seen them in their uniforms. They had dark blue suits and dark blue capes lined with red and little caps. They were so striking that people would stop in the street to look at them —their costumes with their flowing capes were so romantic. Sister and Ella Vaughn lived with Aunt Mamie, but they worked for the Navy as secretaries.

Aunt Mamie then persuaded my father to send me to New York to be polished up. Aunt Mamie and I never got along very well. She told my mother, and I heard her say it, "Virginia is absolutely impossible. She is really impossible. She talks too much, she talks too loud. Her voice is too high, she asks too many questions, and she is very rawboned and nearsighted. Annie, Virginia will never marry well unless you do something to get her polished up."

Aunt Mamie's wasn't a school. She just gave girls a taste of New York life and some culture and social life. It was quite usual for Southern women to go to visit in a city or to go to a school to be "polished." Miss Semple's School was one of the more famous places. Southern families always had a vague hope that their daughter would meet a millionaire Yankee and marry him and bring him home to save the South or the plantation. About the best investment a Southern family who had fallen on hard times could make was to send the daughter north where she might find a millionaire husband.

It is difficult for those who didn't experience it to realize how poor the South was then. Despite Daddy's inheritance from Grandmother Foster, my family lived in genteel poverty, trying to keep our best foot forward on very little money. But we were surrounded by absolutely abject poverty. We lived on the edge of Red Mountain; on the other side of the mountain were the coal mines and the ore mines. On Saturday mornings, mining families would come walking down our street on their way into Birmingham. There was no paved road and none of these people had a car. These great large families were miserable looking, pale and stunted and almost deformed. Pellagra and worms and malaria were common among the poor whites in the South at that time. Pellagra was a dietary disease, and those who had it would break out in white splotches. Late in the afternoon on Saturday the same families would come home; the children would be hollering, and the adults, both men and women, would be drunk and falling down.

These people worked in the iron ore mines and in the coal mines. They lived in company houses and they were paid with company scrip. Every time they tried to form a union, it was broken up. There had been a terrible struggle to get the convicts out of the mines, and these poor whites had replaced the convicts. The struggle between the poor whites and the Negroes for jobs was terrible, and most of the convicts were blacks.

There was such a contrast between the life I led, a fairly secure life—although we were genteelly poor—and the view that I had of the life of the miners, the actuality of which was before my eyes but which I did not comprehend. I was told by my mother and father and everybody whom I respected and loved that these people were just that way. They were just poor white trash. If they had pellagra and worms and malaria and if they were thin and hungry and immoral, it was just because that was the way they were. It was in their blood. They were born to be poor white trash. They dipped snuff and drooled tobacco juice. If they smelt bad and were dirty, well, they liked being that way.

I was told the same thing about the black people. They had pellagra, too. You cannot imagine the change pellagra made in children. The poor white children were very pale and thin with stringy hair. The textile mill children always looked thin and pale and had white hair and white eyebrows and eyelashes. The poor black children always looked ashen. They wore flour sacks as clothes, with nothing under them. And they often had two great streams of snot hanging down from their nose. They were very unattractive looking. I would feel sorry for them and ask my family about them, and they would say, "This is just the way they are. They are born this way. They don't have any pride or ambition. If you gave them anything, they would just get drunk or spend it on something foolish. They are immoral and spend their money unwisely." And here they were living on five or six dollars a week, if they were employed. That was the average wage, which was supposed to be a pretty good wage. The South was poor. The land was poor. The soil itself was washing away.

We were brought up, or at least I was brought up, to believe that the distribution of wealth was ordained by God. It was "in the blood." You were born to be either wealthy and wise and rich and powerful and beautiful and healthy, or you were born to be poor and downtrodden and sick and miserable and drunken and immoral. There was very little you could do to change your fate because it was "in the blood." It was a very comforting thought, you see, because when you saw people starving and poor and miserable, you thought, "Well, it isn't my fault. I didn't do anything to cause it. God just ordained it this way."

There were also a great many genteelly poor, and lots of the poor ladies went to New York and got a house or apartment and took girls. Payment was never mentioned. That was arranged between your hostess and your father or mother, so the girls themselves never actually paid out any board. The girls were paying guests, but they had to remember that they were guests. If you ever reminded your hostess, even inadvertently, that you were paying, she would get perfectly furious and make it very plain that you were her guest and that you were enjoying the privilege of being her guest. That was to save her pride.

New York was always the center of sophistication. If you wanted to get polished and learn to be cultured, the opera was the great thing, whether you enjoyed it or not. And there were the theater and ballet and plays and movies and Times Square and the night clubs and big hotels and Fifth Avenue. It was a perfectly thrilling city. So, my father and mother decided to send me there.

When I arrived in New York, in 1918, Aunt Mamie lived in an apartment on upper Madison Avenue. The neighborhood was not quite fashionable and not quite a slum; it was in between. Her enormous apartment was filled with antique furniture she had brought up from the South, gold pier mirrors and red velvet curtains and mahogany furniture. She lived in some style when I first got there.

I went to Miss Finch's finishing school, which wasn't nearly as fashionable as Miss Spence's school, but I had gotten there late in the year. I adored New York. You cannot imagine what New York was in those days. I would walk in Central Park and up and down Fifth Avenue and back and forth from school.

I went to school from about nine to three each weekday. Miss Finch's finishing school was extremely good academically, and the teachers took a great deal of interest in their students. But we were also trained in the social graces. We took something called the Mesendieck exercises, which were intended to make us graceful, not strong. We learned to enter a room and to cross our legs properly. Then on Friday afternoons, we would have tea. Every girl had to take her turn at the tea table to learn to pour tea and put in the sugar and cream gracefully and not spill it. We were always being lectured on how to deal with a staff, which meant our servants. We also had long sessions on voice training.

The girls at the school came from all around. A few came from the South and all through the Middle West, and many came from New York. The school was fairly new, and the most aristocratic and richest girls didn't go there but they went to Miss Spence's, the most fashionable school. These schools assumed that all the girls were going to be rich and be mistresses of huge mansions with large staffs of servants. I certainly did not feel rich, but I accepted the school's message. I suppose I thought maybe I would get a rich husband and have a large mansion and staff of servants. This was the ideal, to be a popular, beautiful Southern belle and get a rich Yankee husband. A Southern husband would have been all right, I suppose, but most Southerners were just too poor.

The South was and still is, in my opinion, a colony of the North. After we were defeated in the Civil War, they bought us up for a nickel on the dollar, and they still own us. When I lived in Birmingham, it was a company town, just completely owned by Northern corporations. The owners would come down in their private railroad cars. It was like being visited by a king. Everybody would bow and scrape. The South was defeated. The whole atmosphere of the South at that time was that it was a colony. Northern money and Northern energy and people like Mr. Smith of L & N Railroad were the great heroes. Henry Grady, the Atlanta editor, had preached industrialization. Booker T. Washington at Tuskegee was preaching the same thing: Northern money, industrialize and bring in the money. Otherwise, it was just poor tenant farming, and tenant farming was about as low as you could get—moving around from place to place and living in wretched hovels and eating fatback and cornbread and working in the cotton fields all day.

I think the great thing that separates the generations today is the depression. I've had young civil rights workers stay with me who were living on very little money, but they have no concept of what poverty is because they have never actually been hungry. They have denied themselves and lived off hamburgers, but they have never just had nothing to eat. They take buses and airplanes and automobiles and McDonald's hamburgers for granted. They may live on a very simple scale, but they have no concept of real poverty. I think that is the thing that has separated the generations today more than anything else, the poverty that my generation knew firsthand.

The depression in the South started long before the depression in the rest of the country. The South had been poor since the Civil War. Most Southern people were extremely poor. They had been poor during the Civil War, but the rich planter class had given them a feeling of richness. When the Civil War was over, all that was swept away. I don't think that *Gone with the Wind* is the greatest book ever written, but I do think it gives a good picture of the South after the Civil War—the decline of the plantation system and the avariciousness, the desire for money, the terrific desire for money, money, money. That terrific desire grew out of the fact that the South was so damn poor.

I was brought up to think that a Yankee was a very bad thing. I remember as a little girl we would go out and visit some people in Birmingham named Stevens. They were members of my father's church. Mr. Stevens was an old Confederate veteran, and he was a darling man, just as cute as could be. They had a farm on the edge of town and I used to love to go there and visit. I remember talking to him, and I would say, "Oh, Mr. Stevens, I'll never marry a Yankee." "Oh," he'd say, "don't you marry one of those scoundrels." Yankees were bad people and I was a Southerner.

I had seen the equivalent of slavery in its most benevolent aspects on my grandmother's plantation. There was a tremendous abundance and, as far as I could see, an extremely loving relationship between the blacks and the whites. But when my grandmother died and everything in Union Springs collapsed, what happened to old Easter was tragic. Easter had really been the mistress of the plantation, because my grandmother, as sweet and kind as she was, was like a child. Easter ran everything for her. Of course, I suppose the bank and her sons did, too, but Easter actually did the day-by-day, hour-by-hour running of the house and plantation. After Grandmother died, Easter came up to Birmingham to live with her daughter. I never knew she had a daughter, but she had one who was married to a miner who lived across the mountain. He worked in the red ore mines. Well, she had no sooner gotten settled with her daughter than she got in touch with my mother and came to visit. Her daughter and son-in-law brought her in. She looked as she had always looked but a little thinner. She had a spotless white starched dress. She wore a straw hat over her head, and her handkerchief was as white as ever. She wanted to come and live with Mother, with "Miss Annie." I know she hated living out there in that red ore miner's house.

Mother knew that Easter was coming to visit, and to do our duty we fixed ice cream and cake. Of course, Easter and her daughter and her son-in-law went into the breakfast room to eat. The mores had to be observed. When they came back, I could feel that Easter was terribly anxious. Mother was terribly embarrassed because we couldn't take on Easter. We didn't have the money to pay her or even for her just to live with us. Mother knew she couldn't possibly live up to Easter's standards of abundance, and yet she was so sorry for the old woman living over the mountain in an iron ore miner's shack. It was a terrible, emotional period. Here was the old faithful servant who had been a slave, who had belonged to the family, and who wanted to come back to the family. She had been used to living surrounded by the utmost ease. We knew what a wonderful, smart woman she was. We felt terrible that we had not been able to live up to our obligations and had let Easter down. Easter went back to her daughter's shack and died shortly thereafter. I'm sure she just decided that her life was over.

My grandfather Patterson had a body servant during the Civil War named Reuben, old Reuben. Every time Birmingham had a Confederate reunion, the Negroes who had been body servants to the officers would come. By the time I knew Reuben he was in his eighties, and terribly bow-legged, but he would always come. We would never know when he was coming, and he would always arrive at the house at the most inconvenient time, expecting money, food, and whiskey. And there again, Mother felt she was neglecting her duties if we couldn't supply Reuben with a good meal and whiskey and plenty of money. I can remember rushing to the store to buy cake when Reuben came to visit. It was hard to get whiskey then, but Daddy would manage some way to get him a drink.

Reuben would talk about the colonel, Mother's father—"Colonel Jo-siah," or "Colonel Patterson," and what a great man he was. He told us a story one time that may chill your blood, but he thought it was a great story. Although Reuben was bowlegged, he could run fast, so the colonel once had him race against a horse, and Reuben won. He was proud of it. He thought that was wonderful. "I tell you, I beat that horse," he would say. Reuben had never come out of the slavery period, and he expected us to provide for him. We lived in the halfway stage between being benevolent despots or benevolent plantation owners and trying to make a living. It was that awful in-between stage of being genteel but poor. We felt we had all these obligations to the poor blacks, but we didn't have the money to fulfill them.

During the pre–World War I period, the economic base in the South was cotton. Cliff's father was in the wholesale drug business, but the first thing in the morning he would look at the cotton exchange report. Business failed or prospered according to the price of cotton. The South had to sell its cotton on a free market and buy its goods on a protected market because of the tariff. When the price of cotton went down and down, the farmers had to borrow money to make their crop. They would try to make up for it by putting more and more land into cotton, which was the only cash crop they had. Cotton takes a heavy toll on the land and needs a lot of fertilizer, and Southern farmers didn't have the money to buy it. As a result, the land got poorer and poorer in the South and began to erode.

Before the New Deal, one of the noticeable things about the landscape of the South was the gullied farms. Driving down the roads, you never saw a farmhouse with any paint or fences that weren't down. Everything looked miserable. When the New Deal started the soil conservation programs and paid farmers money to get out of these row crops and put more land into pasture and timber, the beauty of the landscape began to return. Cotton was a desperate means of existence. You were really mining the land, which was the expression that we used. I can remember that even during World War I it became a patriotic duty of the businessmen to buy cotton at ten cents a pound. The price was around six or eight cents, and they were trying to bring the price up artificially by buying it at ten cents a pound.

My father, even though he had 9,000 or 10,000 acres, had to "furnish" the tenants, who were all black. He had to provide their seed and fertilizer, and he had a terrible time borrowing enough money to do that. Cotton kept going down and down, and then the boll weevil began to come in and eat up the crops. I was aware that everything I did was connected to the price of cotton, whether I went to school or didn't go to school. For instance, I never could go off to summer camp. All my friends went off to summer camp, but I never could afford to do that.

The great mark of change from that time is not only the landscape, but also the change in the appearance of the children, both the black and white children. The contrast is amazing. Their teeth are so much better now and their complexions and their hair and their clothes. You hardly ever see a child look the way I remember the poor children looking when I was growing up. I suppose that is one reason I am more hopeful than the young people are. I have seen things so much worse.

After my grandmother died, Daddy would go down to Union Springs, but he never ran the plantation. Daddy was never a businessman at all. He was a scholar and a preacher and then he sold insurance, which he always felt was beneath him. He did it because he had to support his family. He couldn't be a gentleman farmer and make a living. Never. I doubt Daddy ever pulled up a weed in his life. He never did anything with his hands that I can recall. Daddy would sit by a fire, and if it started going out, he was accustomed to yelling, "Jim! Joe!" Some black boy would come in and put a log on, or some black woman. When Daddy didn't have any more black people to call, my mother or I would come in and put the wood on the fire. It never occurred to him to just reach over and do it himself.

One day during World War II, Daddy was visiting Cliff and me in Washington, and we didn't have very much oil. We used just enough to keep the pipes from freezing. We had a fireplace in one of the small rooms, and we really lived in there. Daddy was an old man then, but he was still fairly active. We were sitting by the fire, drinking hot coffee, and the fire began to die down. We didn't have any wood, so I went out in the snow and cold with an axe or a hatchet. I never was very good at chopping wood; Cliff usually had some wood already cut. But that night I had to chop us some wood and bring it in and start up the fire again. Daddy looked at me and said, "Dear, I declare, it distresses me terribly to see your hands. You know, my mother had the most beautiful white hands and your mother had such beautiful white hands. I really think that hands are the mark of a lady. Since you have to do all this work, couldn't you wear gloves?" It never occurred to him to do the work himself. I think one of the reasons I became a feminist is because my mother spoiled my father terribly. She never expected him to do anything. She never expected him to wash a dish or fix a meal or do anything around the house, and he never did.

Like my father, I was brought up as a Southerner, too, completely as a Southerner. I had never been North until I went to New York to school. There was only one other Southerner at Miss Finch's, a beautiful girl from Montgomery. We had to take the Mesendieck exercises, and we were supposed to take a shower beforehand and put on our leotards and do our exercises and then take a shower afterward. The water was usually pretty cold, so it was rather disagreeable. The Montgomery girl was a boarder; I was a day pupil. She had a room in the school, so she would arrive at class in her leotard and say that she had taken a shower before she came. Then she would insist on going back to take a shower in her own private room afterward. Well, whether the girls were jealous of her or they thought she was cheating or whether they thought she was taking a hot shower and we were getting a cold shower, I never knew. But I do remember going into the shower room and seeing the girl surrounded by all the others, who were saying, "You are just a dirty Southerner. You don't want to take baths because you are just a dirty Southerner. I am surprised that you even wear shoes." Just direct insults. I was absolutely furious and as shocked as I could be. The girl was crying and mad. She had a wet towel and began to hit at these girls, who were persecuting her terribly and telling her that she was a dirty Southerner and never took baths and probably didn't even have a bathroom in her house at home. So I took up a wet towel and began to defend the Southern girl against the Yankee girls. It was the most absurd, ridiculous thing you could imagine, but we were furious. I wasn't being directly insulted, because I always took my showers, but she was being directly insulted because she was a Southerner. For the first time, I realized that the South was looked down upon. The South was a poor section of the country and Southerners were looked down on.

Aunt Mamie's pretensions were transparent. I could see how hollow they were. How she lived on the little money she had, I don't know. Poor Mr. W—— must have had some little job, because he went off and came back every day. But I never knew what he did. I don't know whether he was still selling shoes or what, but it wasn't much. Aunt Mamie was keeping up all this pretense of the Southern aristocracy with these girls as her guests. When I first lived there, she had a maid come in to serve dinner. She would often invite guests, and we would have a glass of sherry in the parlor and then sit down to a delicious dinner. We would have coffee afterward in the parlor. It was all very formal and rather grand. But as the year wore on, the maid left.

Aunt Mamie did something that I found extremely embarrassing, and I'm sure that Sister and Ella Vaughn did, too. Men were streaming back and forth through New York returning from the war. I remember a procession of them through the apartment. Sister and Ella Vaughn had lots of beaus, and the icebox was always full of flowers and candy. At the same time, Aunt Mamie was having a hard time paying the bills. These adoring young men would invite Sister or Ella Vaughn out to dinner, and Aunt Mamie would say in her high society manner, "How sweet of you to invite us all to dinner." I was only fifteen, but I was aware that the boys really didn't want me along. And not only would they have to take us all out to dinner, but Aunt Mamie would say, "Now, I really think the Waldorf has the best food. Or maybe the Ritz is a little better. Of course, the Plaza is quite delightful." The poor men couldn't embarrass themselves in front of their beloved, so they would end up taking Mr. W—— and Aunt Mamie and Ella Vaughn and Sister and me. Of course, we got a mighty good dinner, but it was a terrible thing to do. Aunt Mamie was desperate and this was her way of saving money on dinner.

I didn't have beaus then. Aunt Mamie still thought that I was impossible. I was so tall and thin and nearsighted. But Aunt Mamie was very active in the Madison Avenue Presbyterian Church, and the church had a soldiers' center, open to soldiers and sailors of all nations. She managed to get the church to take me on as a hostess, and all of a sudden I was plunged into a world of millions of men. No girl could help but be popular. The men were lined up waiting to dance because there were so few girls. I learned to be quite relaxed with men. I can't remember them all now, but one of them was a good-looking Norwegian who couldn't speak English very well. The center was supervised and chaperoned, and I had a wonderful time.

Cliff always claimed that I have a superiority complex. If I have, I acquired it after I married him. When I was younger, I felt terribly inferior to Sister and Ella Vaughn. They were beautiful and extremely popular. The young men were beseeching them and sending candy and flowers all the time. It was painful to me. Aunt Mamie arranged for me once to go to West Point with one of the Hill boys from Montgomery, and that was very nice. But mostly I got practice with the soldiers and sailors and marines and foreign servicemen at the soldiers' center. I realized that if you just smiled and were pleasant and learned how to dance and relax, you could get on quite well. I had always been terribly nervous with men, because I didn't think that I was very attractive and I was trying to impress them.

I did very well in Miss Finch's school. I had no trouble with the work, except that some of it bored me. What interested me most was New York itself. I would get home about three o'clock and I could do anything I wanted, so I explored New York. Above us was a Jewish section and I would walk all over. There were wedding shops where big Jewish women with black wigs would stand in the door and say "Come in, honey," or whatever they called you, "Lovey, come and try on." I would go in and try on wedding veils. But of course, I never bought anything. I was just fascinated with the Jewish section. I would go into a Jewish delicatessen, and for twenty-five cents I could get a roll and a piece of salami and a dill pickle. Oh, it was marvelous. Then there was an Italian section in back of us. The grocery stores there were all wonderful. You could buy a little bit of cheese, and the smells were delicious. Down below that was a German section, filled with the aroma of cabbage. All the sections were designated by food for me. I got these great vignettes of foreign life. I never got down as far as China-town, I'm sorry to say, but I would take rides on the Fifth Avenue bus and sit on top. New York was so beautiful then, and it was so clean. It smelled good, and I never had a moment's fear. I was allowed to go anywhere. I could go to the movies and walk home in the dark.

I was in New York about a year. It was a fascinating experience for me, but I wasn't really happy at Aunt Mamie's. Aunt Mamie never did come to terms with me because I was, I suppose, an obnoxious child. I always wanted to know the reasons for things. Aunt Mamie used to read the society col-umns. She had a passion for New York society, which she was hardly a member of, although she always claimed that she could have been if only Mr. W—— had been a millionaire. But because of Ella Vaughn, some of the young men who came to the house were very rich. Aunt Mamie read *Vogue* and *Harper's Bazaar* and *Town and Country* and was fascinated to find out where the Vanderbilts and the Rockefellers were going. I remember saying to her one day, "Aunt Mamie, why are you so interested in all those people if you don't even know them?" She got perfectly furious with me. I had exposed the myth that I was supposed to swallow. I was supposed to believe that she was an aristocratic Southern lady who had a few guests in her house because she was kind to these poor girls up from the South. My sister had sense enough to be aware of Aunt Mamie's needs. She didn't play up to her, but she accepted her needs and went along. I was always asking questions.

Sister and I were very devoted to each other. I often say that I thought she was prettier and more popular and that my father loved her best, but I was never jealous of her, at least not consciously. In fact, I always felt sorry for her, because Sister was very proud and very sensitive and her feelings were easily hurt. But she was happy in New York. She was in the Navy, making her own money, and having a wonderful time.

Sister stayed on in New York until she was released from the Navy. She had wanted to come home just for a visit and then go back, because she loved being independent. But my father used all the emotional blackmail he could. I remember one of the letters he wrote to her: "If you don't come home, I'll know that you don't love me any more. You are the light of my life, and I have always adored you. If you don't come home, I'll know that you think I'm a failure, that you think I can't support you." Finally she gave in and came home and that summer she met a very attractive man, Hugo Black. While he certainly became a great man and he adored Sister, she never was independent after she married him. He was one of the most powerful characters that she could have married.

Sister and Hugo's courtship was interesting. When she came home from New York, she still had on her uniform. Hugo was just out of the Army, where he had been a major, and was a very successful labor lawyer. He was thirty-five and she was about twenty-one. I was sixteen. He lived up the street from us in a house with a lot of other bachelors. A great believer in exercise, he would walk by the house every day going to his office and coming back, always whistling and bouncing. I thought he was good-looking, and Sister did, too. Whether it was by design or by chance, one day he saw her in her Navy uniform. I must say, she did look absolutely enchanting in it, and he couldn't wait to be introduced to her. He met her the following Saturday night at the country club dance, and he never stopped pursuing her until they married.

I never saw a man work so hard in my life. This was the summer of 1919, and Hugo married Josephine in the winter of 1921. It took him about a year and a half to get her. She was terribly attracted to him, but he was very dynamic and different from her and from everybody in her family. As a labor lawyer he represented the unions, so all the corporation people called him a Bolshevik. All the family friends came to Daddy and said, "Oh, Dr. Foster, you wouldn't let your daughter marry a Bolshevik!" Forney Johnston was the main corporation lawyer in Birmingham and his wife was a great friend of my mother's. Mrs. Johnston and Mother were in the Cadmean Circle together. I know that Mr. Johnston warned Daddy and Mother against having anything to do with this Bolshevik. The Russian Revolution had just taken place, and the word "Communist" wasn't used then; it was Bolshevik, which meant anything radical or particularly connected with labor. In those days, if you belonged to a union, you were a Bolshevik.

The unions had a terrific struggle getting started in the South. When I met John L. Lewis the first time, when we lived in Alexandria, Virginia, he knew the family name immediately. He said, "Durr. From Alabama?"

I said, "Yes."

"I knew your father-in-law very well."

"How in the world did you know my father-in-law?"

"Your father-in-law," he said, "was on Governor Kilby's committee."

There was a big United Mine Workers strike during Governor Kilby's tenure, and the governor appointed a committee to look into it. Cliff's father went up to Birmingham and examined the causes for the strike and came to the conclusion that the mine companies were the most benevolent, paternalistic, high-minded, splendid organizations in the world. They even built churches for their people, and they had a hospital for them. The committee immediately declared that the strike was no good and it was broken. So Mr. Lewis remembered Mr. Durr very well.

Now Mr. Durr was one of the best men in the world, but he thought the coal companies were just wonderful. He thought George Gordon Crawford, the head of Tennessee Coal, Iron and Railroad Company, was one of the greatest men alive. Southerners had a great admiration for the Southern men who had succeeded with Yankee corporations. They had really made it with the Wall Street Yankees. It is almost impossible to realize the power these corporations had and the way they were looked up to as the salvation of the South.

Hugo Black's identification with labor unions had not endeared him to some of my parents' friends. So he had to win over the whole family, not just Sister. When Hugo was courting Sister, he never missed a day to come by. He was dating other people, because he and Sister weren't engaged yet, but he was there all the time. He cultivated me and Mother and Daddy and Sister and everybody. When he started out to do something, he did it.

Hugo was a wonderful influence on me because he would bring me books to read. He thought I had some brains. I remember he brought me books by Mary and Charles Beard, and he brought me Parrington's *Main Currents in American Thought*. I was amazed that he would bring them to me, but he did, and he would talk to me as an equal. He would explain things to me, all about labor unions. He had a tremendous influence on me and I adored him. He was an extraordinarily attractive man, lively and bright and terribly energetic.

I went to the public high school in Birmingham that year, and then that following summer, Sister went up to Mentone. Hugo went to see Sister and took Mother and me with him. She had some beaus up on the mountain, too, but Hugo never left off one single minute.

The following fall—it must have been 1920—I went to the Cathedral School in Washington, along with a lot of my friends. Daddy must have sold something to be able to afford it. The Cathedral School was supposed to be very fine and fashionable, and all the nicest girls went there. My teachers were excellent, but the school itself was snobbish. The headmistress was always telling us that she could have been principal of Westover or Foxcroft or even more fashionable schools. She made us feel she had really come down in the world by being head of the National Cathedral School, because Westover School and the Foxcroft School were even richer and more fashionable. But by that time, I had come to recognize that there was always a rung ahead, no matter what position you achieved. There was always someone richer and grander.

At the Cathedral School I met girls from all over the South. All of them had no idea in the world of becoming anything but debutantes and marrying well and being popular. By and large, young ladies went to finishing school, not to college. Only bluestocking intellectuals went to college. But some of the girls from the Cathedral School did go to college, and they were encouraged to do so. Of course, the great majority of them didn't. Most went home and made their debut and then married well.

Sister would have finished college, but we were poor by the time she had been to Sweet Briar for a year or so. Sometimes we had money and sometimes we didn't. I don't know whether it was cotton going up and down or whether Daddy would sell something or what happened. Mother and Daddy would never discuss money. It was considered common to talk about money.

When I went to the Cathedral School I pretty well accepted its values myself. I did have an intellectual curiosity, and I loved to read and I wanted to go to college, but I had accepted the fact that the world was divided into stratifications, and the important thing was to stay where you were or get to the higher rung. Of course, the poor people, blacks and whites, were poor because they were born that way: it was "in the blood." I was lucky because I had been born to a higher stratum—but I wasn't quite sure that I was going to stay there!

I was always aware that we were not as rich as the girls I associated with. All my friends in Birmingham and the girls at the Cathedral School were richer than I was. For instance, I remember that at spring vacation, I didn't go home because the family just didn't have the money to get me back and forth. I stayed with the Forney Johnstons. Mr. Johnston was in Washington at that time representing the Southern Railroad.

I was always conscious of not having the money that other girls had. Their mothers would go to New York every fall to buy their clothes. I always had somebody come in for three dollars a day to make mine. Mother had good taste, but we were keeping up with the Joneses at great effort—trying to make a fifteen-dollar dress look like a hundred-dollar one.

I came home from Washington for Christmas vacation and at that time Sister was surrounded by young men trying to marry her. Instead of making her conceited, it made her very sorrowful. She couldn't marry all of them, and she was terribly weepy over the ones she couldn't marry. She couldn't bear to hurt their feelings. I remember that feather fans and beaded pocketbooks and boxes of candy and flowers just rolled in that Christmas. I got a few modest things. One of them was a hammer somebody had made in school. But Sister was just besieged by young men at that point, and Hugo was still in there every minute. She was very undecided. She couldn't make up her mind whether to marry him or not.

My mother liked Hugo and Daddy liked him. They realized he was a very successful lawyer and was involved in the country club and had lovely manners. But of course, he came from Clay County, and they couldn't quite place him. They never had heard of the Blacks from Clay County. They found that the Blacks ran a store in Ashland. Hugo's father was quite a prosperous merchant—for Ashland. Mother and Daddy didn't know what a Bolshevik was, but they worried when word came to them that Hugo was one. But even so, Hugo was in the country club and was very popular and considered to be quite a catch, at least by those who weren't part of the corporate fight that was going on. He belonged to the Baptist Church and he taught Sunday school and he belonged to a multitude of fraternal organizations. He knew Birmingham inside out and upside down—poor folks, black folks, white folks, labor folks. He had become quite a figure, but anticorporation.

At that time in Birmingham the corporations and the labor unions were involved in terrible clashes. Hugo represented the carpenters and the mine workers and the railway unions, and he got tremendous judgments against the corporations for employees who had been injured on the job. And he was trying to get the unions organized.

The soldiers had come back from the war by the thousands, determined that they were going to be rewarded for their work. They weren't going back to work for nothing. So they put forth a tremendous effort to form unions and get higher pay. But the white man's fear of the black worked against them. Many black men had also been in the Army, and the corporations spread the word that the blacks had slept with white women in France and they were going to try to sleep with white women in the South.

All the old passions of sex, the dreadful sexual cesspool, I call it, came to the surface, and the white men wouldn't let the blacks into the unions. There were lynchings, and other dreadful things were done to the black soldiers, designed to make the black veterans go back in their place and not think that because they'd been in the United States Army they could take any liberties. Horrible oppressions took place. And, of course, the unions were broken.

In Birmingham the "modern," twentieth-century version of the Ku Klux Klan formed at that time as a kind of underground union. It's commonly thought that the Klan was against the unions, but it wasn't. The workers had tried to form unions to make themselves politically effective and they were defeated, so then they flocked to the Klan. They joined partly because they were determined to get more money and to be politically effective. They felt they could do this only through a secret organization. The bad part of it was that they were determined that the black soldiers should not think they were going to sleep with white women. The Klan was against the Catholics and Jews, too, but not nearly so much.

I never went to a Klan meeting, but I've been to many a Klan parade. I just took it for granted. I never thought anything of it. My grandfather had been in the Klan. He had fought for Nathan Bedford Forrest, who formed the Klan. I thought of the Klan as something noble and grand and patriotic that had saved the white women of the South. I remember seeing *Birth of a Nation,* and oh, I thought it was the most thrilling, dramatic, and marvelous thing in the world when the Klan rode in there and rescued the poor white girl from the black soldier.

You can't imagine the contradictions in my life, the total contradictions. I had been surrounded by black men all my life, sweet lovely old men whose laps I sat on as a child, and the mailman, the yardman, the furnace man. Not one of them had ever been anything but kind and decent to me. I had never been afraid of a single one of them. It never crossed my mind that a black man would make an indecent overture, or a white man, either, for that matter. I kept hearing about rape, but I didn't know what it was, and I was afraid to ask because of the terrible inhibitions about sex that had been driven into me. I was scared that it would be revealed to be something I didn't want to know. But at the same time that I was surrounded by lovely, decent black people, I would go to see *Birth of a Nation* and believe that the Klan was noble and wonderful, and I was proud that my grandfather had been a member of it. So when people said Hugo Black was a member of the Klan it didn't bother me at all.

I used to go to Klan parades, and I remember one thing particularly: I remember looking at their shoes. I wondered why they all had on such worn-out, old, miserable shoes. I had always thought of the Klan as the aristocrats riding off on white horses to save the pure white Southern woman. I was surprised that the Klansmen I saw looked so poor.

The memory of the Confederacy was still very much alive. Lots of Confederate reunions were held in Birmingham, and all the nice girls from the age of about twelve to twenty would serve as pages. The old soldiers all had beards, it seemed to me, and bushy mustaches and they all spit and chewed tobacco. But they were put up in the nicest homes and hotels. The ladies who ran the UDC, the United Daughters of the Confederacy, who were always great big stout ladies or very thin ladies, wore banners and flowers and big hats, and the young girls were all dressed up and were pages. All I could see that we did was to let the old soldiers kiss us. Well, that was pretty horrible, because not only did they chew tobacco, but they were always given liquor to keep them going and so they smelled. The wet tobacco juice—oh, it was disgusting! I came home and told Mother that I wasn't going back, and she said, "Well, darling, they are heroes. They are old Confederate veterans." If some old lecherous man had kissed me, she would have thought it was terrible, but she thought it was perfectly all right to send me down there with these lecherous old Confederate soldiers and let twenty of them hug me and kiss me. They were heroes. I got a terrible distaste for tobacco-flavored and whiskey-flavored kisses.

Then we would ride in the parade and the politicans would make speeches about pure white Southern womanhood—and I believed it. I was pure white Southern womanhood and Southern men had died for me and the Confederate flag was flying just to save me. I got to thinking I was pretty hot stuff, to have the war fought for me.

Nobody ever discussed the Civil War. Nobody ever sat down and said, "Now, you've got to believe that the War Between the States was . . ." You just automatically believed that the slave system had been a benevolent system. I can remember my grandmother telling me, "Well, honey, I just feel so sorry for those poor people. When they lived with us . . ." She never said, "When we owned them . . ." "When they lived with us, they were so happy and we looked after them. We took care of them when they were sick and looked after them when they were old." Of course, I could see them in the backyard in Union Springs, being fed and living in those little clean houses, and I imagined they were being looked after when they were sick and they did look happy to me. "Oh," she said, "the terrible thing for them was when they were freed and had to go back on their own resources and they couldn't make a living." That was the view I got of slavery. Nothing was ever discussed; everything was assumed.

Nothing was ever discussed. If anybody fell by the wayside, it was just never mentioned. I remember it was whispered that a girl had had a baby. Well, she was banished and nobody ever knew where she went. Somebody said that she was sent off to New Jersey, but she disappeared as though she had never existed. Nobody ever spoke her name and she never came back. Her mother and father left town. It was as though the whole family had just died. Nobody ever told you this was the fate that would happen to you if you had a baby, but you knew it. You were aware of it. We knew she was a fast girl and she had done something that had brought on that baby, and we knew if we did it, we would be banished, too. Now, what it was, we didn't quite know. We knew if we stayed in the car and kissed too much that we might do it, too. But nothing was discussed.

Nobody ever told you that you had to believe this or that. It was just assumed that you did believe. Mother divided the world into types of people. The nice people lived on the Southside and were the Presbyterians and Episcopalians. They lived in nice houses and had servants and automobiles and belonged to the country club. They were the people that you associated with. Beneath the nice people was a group that she strongly resented and which she called "the climbers," the new rich. They had money, and they might get in the country club—finally. Of course, they always did if they were rich enough. It was always said, "Well, nobody knows who they are or where they came from. Nobody has ever heard of them before, and I have never been able to place who they were." Then beneath them came the "good plain people." These were the people who might rise eventually into the nice people. They were respectable and they did the work of the world and kept things going. Beyond them were the "common people." Now, these people were mostly Baptists. The fact that Hugo was a Baptist was one of the things that Mother and Daddy held against him. The common people worked, but at inferior jobs. They were, I suppose, the working class. And then, the worst, far beyond them, were the poor white trash. When you got down there, you were at the bottom of the heap on the white side. They were totally uncouth, very miserable people with either tobacco or snuff dripping down their chins. They were always yellow; somehow, I think it must have been malaria. And they had pellagra and hookworms and they bred "like rabbits." They were completely beyond the pale.

The blacks were outside everything. They were just a completely different group. Of course, we were surrounded by them the entire time. They were in the house and our lives depended on them and we loved them dearly, but they were just outside, a completely separate group.

By the time I got to the Cathedral School, I accepted this view of the world, and everybody in the school accepted it. If there was any protest against it, I never heard of it. It was a class society and we Southern girls were just as impressed by it as we could be, because we were not nearly as rich as the Yankee girls were. A few girls finally got to Foxcroft School, which Miss Charlotte Noland ran in Virginia. It was supposed to be the richest school of all and was run on the most snobbish lines possible in order to attract the richest girls. And Miss Noland succeeded. It didn't attract me because I was called back from the Cathedral School when Sister finally decided to marry Hugo.

The wedding was in February of 1921, and I was the maid of honor. When I got home, I found everyone in a great state of excitement because Hugo said to my mother that they either had to have 10,000 people to the wedding—because he was already thinking about politics—or just a very few, a home wedding. Of course, Mother couldn't afford any 10,000 people at the wedding, so they had a very quiet home wedding, just the two families and a few friends.

Hugo was just adamant against liquor. He had a brother who sometimes drank. One night this brother was coming home after he had been drinking. His buggy capsized while he was crossing a stream and he drowned. Now whether Hugo's brother drowned on account of the liquor or on account of the buggy, I do not know, but Hugo was a fierce prohibitionist.

On the day of the wedding my sister was nervous. My Aunt Louise from Memphis, whom we called "Oo-Oo," was a gay old lady in those days.

She smoked cigarettes and took a drink and told funny stories. We all adored her. Sister was so nervous, just trembling and shaking all over, that Oo-Oo gave her a little drink of whiskey. Well, Hugo always said that when his bride came down to the altar and he leaned over to kiss her, the first thing he smelled was whiskey on her breath. He just about fell over in a dead faint. But when they married, he was the happiest man I have ever seen in my life. And I think she was very happy, too.

Hugo absolutely worshipped Josephine. I never saw a man love a woman more than he did or work harder to get her. He did everything in his power to make her happy, except give her her freedom. He gave her everything he could think of. There was not a wish of her heart that he didn't satisfy, but she never had one hour's freedom from that time on. She was Mrs. Hugo Black. He expected her to subordinate herself to his life and his ambitions. It never occurred to him otherwise. He never realized that she might occasionally want to be free to do something she wanted to do. He was kind not only to her but also to her family. He helped us a lot and assumed a great deal of responsibility when my mother and father lost everything. But Sister was always in a state of dependence, total dependence. Their daughter, who was entirely different from her mother, went to college and was much more independent. Hugo wanted to send her to Sweet Briar. He wanted her to be just like her mother. He wanted her to be a sweet Southern lady and beautiful and charming. And Sister was all of those things; she was beautiful and sweet and charming. Everybody adored her, and he above all. But after she married, I don't think Sister ever was able to have a free moment.

That was the way girls were supposed to be anyway. There was no question about that. The suffrage movement was just starting then. A lady who lived in the neighborhood, Pattie Jacobs, was a leader of the suffrage movement in Birmingham. She was a handsome woman, but Mother and Daddy would say, "Oh, poor Mr. Jacobs, think of that wife he's got, running all over the country and the town getting votes for women." And Mother would say, "Well, you know, I think that Mrs. Jacobs likes men." I believed what Mother said, that she was doing it because she liked men.

Liking men was supposed to be quite a sin in those days. Any woman who was considered fast or painted her face or was too forward was accused of liking men. A beautiful woman in Birmingham named Mrs. Barrett had been married three or four times, and it was whispered that she liked men, which meant she was a fast woman. That was a terrible sin. You were supposed to be "chased and chaste." You were supposed to be totally pure and terribly attractive to men but not give them an inch. If you did, you would be banished, packed off to New Jersey. You can see the inhibitions that had been built up in us and the class barriers and the sex barriers and the idea that marrying and marrying well was the only fate you could possibly want.

Now, I had no objection to this. Not then. My great fear was that I wouldn't be popular. I had been told from my infancy that I was too big, too rawboned, nearsighted, and that I asked too many questions. I never was given a good image, except by my mother. She always said, "Now, dear, if you will just do this or that, you will be beautiful and you will be charming." I wasn't any great belle. I had a few boys who came around, but they weren't much. In my teens, I really wasn't one of the most popular girls.

We had the most awful system then. The hostess of a party or dance would make a list of the girls who had been invited and put it on the cigar counter at a drugstore. The boys would go in and check the names of the girls they wanted to take to the event. No matter what you were invited to, whether it was a buffet supper or a picnic or anything, the boys would check the names. The boys were totally in control of the social system. If you didn't get checked, you didn't go, even if it was a private party. The hostess would make frantic efforts to try to make some boy bring you! We were in a state of absolute terror all the time because we were totally dependent on popularity with the boys. If they didn't check your name, you were disgraced.

Sometimes I wasn't checked. My mother's fashionable friend Mrs. Cabaniss knew that my mother was worried about me because I wasn't very popular. This was when I was only fifteen, before I went off to New York. I had a few beaus but not nearly enough to make me a belle. One of them wouldn't take me to a dance because he came up to my elbow, and the other one couldn't dance. So Mrs. Cabaniss said, "Now Virginia, men are like sheep. If they see a lot of men around a girl, they will always be attracted because they follow a crowd. The thing for you to do if you want to be popular is to be nice to all the 'drips,' the dull boys and the ugly boys and the boys who can't dance well and the shy boys and the boys who aren't much with it. You just start being nice to all the drips and then no matter who they are, the 'dashing' boys will see you being surrounded by all these boys and they'll want to know what that girl has got. She must have something, you know, or she wouldn't be surrounded." So I made an absolute, desperate effort to be nice to all the drips. I collected around myself some of the drippiest drips you've ever seen. I really blush to think how false and hypocritical I was—I'd go with the short boys and the tall boys and the shy boys. Some of them turned out to be the nicest, of course, when I made them feel at ease. But lots of them were rather dull. Oh, what I suffered, the boredom I put up with. Finally I got to be fairly popular. Boys would break in on me at the country club dances and they would check me off for the dances. But I was always a little anxious. I never had the feeling that the belles had of being irresistible.

Now the fact that I had gone away to New York and to the Cathedral School didn't mean anything. Nothing gave you status in those days but being popular with the boys. You could be beautiful, you could be rich, you could go to Paris to school, but if you weren't popular with the boys, none of it counted. Some of the richest girls in Birmingham, ones who went to Foxcroft and had clothes worth thousands of dollars and gave the boys eight-course dinners at their homes, never got checked for the dances. The boys absolutely ruled the social life. They were the ones who determined whether a girl was or was not popular. We were totally at their mercy. Attracting men and being attractive to men and getting a nice beau and the best marriage that we could was our only ambition and our only future, our only career. So naturally the boys were in total command of the situation. Only the girls who were so popular that they could play one man off against another had any power.

A girl who lived across the street from me was engaged to five men at the same time. She played one man against the other. The same thing was true of my sister. She had all these men trying to marry her and she was totally in control of the situation. Of course, Sister was so tenderhearted that she was always crying because she couldn't marry them all. She was afraid to break their hearts.

I was different. I wanted to be popular and marry well, of course, but I also wanted to go to college. Daddy thought I had some brains and he wanted to see that I got a college education. Daddy had a splendid library and I had read everything in it. I had read Macaulay's *History of England,* Green's *History of England,* all of Dickens, all of Scott, most of Eliot, and a good bit of Guizot's *History of France.* I was such an omnivorous reader I had even gone through the *Book of Knowledge.*

One reason I read so much was that I was nearsighted and very poor at sports. I never could play tennis or golf. I could swim, but that was about all. I didn't get glasses until I was sixteen, and after that my parents seldom let me wear them. Mother thought glasses would just ruin my chances. When I dated, my mother would hide the glasses, and she would never let me wear them at dances or parties. In the days before talking movies, they would flash signs up, and I never could read them. I could hardly see Marguerite Clark or Mary Pickford or Wallace Reid, who was my hero. I couldn't see the leaves on the trees. Everything was a blur.

I never belonged to the Jazz Age. In Birmingham, there was a fast set that drank gin, but I never belonged to that, because I was a "nice girl." I went mostly with nice young men. Occasionally I would get caught with a drunk, which was pretty sad. We girls would spend all day fixing ourselves up for a dance we'd been invited to. Everything would have to be just right— our slippers and stockings and underwear and our powder and paint and lipstick and rouge. We would take bubble baths. Somehow we thought a bubble bath would make us irresistible. Our mothers would powder our backs, and we'd curl our hair. Our dresses were usually made of satin or tulle or chiffon, and we would have to have the right kind of little evening bag. When we finally got it all done, we would look like beautiful flowers.

Then, after all this preparation, we would go to the dance with some boy, and by God, he would get drunk.

In those days, the liquor was mostly bootleg liquor, and some of the boys got what they called jake-leg. And they'd throw up. The country club would just be lined with the aristocracy of Birmingham throwing up over the balustrade because they had drunk this horrible liquor. There was no temptation for young ladies to take a drink because it tasted so bad. But it was very disappointing to want to be the figure of romance and have your beau turn into a sick young man. He couldn't bring you home, and somebody else would have to.

My brother had been in the Sigma Alpha Epsilon fraternity at the University of Alabama; the SAEs were the top dogs in Birmingham society then, and many of them were big drunks. My brother never let me go out with any of his fraternity brothers. A few of them would ask me for dates, but he said, "No, Jinksie, you can't go with that boy." The caller may have been one of his best friends, but he knew that he drank heavily or he made passes. He protected me from such behavior.

That summer after Sister got married I was just dying to go to college. I had passed my college boards, though I had to take Latin twice. I never was very good in Latin. I had a splendid teacher at the Cathedral School, Miss Webster, and she finally interested me in Latin because she taught it as a history course, the history of the Roman Empire. Anyway, Daddy finally agreed to send me to Wellesley, because he was convinced I had brains enough to go to college.

3

College Student and Debutante

THE TUITION AND BOARD at Wellesley in those days was $800 for the year. But of course, I had to have railroad fare back and forth and clothes and an allowance of $25 a month. It all added up to about $1500 a year, which was a lot of money for my family. We were getting steadily poorer in those days, but Daddy agreed to my going. I really think my mother thought that maybe I would catch a rich beau up there, but she never said it. She bought me a squirrel coat. I was so proud of it—a fur coat, the first one I ever had. I thought it was the most gorgeous thing in the world, gray and very pale.

Hugo was doing very well then, and he encouraged my parents to send me off to college. Whether he helped with the fees or not, I don't know. I know he helped the family a lot, but exactly when and how much was always a matter of mystery.

I went to Wellesley in 1921 and was told I was to room in the village. The freshmen at that time all lived in the village, and the upperclassmen lived on the campus. I arrived at an old-fashioned wooden house and found that I had a room on the second floor. When I reached the room, I saw a beautiful girl sitting on one of the beds. Her name was Emmie Bosley, and she was from Buffalo. She was lively and vivacious and very attractive. It was just a mutual meeting of the souls; we adored each other. It couldn't have been a happier combination.

Emmie's father was a lawyer, and they weren't very rich. They were like me—they went with all the rich people and were part of the society group, but her father was not very wealthy, so they always had to worry about money, too. Her sister was a sophomore, and she, too, was a beautiful girl. Emmie was a brunette and her sister Kay was a blonde with blue eyes. Emmie's relationship with Kay was like my relationship with my sister. She thought Kay was the most beautiful creature in the world and the most popular. She was always sorry for Kay because Kay was so sensitive and wept and cried and was always breaking hearts and then sorry that she couldn't marry all the boys who wanted to marry her.

Wellesley was sheer delight to me. I never felt so well or so happy in my life. I felt completely free.

In Birmingham, the mothers at the country club would all watch the ballroom from the back porch. The country club had big French windows leading from the ballroom to the porch, and the mothers always watched to see how many breaks their daughters got and how popular they were. If a girl danced too close to a man or a man danced too close to a girl, or the mothers saw any kind of hanky-panky going on, don't think that they didn't come right in and make a scene about it! We were just watched constantly. It wasn't that our mothers thought we were going to do anything immoral. They wanted to see how popular we were. It was like a race, like a horse race, and they wanted to see whether their daughter was coming out ahead and who danced with her. This was a serious business of life. This wasn't anything frivolous. Mothers had to get their daughters married well. Now, by marrying well they meant a boy who was white, was a Presbyterian or an Episcopalian, was well off, came from a good family, could be placed, and was able to support a wife in style. They hoped it would be a love match, but the main concern was that they wanted their daughters to marry well.

There was no other future for us; what could we do? Women had gotten the right to vote in 1920, but in Alabama, the legislature had voted against the amendment. Women in Alabama could vote, of course, because the amendment was ratified in enough states over all, but women in Alabama had few job opportunities. You could teach school. That was considered respectable. But when you started teaching school, that meant you had lost all hope of getting a husband. As Daddy would say to me when he saw me putting my glasses on, "I think you are going to be an old-maid schoolteacher, the way you wear those glasses. That's all the future I see for you." He would really get mad at me if I didn't look pretty and charming. He would look at me and say, "Well, I don't see any future for you but to be an old-maid schoolteacher." That may be the reason he sent me to Wellesley. He thought that was the only future I had. He loved me in a way, but I irritated him. I was too much like him and I would argue with him.

Daddy may have been pleased that I liked his books, but he really wanted me to be like my sister. He didn't think I was as sweet. He irritated me, too. We would have terrible arguments about things. And he would make Mother cry quite often, and I didn't like that. Daddy was either very up or very down. Mother used to say it was like riding the elevator. He was always busy with some scheme to make a million dollars. He was always investing money in oil, for instance, and the oil wells always came out dry. But whether up or down, he was always articulate. And when he was down, he was the downest you can imagine. Everybody else had to be down with him. He would say he was a failure and make everybody perfectly miserable. He would just pour out his frustrations and his grief and his disappointments, just drown Mother and all of us in them.

Daddy was such a contradictory man. He was highly educated and he was terribly interested in things. He read the entire newspaper every day and kept abreast of foreign affairs and what was going on in Washington. He always woke up about three o'clock in the morning and read until about five. He would read the *Literary Digest,* the intellectual journal of the day, from cover to cover. At the same time, he was full of contradictions about race and class and women. His mind and emotions were totally at variance.

Daddy felt guilty because he wasn't making money and wasn't rich. He thought he was a failure. In those days, if a man didn't make money and couldn't support his family in the right style, he was a terrible failure. His brothers had done better. His oldest brother, Robert, was a judge in St. Louis and had made a lot of money in rice. One of Robert's sons later was head of Arkansas Power and Light. Daddy's other brother, Hugh, was head of the bank in Union Springs and later was in the Federal Reserve System.

Daddy wasn't a good businessman. He was always trying to get rich by investing in real estate. Of course, Birmingham had booms and busts. A lot of the real estate, if he could have held on to it, would have made us rich. But if Mother wanted a big house or a Packard automobile, he got her one whether he had to borrow money for it or borrow on the real estate or the farms or the plantation. He sent me to Wellesley even though I'm sure he couldn't afford to. He was always doing more than he could afford to do. He just couldn't admit to Mother that he was broke, that he was getting so poor. She knew it, but she couldn't accept it either. She would get the bills and hide them. She would stick them behind the cushions of the sofa or the pictures on the wall. She couldn't bear to give him the bills. Then the creditors would start calling up on the telephone. Daddy was like Mr. Micawber in *David Copperfield,* but he was never as cheerful as Mr. Micawber.

I was conscious of all this at the time and it made me unhappy. At the same time, I was only eighteen, and like most young people I was absorbed with myself. Then at Wellesley I really began to bloom as far as boys were concerned. The first month I was there, I was invited to the Southern Club.

A very nice Southern lady in Cambridge named Mrs. Gay had several daughters, whom they called the Gay girls. They were nice young Southern girls, but Mrs. Gay was indigent and she kept up by giving Southern Club dances, which you paid to go to. There again, you were Mrs. Gay's guest. She would hire Brattle Hall or some hotel ballroom, and she and her daughters were the hostesses. Everybody was introduced to everybody else, and the band would play "Dixie" and we would all stand and cheer.

I was first invited to a Southern Club dance because of a girl I knew at the Cathedral School named Sarah Orme. She was from Atlanta and was one of the greatest Southern belles. She would get forty-five letters a day from boys. She would get fourteen corsages on Sunday or four boxes of candy on Tuesday, special deliveries and telegrams. She was like Zelda Sayre, except that she always knew where she was going and she was a very sensible, down-to-earth girl. She wasn't beautiful, but she was very attractive and totally at ease and self-assured. I think that made the young men feel comfortable. When she came to see me one Christmas, all the boys in Birmingham fell for her. She had a friend named Clark Foreman whom she had grown up with in Atlanta. Clark was at Harvard, so Sarah wrote Clark about me when I went to Wellesley. I don't know whether he was ever Sarah's beau. We divided boys then into friends, beaus, and suitors. The suitors were the ones trying to marry us. I think Clark was just a friend of Sarah's.

Clark called me up and said he wanted to take me to the Southern Club dance. I said I had a beautiful roommate and didn't he want to get a boy for her. He said yes, that Bill Sibley would come. Bill also came from Atlanta. His father was a federal judge there, and Bill was in law school. Then I said that my roommate had a beautiful sister and didn't he want to get a boy for her. He said yes, there was a boy there from Virginia Military Institute named Bill Winston and he would get him.

The girls today have no idea of the restrictions placed upon us. We may have resented them, but they made us feel we had something very precious and valuable that all the boys wanted. And if we didn't guard it carefully, it was gone. It made us feel terribly desirable, irresistible.

At Wellesley we could go to a dance only on a Saturday night. We could go into town on Saturday and stay overnight. There were certain guaranteed houses where we could stay in Boston or Cambridge. In Boston, on Commonwealth Avenue, we stayed in a guaranteed house that was run by an extremely respectable lady. We would leave Wellesley and take the train to the South Station. When we got to this lady's house she became our mother, guardian, and chaperone. She was responsible for us. We signed in and told the lady what time we would be in that evening. (We had to come in by twelve o'clock, and she would wait up for us.) Then when the young men came in to take us out, she would have to meet them and know exactly what their names were and "place" them—did they go to MIT and what class were they in and where did they live, or did they go to Harvard Law School. She had to know exactly where they were from. And of course, if anything happened, she knew exactly how to get hold of the boy or the people at his college.

The Southern Club was in Cambridge, so we had to go over to Cambridge for the dances, which were usually held at Brattle Hall. Everybody would come into the South Station. It was a great big gloomy place, but it always meant for me romance and fun. We never ate supper on the day of the dance because we were so excited. We would get all dressed up. We would fix each other's hair and powder each other's backs. Then we would come down and meet the young men.

Well, here the three were. There was Bill Sibley, who was tall and handsome. He was a suitor of Sarah Orme's, but that night he was Emmie's date. I was with Clark Foreman, who was also crazy about Sarah. He was short and dark and very lively. Bill Winston was a figure of romance! He was about six feet two and had a bulldog jaw. I thought he was the handsomest creature I had ever seen. He wore a great big swirling VMI cape, pale blue and lined with red. Can you imagine anything more romantic? Of course, they all had on tuxedos. Bill Winston was Kay's date.

In those days, the boys didn't have cars. You went on the subway or the streetcar or you walked. I walked in Cambridge more than I ever walked in my life, and walking in silver slippers was always rather difficult. But we finally got to the Southern Club dance. We went in and were introduced to Mrs. Gay.

"Where are you from?" she asked, trying to "place" us.

"Alabama," I said, and she then recalled that she knew someone who came from Montgomery.

After Mrs. Gay placed us, she introduced us around. Then we joined a circle dance. When the music stopped, the girls would dance with the boy opposite. This was a way of getting people introduced. Then the boys would break in on the girls. On occasion, they did something that we never did in the South; the girls would break in on the boys. I thought this was extremely daring. Of course, I broke in on Bill Winston. By that time, I thought I had found the romance of my life.

Clark Foreman was a marvelous dancer. He was "absolutely divine," as we used to say. I was a pretty good dancer, so we would give exhibitions. The Southern Club became a fixture in my life. All the Southern boys went there.

Clark and I became great friends. So did Bill Sibley and I. Both of them took me out a lot. They were in love with Sarah, at least Bill was, but Clark began to be as good a friend of mine as he was of Sarah's. They introduced us to everybody and we were launched on Cambridge society.

I had a perfectly marvelous time that first year at Wellesley. I loved every minute of it. I fell in love with Bill Winston and was just delighted. I suppose it was love, anyway. Bill went to Harvard Law School. At VMI he had been first captain of the football team, which meant a great deal then. Once he took me home to meet his family. They had a huge mansion on the Hudson River and raised horses and cows. His father was a contractor and built dams and reservoirs. He built the reservoir for New York City. I had gone to National Cathedral School with Bill's sister, Jacquelyn Winston. She was younger than I was, but we were great friends, and she invited me to visit, too.

I never did learn to ride a horse, and I was scared to death of them and of cows all my life. That weekend at Bill Winston's house I was supposed to ride. Every Southern lady was supposed to know how to ride. Well, I didn't know how to ride. I did have sense enough not to get up on a horse and disgrace myself. I remember when they took me out to see the cattle, I didn't know anything about cattle either. I wasn't a country girl.

"What kind of cow is that?"

"It's a young heifer," Bill answered.

Not knowing a thing about cows and trying to impress him with how interested I was, I said, "Oh, I think heifers are so much prettier than Jerseys." I didn't know anything. I was just trying to impress him.

When summer came, I still had a beau up at Mentone, Carlton Wright, and I also adored him. He was a bit younger than I was and a beautiful young man. I kissed and hugged him, and I had since I was about thirteen or fourteen years old. He was my secret love, I suppose. Mother and Daddy and his aunts never thought anything about it because we were so young. I told Carlton that I had met this other boy named Bill Winston and that I had fallen madly in love with him. There was this great sorrow for a while, but it did not last long. We went back to kissing again!

I went back to Wellesley for my sophomore year and got to live on campus instead of in the village because I was an upperclassman. We drew lots for rooms on the campus, and my roommate and I drew a low number and got a beautiful set of rooms with a study and a bedroom on the first floor.

The first night, I went to the dining room and a Negro girl was sitting at my table. My God, I nearly fell over dead. I couldn't believe it. I just absolutely couldn't believe it. She wasn't very black, sort of pale, but she was sitting there eating at the table with me in college. I promptly got up, marched out of the room, went upstairs, and waited for the head of the house to come. She was a tall, thin, New England spinster. She wore glasses attached by a string to a small round pin on her bosom. The glasses teetered on her nose and she would cast her head down and look over them at us. I told her that I couldn't possibly eat at the table with a Negro girl. I was from Alabama and my father would have a fit. He came from Union Springs, Bullock County, and the idea of my eating with a Negro girl—well, he would die. I couldn't do it. She would have to move me immediately. She looked at me.

"Well, Virginia, why do you feel this way?"

"Because I'm from Alabama and my father would have a fit. I just couldn't dream of it." I was rather irritated with her for thinking that I could do such a thing.

"Well," she said, "you think then that it is just impossible for you to eat with a Negro girl?"

"Why, absolutely," I responded. "I couldn't think of it. You'll just have to move me."

"You know, Virginia," she said, "Wellesley College has rules, and the rule is that you eat at the table to which you are assigned and that you change your table after a month. But you can't change your table until the month is up. This is the rule. Now if you don't want to obey the rule, then that is up to you."

I was amazed. "You mean that I have to eat at a table with a Negro girl?"

"Well, you have to obey the rules of Wellesley College."

"What happens if I won't do it?" I asked.

"We'll just say that you chose to withdraw. We won't expel you or suspend you. You'll have nothing on your record except that you are through and that you chose to withdraw." There were no threats at all, just calm but firm insistence on obeying the rules.

"But my father would have a fit."

"He's not our problem. He's your problem. You either abide by the rules or you go home. You can withdraw, but you won't be expelled. Now you go to your room and think about it and let me know in the morning what you want to do." I couldn't believe it; I was absolutely amazed that anybody would take such an attitude.

This was the first time that my values had ever been challenged. I told Emmie that I was upset, and Emmie said, "I don't know what's wrong with you. I just think you're crazy. Last summer when I was visiting you down in Alabama, you kissed and hugged that old black woman who was cooking for you. I wouldn't have kissed and hugged an old black woman, but you did. Why would you kiss and hug them and not eat with them?"

Well, it was difficult to explain. I said, "Why, I just love the cook, but I don't eat with her." I had a hard time making any sense out of it.

"I just think you're crazy. You're dated up for the Harvard game and you're dated up for the Yale game. If you want to go home and give all that up because you don't want to eat with a Negro girl, I just think you're crazy."

Emmie went to sleep and I stayed awake all night long. It was terrible for me, because I knew if my father ever heard of it, he would be furious. I could just hear him, "My daughter eating at the table with a Negro girl! I send her up to Wellesley with the Yankees and they make her eat with Negroes!" Now, I was having the time of my life at Wellesley. I had never had such a good time. I was in love with a Harvard law student, the first captain of VMI, and life was just a bed of roses. But I had been taught that if I ate at the table of a Negro girl I would be committing a terrible sin against society. About dawn, I realized that if nobody told Daddy, it might be all right. If I didn't tell him, nobody else was likely to tell him. That was the only conclusion I came to. I didn't have any great feeling of principle. I had not wrestled with my soul. I just told myself that Daddy would never hear about it and I would get to stay at Wellesley.

The next morning I went to the head of the house and told her I was going to stay. I thought she was going to give me a lecture, but she said simply, "Well, I'm very glad." And that was it. I did eat with that Negro girl for about a month, and I came to realize in that time that it wasn't the Negro girl I was afraid of. It was my father's reaction I feared. She was a perfectly nice girl, well-mannered and intelligent. She used the right fork and all. She was a Southerner, too. They served us Indian pudding on Saturday nights, which was nothing in the world but cold grits with molasses on it. The first time they served it, we both said, "Cold grits! With molasses!" We thought it was the most horrible concoction we had ever tasted.

So I didn't tell Daddy and I stayed. But that was the first time I became aware that my attitude was considered foolish by some people and that Wellesley College wasn't going to stand for it. That experience had a tremendous effect on me.

There were other Southern girls at Wellesley. We were all a little ashamed of breaking the Southern taboos, and yet we didn't want to leave. I didn't know whether I had acted rightly or wrongly, whether I should have stood by Southern tradition and gone home or not. I only knew I had stayed because I didn't want to miss the good times I was having.

I remember only one other incident that involved an awareness of race. Wellesley is on a big lake, and once we went swimming in it. One of the black students was also swimming. One of the other Southern girls climbed up by me on the dock and said, "My God, I never thought I would be swimming with black people." She had accepted the fact that she could eat with them, but not that she could swim with them. All of us were a little bit in conflict. We didn't want to repudiate our Southern traditions, but we didn't want to leave Wellesley, particularly Harvard and Cambridge. So we never discussed it. There was no great soul searching.

I didn't become friends with the Negro girl, but I was pleasant. I was polite. There were not only a number of Negro girls in the college, but there were Chinese and Indian girls, too, and I had to get used to that. One of the Chinese girls was named Lillian Chen. She was a member of the famous Chen family of China, immensely rich with jewels. She was a rather special kind of girl because she was so rich and had such beautiful jewels. I never made friends with the foreign girls either. We were all polite and pleasant, but I never made friends. My friends were the white Southern girls and my roommate and her sister.

That winter my roommate was invited to a dance at Exeter Academy by a friend from Buffalo. She took me along and I met a boy named Corliss Lamont. He was at Harvard, but he had gone to Exeter. He was a wonderful dancer, unlike Bill Winston. My relationship with Bill hadn't come to anything more at this point than my romantic feeling toward him. I had never kissed him. Oh, my God, no. Kissing was supposed to be awfully fast.

Corliss drove us back to Wellesley and became a beau of mine. I had never heard of the Lamonts. I didn't know who he was. He wore a thin overcoat with a raggedy collar. The rich boys in those days wore big coonskin coats and had great red Stutz automobiles. He didn't have anything like that at all, and I thought he was just a poor boy. When we went out, I would always take the fifty-cent lunch and thirty-five cent drink or something that was cheap, because I thought he was just a poor Harvard student and barely getting along.

One night, Corliss called me and said he had two friends he wanted to bring out. He asked if I would get Emmie and Kay to go along. When he arrived with the two boys, he introduced them as Rockefeller and Vanderbilt. Of course, we thought it was a huge joke. It never occurred to us that they really were Rockefellers and Vanderbilts. We called Mr. Rockefeller Mr. Rockebilt and Mr. Vanderbilt Mr. Vanderfeller. That was the end of the Rockefellers and the Vanderbilts for us, but Corliss kept coming back. I used to go out with him a great deal. He became a beau, but not a suitor.

Corliss took me out on the lake in a canoe one time, and he made some advances toward me. But we were so afraid we were going to tip over that we couldn't do much courting. That was one reason, I think, that they had canoes on the lake. We never did get to the courting stage, but I was very fond of him and I still am. I think I am one of the few people in the world who ever liked Corliss Lamont and didn't know he was rich. His father, Thomas Lamont, was J. P. Morgan's partner, but I didn't know who J. P. Morgan was. We were totally ignorant of such matters. Romance was the great thing.

The incident with the black girl at Wellesley may not have been crucial at the time, but it was the origin of a doubt. It hurt my faith, my solid conviction of what I had been raised to believe. But that was not the only new idea I encountered at Wellesley. I also realized for the first time that women could be something. This was the real liberation that I got at Wellesley. I realized that women didn't have to marry to be somebody. I remember the woman who taught us Shakespeare. She was an old lady with white hair, and she was one of the happiest creatures I have ever seen. She had never had a husband. She taught Shakespeare all of her life. She adored Shakespeare. When she read Shakespeare, it was the only time in my life that I ever liked his work. She read with such passion and conviction. This lady had never married and yet I could see that she was perfectly happy. She didn't have to have a husband. I realized that women could be happy without getting married, and they could use their minds and accomplish things.

Wellesley was a very enlightened college. It even had a course on sex. We didn't know anything about sex. My roommate was extremely popular, but she was just as innocent as I was—and she came from Buffalo. She regarded herself as far more experienced because she had kissed a few more boys than I had, but she really knew no more than I did. The course on sex was for freshmen students and was supposed to prepare us for marriage. All the freshmen class went to the chapel, and we looked at a movie for several nights running. The first night of the movie a young lady and a young man met each other at a party. He asked if he could come to see her. After the first segment of the film one of the professors gave us a talk about meeting men, about manners and the rules of the college, about how you couldn't go into Boston without a chaperone. We were taught the proper way to act as a Wellesley student.

The second night of the course, the young man and the young lady were taking a walk in the woods. They sat down in a hammock and the apple blossoms began to fall on them. He leaned over and kissed her and asked if she would marry him. She said yes. That was the second lesson. The lady who lectured us that night didn't advise us not to sit in hammocks, but she did make it plain that you didn't sit in hammocks with young gentlemen until you were ready to marry them. And you certainly didn't kiss them until you were ready to marry them.

The third night of the film, the young couple had the wedding. It made us all just drool with envy—white veils and white satin and long trains and candles and bridesmaids and flowergirls and the handsome groom in full dress. They had the most beautiful wedding you've ever seen. The moral was very plain: if you conducted yourself properly, if you didn't sit in the hammock with a young man and kiss him until you got ready to marry him, you would get married and have a beautiful wedding and live happily ever after.

We had one more class. The young couple was leaning over the cradle with the baby. But we never knew how the baby got there. I know you will think this is absolutely insane, but there they were married and we couldn't figure out how the baby got there. They were both so proud and so happy, and they were going to live a life of joy and bliss forever afterward. But how that baby got there, we couldn't figure out. We discussed it at great length, and most girls, including me, thought it was the kiss. That scared us. We had kissed boys.

I wasn't raised on the farm, so I had no idea about births and such. Later, when Cliff and I had been married several years, we would occasionally drive down to Montgomery for weekends. We didn't have superhighways then, and we would drive through country farms and see chickens and cows. I said to Cliff, "Why do the roosters treat those hens so bad, jumping on top of them and trying to pull their combs out? Why are they so cruel to the hens?"

I was as ignorant as I could be, and I was frightened. Inhibitions had built up in me. One girl thought it might be the apple blossoms, but we laughed at that. We knew that was silly. But we knew that hammocks were very dangerous—and kissing. Emmie was braver than I was, so she went to Kay, her older sister, who *did* know where babies came from, and she came back with the word that kissing didn't do it. That was all she ever said. She never discussed it.

The great ideal was to be chaste and absolutely pure, but also to be so attractive that you were always chased by the boys. It was a difficult combination, as you can imagine. But still, that was the ideal. Anyway, I was relieved to know that if I kissed, I wouldn't have a baby. Of course, I didn't know what else could happen.

We had these strictly traditional lectures at Wellesley on preparation for marriage and how to conduct ourselves properly, but we also had zoology courses. This was typical of Wellesley. We started out having to stick one crayfish with another so they would breed. Well, they did, you know. Then we would cut them up and see all the interior workings. And we would cut up frogs and look at them under microscopes and watch the development of the egg. Somehow I never related this to humans. I saw it just as something that frogs did and crayfish did. We never got beyond the frogs and crayfish, but we studied the reproduction system of frogs and crayfish rather extensively!

Then in the laboratory, there were horrible objects in bottles of alcohol. One bottle held a curious creature with a tail like a fish. Then there was a strange little creature all doubled over, and the tail had gone. We were being taught that the development of man corresponded to the ages of mankind. I was also taking anthropology and geology courses, where we studied about the first little fishes that came up out of the sea. It was all related to the development of man. The final development of man was these little fetae in the bottles of alcohol. The exhibition in the laboratory went right on through to a big bottle that had a real baby in it, dead of course, all in alcohol, pickled. Well, you can't imagine the horror that thing was to me and all the other girls. We thought, "My God, imagine." We did know that babies came out of the mother's stomach. We just didn't know how they got in. But the idea of having such a disgusting object inside of you horrified us. And the afterbirth—the whole thing was just vile and disgusting. So we promptly ruled it out of our minds. We had a great way, like Scarlett in *Gone with the*

Wind, of just forgetting about it. We just pushed it aside. We didn't really believe it.

Instead of making us think how wonderful it would be to have a baby, we developed a real horror of such a disgusting performance. But that was typical of Wellesley: they would teach you one thing on a scientific basis but never tell you how the baby got into the mother's stomach. Now, I'm sure there were girls at Wellesley who did know, but not the group I was with. We had been so inhibited by that time that we didn't want to know. We didn't discuss things like that. We talked about romance and beaus and lovers and sweethearts but not sex.

I'm sure the Southern girls believed, as I did, that sex was something connected with black people. It happened in the basement and was dirty and ugly and smelled bad, with a man leaving in the middle of the night or early in the morning and Mother getting upset and saying, "She's had a man down there all night." Something was ugly and disgusting about it.

We had some excellent teachers at Wellesley. I had a marvelous teacher in economics, Professor Muzzy. He was a socialist, a Fabian. The Russian Revolution had taken place, but I never heard about it. Communism and Russia were far removed from my world. Muzzy was a follower of the Webbs. He read their great massive volumes with the details about how many out-houses there were in a certain road in London and the terrible plight of the poor. There were all kinds of tables and statistics that I had difficulty following. But I did get the impression that the great majority of people in the world had a pretty hard time. Once Muzzy gave me a paper to write. He knew that I came from Birmingham, so he said, "Mrs. Smith is the wife of a steelworker and her husband makes three dollars a day. Now tell me how Mrs. Smith with three-children is going to arrange her budget so that she can live."

Well, I tried to do it. I had to look up the price of food and rent and doctors. It was an active lesson in economics. I soon realized that Mrs. Smith couldn't possibly live on that amount of money. She just couldn't do it. When I handed in my paper, I had written at the end, "I've come to the conclusion that Mrs. Smith's husband doesn't get enough money, because they can't possibly live on what he is paid as a steelworker in Birmingham, Alabama." Not that I had ever been in a steel mill or knew anything about it. But Muzzy gave me an A, because he said I had finally realized that people can't live on what they are paid.

I had another great experience, too. Bible was a required course at Wellesley, but it was taught as history. So I learned that my father had been right about Jonah and the whale. You can't imagine what that meant to me. I had always felt that Daddy did a very noble act by saying he did not believe the whale swallowed Jonah. He refused to lie and be a hypocrite. But I had always been uneasy that my father had been thrown out of the church for being a heretic as a result of that. It was a great relief to learn that he had been not only noble but also right about the Bible stories as symbolism and myth.

These incidents at Wellesley had a delayed effect, but the main thing I learned was to use my mind and to get pleasure out of it. I also learned I could be comfortable about the Bible, and I could be comfortable that a woman could make a living and be happy even if she didn't have a husband. And I began to realize that people had a hard time living and didn't get paid enough. I began to get some inkling of economics. So my Wellesley education was quite liberating. On sex, there was a tremendous breakthrough, although it is hard to realize. I began to kiss Bill Winston and enjoy it thoroughly. Oh, he was so handsome and he used to wrap me in his VMI cape. My goodness, what romance! That was more dangerous than a hammock. So I was liberated to a degree. In sex, religion, and economics—in those three in particular—I was liberated at Wellesley.

At the end of my sophomore year, I had to go home. The boll weevil ate up my education. An English teacher thought I had some writing talent and she came to me and said, "Now, Virginia, I think you have a certain talent in writing, and you could come back next year and work in the Self-Help House." In the Self-Help House, the girls did all the work: they did the cooking and the cleaning up and everything for themselves. And they paid practically nothing, a very little amount, for their room and board. "I think I can arrange for you to get a scholarship," she said. I was thrilled. I was dying to come back to Wellesley. So I wrote my father and mother. And oh, my father! The idea of my going into the Self-Help House! Daddy felt he was a failure financially, and for me to go into the Self-Help House would prove he was a failure. I thought I was in love with Bill Winston, and I longed to go back to Wellesley. I'd have gladly worked in the Self-Help House, but my father's pride would have been hurt. No indeed, no daughter of his was going to go to Wellesley and go into the Self-Help House. That was just impossible, to do the cooking and the cleaning and washing up. Oh, no. It was his Southern pride and the fear of being a failure, of being considered a failure. I realized when I left that I couldn't go back.

When I left Wellesley, I thought I was engaged to Bill Winston. I told my mother I had met this marvelous boy that I was going to marry. I got two or three letters from him and that was the end. I never heard from him again. He just faded out completely. About a year later I learned that he had committed suicide. That was always one of the great mysteries of my life. I can't imagine why that boy committed suicide. He was so handsome and smart.

The first thing I had to do when I got back to Birmingham was to make my debut. All that summer of 1923, great plans were made. I was "introduced" and I went to party after party. All the debutantes had luncheons and teas and we felt terribly important. Then I visited my aunt Oo-Oo in Memphis and went to the parties there.

I had a horrible experience in Memphis, a really frightening experience. The depression had hit the South much sooner than it hit other places, particularly in cotton. While I was in Memphis I met a boy named Jim Rainer at a party. His family had a plantation in Mississippi. He was a big, tall, good-looking boy and a wonderful dancer. I always went with wonderful dancers—except for Bill Winston.

W. C. Handy was playing on Beale Street then, the most marvelous music you can imagine—the "St. Louis Blues" and the "Beale Street Blues." To dance to Handy's band was one of the most wonderful things in the world. There were also the two-bit bands. A group of boys would each put in two bits, a quarter, and hire a band on Beale Street. The band would play and we would have a wonderful dance. I just danced, danced, danced.

Jim Rainer took me out after one of the dances to a road near the country club. By that time, I was used to all the boys wanting to kiss me. It was a game they played, and it didn't mean a thing, of course. They just wanted to see if they could. We were having the usual argument about whether to kiss or not to kiss and did I kiss or didn't I kiss.

This was the Jazz Age, which was supposed to have been such a terrifically gay, drunken, sex age. Well, it really wasn't. I mean, there were some people who might have engaged in all that, but the nice girls didn't. I don't bet that Zelda Sayre did even. I bet kissing was the limit that she went to, in spite of what they all said about her. If you read Fitzgerald's books, they are not as sexy as you would think they were. Zelda always did things to shock people, but that was it. She used to come up to the dances in Birmingham and she was just gorgeous. She had a golden glow around her. When she came into a ballroom, all the other girls would want to go home because they knew the boys were going to be concentrating on Zelda. The boys would line up the whole length of the ballroom to dance with her for one minute. She was just pre-eminent. And we recognized it.

But anyway, Jim Rainer and I stopped on this lover's lane, and all of a sudden, two black fellows appeared on either side of the car, one of them with a pistol and one of them with a knife. They said to Jim, "Get out of that car or we'll cut your heart out, and give us what you've got." Now Jim had this plantation in Mississippi and was used to the blacks. So he got out and stayed very cool and said, "Okay, I'll give you all I've got. I'll bet you are on your way to Chicago." They said, "We are." He said, "Well, I'm sorry we don't have anything for you in Mississippi." They were all leaving Mississippi then. A lot of them were going north. He talked with them and kind of joked with them and laughed and gave them the money he had in his pocket, and they went on off. Of course, it scared the hell out of me. I was terrified. I kissed him in gratitude then! He took me home and told me, "Please don't tell your aunt, because I will be blamed for it. I'll be in a lot of trouble. So please don't tell your aunt."

Honestly, I read in the paper the next morning that there had been a series of robberies and rapes on the borders of Memphis. Now whether these men who held us up were the robbers and rapers or not, I don't know, but it did scare me. When I got home, I began having nightmares. I was just terrified. I would wake up in the night screaming. Finally I told Mother what it was and after I told her, I got it off my mind. But that was the first time in my life I had ever been afraid of a black person. I had been surrounded by them all my life. They had waited on me and taken care of me and cooked for me and washed for me, but I had never, never been frightened of one before. That was something new.

I spent that whole year making my debut, going to parties and having dates and going to dances and visiting my aunt. I went up to Knoxville and visited a friend of my mother's and there were more dances and more dates. All this may have been as expensive as going to school would have been, but at least Mother thought it might have been leading to something more profitable. And it wasn't very expensive. The rich girls had big rich balls that cost hundreds of dollars, but I never had any like that. I think Mother had a buffet supper for me, but that was all. We couldn't afford any big parties.

I did have one or two proposals that year, but nothing that appealed to me or amounted to anything. The next year, we really were hard up. The furnace didn't work well, and the roof leaked, and the plumbing was going bad. So I said to Mother, "I'm going to get a job." This was unheard of, but I did it. I went downtown on my own and got a job at the county bar association's law library at twenty-five dollars a month. Mrs. Thach was the law librarian, and she hired me to come in half a day. Twenty-five dollars a month was a lot of money, and I got the furnace fixed and the plumbing fixed and the roof fixed, and I began to paper some of the rooms in the house where the paper was falling down.

Poor Mother and Daddy were terribly embarrassed about that. They thought it was a confession of dire failure, a daughter working. I could hear Mother saying to her friends over the telephone, "Well, you know how these girls are. They just can't have enough ball dresses and silver slippers." She had to pretend I was just working because I was frivolous and wanted more ball dresses. She couldn't bear to think I was working because we needed the money. And Daddy said, "You realize that with a daughter working downtown, my credit is destroyed. My credit at the bank is completely destroyed." It really was tough. By that time, the price of cotton was down to nothing, and Daddy was beginning to sell off what land he could. Then Mrs. Thach got sick and I got the job as law librarian. It paid one hundred and fifty dollars a month.

4

Marriage, Junior League, and the Depression

WHILE I WAS being brought up to be attractive and to have a lot of beaus and get married, all around me things were happening—antilynching fights and child labor fights and the suffrage movement. It was only after I was safely married that I could really be interested in anything else. I led an egotistical, self-centered life because I was always trying to do what other people wanted me to do and make everybody love me. The consequences of not being loved were plain: you didn't get married. You got to be an old maid and that was the worst fate that could befall you. A lot of old maids used to come to stay with us. They couldn't do anything, except maybe teach Sunday school and work in the women's exchange. And when they finally got so poor they had to work in a department store, that was just the end. They had reached the bottom then. The only safe economic route was to get a husband. Romance was nice, but having a man to provide for you was what was important. Old maids were pitied not just because they had no husband but because life without a husband meant a life of poverty.

I met Cliff at church. I didn't care for any of the various gentlemen who offered themselves before Cliff, but I was under terrible pressure to get married. Everybody else was getting married, and my family was getting anxious that I was not.

My mother and father were sitting on the front porch after dark one April night in 1925. I was twenty-one years old and the family had about given up on me. I had had some proposals, which I hadn't accepted, but I hadn't had very many serious love affairs. They decided I was an old maid. My brother said to me, "Look, nobody would ever suit you. Everybody that comes around, there is something wrong with them. You'll never get married. Nobody suits you. You are just always critical of everybody."

Daddy said, "What do you expect? Who are you looking for?"

Mother, who was always trying to protect me, said, "Now, Virginia doesn't want to marry somebody she's not in love with, you know."

So my brother asked me, "Have you ever seen anybody, any human being, that you wanted to marry?"

Of course, there was Carlton Wright, whom I still adored, but he had no money and was impossible from the husband point of view. Our relationship was just beautiful and romantic. Then there was Bill Winston, who was certainly eligible in every way, but he jilted me and then committed suicide. So I thought really hard and I said, "Well, I'll tell you. I met a young man in church last Sunday and I think he is the handsomest young man I have ever seen, or one of them." I really thought he was more handsome than Bill Winston. He was tall, blond, and blue-eyed and wore English suits, not the seersucker suits that looked like pajamas that most Southern boys wore.

My brother asked, "What's his name?"

Daddy spoke up then and said, "Oh, that's John W. Durr's son. His name is Clifford Durr."

My brother said, "That's who you want? That's easy. I'll get him around for dinner next Sunday." They had been fraternity brothers at the university.

The Durrs were from Montgomery, and my father had known Cliff's father from his preaching days. Cliff's family was Presbyterian, and they would invite Daddy to stay with them when he went to Montgomery to preach or on church business. Cliff's great-uncle, Willie Johnson, and my great-uncle, Willie Foster, had fought in the Civil War together and had been good friends. So our lives were connected in various ways. The Durr children thought Daddy was a lot of fun. He was lively. The children called him Dr. Foster from Gloucester. They'd stick their heads in the door and yell, "Dr. Foster went to Gloucester in a shower of rain; He slipped in a puddle, right up to his middle, and never went there again!"

The next Sunday, Cliff came to dinner. Mother got out the damask table cloth and the damask napkins. We had a delicious dinner, served by the cook. Mother also bought a marvelous cake from a lady in Birmingham who charged five dollars for her perfectly beautiful creations. This was a lemon meringue cake, piled high with white icing and filled with lemon meringue. When the cake was brought in, Mother said, "Well, Virginia, this is certainly a delicious cake." She didn't say I made it, but of course Cliff assumed I had.

After dinner, Mother went to take a nap. Brother and Daddy went out to play golf at the country club, and I was left with Cliff. My opportunity. Cliff didn't have a car, so we got in my father's old Studebaker, which ran out of gas before it ever really started. Fortunately, the car was parked on a hill, only five or six blocks straight down to a filling station. We used Daddy's car all the time we were courting and every time we got in it it was out

Clifford Judkins Durr.

of gas. Cliff would have to fill it up. I don't know why he didn't suspect then that he was courting a pauper.

Cliff and I started dating that summer. Those were such happy days. He'd come to the house for dinner, or I'd meet him downtown. He came up to the law library where I worked one day, and asked for a certain book. I asked him what the problem was; I remember it was something on municipal law. I not only went and got the book, but I also began to look up the law for him. Cliff was impressed with that. He complained that I never would do that for him after I became his legal secretary! In the fall, Cliff took me to Montgomery to meet his family. While we were there, an old Negro man, George Washington Daniels, who had joined Cliff's family like a stray dog, said to Cliff, "You say her name is Miss Foster?"

Cliff said, "Yes."

"Is she one of them Fosters from over there at Union Springs?"

"Yes, her people came from over there."

"Well," said the black man, "you latch on to her and you'll be getting some sugar. Her folks own the county." Well, we got engaged, and inside of six months after we were married, the last of the great plantation was gone for taxes. Cliff had grounds for annulling the marriage, I suppose, but he didn't do it.

Actually, kissing was what prompted Cliff to propose. I still wasn't too clear about the consequences of kissing. We drove down to a football game in Montgomery one weekend and we stayed with Cliff's mother and father. Cliff had been trying to work himself up to proposing for some time. Once I was babysitting with the two Black boys while Hugo and Sister were out of town. Their youngest child was then about eight months old. Cliff had rehearsed a proposal and was working up to it. I was getting rather interested when all at once in the kitchen there was the damnedest explosion you ever saw. We rushed into the kitchen and there was milk dripping from the ceiling. I had been warming milk for my nephew, and the bottle had exploded. Well, that set Cliff back for two or three months.

Later Cliff decided that the trip to Montgomery might be the time for proposing. He got his father's car and we drove around. He wanted to find a nice place on the side of the road to park, but he realized that the Ku Klux Klan had taken over the job of policing the highways. They were going to stop this "necking." He thought it would be embarrassing if he got just in the middle of the proposal and the Ku Klux Klan interrupted. So finally, we drove back to his father's garage, and he kissed me. He didn't say anything about marriage that night, but the next day as we were driving back to Birmingham, I was very concerned and wanted to know if Cliff was really going to marry me. I didn't know what the consequences of this kissing would be! And so we got engaged.

We planned to marry in the spring, but in the meantime I realized that in marrying Cliff, I was marrying someone different from anybody I had ever known, someone who always told the truth. Cliff wanted to get married immediately and I was just thrilled. I asked him why he wanted to get married so quickly. I thought he was going to say it was because he loved me so much he could hardly stand waiting. Instead, he answered, "Well, I get awfully tired of coming home from the office every afternoon and having to take a bath and get dressed and come over here and get to bed late. It is just wearing me out. I want to get married and quit all this." I should have realized what kind of a family I was marrying into.

Cliff's whole family was like that— absolutely truthful. His mother and sister came to Birmingham for a tea, and my mother said to Mrs. Durr in a rather tearful way, "Oh, I hope your son will be kind to my daughter. She is such an innocent young thing." Mrs. Durr said in a perfectly practical way, "Well, Mrs. Foster, you needn't worry about Cliff. Cliff always looks after what is his. He had a dog named Shiloh and he was the faithfulest thing in the world to that dog. He will always take care of what is his."

Now I don't know what my father did to manage the expense of my wedding. He probably had to sell the last piece of the plantation, but I had the biggest wedding you have ever known in your life. Josephine had had a small family wedding, but every mother has to have at least one big wedding, so I had a big wedding. It was in the new Independent Presbyterian Church on Easter Monday, 1926. Easter lilies were everywhere. Of course, the church had paid for these. I had eight bridesmaids, and Sister was my maid of honor. We had sent out fifteen hundred invitations and there were more than five hundred people at the reception. I am sure it cost money that my father didn't have. My mother was triumphant. Here was a daughter who had married well.

Everybody rejoiced when I married Cliff. They thought I had not only married well but had married above myself. Clifford had been a Rhodes scholar and a Phi Beta Kappa and head of a fraternity at the University of Alabama. His family was well off, and he was in a corporate law firm in Birmingham. My mother and father thought I had married very well indeed.

We were married in April of 1926, while Hugo was running for the Senate. He was running against former Governor Kilby, John Bankhead, L. B. Musgrove, and Judge Mayfield of Tuscaloosa. It was a bitter campaign. Hugo won, but it was a hard fight. He was away from home campaigning all that spring, but Sister was my maid of honor.

I had quite a few parties given for me before the wedding—showers and luncheons and teas and buffet suppers. But Cliff couldn't go to any of the parties; he had had his wisdom teeth pulled. He wanted to be in good shape for the wedding, but he didn't know the dentist was a butcher. His face swelled and his jaw ached. The dentist had fractured his jaw and bits of bone kept working their way out. Cliff was miserable.

Me in wedding gown, 1926.

Marrying Cliff was a triumph, but the wedding was not without its difficult moments. The preacher forgot the date and came late. The organ wouldn't play, and we had to get a little black boy to come in and pump the bellows. The wedding was at eight in the evening. After the reception we were supposed to take the train to New Orleans. We were in full dress for the wedding and Cliff was to change after the reception and go down to the train. But eight o'clock came and no preacher. Finally, the preacher arrived at eight-thirty. He was the only calm person in the church.

After the reception, Cliff went to change clothes and his britches were gone. One of Cliff's brothers dashed off to his apartment to get another suit and about that time, the maid came around and asked Cliff if he was looking for his britches. She went on to say, "This is Miss Josephine's room and I didn't think it was right for no man's britches to be hanging in the closet of Miss Josephine's room, so I took them over and put them in Mr. Sterling's room." Cliff finally got the britches and we rushed off to the train station.

We took the train down to Pass Christian, a great place for honeymoons. It was just full of spring blossoms and the air smelled fresh and sweet. We had a big room in a lovely hotel on the Gulf. Getting used to having a man in my room was quite an adjustment. We were still rather strangers, but a series of incidents brought us closer together. First we woke up in the middle of the night to the sounds of a hurricane. I never heard such wind in my life. We were terrified. The doors and windows flew open and the water and wind came pouring in. We couldn't get out of bed and we just knew that we were going to die there together. That brought us closer together, I must say. When we went down to breakfast, we were still shaking with fear of the terrible night we had been through. Out in the yard was a big boat that had blown in from the Gulf. Everybody in the hotel said, "Well, that was a rather mild blow we had last night. It only got up to eighty miles an hour."

Next, a friend whom we saw on the beach invited us to dinner at a hotel in Biloxi. Cliff always had a very good appetite, and since you could choose as many items from the menu as you wanted at the same price, he decided to eat it all. He started out with oysters and then he ate crab, then clams, then shrimp, and then fish. He went right down the menu. He ate it all and enjoyed it all. The next morning my bridegroom was green, bright green. I went rushing downstairs, absolutely terrified, "My husband's turned green!" The lady said, "What did he eat for supper?" "He ate a lot of seafood." She said, "Well, that's it. Just go upstairs and tell him to throw it up." When I got back upstairs, he had already begun to throw it up. And he threw it up all day long.

All through our honeymoon, bits of bone were still coming out of Cliff's fractured jaw. He had to lie on the bed with his mouth wide open and I would pull out the bone. By the time we got home, we were really very friendly indeed.

I came back from my honeymoon pregnant. I had not known the first thing about marriage, to say nothing about birth control. In those days no one was concerned about controlling it. A girl got married and had babies, and that was that. We thought that a perfectly innocent and ignorant girl had a better chance of getting a good husband. It was pretty hard on the man, I must say, to marry a woman who didn't know what it was all about.

I had an old maid aunt who stayed married two days. She came home and said, "My goodness, I am sure my brothers would never do anything like that." She had seven brothers. And she never did go back to her husband. She was very dressy when she came to visit us, and she stayed for months at a time. She loved society and was quite coquettish and flirtatious. She was "Mrs.," but of course she was a virgin still. She seemed to have it both ways. Everyone admired her because she was so pretty and attractive. Yet she had left her husband three days after the wedding. I remember asking her one morning, "Well, Aunt, why in the world did you leave him?" She said to me (I can remember this as if it were yesterday), "My dear, I don't want you to think I am critical of people who get married. I know marriage is necessary to carry on the human race. You know, my dear mother and father were married, and I had the highest respect for them. But," she said, "personally, dear, I have never seen how a lady could do it." That was the sort of atmosphere I was brought up in. Naturally, I came back from my honeymoon pregnant.

I really thought I was the only human being in the world who had ever had a baby. I was so conceited: the bigger I got, the prouder I was. I had an old doctor, and instead of saying, "You must diet and keep the baby small," he would say, "Oh, Miss Virginia, you've got to eat for two now." I weighed 120 pounds when I married, and when the baby was born, I weighed 185. I was absolutely immense. I could hardly walk. And Dr. Lupton was saying, "Nobody in the world is as healthy as a pregnant woman."

Cliff and I lived with my mother and father in the house on Niazuma. That was part of the myth. We wanted to get a little apartment and be by ourselves, but Mother said it would be bad for me to be cooped up in a little apartment. Mother really wanted to bring in a little income and to keep me from leaving. She was clinging to me in those days. Mother and Daddy owed everybody, and Mother realized things were just going down the drain. But Cliff and I were very happy. We turned one of the rooms upstairs into a sitting room, and we had people in. We had a portable grill and could cook things.

Having a baby in those days was different from now. To have a baby, you went to the doctor once every two or three weeks. Everybody pampered you. I had terrible morning sickness for a while, and I was treated like the queen bee. And I felt like the queen bee. I felt as though I was doing something that nobody had ever done before. It was the most marvelous thing in the world. I was simply thrilled.

I woke up one morning after Cliff had gone to work and realized the baby was coming. I called Cliff immediately. He came home, and we finally got to the hospital. A trained nurse, Miss Taylor, had been engaged for me and I had a private room. Cliff and Mother stayed with me until I went into the delivery room. I delivered a healthy baby girl—Ann—and about an hour afterward I was sitting up eating breakfast and feeling wonderful. Here I was, a healthy young girl, and I had a trained nurse around the clock and stayed in the hospital about two weeks.

The nurse came home and stayed with me another two weeks. I wasn't allowed to walk up and down the steps and was generally treated like an invalid. Everyone made me feel I had done something just spectacular. This was the reward of all my life. When my daughters have babies, they are up the next day. It is the most remarkable change.

We lived with Mother and Daddy for a few more years, and then Cliff became impatient to get our own place. He was making more money and had been made a member of the law firm. Mother and Daddy were harder up than ever, and when Sister and Hugo came home in 1931 to stay a year in Birmingham while Hugo ran for the Senate again, we decided to move. We bought a darling little house in the same neighborhood.

Hugo and Sister took over the house on Niazuma. Both Mother and Daddy hated to admit they were dead broke, and so we all had to pretend they were doing Sister and Hugo a favor to let them stay in their house. We had to protect their pride, because they both felt terribly ashamed at losing everything they had.

In the meantime, I had an extremely bad miscarriage. The situation at home worried me, and then I had the flu and had a miscarriage shortly afterward. So Cliff and I were delighted to get on our own.

I was leading the life of a young married woman in Birmingham. I was active in the Junior League and in the church and belonged to a bridge club and a sewing circle and made clothes for Ann. But I was becoming more and more aware of the terrible state of the economy. Cliff's firm represented the power company, so we were comfortably established even though we were helping Mother and Daddy. But around us was just ruin; smelting furnaces were shutting down and people were losing their jobs. As the city became poorer, more and more beggars came to the door. People were absolutely desperate, and there were any number of muggings and robberies. You didn't want to go from your door to the garage, because people were lurking in the alley. Things in the city were getting very bad indeed, as they were all over the state.

In 1931 I had another terrible miscarriage and nearly died. I had what

Cliff's father, John W. Durr, Sr., and me just after the wedding.

they call *placenta previa* and nearly bled to death. While I was in the hospital, I was very ill and had to have blood transfusions. My nurse, Mrs. Van Merkenstein, was a devout Catholic and had I don't know how many children. She thought birth control was a sin, but she and her husband were separated, although sometimes they got back together. Maybe he felt they had too many children.

At that time, the dairies in Birmingham had a terrible price war. The dairies were losing money because people couldn't afford to buy milk, so they engaged in a cutthroat price war to try to stay in business. One day Mrs. Van Merkenstein's son went to a place called Southern Dairies, just to get a milk shake or ice cream cone, when some people from another dairy came by and threw a bomb. He was killed. It was the most awful, unnecessary killing and the most horrible thing for this poor woman. She was the one who was called in on the emergency, and she found that it was her own son. The death of Mrs. Van Merkenstein's son woke me up to what was going on, on a personal basis.

While I was in the hospital I saw children with rickets. I thought they had cerebral palsy, but it was rickets—just because they didn't get enough to eat, no calcium. That shocked me.

Another shock came after I was well enough to be wheeled out on the gallery that surrounded St. Vincent's Hospital. A woman sat next to me one day and we began to talk. By that time I had had one child and two miscarriages. She was a rather nice-looking, comfortable woman in her late thirties and she came from Chicago. She told me she had just had a baby, so I asked her where it was. She said, "I've never seen it. I'm going to put her up for adoption and I don't want to see her because I'm afraid I might get fond of her." I was shocked and asked her why she was doing such a thing. She said, "The fact of the matter is that I don't know who the father is. I worked at the ready-to-wear at a big store in Chicago and we were expected to entertain all the salesmen and customers. They would take you out to dinner and then ask you to go to their room afterward. I was always very careful, but somehow I got pregnant. I didn't want to have an abortion. I was afraid something would happen. So I decided to come down here and have the baby." She took it very calmly. It seemed to me just awful. She added, "Well, how else are you going to make a living?"

Here was a woman who had to make a living not only by selling ready-to-wear, but also by being ready-to-wear, as it were. I thought that was horrible. I had been surrounded by Mother and Sister and Cliff and the nurse and flowers and doctors and everybody acting as though having a baby or not having a baby was the most important thing in the world. And this poor woman was having a baby all by herself down in Birmingham where nobody even knew her. She would never see the baby because she knew she had to give it away. For the first time, I became aware of how badly women could be treated and how helpless they were in situations like that. I think that was the first dawn of a feeling of wrath and rage against women's lot.

I had nothing against my life. I had no feeling that anyone was at fault for what went wrong. The miscarriages were just something that happened. But I began to have a feeling of rage at this woman's fate.

I began little by little to wake up to the world. Mrs. Van Merkenstein had told me that the dairies were pouring milk into the gutters because they couldn't sell it. I talked the Junior League into starting a milk project so that the milk could be given to poor people instead of thrown out. I thought that would help the rickety children, anyway. The project took an immense amount of time and trouble, because the dairy owners were afraid that if they gave away milk, nobody would buy it. The Southern Dairies Association didn't have a very good reputation, so we convinced them that here was a chance to reinstate themselves in the public's esteem. We persuaded the dairy owners to agree to the project by arguing that they would eventually profit from it. "Now look," we said, "if you give these people a taste of milk, they will get used to drinking milk. Then when they get jobs and there is some money available, they will buy milk." We also told them that the Junior League would pay them something for the deliveries. But then the city objected to the plan because the dairy owners said the milk would have to be delivered in five-gallon cans, not in bottles. Finally, however, the city agreed and the dairy owners began to deliver the surplus milk in five-gallon cans to feeding stations run by the Red Cross.

Slowly I was becoming aware of how bad conditions were for so many people in Birmingham. Many families had nothing, not even a dime for the movies. They had no outlet at all, and they took it out on each other. I thought if they just had some kind of recreation, they would be better off.

One night when I was talking to Cliff about it, I suddenly had an idea and broke off the conversation and called the chief of the fire department. "Every time I pass the fire department down there at Five Points," I said, "I hear somebody tooting away in the back on a trombone or a bass horn. Have you firemen got a band?"

"Well, sure," he answered, "we've got a good band down here, but there is nobody around to listen to us."

"If I get an audience for you, will you put on a concert?" He told me there was nothing the boys would like better. Well, then I called the mayor.

"I want to get the city auditorium next Sunday at 2:30."

"Well, I don't know what you want with it," the mayor said. "Nobody else wants it. If you promise not to tear it down, you can have it."

The next day I called the newspapers and announced there would be a free band concert at 2:30 on Sunday in the city auditorium. The chief of police called me as soon as he heard about it. He said, "What is this about you putting on a concert with the firemen's band? The policemen have got a hell of a lot better band than the firemen." "Bring them along," I told him; "let's see." So the idea began to build and volunteers began to flock in.

I insisted that there be sing-alongs to give the people a chance to participate, too. A young man—an insurance salesman, I think—volunteered to be the master of ceremonies and he turned out to be one of the best I have ever heard, with a magnificent line of chatter. So every Sunday we had a free concert and show that really got going about the time we moved to Washington.

In those days, I still wasn't really in contact with the terrible poverty, hunger, and distress around me, but I was beginning to see it. There was no relief—no city relief, no county relief, no state relief, and no federal relief. Hoover was the president, and in that idiotic way he was talking about two chickens in every pot. Prosperity was just around the corner. But worse was his attitude that it was the poor people's own fault. If they had saved their money, if they had been more provident, if they had stored up, something like the grasshopper and the ant, they would be okay. President Hoover's attitude was typical of people who were well off. They all blamed the poor people for the poverty. I didn't hear anybody say that the problem was the economic or political system.

Now, my mother and father were losing everything. Everything Daddy had was going down the drain. The banks were taking over all the things he had mortgaged or borrowed money on. Daddy finally sold the plantation to Mr. Maytag of the Maytag Appliance Company—for eight dollars an acre, little more than the accumulated taxes. It's the richest land in Alabama and is now worth more than a thousand dollars an acre. Everything just went.

Through the Junior League I began to work with the Red Cross, which was the only relief organization in town. Its money came from donations. The Red Cross gave a family of five $2.50 a week, but not until a Red Cross worker had certified that they were completely impoverished—that there was no money left whatever and there was nothing they could sell and nothing they could borrow and nothing they could do except starve to death.

The Red Cross workers at that time had no cars, so they had to travel by streetcar to investigate the cases. The worst destitution was in the towns around Birmingham, the industrial suburbs like Ensley and West End and Gate City, where the big corporations like the Tennessee Coal, Iron and Railroad Company and Republic Steel were located. Rachel London Lamar, whose husband Dr. Clifford Lamar was our baby doctor, was president of the Junior League then. She suggested that we form a motor corps and drive the Red Cross women around so they could certify more people.

I began driving a Mrs. Bishop. She was a very intelligent and fine person, and she was just overcome with the weight of the misery she was trying to deal with through the Red Cross. So I began to take her out one day a week. Later I took her out more often—every day, Cliff said. He had to walk to work and back on the days I had the car.

I had a cook and a nurse. I don't know what I paid them. It was mighty little, but they were so thankful and delighted to have a job and food. Every day, black men and black women would come to the door begging for work.

They would work for fifty cents a day or for anything. Then the white people would come begging for work and they would work for anything. It was just mass misery. I began to see this when I took the Red Cross worker out and saw whole areas just flat-out broke. The corporations had shut down everything because they couldn't operate at a profit. The people who were living in company houses had no place to go. The Tennessee Coal, Iron and Railroad Company, which was part of U.S. Steel, let the people stay in their houses, but they cut off the lights and water. There was one water tap on every block. There were no lights, no electricity, and no heat. Tom Girdler, the president of Republic Steel, wouldn't let the poor people even stay in the company houses. The company drove them out and posted guards to shoot them if they came back. A lot of those people started living in the coke ovens, which are brick beehives where coal is smoked to make coke. People would crawl in there like animals to keep the rain off.

I saw more accumulated misery than you can imagine. What bothered me most was that these poor people blamed themselves for their situation. They never said, "We are destitute because U.S. Steel doesn't treat us as well as they treat the mules." The mules got whatever they needed to stay alive, but the people got nothing. They never once said that the U.S. Steel Company or the Republic Steel Company was to blame, that they were the ones that laid them off. There was no wrath or indignation. They would always say, "Well, if we hadn't bought that old Ford," or "If we hadn't gotten that radio." They were full of guilt about themselves.

I got a strong bias against preachers in those days—particularly the hell-fire and damnation preachers. We would be in some cold house trying to certify that a person was absolutely penniless so that he could get the $2.50 a week, and some damn preacher would come in. He would tell these people they had sinned and that was why they were suffering. He would pray with them. I got so I wanted to kill these preachers. I thought it was dreadful to tell these people they were poverty-stricken because they had sinned! And to tell them they had to come to God or they would all go to hell!

The early thirties were terrible times. The accumulation of misery mounted so that I found myself just dreading to go with the Red Cross workers. I thought I couldn't stand it. It was too much. I couldn't bear to hear another complaint.

When I was working out in the industrial areas, I didn't meet any organized political groups, but I did come in contact with the Communist party. This was 1931 or 1932, in the depths of the depression. It was just the period that Ted Rosengarten wrote about in his book *All God's Dangers*. The Communist party was organizing the sharecroppers in Tallapoosa County, and H. L. Mitchell and Claude Williams and the socialists were organizing the sharecroppers in Arkansas in the Southern Tenant Farmers' Union. But I didn't know any of this at the time. I had no idea of it.

I went down to Montgomery with my little girl to visit my mother-in-law and met a dear friend of hers, Mrs. Nash Read. Jean Read's mother was a Baldwin before she married, and the Baldwins were one of the richest and most aristocratic families in Montgomery. Jean Read's mother and father believed in culture and travel, and while they were never terribly rich, Jean and her sisters Dolly and Sheila went abroad and studied and spoke several languages.

As an adult, Jean became very much interested in the child labor movement. Seven-year-old children were working at the mills in Alabama. Cliff's grandfather was president of the Tallassee Mills at one time, I'm sorry to say. I never knew him, but Mrs. Durr was always rather ashamed that he had been president of the mills when this was going on. The mill owners argued that they were saving the children from starvation, that the tenant farmer was so poor that they were helping the poor little children by giving them jobs in the mills. It never occurred to them that they were not being benevolent. Of course, mill owners in England had the same attitude when they put the women and children to work.

Jean Read's sister Sheila married Paxton Hibben, a famous journalist who covered the Russian Revolution. He was the nephew of the president of Princeton and a contemporary of John Reed, who wrote *Ten Days That Shook the World*.

Her other sister, Dolly, married a Mr. Speed from Louisville, who was extremely aristocratic. But Mr. Speed died and Dolly was left with a girl and boy. Their fortunes had fallen by then, so she took them to Vienna to educate them, to give them culture and teach them music and languages. They arrived during the Dollfuss period when the socialists were in control and were fighting against Hitlerism. The Communist movement was very strong, and Dolly's two children, then in their late teens, joined the Communist party. When Hitler came into power, and the situation got very bad in Vienna, Dolly Speed—who had become a Communist, too—brought her two children back home. She had no money, so she went to Montgomery to live with her sister, Jean Read.

Jean had married a wealthy man and had a beautiful old house. She was the leading society lady of Montgomery. Her food was the most delicious, she wore the prettiest clothes, she gave the nicest parties, her garden was the most beautiful, her house was the most tasteful. She was head of the little theater. If anyone had a ball, she decorated the ballroom. She was a woman of tremendous artistic talent.

My mother-in-law took Ann, who was three or four, and me to Jean Read's for tea. Dolly and her daughter, Jane, were there, too. It was early summer, and we sat by a lovely pond with water lilies. Jean was a gracious hostess, and Ben, the butler, served the most marvelous food, things like puff pastries. Dolly was trying to make some money by taking pictures, and we arranged for her to take pictures of Ann by the pool.

I knew that Dolly and Jane were Communists, but I didn't know what a Communist was. Hugo had been called a Bolshevik because he was on the side of the labor unions, so I thought everybody who was in the labor unions or for labor was a Communist. Mrs. Read, who had sort of a high society voice, would say, "Oh, isn't this darling? This is amusing; Jane and Dolly are Communists! What do you know about that!" Jane didn't find it a very laughable matter. Dolly and Jane talked about the horrors of what had happened in Vienna, but it made very little impact on me. Hitler and Dollfuss and Vienna were even more remote from my world than communism was.

Dolly and Jane were helping the sharecroppers' union in Tallapoosa County, and soon after I met them a strike broke out. When the shooting started, Mrs. Read, as I understand it, stopped laughing about Jane and Dolly's being Communists and told them to leave. She was afraid they might influence her son, Nicholas Read. I found out later that a Marxist study group in Montgomery also supported the union strike. Today some of the members of that group are among the richest people in Montgomery. They will talk about it, but they won't let their names be used, because they are terribly respectable. Jane and Dolly moved to Birmingham after they left Mrs. Read's house in Montgomery and eventually ran a Communist bookstore there.

Hugo won the race for the Senate, and he and Sister and their two boys went back to Washington in 1932. He had run against former Governor Kilby. Sister had gone all over the state with him as his secretary, and he paid her a secretary's wages. She had been in the Navy and she knew how to use a typewriter. In the course of the campaign, Kilby accused Hugo of paying his wife and cheating the government. I never saw a man get as angry as Hugo did then. After that, he lit into Kilby tooth and toenail. And he beat him.

In 1933, Mother and Daddy came to live with us. They rented their house out. By then everything they had in the world had gone except the house, and Mother began to develop symptoms of what in those days they called "melancholia." She wouldn't eat and she couldn't sleep and her mind seemed confused. She finally went to an institution in Birmingham called Hillcrest. That was a horrible period, because she begged and begged to come home. She cried and cried. That was a horrible, horrible period.

Meanwhile, Daddy plunged head first into the Roosevelt campaign and that saved his life. He and Judge Fitts from Tuscaloosa had gone to Warm Springs in 1931 and begged Roosevelt to run. Daddy became a pas-

Hugo Black as Senator, the 1930s.

Sister with Hugo, Jr. *(left)*, and Sterling.

sionate Roosevelt supporter and worked hard for him during the campaign. He hoped he would be rewarded with a job, and sure enough, when Roosevelt was elected he was given a position on the National Emergency Council.

In early 1933 my father came to live with us, my mother went into the sanatorium, and Cliff left the law firm. He was a full partner, and there seems to be a difference of opinion about whether he resigned or was fired. The senior member of the firm, Logan Martin, was the brother of the president of Alabama Power Company, Tom Martin, a hard-working and rather decent fellow. Logan was a bachelor and had no family responsibilities at all. He also, as top member of the firm, drew a higher share of the profits than anyone else. Cliff's percentage was low, although he did get a share. A whole series of unpleasant incidents happened at the office, and finally Logan just started firing people, young lawyers and stenographers, without even having a meeting of the members of the firm.

The head stenographer came to Cliff one day in a great state of excitement. The firm had had one stenographer whose husband had left her, and she had a baby. Mrs. Cole went to Cliff and said, "Can't you do something about Mrs. So-and-so? Judge Martin has just fired her. She's got no family and she has this baby. I'm afraid she is going to kill herself." So Cliff went in to see Logan and asked if they could keep her on. Logan said, "Will you pay her salary?" Cliff said that he had a wife and baby to support, but he was willing to take his share of a cut in pay so that they could keep everybody on. Also, some of the younger lawyers who had been let go were married and had children and Cliff protested against their summary dismissal. They didn't even get a week's notice; they were just fired. Logan's answer was "Well, we can't keep them unless you are willing to pay their salaries. I'm not." Some of the other members of the firm agreed with Cliff and were upset about it, but they wouldn't take a stand.

Now, Logan just despised Hugo Black, and Logan ran the politics of the firm. He never did any legal work, and he had separate files and a separate secretary. When Hugo ran for the Senate the second time, Cliff found out that one of the vice-presidents of the Alabama Power Company, Colonel Mitchell, didn't like Kilby, so they began talking about the situation. He would call Cliff up to his office and would get on the phone with the power company local managers and tell them all to vote for Hugo Black. Between Colonel Mitchell and Cliff, the power company went for Hugo. Logan didn't like that.

There was a good deal of argument about whether Logan Martin fired Cliff or Cliff resigned. Anyway, Cliff soon found himself out of the firm and about to start practicing law in Birmingham on his own in the depths of the depression.

We had a fishing cabin down along the river, near Clanton. The river was not too crowded in those days. Cliff said the best time to take a vacation was between jobs. So we sold our little Chevrolet for $350, and Cliff's brother drove us down to the river with some groceries. It was spring, beautiful down there, and we found out where the fish were biting.

The power company owned a great stretch of vacant land on the river, and a lot of poor people had built shacks on it. These settlements were called Hoovervilles. The people fished in the river and lived off the land.

One night while we were down there, Mr. Mims, who had a fishing camp, brought his whole family over. Nobody went to the fishing camp because nobody had any money. Then another family came over. Mr. Mims was a funny fellow who played a guitar. Our ten or twelve welcome but uninvited guests sang a lot of the old songs and somebody got up and danced a buck and wing. But I knew I had to feed them something, and I was terrified because I didn't know what to give them.

I went back in the kitchen and fortunately found a five-pound sack of sugar. I found some chocolate and made some fudge. Well, those people had not had any sugar for months and months. They hadn't had anything sweet. Sugar was one thing they couldn't buy and they couldn't grow. If I had given them the most marvelous meal in the world, they couldn't have been any more thrilled than they were. They not only ate every piece of fudge I made, but the children came in and licked the bowls and spoons.

We thought we were having a pretty tough time. Cliff didn't have a job and we didn't know what we were going to do, but we knew we always had somebody to fall back on. Cliff's brother had offered to lend him any amount of money he needed. I realized that these people on the river were completely desperate.

After we'd been on the river about a week, a fellow drove over in a truck and said, "I think somebody in Washington is trying to get Cliff on the telephone. They said it was important." So we went to Clanton, and it was Hugo. He told Cliff the Reconstruction Finance Corporation, RFC, was looking for corporation lawyers and they had asked him for recommendations. He had given them a half-dozen names of people in Alabama he thought were qualified. He said if Cliff was interested he had better go right on up there. Cliff left right away.

PART TWO

WASHINGTON, D.C.

1933–1949

5

Seminary Hill

STANLEY REED, THE GENERAL counsel for the RFC, hired Cliff to head up the bank insurance program, but the legislation never got through Congress. The next thing Cliff knew, he and another fellow, Jim Alley, were setting up the whole program for the recapitalization of the banks. Reed was then appointed solicitor general, and Jim Alley was made general counsel. Now, Cliff had never represented a bank in his life and knew nothing about banking, and all of a sudden he found himself head of the program to recapitalize the banks.

When Cliff first got the job in Washington, he thought he might be there for only a few months. Roosevelt had taken office in March and we arrived in April. But just before I left Birmingham I went to the Junior League Convention in Philadelphia. I was vice-president of the Junior League in Birmingham at that time.

At this convention of well-off young ladies from all of the eastern seaboard, I first began to hear criticisms of President and Mrs. Roosevelt. I heard remarks about the rich and aristocratic and socially prominent Roosevelts taking up the cause of people who were completely improvident. That was a great word people used—improvident. You hadn't provided for the future, you see. You were poor and it was your own fault. No one in Birmingham blamed the Tennessee Coal, Iron and Railroad Company. Even the people out of work didn't blame them. Now, I did. By that time, I was getting furious at these Yankee corporations.

Cliff was already in Washington, and after the Junior League Convention I joined him there. We lived with Sister and Hugo for a week or two; then I returned to Alabama to get Ann, who had been staying with her grandmother. For a time we lived in an apartment building on Wisconsin Avenue near Sister and Hugo, but soon I began looking for a house. Cliff was making $6,500 a year. During the depression we thought that was a pretty good salary. I didn't want to live in Washington. I wanted to live out in the country, or somewhere in the suburbs anyway, on account of Ann.

Living in the apartment was awful. We were twelve stories up, and Ann would ride the elevator all the time. I was in a constant state of chasing her up and down, going back and forth getting her. I was worried to death about her. Sister was extremely nice to me and took me to all the events she went to at the Senate. I could leave Ann with Sister's cook, Mary Marble, who had worked for my mother, but I was really anxious to get out into the country.

While I was at the Junior League Convention, I met a real estate agent from Washington, and she said, "Where do you want to live?" Her name was Ann Carter Green. I said, "Well, I would like to live out in the country where people are poor and genteel." She laughed and said, "You have described Seminary Hill." This is where the Virginia Episcopal Theological Seminary was. "It is out in the country and everybody is poor and everybody is genteel. They rent their houses for the summer."

I really took her seriously, so when I started looking for a house I told the real estate agent that I'd like to live on Seminary Hill. She said, "Oh, my heavens, there are never any houses to rent on Seminary Hill except in the summer. The professors go away for the summer and they rent their houses sometimes." She said, "I'll call up and see, but it's very, very chancy." She did find a house to rent; it belonged to the Zabriskies. At that time Mr. Zabriskie was one of the professors at the seminary. He came from New York and had a lovely wife named Mary. Their house was a perfectly beautiful old place built in the shape of an octagon and surrounded by oak trees. It was very nicely furnished. I went out there and immediately rented it for $75 a month, but that was just for the summer.

As it happened, we lived on Seminary Hill all the rest of the time we were in Washington. We later bought a house there, an old farmhouse with two acres of land, for $6,500. Land was so cheap then.

I had brought a nurse with me, who also acted as cook. I still thought I could never get along without servants. I just never dreamed it was possible. Celeste had been Ann's nurse for a long time. She was a very pretty black girl who had had a disastrous marriage and was glad to get away from Birmingham. She was the niece of the sister of my old nurse, Alice. Alice's sister, Mary, was the washwoman for the whole household in Birmingham. Celeste had stayed and helped with Ann after my two miscarriages. She was a sweet person, and I was fond of her, but we hadn't been in Washington very long when she got lonesome and wanted to go back to Birmingham. She didn't like the people in Washington and didn't know anybody and didn't know the right church to go to. So she left.

Cliff was working day and night at the RFC and was gone all the time.

He'd go to work in the morning, come back home for a hurried dinner, then go back to work, and finally return at two or three in the morning. They were trying to save the banks. He was awakened at night by people calling from every point of the compass saying, "If we don't get money here by tomorrow, I'll commit suicide. We'll all be ruined." Cliff and the other people at RFC were working as hard as they possibly could, but some of the bankers did commit suicide. That was the awful part about it.

Cliff would talk about his work if he wasn't too tired, but he'd usually come home and just go to sleep. He was in a state of exhaustion. He was putting his finger in the dike, but at that time everyone was afraid the whole country was going to go bankrupt. It was the strangest kind of time.

One thing happened that I thought was amusing because it was so unlike Cliff. Cliff was a model gentleman and rarely showed any irritation or anger or resentment. The head of the biggest bank in Birmingham came to Washington. His bank was in trouble. He thought he was a big shot, so he went directly to Jesse Jones, who was head of the RFC. He wanted to see Mr. Jones immediately. Mr. Jones said, "You'll have to go down and see Mr. Clifford Durr, who is head of the general counsel for the bank reorganization division." Now this Birmingham banker, Oscar Wells, was a rather pompous man. We had known him, but only slightly. So he said, "Oh, Mr. Jones, I couldn't deal with an underling like that. Why, that's just a local boy from Birmingham. I want to deal with the head man." I think he thought Mr. Jones ought to get busy and draw up the papers himself, but Mr. Jones said, "Well, if you don't deal with Clifford Durr, you just don't deal with anybody, because he happens to be the lawyer who's drawing up all these papers."

Mr. Jones called Cliff and said, "Cliff, there's a man on the way to see you from Birmingham named Mr. Wells. He says he doesn't want to deal with you because you're just a local boy from Birmingham. I think you'll have to keep him waiting for a while." So Cliff did keep him waiting, I think an hour, sitting in there cooling his heels. It was unlike Cliff to do anything like that, but Mr. Wells had been so arrogant, so scornful of having to deal with just a local boy.

That summer I made friends on Seminary Hill. The dean of the seminary was there, and I became fond of him. He was a widower, and his niece kept house for him. There were a lot of people around the Hill who were very nice. Seminary Hill is right outside of Alexandria. The Episcopal high school is there and the Virginia Episcopal Seminary. A paved road ran from Alexandria to Washington, but the road from Alexandria out to Seminary Hill was just gravel. A bus ran twice a day. It was isolated, but it was a real neighborhood. The people in Virginia have the most beautiful manners in the world, and everybody called. Those were the days when people called

—to visit, I mean, not by telephone. You were supposed to be prepared for visitors in the afternoons and have iced tea and cookies ready.

Seminary Hill is a perfectly beautiful place with the old brick buildings of the seminary and the brick buildings of the Virginia Episcopal High School. This is where the gentility of Virginia had gone for generations. They would refer to "the High School," "the Seminary," and "the University," which meant the Virginia Episcopal High School, the Virginia Episcopal Theological Seminary, and the University of Virginia.

Cliff and Ann and I would take a walk after supper if Cliff was there. Even when Cliff wasn't there, Ann and I would take a little walk in the grove. One night we overheard a very one-sided conversation, and we came up on Mr. Jim. He had an old house up there on Seminary Hill that his family had lived in for generations. He was extremely courteous and told us his name and where he lived. He said he came out every night to talk to his trees, his friends. Nobody regarded him as insane, just a little strange.

Then there were the Herberts, who lived in Alexandria but had come up to Seminary Hill to get out of the city. They were great aristocrats from Virginia. In some way they were related to the Fairfaxes who had settled Virginia. It had been discovered that the heir to the Fairfax title lived in Virginia. He had gone back to England and claimed his patrimony and had taken Mr. Herbert, who was a bachelor, with him. For years Mr. Herbert had lived in England and been part of the British aristocracy. Lord Fairfax didn't have much money, but he had the title and a castle. When Lord Fairfax either fell on hard times or died, Mr. Herbert came back to the United States and lived with his three old-maid sisters, who had rented a house for the summer right across the road from us. They were all very Virginian and talked with that beautiful Virginia accent.

The Herberts would invite us to dinner. They were marvelous cooks, but they didn't believe in eating cooked food. They would offer guests delicious meals of broiled chicken and puffed pastry and biscuits and corn pudding. Then they'd say, "I hope you'll eat this, but I want you to understand that while you're eating it, you're killing yourself. This is the kind of food that kills people." They would be eating bananas and drinking herb tea. Everything raw or natural. But no one thought they were odd, either. They were just taken as a matter of fact, too. Everybody accepted them. They would tell terrible tales about old Cousin Annie who came to visit them. Cousin Annie was eighty-nine years old and she still seemed to be healthy. "But, you know, that woman is killing herself. We took her out and do you know what she had for dinner? She ordered and ate a dead lobster."

One of the reasons people were so nice to us on Seminary Hill was that they had "placed" us. Dr. Crawford, who had been dean of the seminary, had had several beautiful daughters. One of them, Alice, had gone to Birmingham as the wife of an Episcopal minister, Dr. Randolph. My mother and she were friendly and I had known her, so she vouched for us. She and her husband had returned to Virginia when he took a position teaching in an Episcopal school.

Mrs. Randolph was an absolute beauty. She had perfect features and masses of shiny, curly black hair. She also had lovely white skin and a slender figure. She had been proposed to, we always understood, by every million-aire in the country, but she married Dr. Randolph, an Episcopal minister, with whom she had fallen in love. She was a devoted wife to him. We got to know them quite well. He had been head of an Episcopal school some-where in south Virginia and he had failed the sons of some very prominent people in the Episcopal church. He would just fail them or expel them if they didn't do right. The board of trustees warned him he was losing money for the school and for the Episcopal church. But he was a man of total integrity and honesty, and he kept on failing the students who did poorly, so the board fired him. He came up and lived in the little house next to us after we'd bought a house on Seminary Hill. During the war he got a job in a torpedo factory. He'd go off in the mornings with a lunch basket in his hands. And Mrs. Randolph would come out and empty the garbage. I never will forget, she always wore gloves and always looked beautiful—her hair fixed and beautifully dressed. After the war was over, he became director of the church in Rome, Italy. Mrs. Randolph went with him, and I understand their later years were very comfortable and happy. They were lovely people. There were a lot of Virginians I didn't like at all, but there is a strain in Virginia of men of integrity, men like Cliff who insist on doing right in spite of hell and high water. Dr. Randolph was one of them. And he did it in such a matter-of-fact way.

Mr. Reid was a lovely old Englishman who had taught at the Virginia Episcopal High School. I would go over often in the afternoons and have tea with him, because being English, he made delicious tea and he loved to have people drop in for tea. When the Germans started bombing England, Mr. Reid, then in his eighties, was terribly concerned about his relatives. I said, "I declare, what do you think is the cause of all the trouble in the world?" He said it was very simple: it was on account of the gasoline engine. He said as soon as we got away from horses, the world began to go to hell. He was absolutely convinced that everything was the fault of the gasoline engine. He had rather old-fashioned ideas and that's what he stuck to.

Birmingham had been a bustling place where everybody was striving to get ahead and get money and give big parties and impress people, but the people in Virginia were already sure they were the absolute top of the heap, so they didn't have to impress anybody. If they were poor, they were still absolutely Virginian. The atmosphere on Seminary Hill was of people who were genteel, extremely genteel, and not rich, but who had beautiful manners and were absolutely secure in the knowledge that they were Virginians.

I remember there was one woman in particular who was like that. Tinsley Harrison's mother, a Birmingham friend, asked me to go see her cousin. So I went there, and my heavens, here was this handsome woman with a brood of handsome children. The house looked like a wreck. Some of the windows were out, and the woman's poor old mother was huddling over a little fire. She greeted me with perfect grace. So when I went back to Birmingham to visit, I told Mrs. Harrison about her cousin and what a desperate time she was having. She said that was because her grandfather had been a gambler. There was a streak of gambling in the family, and they had lost all their money. She said, " You know, this cousin of mine has all the family silver. It must be worth several thousand dollars. When you go back, ask her if I can buy the silver from her. Maybe that would help her out of her desperate condition."

So I went out there one cold day. It was after Christmas, cold as it could be, and the house was freezing. The empty windows had been covered with wood. I told the lady that her cousin in Alabama, Mrs. Harrison, would like to buy the family silver. She said, "Dear Ella wants that silver? Why it had never occurred to me that she'd like that silver. If she feels that way about it, I'll send it to her tomorrow." I said, "But she wants to buy it from you." "Oh," she said, "I couldn't think of selling the family silver. But I'll certainly share it with her, and give it to her if she feels strongly about it." Well, what could you do about that? She was not going to accept any money for the family silver; that was something that was sacred.

Virginia was a fascinating place to me because it provided a haven from the hubbub of Washington. After the Zabriskies came back, we rented a house off the hill and then we bought one next door to the Zabriskies. Seminary Hill was a wonderful place for children because there was plenty of space and it was safe. It was a neighborhood. Later, when our little boy died, I can remember everybody coming over with jelly and custards and cake and casseroles. On the social side, on the personal side of pleasant living, it was delightful, an absolutely lovely place to live.

We were the first New Dealers on Seminary Hill, so initially we were completely in the world of old Virginia. Later, other New Dealers began to move in. Much later, Sister and Hugo bought a house out there, when he was appointed to the Supreme Court. We were guaranteed by Mrs. Randolph, who had known my mother in Birmingham. It was a guarantee that we would not create any disturbance, I suppose. But, of course, we did.

For the first year we were on Seminary Hill, I didn't have much to do with Washington. We had lots of visitors—people coming up and staying overnight and having dinner with us, people from Alabama. Then the family all came up, Cliff's family and some of my family. Of course, Sister lived

Clifford Judkins Durr, Jr., whom we called Brother, and baby Lucy with me, Seminary Hill.

in Washington, too, and Hugo was in the Senate then, but I was really more or less cut off from Washington. Sister took me to a lot of the official receptions, but I wasn't really part of that life. And after I'd been to a few, I wasn't so anxious to go again. At all those Washington receptions, unless you're really part of the group, you're just kind of an outsider looking on.

One thing that I did get freed from was the ladies at the RFC. Many men at the RFC had extremely ambitious wives. Their husbands were ambitious men, and the wives wanted very much to get into Washington society. They would give luncheon parties, bridge parties, and tea parties, where you'd go and play bridge and have lunch at a hotel—oh, those awful peas and half-done chicken lunches! They were a horrible bore. I finally said to Cliff, "Look, if your future depends on my going to these luncheons and teas and dinners that I'm invited to, I will, but they are the most boring things in the wide world. A lot of strange women who play bridge." And he said, "If my future depends on your playing bridge, I don't have much future anyway." He said I was the poorest bridge player in the world. So he relieved me of that.

My life was encompassed by Seminary Hill. I liked the people tremendously. I joined the Episcopal church and Ann started going to this Episcopal Sunday school. I'd go to the Ladies' Auxiliary that met for tea every week. I just loved it. It was a tremendous rest for me and I enjoyed it thoroughly.

My father came to visit us quite often. We'd sit out in the garden if it was warm and by a fire in the winter. The ladies would always invite Daddy to their teas because he was very chatty and always pleasant. But at one of these teas he began to tell how he was from Virginia. His family came from South Boston in Virginia. He was met with the usual sort of cool acceptance of the fact that he, or his people, had left Virginia, and the ladies started talking about whether the Fairfaxes were kin to the Washingtons or the Washingtons were kin to the Randolphs or the Randolphs were kin to the . . ., so on and on.

I don't know whether he got irritated or whether he thought he was going to be funny, but out of the clear blue sky, Daddy said, "This reminds me of a story from an old man up in Walker County." That's one of the roughest counties in Alabama, up in the coal mining region. "They were looking for a man to teach school and an elder in the county wrote up to the University of Virginia. The old man could hardly write. He got a tablet and a pencil and wrote up to the University of Virginia in Charlottesville and said, 'Dear Sirs, Beat Eight of certain district in Walker County is looking for a schoolteacher, and can you recommend a good young man? We'd pay him $800, year basis, free board, whatever.' So he got this beautifully written letter back, beautiful handwriting and addressed properly: 'Dear Sirs, My name is St. John Washington Jefferson Randolph, or whatever—a very old Virginia name. On my mother's side I am connected to the Jeffersons, and on my grandmother's side I'm connected to the Lees, and on my great-grandmother's side I'm connected to the Fairfaxes.' He gave them about four pages of his genealogy. And then he ended by saying he would like to apply to teach at the school in Walker County. Well, the writing was very delicate, beautiful, very legible, but very fine. So the school board got together and read the letter. They figured out page by page. And they discussed what to reply. Then the old man got out his tablet again and wet his pencil and wrote: 'University of Virginia. Dear Sir, We have read your letter. N'er mind. You needn' come. We weren't lookin' for no man down here for breedin' purposes, jus' one to teach school.' "

Nobody laughed, I can assure you of that. Daddy was just disgraced. They really didn't think that was funny at all. They spent hours developing these family themes. Daddy came from an old Alabama family, so family heritage talk wasn't totally alien to him. But these Virginians made him feel that being from Alabama was a disgrace. If you weren't from Virginia, you really didn't count. Of course, you could be away from Virginia temporarily, but to leave Virginia, to have your ancestors pick up and leave Virginia, was inexcusable. They always thought there must have been something peculiar about you if you did that.

I've lived on so many different levels. Here, by chance, we got in the middle of the most conservative, genteel community in northern Virginia, where the people had lived for generations. So the first year, until I got used to Washington, I lived in this completely pleasant, genteel atmosphere and went to tea parties.

I was anxious to get pregnant again. The doctors in Birmingham had told me I could never have any more children because of the two miscarriages. But I went to a good doctor in Washington and the second year we were there I had a beautiful little boy. He was born on September 18, 1935, and named after Cliff, but we called him Brother.

Ann started school at St. Agnes, the Episcopal school. I asked the ladies about the public school. They said I couldn't think of sending her to a public school because of the nits. All the children there had nits in their hair. The public schools of Virginia were so bad that nobody went there—no nice person went there. So St. Agnes was the only school they ever considered.

After the Zabriskies had returned at the end of that first summer and we rented a house off the hill, by the greatest luck in the world, my next door neighbor was Stella Landis. Stella came from Mississippi. Stark Young's *So Red the Rose* was written about her family and their plantation. Stella's grandfather was Bishop Galloway, the presiding bishop of the Methodist Church of Mississippi. Stella had gone to Millsaps College. She was a tall, thin, beautiful woman who had originally come to Washington to look for a job. She didn't want to stay in Mississippi. If you ever heard anybody strong against male oppression, she was. She had several brothers, and maybe it was the bishop, too, but anyway she felt the women in Mississippi were badly treated. We were similar in a way, tall and thin. Both of us read a lot and were nearsighted. But Stella was beautiful. She had lovely fluffy dark hair and great big gray eyes and white skin. Stella had worked for the Scripps-

Howard papers, and old man Scripps had taken her around the world with him on his yacht. There was certainly no scandal connected with that; he was about eighty-seven then. He just found her to be a delightful companion. She was, I think, one of the most charming women I ever met.

Jim Landis's people had been missionaries in China. He was brilliant and had been sent home to go to Harvard. When he was still quite young he had become dean of Harvard Law School. In Washington he worked in the Securities and Exchange Commission with Joe Kennedy.

Stella and Jim had two little girls. Their Ann and our Ann were about the same age. And then their Ellen came along and our Lucy came along. Stella and I became close friends, and through her I became interested in the New Deal.

Jim Landis had been a law clerk for Justice Brandeis, and Stella loved to go to the Supreme Court to hear the cases. She had lived in a law school atmosphere and knew a lot of the lawyers. We would go to the clerk's office and Justice Brandeis's messenger would come and usher us to the front seats. Mrs. Brandeis never came, so we would sit in Justice Brandeis's private enclave. I loved all that. I was a country girl from Alabama and I thought all the pomp and ceremony and being ushered into the seats was fun. I began to enjoy Washington. I also got interested in the law cases. All the great New Deal cases were being tried, cases such as *Schechter Poultry Company* v. *United States,* the 1935 case in which the Supreme Court invalidated the National Recovery Act (NRA), and *United States* v. *Butler,* the 1936 decision in which the Court held the Agricultural Adjustment Administration's processing tax unconstitutional.

Stella was also interested in congressional hearings, and I began to go to them with her, too. Then she began to take me with her to visit the Supreme Court justices' wives on Monday afternoons, when they received. We went to see Mrs. Brandeis a number of times, because she was crazy about Stella. Mrs. Brandeis was a marvelous, interesting woman. She must have been eighty, but she was still absolutely beautiful. She always wore cotton stockings. She said, "You girls are very extravagant, I think, to wear silk stockings. I never wear silk stockings, unless it's an evening entertainment." Through Stella I got to know her. She was very nice to me and began to invite Cliff and me to her Sunday afternoon teas. But that was more on account of Cliff than on account of me.

Cliff got to know Jim Landis pretty well because they'd go to Washington in the car together in the morning, but he never did like Jim much. Cliff judged people more by character than by their accomplishments. He said Jim was one of the most cold-blooded, selfish people he'd ever met. He didn't think he was arrogant; he was just unaware. He was that way with Stella. I remember their little girls went to St. Agnes, too, and when the children would put on plays, Stella would have to beg and beg Jim to come. The girls wanted their father to be there. Jim was just unaware. Whatever he did in his work, he did with his entire concentration, his entire mind. He talked very little, but when we'd go to his place for dinner, if he drank a great deal he'd start talking along about 12 o'clock and keep talking until 4 o'clock in the morning and be absolutely brilliant. But by that time, we'd be in a state of total exhaustion. He really was just shy, and he was a difficult husband. Later he deserted Stella.

I met a lot of New Dealers at parties given by Aubrey and Anita Williams. Aubrey was the assistant administrator of the Works Progress Administration, under Harry Hopkins. Later he became head of the National Youth Administration. The Williamses lived with their four boys in an old house in Arlington County, several miles from where we lived, but on the Virginia side. They often had parties on Sunday, with a bright fire and delicious food and drink. All kinds of people would come. Anita was a wonderful cook, and Aubrey was very gracious and funny and hospitable. People loved to gather at the Williamses' on Sunday afternoon.

I remember meeting Helen Gahagan Douglas at Aubrey's. She looked like a Greek goddess, and she was a sweet person, too. Cliff was very admiring of her. Pete Seeger and Alan Lomax would go to the parties and play folk music. Alan Lomax's father was head of the folk music section of the Library of Congress, and Pete Seeger's father was head of the entire music division. Pete and Alan were the founders of the folk music revival. When I first met Pete, he was wearing a dirty sweatshirt and a pair of dirty jeans. He'd left Harvard and was going all over the country with a guitar collecting folk music. I adored him from the very start. He's another pure character for whom I never had anything but praise and love.

Another place where we met a lot of the younger New Dealers, such as Jim Rowe and Jerry Reilly, was in a house next to us on Seminary Hill, which seven or eight girls rented for the summer. They all had jobs in New Deal agencies. One of them, Lois, later married Tom Eliot, a congressman from Massachusetts and the grandson of a president of Harvard. Tom Corcoran's place, the "little red house," was another gathering spot. A lot of the young bachelors lived there and would have parties.

As I got to know a lot of the people in Washington who were in the New Deal, I decided I wanted to do something, too. I had heard that Mrs. Roosevelt worked for the Women's Division of the Democratic National Committee, and I admired her greatly. I had met her at a garden party that Sister took me to, and I thought she was absolutely lovely. She was a tall, slender woman and had brown hair and beautiful eyes. The lower part of her face was not very attractive, but she was such a lovely person to be with that she gave the impression of beauty and graciousness and charm and cordiality. So I decided I would volunteer for the Women's Division, mostly because I knew Mrs. Roosevelt worked with them.

At that time we were sending money back home to my mother and father, who had moved back to their house. We had hired a lady to live there with her family and look after my mother. My brother had a job then with the New Deal and was also sending them money. Although Cliff was making only $6,500 a year, we could afford a cook, a nurse, a yardman, and a washlady. In those days everything was so much cheaper. I feel a little ashamed when I think what we paid the servants: the cook and nurse got $8 or $10 a week, plus room and board, and the yardman and washlady got $2 or $3 a day. I paid the going wage; it never occurred to me to do otherwise. Because of the servants, I could leave the children at home for a morning or an afternoon without feeling guilty, and so I began to go into town and work at the women's section of the Democratic National Committee.

6

Initiation into Politics

WORK AT THE WOMEN'S DIVISION of the National Democratic Committee was very pleasant. I started going there as a volunteer two or three times a week. I'd clip newspapers and answer the telephone and do whatever volunteers were supposed to do. Dorothy McAllister, from Grand Rapids, was in charge, and May Thompson Evans, a very attractive girl from North Carolina, was second in command.

An interesting lot of women came through the office, and I became fond of them. Mrs. Roosevelt came in quite often. And old Mrs. Daisy Harriman would sweep in. She was a great figure in the Democratic party, a very handsome woman who gave a lot of parties.

At that time the Women's Division was trying to put into effect the 50-50 plan—all Democratic committees would be 50 percent women and 50 percent men. Women would have equal representation. That was considered a radical proposal—I should say it was! In the Southern states there was not a single woman on a single local Democratic committee. The women on the Democratic National Committee were usually pretty Southern women who wore big hats and sang "Dixie." The people in the Women's Division were particularly worried about the South because there were no Southern women on any Democratic committees—local, city, or state. Except for the few token Southern women on the Democratic National Committee, Southern women were completely outside the party.

The Women's Division made quite a study of the South and decided that the problem was the poll tax. After the Populist uprising, about 1900, the Southern states disenfranchised the Negroes by the white primary and by the poll tax. The poll tax also disenfranchised the poor whites. Even after the woman's suffrage amendment in 1920, very few women voted in the South. If a poor tenant farmer had scraped up a dollar and a half to pay his poll tax, he sure as hell wasn't going to pay a dollar and a half for his wife. And the women themselves never had any money.

In Alabama the poll tax was retroactive to age twenty-one even if you started voting when you were forty-five. It was retroactive in Virginia for three years. Texas had the highest proportion of people of voting age who voted, about 30 percent; Mississippi had the lowest—12 percent. As a result, much of the South was run by an oligarchy composed of white, usually middle-aged, gentlemen, or men—some of them were gentlemen and some of them weren't.

The goal of the Women's Division was to get rid of the poll tax so white Southern women could vote. There was no mention in the Democratic Committee at that time of black people. And there were no Negroes around the Women's Division. Of course, very few black people in the South voted, but the Southern white women didn't vote either.

I had a personal experience with the poll tax in Birmingham that made me realize how stupid it was and how difficult. When I was twenty-one years old—before I married Cliff—I went to register to vote. My father was always a registrar, and one reason was because they knew that he had never registered any black man. He used to come home from the board of registrars and say, "I swear to God, there was a damn nigger there today who had been to Harvard. Harvard, mind you! And you know, you just couldn't hardly think of enough questions to ask him that he couldn't answer. But I did." So he never registered a single one. I took this completely for granted, of course. Daddy was just upholding pure white Southern womanhood and white supremacy, and I accepted it. I had been surrounded by that attitude all my life.

Anyway, I registered when I was twenty-one, and I paid a dollar and a half for my poll tax. From then on, when I would go down to vote, they would say, "You haven't paid your poll tax." I would say, "But I did pay my poll tax." I didn't know you had to pay it every year. I was as stupid as that, and I had gone to Wellesley for two years. So I would sign an affidavit that I had paid my poll tax. When I got married, Cliff went with me to vote and found that he had to pay about fifteen dollars so I could vote, because all these affidavits I had made out didn't mean a thing.

When I started working for the Women's Division of the Democratic National Committee and found that getting rid of the poll tax was one of their concerns, I was interested. Here I was a young married woman on Seminary Hill in an old farmhouse that we fixed over, with a little boy and two little girls. The youngest at that time was Lucy, who was born in January of 1937. I had two full-time servants and two part-time servants and an automobile. I lived in a lovely, quiet neighborhood that I adored. But I also wanted to be in Washington in the midst of all the excitement, because the

New Deal to me was perfectly thrilling. Cliff was saving the banks and the telephone was ringing all the time. It was an exciting time to be there.

I was also slowly becoming something of a feminist. I had had a great resentment, I now realize, of the role that Southern girls had to play. Nice Southern girls were supposed to try to get husbands, and so they were always fooling the men and being pleasant and putting up with almost anything to be popular. My resentment hadn't come to the surface yet. It was still gestating inside of me. But I must have felt it, because I plunged into the fight to get rid of the poll tax for the women of the South with the greatest gusto. I began to go to the headquarters every morning.

About this time, Clark Foreman came back into my life. I saw in the paper one day a picture of a very handsome dark-haired girl walking on Connecticut Avenue with a big cape swinging behind her, and the caption said, "Mrs. Clark Foreman, one of the young beauties of the New Deal set . . ." Her father was the Canadian assistant governor-general. Mairi was quite fashionable and beautiful and very stylish. Her name had been Mairi Fraser. Her family were all Scots. I wondered if she was possibly the wife of the Clark Foreman I knew. I hadn't seen or heard of him since I left Wellesley. I looked in the telephone book and called and said, "Mrs. Foreman, are you the wife of Clark Foreman from Atlanta?" She said yes, she was. I said, "Well, tell Clark that I called. I was Jinksie Foster from Alabama." So Clark called that night, and he and Mairi came to visit us the following Sunday.

After he had left Harvard, Clark had gone to the London School of Economics and had studied socialism, the British brand. Then he had gone to Russia and studied communism. While he was over there, he became aware of the race issue. He had been brought up as I had been; he just took all the Southern attitudes for granted. After his education and travels he didn't become a socialist or a Communist, but he did decide he would come back to Atlanta and attack the race issue. He had had the horrible experience of witnessing a lynching while he was a young student at the University of Georgia. So when he came back he worked with Will Alexander in the Interracial Council. Then he worked for the Rosenwald Fund.

Harold Ickes, who was secretary of the interior and head of the Public Works Administration, had asked various interracial groups to recommend someone to work in the Department of the Interior to see that blacks got a fair share of jobs in public works. He also was trying to desegregate the Department of the Interior, where the bathrooms and the cafeteria were still segregated.

Clark arrived in Washington to work for Ickes and promptly hired a Negro secretary. Well, this caused an absolute storm throughout the whole government. No one could understand how a young white Southern boy who came from a good family, the Howells of Georgia, could do such a thing. Of course, they immediately accused him of having the woman as his mistress, which was absurd; she was simply a very efficient secretary. Clark was the first person to break that barrier; he was a great believer in racial equality and was working at it.

That Sunday afternoon when he came out to our house, he began telling us what he was going to do and what he was doing. Well, my Lord, I just fell into a fit! I couldn't believe it. We got into the most awful fight you have ever known in your life. Cliff said he had to take the wood basket out of the way because I would have brained Clark or he would have brained me. Clark is not tactful at times. He said, "You know, you are just a white, Southern, bigoted, prejudiced, provincial girl." Oh, he just laid me out. I got furious and I said, "You are going back on all the traditions of the South. You, a Howell of Georgia, going back on all of it. What do you think of the Civil War? What did we stand for?" White supremacy, of course. When they left, Cliff said, "Well, I don't think you'll ever see him again." Amazingly enough, they called us up the next week and invited us to dinner.

Of course, Cliff thought pretty much the same way I did, but he didn't holler about it. I hate to say it, but we had both been surrounded by these beliefs since infancy and we didn't question them. We had both been raised by black women whom we had adored and trusted and on whom our lives depended. Yet, at the same time, we were brought up to think that all black people were inferior. So we had acquired a double vision of blacks which I am sure contributed somewhat to our later change in point of view.

In spite of the stormy beginning, we began to see a great deal of the Foremans, and through them we met Wicki and Tex Goldschmidt, who were from Texas. Wicki worked for Aubrey Williams at the WPA, and that's how I met Aubrey.

By this time, I was beginning to enlarge my circle of friends and my ideas. But there were no black women in the Women's Division. Not a one. The only black woman I ever saw at that time was Mary McLeod Bethune, and she worked for Aubrey Williams. Through Clark I met some black people, his secretary, for instance, and his assistant, Robert Weaver. Clark had blacks to dinner and that's where I met Mattiwilda Dobbs. She was Maynard Jackson's aunt. Maynard Jackson was elected mayor of Atlanta in 1973.

Neither Cliff nor I had any musical or artistic taste, but Clark and Mairi were very much into the cultural life of Washington, the symphony and the arts. They both loved it. Mairi painted, and they enjoyed modern art. We didn't know what it was. I remember we went to Clark and Mairi's one night, and they had a new painting that they were thrilled about. They asked us what it was and we said all we could see was an old tin wastebasket. It turned out to be a new work by Ben Shahn. We were completely outside of that part of their lives. We couldn't recognize good art and music or appreciate it. I never had any training in art, and I was—and am—as blind as a bat. If it doesn't look like what it is supposed to look like, I am just lost. Even works by Picasso. And oh, they adored Picasso and all those one-eyed people. In music, the only people I could ever appreciate were Pete Seeger, Alan Lomax, and the country folk singers. I still love them, but above them I'm lost.

Clark had known Mr. Dobbs very well in Atlanta and had worked with him in his interracial work. So they arranged for Mattiwilda, who was a grand opera soprano singer, to have a concert in Washington at the Phillips Gallery. Mairi called me up and said, "Jinksie, could you possibly come over and arrange about the tea? I have to go to the reception. I don't want to leave the cook in the kitchen with nobody to help her out." So Cliff and I went over and we set up the teatable and I made sandwiches.

When the Dobbses all came back, they told us Mattiwilda had made a tremendous hit. Everybody stood and cheered. They were all thrilled beyond words. Mattiwilda later sang at the Metropolitan Opera in New York— just one year after Marian Anderson broke the color barrier at the Met in 1955.

I don't know how many Dobbses were at the Foremans' the night of Mattiwilda's concert at The Phillips Gallery; there must have been fifteen. I served the tea—quite a reversal of roles for me, as you can imagine. Here I was serving tea to this black family. And they were so charming and sweet. Mattiwilda's mother, Maynard's grandmother, was one of the sweetest, most charming women you have ever known. She made everybody thoroughly at ease. She had those wonderful Southern manners that are like oil on troubled waters.

Through the Goldschmidts, I met Lyndon and Lady Bird Johnson. Tex Goldschmidt was in the water conservation division of the Interior Department. When Lyndon first got elected to Congress, another Texan, Alvin Wirtz, was assistant secretary of the interior, and they were both just hell bent on the Lower Colorado River Project—to dam up the river to irrigate the land. Tex was active at the bureau that controlled all of this. Anyway, there were the Lyndon Johnsons, the Alvin Wirtzes, the Clifford Durrs, the Clark Foremans, and Nancy and Mike Straus. Mike was also in the Interior Department. Abe Fortas and his wife were in our little circle, too. We began to meet once a week for dinner.

Lady Bird had just come up from Texas, and Lyndon was a young congressman with a great big adam's apple, as thin as a stringbean. We used to laugh and call him the "drugstore cowboy," because he always wore cowboy boots. In Lyndon's later life he was so maligned and was called vicious and cruel, but I remember him as the sweetest young man. Of course, we were older than he was, ten years older, but I adored him and Lady Bird. Lady Bird and I are still friends.

The thing that impressed me about Lyndon in those days was that when he wanted to go after something like the Lower Colorado River Authority, he did not miss a trick. He cultivated everybody in the Interior Department. He was always on the job and always remembering birthdays and Christmas presents and everything else. He was a constant politician. He never took his eyes off the Lower Colorado River Authority. He got the irrigation project through, and then he got electricity for the Pedernales River where his home was. Everything around there is electrified now, but when he was growing up, there was no electricity at all.

Hugo and Josephine weren't really a part of our circle. Heavens, they were much higher. He was a senator then and by 1935 he had become one of the great New Deal senators. He worked on all of the Roosevelt projects. We did see them often. At their house we met an entirely different set of people, people like Lister Hill of Alabama, who was in the House then, and Claude Pepper, who also came from Alabama, from Clay County, the same county that Hugo came from. Pepper was a senator from Florida, and he later became a great champion of the anti–poll tax bill. We met Lowell Mellett, head of the National Emergency Council in the White House at that time, and he became a dear friend. We met the Thurmond Arnolds, who became friends of ours. Thurmond was in the Department of Justice. We also met Bob La Follette.

During this same period, I also met John L. Lewis. Under the first National Recovery Administration, business had the power to form organizations that regulated themselves. Labor, under section 7(a) of the National Labor Relations Act, also had the right to organize. The NRA was later declared to be unconstitutional, but then Congress passed the Wagner Act, which gave labor the right to organize. Mr. Lewis had fallen out with the American Federation of Labor and was forming the Congress of Industrial Organizations. He used section 7(a) of the NLRA to organize the CIO. There were tremendous labor struggles going on, and John L. Lewis loomed over Washington like some great big giant. He had tremendous character. I met him on a purely social level, as I did most of the leaders in Washington. One of my neighbors on Seminary Hill was named Brookings. Her husband was with the Brookings Institution, which his father had founded. Mrs. Brookings went to the Wellesley Club and was always begging me to go. I did go occasionally, but it bored me. The women who attended were as remote from what was going on as the man in the moon. But through Mrs. Brookings I went to a tea one afternoon and met Mrs. John L. Lewis, a charming woman. Mrs. Lewis had been a schoolteacher and she spoke beautiful English and dressed well. She wasn't a fashionable woman, but she was very ladylike. She was very pleasant to me and asked me to come and see her. She said, "You know, I have a daughter, Kathryn, whom I want you to meet."

I was longing to meet Mr. Lewis because he was so prominent in the news. So Cliff and I called on the Lewises one Sunday afternoon. They lived in a marvelous old house on the corner of Lee Street with a beautiful garden in the back. It was one of the Lee houses, a house built by one of the famous Lee families of Virginia, and it had high ceilings and was beautifully furnished. The Lewises lived in great style and in very good taste.

Mr. Lewis had come from a mining family in Wales and had been a miner himself. Mrs. Lewis taught Mr. Lewis to read and write. He was a massive and brilliant man with big eyebrows and a courteous manner. He talked with such an accent and with such resonance that he sounded like a Shakespearean actor. Mrs. Lewis wanted to associate with ladies and gentlemen. She loved northern Virginia. She loved the gentility of Alexandria and the old houses and gardens. I think she loved the black servants, too, the butler, the maid, the cook.

The Lewises' daughter, Kathryn, was a very bright, witty girl in her late twenties. Unfortunately she had some sort of glandular trouble and weighed about three hundred pounds. She was her father's assistant. Cliff and I got on well with the Lewises, and the friendship slowly grew.

In the South, the Wagner Act and the NRA were fiercely fought. John L. Lewis was one of the people who tried to organize the South. He sent down lots of young radicals, some of whom were Communists, although Communists were barred from his Mine Workers union. Quite a lot of young people became Communists at that time, because the capitalist system appeared to have fallen on its face. The Communist party at that time was much more open and had organized many of the unemployed. The young Communists were not welcome in the South and were often beaten up and held in jail incommunicado. A number of them were even killed. I still had no idea what communism was; I just thought Communists were people who were for labor and the unions.

About that time, I met a girl named Ida Engeman who was from Mississippi and had gone to Wellesley. Her name had been Ida Sledge. Ida was Tallulah Bankhead's half-aunt. At that time Will Bankhead was Speaker of the House. Will was from Jasper, Alabama, and had married Miss Ada Sledge from Mississippi, a very beautiful and aristocratic lady. She bore him two daughters, Eugenia and Tallulah, and died when Tallulah was born. Ada's father had another daughter from a second marriage, and she, Ida, was the one I knew.

Ida was extremely upset about the plight of labor in the South and was much more radical than I. She worked for the International Ladies' Garment Workers Union, the ILGWU, which was trying to organize in Mississippi. Twice she was run out of Mississippi by a mob, although she was kin to the aristocracy of Mississippi. Her mother and my aunt were friends, and they got us in touch with each other because Ida was also living on

Seminary Hill. She was married to George Engeman, and her children were more or less my children's ages so we got to be friends and remained so until her death a few years ago. Ida told me what was happening in Mississippi, that the people were being put in jail and killed in the fight to organize labor.

Then Bob La Follette started the Senate subcommittee hearings on civil liberties, which is one of the most significant set of hearings that has ever been held. This is where I got my education. La Follette held hearings in Washington for months on end about every part of the country—California, Ohio, Alabama, Mississippi, and Harlan County, Kentucky—and I began going to them regularly in the summer of 1938.

That spring, our son had died. He had appendicitis and the doctors didn't diagnose it correctly. We took him to the hospital, but his appendix burst. Penicillin was unknown in those days, and he died. He was only three. I was terribly depressed, and the La Follette hearings diverted me. Then I got interested in them and I learned a great deal. I would go in every morning with Cliff and come back with him. It was an exciting summer, and it did take my mind off my little boy's death, at least during the day.

The La Follette committee hearings lasted from 1936 through 1939, but the most dramatic ones were those on Harlan County, Kentucky, in 1937. Harlan County was known by then as Bloody Harlan because of the violence of antiunion activity there. Great big tall people out of the woods of Harlan County would come into the committee chambers and then in would come a deputy sheriff with a gun on his side. They were the scariest looking people I ever saw. And the thing that was so horrible about the trouble in Harlan County was that the man who had shot down the fellow they were complaining about—they were all kin! First cousins, second cousins, brothers, in-laws. Harlan County was divided between the operators and the United Mine Workers, but every family was split. You could just feel murder and death in that hearing room. You didn't know if one of those tall men would haul out a gun and shoot somebody. It was dramatic because the mine owners and the labor organizers would face each other in confrontation. Of course, the mine owners would say that they had nothing to do with the shootings and killings. They were just for law and order; they didn't do a thing. All the guns and dynamite and all, they had nothing to do with it. Oh, such a bunch of pious lies you've never heard!

Then I heard about the Little Steel strike in Ohio. The people who owned the steel mills had started cities like Canton, Ohio, and they were nice-looking gentlemen with white hair. They owned the steel mills and they owned the town. They would say, "But we started the town." And La Follette would say, "But you bought all these guns and machine guns and killed all these people at the strike." "But it is our steel mill. What a preposterous idea—these people even thinking of organizing the workers! We treat our workers nicely. We've always treated our people nicely." It was exactly like slavery times, except they paid the workers. The workers lived in company houses and had no union at all.

I remember one preacher had taken the side of the strikers and had been promptly fired. At the hearings, a benevolent old gentleman was asked, "Why did you fire Reverend So-and-so? Was it because he encouraged the strikers?" He said, "That was my church. My father built that church. My grandfather built the town." It was his town, his church, his steel mill. The hearings on that strike were as dramatic as you can imagine.

The automobile workers' strike was also violent. Our friend Walter Reuther, who later became president of the United Automobile Workers, was a big organizer at that time. At the hearings, an automobile worker would get on the stand and say he had tried to organize the automobile workers. He would tell about what he had done and how the organizers had been beaten up and forced out. He would be asked if he knew of any informers in the union and he'd say, "No, not to my knowledge." So a man who looked like an automobile worker would be brought out, and the first man would be asked, "Do you know this man?" "Do I know him? He's my best friend. We have a cottage up on the lake together. My children and his have played together since they moved into the neighborhood." Of course this fellow had been an informer the whole time. Well, at that point, you never knew what was going to break out. Some of the union organizers had to be physically restrained from rushing up and socking the men who had betrayed them.

When the committee got to old Tom Girdler and Republic Steel and what he had done to the people in Birmingham, Girdler himself took the stand. It was a great day.

By this time, I had become friends with all the people on the committee, and we often lunched together. I had met Bob La Follette at Sister and Hugo's. John Abt was the head counselor, and Luke Wilson, Charlie Flato, Harold Weinstein, and a big fellow from Kentucky named Ed Prichard were on the staff. Ed had been loaned from the White House, where he was one of Felix Frankfurter's law clerks, a "hot dog boy." He always wore beautiful linen suits and was just the picture of the old Kentucky colonel. We all liked him very much. Later he was put in jail for stealing votes, and the people who knew him never could believe it.

Finally, the La Follette committee hearings got to the Tennessee Coal, Iron and Railroad Company, and was that a fight! Tennessee Coal, Iron and Railroad (TCI) had become a division of U.S. Steel in 1907, and it practically ran Birmingham. Everyone ate when it was prosperous and didn't when it wasn't. Like other steel companies at the time, the company had a private police force. Eugene "Bull" Connor had been head of the U.S. Steel private police force at TCI, and so the company helped Connor get elected police commissioner of Birmingham, and Walter "Crack" Hanna took Connor's place as head of the U.S. Steel police in Birmingham. Hanna later became head of the Alabama National Guard. Bull Connor, of course, became famous—or infamous—in the 1960s when he oversaw the use of fire hoses and dogs to break up the civil rights demonstrations in Birmingham.

Witnesses at the TCI hearings before La Follette's committee told all about the many fine Birmingham gentlemen who had formed a committee to keep out labor organizers. They also told about what happened to the labor organizers in Birmingham. One young organizer was held incommunicado for six months by the police. He couldn't contact anybody. Nobody knew whether he was dead or alive. When he got out of jail, he had to go to Colorado because he had tuberculosis. I don't remember his name; the young Communists in those days often changed their names. I remember running into him in Denver years later and saying something to him, and he refused to recognize me. He wouldn't admit he had ever been in Birmingham. Many of these labor organizers had a rough time, and the ones who got out and went their way didn't want to be reminded of those times.

Some of the fine gentlemen who had formed the Birmingham committee were my father's friends and my friends' fathers. They had been so sweet to me all my life and were the leading men of Birmingham, the men I had been brought up to think highly of. I just couldn't believe it. I believed it about the men in Harlan County and all the other places, but I didn't know them, you see. I knew these men. I just didn't believe these men could do the things they were accused of—holding people incommunicado or having them beaten up or disappear. I had seen poverty in Alabama but never violence. I was terribly shocked by all this, so I did something that I now see just shows how foolish and stupid I was: I sent telegrams to my friends' fathers, these high-class gentlemen, saying "I have heard today in the La Follette committee you accused of such and such, and I am sure it is not the truth. Please refute this unwarranted lie." Well, I got some of the most embarrassed letters back that you have ever seen. "My dear Virginia," they would say, "I do not think you understand what has gone on here in Birmingham. I can assure you that our only objective has been to maintain law and order and we had nothing in the wide world to do with all this shooting and killing and holding incommunicado. That was absolutely not our intention." They just excused themselves completely.

It was during the Birmingham hearings that I first heard the name of Joe Gelders. He had been picked up one night while walking home. The fellows who picked him up took him over the mountain with a whole bunch of other men. They beat him and stamped on him and then took all his clothes off and left him for dead. He managed to crawl to the roadside and somebody picked him up and took him to Clanton. He was terribly hurt.

When he died, in his fifties, an autopsy was performed and they found that his chest was just a mass of cartilage and bone that had been crushed by their stamping on him. But he had survived, and at the La Follette committee hearings he became the central figure. Testimony there pointed to Walter J. Hanna, "Crack" Hanna of TCI, as the one responsible for Gelders's beating, in spite of the fact that two grand juries in Birmingham had failed to indict Hanna.

I was terribly interested in this fellow from Alabama who had been beaten and left for dead. He was the hero of the hearings. He didn't testify because he was still in the hospital, as I recall, but I heard all the testimony about him. I came home and asked Cliff if he had heard of him. Cliff said, "Why, yes. He was at the university with me." Cliff knew him well. Then I remembered that I knew his brother, and it all came back to me who Joe Gelders was.

Birmingham had always had a very rich Jewish community, owners of big department stores and a lot of other businesses. There were poor Jews, too, I suppose, but I didn't know them. The Gelders lived in a big house on Red Mountain, which was the fashionable Southside area. Louis Gelders, Joe's brother, and I went through school together for years and we were friends, although not close friends.

Finally I remembered Emma Gelders, Joe Gelders's older sister. Emma was quite well known in Birmingham. She had graduated from Smith College, which was very unusual in those days. That was before my era. She and several other girls in Birmingham—Amelia Worthington and Mary Park London and Martha Toulmin—were called the bluestockings because they had gone to college and they read books and gave papers. I can hear my father saying, "Well, I saw Mary Park London downtown today. She'll never get a husband. Never. Mary Park London is just entirely too educated for a woman." So I thought these women were rather set apart because they would never get married. Everybody said so. But they all did, and they were suffragists.

I decided to look up Joe Gelders and see what kind of a fellow he was, so I went to see him at his office in Birmingham the next time I was there. Joe was tall and thin, a good-looking fellow. He looked like a Jewish prophet, with beautiful eyes and lovely manners. I also met his darling wife Esther, who was Esther Frank from Montgomery. She worked with Joe and she was very lively and pretty and a typical Southern belle type who made you feel at home. Joe had never heard of me before. He suggested that we go out in the park, so we went down in the elevator and sat in the public park.

"You know my office is wired," he said.

"What for?"

"Well, I just know that it is. They've got taps on my line everywhere, and everybody who comes in, they know who it is." That was the first time I had ever heard of the FBI's wiretapping people.

Joe Gelders's story was fascinating to me. He was teaching physics at the University of Alabama when the depression came. His wife taught English. They were a very popular young couple at the University of Alabama, and both of them were totally unpolitical.

When the depression came, the farmers were desperate. Prices had fallen to almost nothing. To raise prices, the government began a policy of destroying baby pigs and plowing up cotton and corn. Meanwhile, people were starving and had nothing to wear. Young people today understand little about the rickets and pellagra and the hookworm, because they've never seen them. A child who's shaking all over with rickets because he doesn't get any calcium is a pretty horrible sight. Aubrey Williams used to tell me about a lot of his relatives who were poor as Job's turkey. I'd say, "What do they do?" He'd say, "Well, they just sit and spit all day." That's from hookworm. Everybody said the Southerners were lazy, that they didn't like to get out and work. Well, they had hookworm and they had parasitic diseases and nutritional diseases. Young people today have never seen that. They've never seen children in the mill villages who worked in the cotton mills. I was in my twenties before I woke up to it, and it had been right around me all the time.

Joe Gelders saw the starving people all around him in Tuscaloosa and got terribly upset. Killing pigs when people were hungry and plowing up cotton when they didn't have anything to wear seemed wholly irrational. Now, Joe didn't know a thing about economics, so he went to the library and began to read. He started out with Adam Smith, and he went right on through, reading all the books he could find on economics. He read Charles and Mary Beard and the socialists, the English Fabians, the Webbs. I had read them at Wellesley, but they were hard reading. They stirred me up a little bit there, but not much. When he got to Engels and Marx, he said, "This is it! This is the answer to all the poverty and all of this killing the pigs and burning up the corn and cotton."

Joe was still teaching at the university at the time and had never met a Marxist in his life, or a socialist either. He had never even heard of the Communist party. He had simply read about socialism and the ideas of Marx and Engels and had decided that he had found the answer to poverty. So Joe began to have meetings at his house, and he'd tell everybody that the cause of the depression was capitalism. The next year the university officials told him they didn't want him to come back. Well, he was very much surprised.

Joe then went to New York to visit his sister Emma, who had married Roy Sterne from Anniston and who lived on Long Island. The Sternes had two girls, Barbara and Ann, and were very conservative intellectuals. They

Joseph S. Gelders, photographed in California about 1947. (Courtesy of Esther G. Zane)

kept up with everything but were not radical in the least. Joe began to take courses and later contacted the Communist party and got in with the radical groups in New York. I don't know whom he dealt with. He always said he never joined the Communist party, never was a card-carrying member. Maybe the party thought it was better for him not to be. Anyway, he was told that the best thing he could do was to go back South to help the labor organizers who were being thrown in jail.

Joe stayed in New York that summer, and then he returned to Birmingham as the Southern representative of the National Committee for the Defense of Political Prisoners. His wife worked with him as his secretary. They were involved in a number of law suits, and as Ted Rosengarten makes clear in *All God's Dangers,* Joe tried to help the sharecroppers' union in Tallassee, Alabama, get organized.

Joe and Esther Gelders were a lovely couple, just a few years older than I. He was handsome, charming, and well mannered. I talked to them about how terrible I felt when I went back to Birmingham and found that everyone was so against the New Deal and hated Roosevelt. The rumor had spread that the blacks had formed Eleanor Clubs and were being encouraged to push white people off the sidewalks. People claimed that blacks would make an engagement to come and wash or cook and wouldn't come. They were supposedly doing everything to irritate the white folks. I heard it a thousand times. "I'm sure my cook has joined the Eleanor Club." Or, "I'm sure the washwoman has joined the Eleanor Club. Every one of them has. You can't walk downtown anymore because they will come up and just push you in the gutter." This really distressed me. The race issue was not my primary interest at that time, but I hated for Mrs. Roosevelt to be so maligned.

In the meantime, the Women's Division of the National Democratic Committee was working quietly on the 50–50 plan. We were getting out literature against the poll tax and trying to get somebody to introduce a bill to abolish it. The poll tax became a great political issue.

One day when I went down to do volunteer work at the Democratic National Committee, everybody looked as though there had been a death in the family. The chairman of the Democratic National Committee, Jim Farley, had brought discouraging news. Farley was a big genial Irishman from New York who later became head of the Coca-Cola Company. His wife never came to Washington. They had come from humble origins, and she was very sensitive about it. Actually, the break between Farley and Roosevelt came because Mrs. Farley thought Mrs. Roosevelt snubbed her. I'm sure it never crossed Mrs. Roosevelt's mind to snub Mrs. Farley. Mrs. Roosevelt was just such a busy woman, into everything. She was so different from most first ladies.

Mr. Farley had come down to see Dorothy McAllister, who was head of the Women's Division of the National Democratic Committee. Then he had gone to the president of the United States and said, "You've got to shut up these damn women in the Democratic Committee because it's making trouble on the Hill with the Southern senators and congressmen." They weren't going to pay any attention to the 50-50 plan, particularly when relatively few women voted. Farley was terribly upset about the poll tax fight because it was beginning to catch on.

We had a meeting right away. We discussed setting up an independent committee to work for the abolition of the poll tax. Nothing was done for a while, however. The poll tax fight was put in a state of abeyance. The Democratic Women had been forbidden to work on it.

7

The Southern Conference
for Human Welfare

ABOUT 1936 CLIFF joined the Southern Policy Committee, a group of young Southerners in the New Deal who met for dinner together once or twice a month to discuss the South. It was all white and all high-echelon people in the Senate and the House and New Deal agencies: Cliff, Lister Hill, Senator John Sparkman, Clark Foreman, Tex Goldschmidt, Abe Fortas, and some others.

At one of these meetings of the Southern Policy Committee, Clark Foreman and a very bright fellow named Jerome Frank, who had been general counsel of the Agricultural Adjustment Administration, had the idea that a pamphlet should be written on the South. In 1938 they sold the idea to the president, and he asked Lowell Mellett of the National Emergency Council to direct the project.

The result was the *Report on Economic Conditions of the South,* referred to as *The South: Economic Problem Number One,* written mostly in my living room. Arthur Raper, a noted sociologist from North Carolina; Jack Fisher, who later became editor of the *Atlantic;* Tex Goldschmidt; and Cliff all worked on the pamphlet. I wasn't included in the group—no women were—but I was always bringing in coffee and food and hearing the fights among them. Sometimes they worked at Lowell Mellett's house, right down the road from us. The report had articles on agriculture and industry. Cliff wrote an article for it on credit and he wrote the letter that the president signed that introduced the pamphlet. The pamphlet was written as a manifesto of what had to be done in the South and is really very good. Today it's a collector's item.

When the pamphlet was finished, they got a lot of very distinguished people from the South to certify it. It was all about the South—the lack of credit and the poverty. You didn't have to be very bright or ideological to know that something was wrong when people were dying of starvation not because there was too little, but because there was too much. You felt you were living in a mad world. Cliff wrote to the president about this time saying the South was the paradox of the nation, rich in natural resources and yet the poorest region of all.

Hugo was on the Supreme Court by the time the pamphlet came out. He had supported Roosevelt in the Court-packing fight and had fought for the thirty-hour work week, too, which finally became the Wages and Hours Act, a forty-hour work week bill. Roosevelt had appreciated his support, particularly on the Court-packing bill, and had appointed him to the first vacancy after the effort to enlarge the Court failed.

Many of the other Southerners fought the Wages and Hours Act. In the summer of 1937, just before Hugo was appointed to the Court, I went with Sister to Point Clear, across the bay from Mobile. Hugo was preparing to run for reelection in the Senate and was going to come down and join us and begin his campaign in Alabama. He was delayed by the Senate debates over the wages and hours legislation and he never did get there. The people around us at Point Clear were big turpentine and lumber people. They owned the turpentine and lumber companies, and they were paying their labor ten cents an hour. Good God, the way they treated us, you would have thought we had smallpox. The children would come in from the beach saying that these people had said Uncle Hugo was a crook and a thief and a liar.

The year before, Roosevelt had been reelected by an enormous vote. After that great victory, he decided to purge the conservative Southerners who were blocking his programs in Congress. Many of the Southerners, particularly Walter George from Georgia, were anti–New Deal, and mainly they opposed wage controls. Aubrey Williams and Harry Hopkins were paying the WPA people, white and black, the same wages, and this was "ruining the nigras." Cotton Ed Smith of South Carolina said paying the "nigras" more than a dollar a day was going to ruin the South. They felt all the South really had to offer the North was cheap labor. We Southerners had such a low opinion of ourselves in those days. A lot of Southerners still do.

Roosevelt had lost the fight to enlarge the Supreme Court, and his other projects were threatened, too, so he launched his famous purge. He tried to defeat some of the people who'd been blocking all his programs, but he took on too strong an opponent when he attacked Senator George of Georgia.

Roosevelt spoke at Barnesville, Georgia, and came out publicly against Senator George with the senator sitting right up on the platform with him. Roosevelt told the audience that fascism and feudalism were very much the same and that fascism was rising in Europe and the South was feudalistic.

Feudalism and fascism both meant society was controlled by an oligarchy and the people had no rights or freedoms or powers. Then Roosevelt quoted from the National Emergency Council report. The South was the nation's number one economic problem. It was a powerful speech.

Well, not only was Mr. George reelected, but he won by one of the biggest majorities in Georgia history. Everybody in Georgia was perfectly furious at the president's coming down and telling them whom to vote for. All the Southerners opposed by Roosevelt won, overwhelmingly. The purge was a total failure as far as the South was concerned. This was a great crisis, because Roosevelt had put his prestige on the line to change the South, to try to get rid of this bloc that was defeating him on many of his New Deal measures.

Now, I was aware of Roosevelt's various successes and failures, the programs he was trying to put in place and the goals he was aiming for, but I was not directly involved. Cliff and Hugo were involved in the New Deal programs intensely, but my acquaintance with the important people and issues of those days was strictly on a voluntary and social basis.

As I began to meet people, though, who were working seriously with the problems of labor and unionization, I began to get more serious about some of the issues. Through the John L. Lewises I met Mrs. Bryant. The Bryants had a big bank in Alexandria and were leading citizens of the town. Mr. Bryant was on the board of trustees of the Episcopal Theological Seminary. Mrs. Bryant had been a Mason, a Virginia Mason, and they lived in the old Mason house down the street from where we lived. She was the granddaughter of James M. Mason, who went to England with John Slidell as an emissary of the Confederacy. She was also the descendent of George Mason, the author of the Virginia Bill of Rights.

One day Mrs. Bryant invited me to a luncheon, where I met Mrs. Bryant's sister, Lucy Randolph Mason. Miss Lucy was a pretty, dainty, white-haired Virginia lady who wore glasses. She was extremely aristocratic and had a lovely soft Virginia voice. Miss Mason told me that she was a YWCA worker but she was very anxious to get into the New Deal or into some other line of work because she realized that the YWCA, as good as it was, wasn't attacking the problem of poverty.

Miss Lucy's brother-in-law, Mr. Bryant, went to see John L. Lewis and told him that Miss Lucy wanted to get into the labor movement. Mr. Lewis was a very bright man in many ways, and he immediately saw that Miss Lucy could be a great advantage in the South. As his public relations person Miss Lucy would be very disarming. All the fierce police chiefs and sheriffs and newspaper editors would be looking for some big gorilla to come in, and Miss Lucy would appear. She was the kind of perfect Southern lady for whom men would instinctively rise to offer a seat. So Mr. Lewis hired Lucy

Randolph Mason as his public relations representative in the South and gave her an office in Atlanta.

Miss Lucy was delighted to be the CIO representative in Atlanta, because she was so discouraged with her YWCA work. How could you work with a lot of girls in a tobacco factory if they just weren't being paid enough? How could you save them from a life of sin or bring them to Jesus or whatever? They were making fifteen dollars a week or less. That just wasn't enough. Miss Lucy had a strongly developed social consciousness. She had met Mrs. Roosevelt through these various YWCA, laboring-girl projects, and they had become friends.

About the middle of the summer of 1938, I got a call from Joe Gelders, whom I had met just once before. He said he and Miss Lucy Randolph Mason were in Alexandria and wanted to come out and see me. Joe and Miss Lucy said they had been to see the Roosevelts up at Hyde Park and had told them the terrible things that were happening in Mississippi because of resistance to the labor movement—burnings and murders and beatings and defiance of the law. Jimmy Collins, an organizer for the textile workers, had been beaten up and arrested in Tupelo. Ida Sledge got into trouble in Tupelo, too. She had been sent to Mississippi by the ILGWU. The union thought she wouldn't have much trouble because she couldn't be called an outside agitator. She was a native of the state and kin to the Bankheads of Alabama. But Ida was run out of Tupelo twice, once in her nightgown. Now, John Rankin represented Tupelo in the Congress. Although Rankin had supported many New Deal measures, he was anti-Semitic and anti-black and very much against unions. Everybody who joined the CIO was a Communist, according to John Rankin. Of course, I still thought that if you belonged to a labor union then you probably *were* a Communist. That was how little I understood about it at the time.

Miss Lucy and Joe Gelders had gotten together in Mississippi during the trouble in Tupelo involving Ida Sledge and Jimmy Collins. They decided to go to Hyde Park to talk with the Roosevelts. They wanted to create an organization to bring together the New Deal elements in the South, the labor unions, the people who were benefiting by the New Deal, like the WPA people. After talking with Joe and Miss Lucy, President and Mrs. Roosevelt agreed to call an organizational meeting.

When Joe and Miss Lucy stopped in Alexandria, they asked me if Hugo Black would speak at the meeting. I told them, as I always told everybody, that the only way to approach Hugo Black was directly. Hugo hated people to approach him through the family. So Joe went to see him, and Hugo agreed to speak at the meeting.

In the meantime, I told Joe and Miss Lucy about the group of people who had written the pamphlet *The South: Economic Problem Number One*. I suggested they get in touch with Clark Foreman, and Frank Graham, president of the University of North Carolina, Arthur Raper, and all the North Carolina people. In the end, the New Dealers, the Southern Policy Committee, the labor people, and the black people all got together in Birmingham in November 1938, for the first meeting of the Southern Conference for Human Welfare.

A variety of groups came together at the conference in Birmingham. I attended as a delegate from the Women's Division of the Democratic National Committee. Miss Lucy and Joe Gelders represented labor. Cliff and Clark Foreman and Tex Goldschmidt represented a group of young Southerners in the New Deal. Jane and Dolly Speed, who now ran a Communist bookstore in Birmingham, and Rob Hall, the Communist secretary for Alabama, were there. Bill Mitch and others represented the mine workers and the steel workers. I understand that Mrs. Roosevelt was the one who insisted that blacks be included, and Mary McLeod Bethune was her emissary. Frank Graham and many other University of North Carolina people were there. Myles Horton was there with the people from the Highlander Folk School, a settlement house in rural Tennessee that had become involved in the union movement.

The conference leaders had decided to give Hugo the Thomas Jefferson Award, so Hugo and Sister came too. They had traveled on the train with William Dodd, who had been a well-known professor of history at the University of Chicago and who was then ambassador to Germany. Dodd was to introduce Hugo and present him the Jefferson Award. When Hugo and Sister arrived at the house, they were concerned that Ambassador Dodd didn't seem well. When the time came at the conference for him to introduce Hugo, he couldn't speak and he had to be led off the stage. Apparently he had had a slight stroke. The Birmingham newspaper columnist John Temple Graves took over and introduced Hugo. Hugo gave a perfectly marvelous speech, quoting Jefferson all the way through.

The conference opened on a Sunday night in the city auditorium in downtown Birmingham. Oh, it was a love feast. There must have been 1,500 or more people there from all over the South, black and white, labor union people and New Dealers. Southern meetings always include a lot of preaching and praying and hymn singing, and this meeting was no exception. The whole meeting was just full of love and hope. It was thrilling. Frank Graham was elected temporary chairman and he made a beautiful speech. He set the tone for the meeting, and we all went away from there that night just full of love and gratitude. The whole South was coming together to make a new day.

We were to meet the next morning to elect a permanent chairman and then break up into workshops, but when we got there we found the auditorium surrounded by black marias. Every police van in the city and county was there. Policemen were everywhere, inside and out. And there was Bull

Connor saying anybody who broke the segregation law of Alabama would be arrested and taken to jail. No ifs, ands, or buts about it.

The city auditorium had a central aisle, and Connor said the blacks had to sit on one side and the whites on the other. Then a great debate began about whether blacks and whites could sit and stand on the stage together.

That same day Mrs. Roosevelt arrived. She was ushered in with great applause. Everybody clapped and clapped and clapped and clapped. She got a little folding chair and put it right in the middle of the aisle. She said she refused to be segregated. She carried the little folding chair with her wherever she went. The workshops were held in various churches and other buildings, and of course they had to be segregated too. Policemen followed us everywhere to make sure the segregation laws were observed, but they didn't dare arrest Mrs. Roosevelt.

The South's etiquette of race was challenged in another episode during the conference. Louise Charlton, who had been one of the organizers, was presiding until Dr. Graham was officially elected president. At one point she called on Mary McLeod Bethune. She said, "Mary, do you wish to come to the platform?" Mrs. Bethune rose. She looked like an African queen, a large woman and homely but with an air of grandeur. She always carried a stick engraved with her name on it that President Roosevelt had given her. She was very proud of that stick. Mrs. Bethune got up with that stick and she said, "My name is Mrs. Bethune." So Louise had to say, "Mrs. Bethune, will you come to the platform?" That sounds like a small thing now, but that was a big dividing line. A Negro woman in Birmingham, Alabama, was called Mrs. at a public meeting.

By that time, I had come around to thinking that segregation was terrible. Just by osmosis mainly. I had met Mrs. Bethune and I had met other Negro people at the Foremans' house. Before that, I had always known them as servants. The mailman was probably the best educated Negro I had met before I went to Washington, except for the few black students at Wellesley. I had never met an adult Negro who could read or write well except the postman. I remember going back to Birmingham and shaking hands with him and saying I was so glad to see him, and I called him Mr. I got hell on that. Cliff's brother heard me and said, "Now look, Virginia, if you think you are going to get by with calling the postman Mr. you are wrong. Birmingham won't stand for that." Cliff's brother is a lovely man, but he was just as rigid as he could be.

I get so upset over the black separatists, who want to put themselves back in a cage, because it was a terrible thing to be white and have to think everybody who wasn't white was inferior, to look down on them and think they smelled bad and were common and vulgar. It's just terrible. It was so rude, too. You know, I was brought up to be a Southern lady, and it dawned on me how rude it was to think a black was too dirty and smelled too bad to sit by me. I had been raised by them and sat in their laps, slept with them and kissed them all my life. This was what was so crazy about the South.

We grew up with such contradictory feelings. "I loved dear old Suzy. She raised me from a baby and she treated me like a mama. She is the sweetest thing in the world." But, "Of course, I wouldn't sit by her son on the bus." Think of the men who repudiated their own children. I mean, why didn't it ever occur to us that most of the light Negroes had white fathers or white grandfathers? What did it do to a man to repudiate his own child? And to say that that child was so inferior his father couldn't sit on a bus beside him? Can you imagine? Wouldn't you think that would do something funny to their brains? To say, "That's my son, but he can't . . ."

Clark Foreman told me two of the funniest, most awful tales, and he said they were true. He said there was a country white girl who got pregnant by a black boy—voluntarily. She had the baby and sent him to a black orphanage, because her family had found out about it. But she wanted to see him after he had been there some time, so she went to the black orphanage where the child was. I guess the child was four or five. He was eating at the table with the other children. The people who ran the orphanage said to her, "Don't you want to sit by your child?" And she said, "Well, I couldn't do it. Eat with niggers?" This was her own child! She couldn't sit by her own child! She could have nursed him at her breast, but she couldn't eat with him.

Clark told me an even more peculiar story. He had an uncle who lived on the Howell plantation in Georgia and had several half-black children. Clark's aunt brought them up with her own children. The children knew they were kin. There wasn't any doubt about that. Everybody knew it. Eventually the black children went to Philadelphia. One of the girls in particular did very well, and her son became a doctor. When she went back to Atlanta one time, she called one of her white half-sisters and said she wanted to see them all. She had been gone so long and she remembered so much about them. Clark said they had a family meeting to decide about seeing this woman, this half-sister. They couldn't meet with her in the parlor. That would be absolutely breaking every taboo in the South, since she was half black. They couldn't take her into the kitchen, because she had risen in the world and her son was a doctor. So they decided the lady who would receive her would go to bed and pretend she was sick. Then they could bring the black guest up into the bedroom and all the other aunts could come visit, and they could all sit down! He said they had a whole family gathering to decide this. That's the way things were. It's hard to believe now. By the time of the first Southern Conference for Human Welfare meeting in Birmingham in 1938, my thinking about race had certainly changed.

On the first full day of the conference there were meetings all day. Cliff made a speech on credit, and I went to the meeting on the poll tax. That

night, Frank McCallister came up to me. He was a socialist with the Southern Workers Defense League. He was like Uriah Heep, smiling all the time,
and he wanted to know if he could take me home. Cliff wasn't there at the
time, so I needed a ride. I said that was very nice, and so he and another
fellow, who was also a socialist, took me home. Right away, they wanted
to know if I knew Joe Gelders was a Communist. I said I guessed he was. I
hadn't thought about it very much. They wanted to know if I knew Rob
Hall was a Communist and Jane and Dolly and all sorts of other people
were Communists. I said, "Mr. McCallister, these people are all working for
the same thing we are working for. They are trying to fight against the poll
tax and get labor organized. They are doing what the New Deal wants to
do." "Well, Mrs. Durr, you are young and naive. . . ." H. L. Mitchell later
told me that at that time the socialists thought I was a Junior League dilet-
tante. Of course, I thought I was the greatest thing in the world, facing up
to the lions of Birmingham by coming down to the meeting. I can assure
you that none of my friends came, the ones I was raised with. McCallister
continued to throw suspicion on this one and that one. I finally got angry
at him and I said, "I think you are just trying to break the whole thing up."
And he was.

Here we were in Birmingham, Alabama, sitting down together to try
to protect the rights of people to organize so they would make more than
two dollars a day, trying to get people the right to vote so they could have
some influence on their own lives. We were trying to do things that were
absolutely fundamental, right on the lowest level of political and economic
democracy. And these socialists and Trotskyites did nothing in the world
but red-bait. It made me mad. And if you didn't go along with them, then
they'd red-bait you. McCallister red-baited me to a fare-thee-well from then
on out. I still get mad when I think about it. And I didn't even know what
a Trotskyite was. I used to think the Trotskyites were some form of fleas.
They always made me itch when they were around.

Then things began to get tough. Mabel Jones West, a hired hand for
the Ku Klux Klan, launched a terrible attack on the Southern Conference
for Human Welfare from the extreme right wing. We were all a bunch of
reds. She said she "didn't know what the niggers and the white women were
up to." They were eating together and "what did they do at night and where
were they staying?" The same old dirt—just get a black man and a white
woman in a big auditorium, and by that night, they'll be in bed. Well, that
made me mad, too. It was disgusting, and I was feeling pretty badgered.

Some childhood friends of mine—sweet, dear people—took me out to
lunch. One had been in my wedding, and both were very devoted friends.
One of them said, "Now, Jinksie, I think I should tell you frankly that I
think it's awful for you to come down here and encourage this rabble to
take over. You are going to go back to Washington and we are left to deal

with it. I just have to tell you I think it is the most horrible thing you have ever done. I don't think you could possibly know what you are doing. You are going off and leave us with this rabble on our hands that will just try to take over everything." She was serious about it, too. And her husband was serious about it. I was meeting with quite a lot of opposition.

Then Aubrey Williams came to make a speech. Aubrey was a very jolly, funny fellow, always cracking jokes. He was presiding over a workshop on relief and somebody said to him, making a joke, "Oh, come the revolution, we'll do that." It was a joke, just a remark. And Aubrey said, "Hooray for the revolution," or some joking remark. Well, it came out over the radio that Aubrey Williams, one of the heads of WPA, had said we welcomed the revolution.

The first thing we knew, Mr. Roosevelt was on the telephone to Aubrey saying, "What are you and my wife doing down there? What do you mean by coming out and saying you are for the revolution?" Mr. Roosevelt was in no way a socialist, you understand. He didn't believe in a revolution. He believed in restoring capitalism, which he did. Aubrey tried to explain it was a joke, but Mr. Roosevelt was angry. Of course, all the newspapers immediately seized on Aubrey's remark. "Aubrey Williams, deputy director of WPA says, 'Welcome the revolution.' " You cannot believe the extent to which this went on. The opponents of the New Deal and of labor's efforts fought the labor unions on the Communist charge, they fought the New Deal on the Communist charge, they fought Mrs. Roosevelt on the Communist charge. They used it against everything.

The only active Communists I met at the Birmingham meeting were Jane and Dolly Speed and Rob Hall. Not only were Jane and Dolly active; they might as well have carried a placard. Miss Jane was handing out Marxist literature to everybody. Dolly and Jane embarrassed a lot of people, especially the more conservative ones. We never saw some of the North Carolina people again. Jane and Dolly just scared them to death. Rob Hall was playing a very quiet part, but he was there. He later became a Rockefeller Republican.

Now I haven't the slightest idea whether Joe Gelders was a member of the Communist party. If Joe was working with the party, he wasn't an open member, but I was pretty naive about these things. All the intricate distinctions about who was a Trotskyite and who was a Communist and who was a socialist and who belonged to this block went over my head like the wind because I didn't know what they were talking about and it didn't interest me in the least. What I was trying to do was get rid of the poll tax. I thought that was the first step to getting the South freed of all the terrible burdens it had. I was very strong for the labor unions because I had seen the suffering out in Ensley and Pratt City.

All the different groups and isms used to bore me to death. I always felt it was exactly like the distinctions in religions—are you going to get to heaven by dipping or sprinkling or total immersion. I'd been brought up with that all my life, and it seemed to me exactly the same thing. Church people would talk about building a new society, a utopia where everybody would have peace and plenty and love each other. But, by God, if you weren't dipped, you'd never get there. I had been brought up in the Presbyterian church and had been through all of Daddy's troubles about Jonah and the whale and walking on the water. I must have irritated the Southern Conference ideologues very much, because I thought it was a joke. I really thought it was silly, and I still think a lot of it was just the silliest thing in the world.

Maybe I'm wrong about it, but I went through that all the years of my life when Daddy was a preacher. I think the teachings of religion have been very nearly ruined by theology. Every religion that I know has gotten bound up in theology. When I was at Wellesley, we had to take Bible, and we studied comparative religions. It seems to me that the essential point of every religion I've ever studied is the golden rule, to treat people as you want them to treat you. Well, very few people ever accomplish that, and I think the theology is silly: whether Buddha has four arms or two, whether you bathe in the river or whether you have foot-washing.

In Mentone, Alabama, I'd gone to the Holy Roller meetings, and I'd seen people let themselves be bitten by snakes and pick up hot lamp chimneys and drink poison green. We'd go to these Holy Roller meetings, just as a joke really, and these crazy country folk from way back in the mountains would let themselves be bitten by snakes. Scariest thing you ever saw. It scared me out of my wits. I'd get out of there as quick as I could when they started handling the snakes. The idea was that the snake couldn't bite you and the hot lamp chimney couldn't burn you and the poison green couldn't poison you. The spirit of God was with you and nothing could hurt you. And then they'd get the jerks. They'd dance before the Lord. They'd have these movements where they'd get up and dance. They would finally get so possessed by the spirit, they'd roll on the floor, just roll from side to side and scream and yell. The meetings were always held in the lay-by period after crops had been gathered, at the end of August, usually, before they started picking the cotton and corn.

The divisions in the Christian religion have obscured and badly hurt the meaning of Christianity. Every religion you look into is really founded on a worship of one god who is the father of all mankind, and the central idea is to treat each other as you'd like people to treat you. That's my idea of religion.

It had been difficult being brought up in the Presbyterian church, with my father a preacher and having him thrown out of the church because he didn't believe in Jonah and the whale and walking on the water. I just could never believe you got to heaven because you told your beads four times or because you had your feet washed or because you were sprinkled or dipped or totally immersed.

So much of the political agitation that goes on today seems to be very much like the great fights in religion. Instead of the fights being about whether you're going to get to spiritual heaven and be sitting on the right hand of God and playing the harp and forever living in bliss, they fight now about heaven on earth. People want to get their share while they're alive. But instead of working together and trying to figure things out so that people will have a fair share and won't all suffer, they keep getting bogged down in words. Now, I think a lot of people are working on real solutions, but there are so many who are working against them. And the people who are working for solutions are working for them in such different ways.

This is the way I felt in 1938 at the Southern Conference meeting in Birmingham; it was silly to argue ideology when there were so many hard jobs to be done. I was concentrating on the poll tax and on getting women to vote. As time went on, I felt more strongly about women's rights. I had a good husband, so I don't personally have passionate feelings about women's rights. But I had passionate feelings about the way Southern girls were treated and the position I was in as a young girl. It was supposed to be bad for you to be smart and to go to college, because men liked dumb women. My aunt, I remember, would say, "Don't discuss books with boys. That always scares them off."

A lot of talented people worked with the Southern Conference for Human Welfare, people who were not scared away by the ideological fights. Clark Foreman was one of them, and there was Howard Lee from Arkansas and Alton Lawrence from North Carolina. Howard was executive secretary of the conference from 1939 to 1941. He was a big country boy who had been inspired by Claude Williams from Arkansas and was very dedicated. He greatly admired Mrs. Roosevelt, and he had her picture by his bed when he later shot himself. At that time a lot of the young men who would have gone into the ministry went into the labor movement instead. Alton Lawrence, who was elected secretary in 1942, had prepared for the ministry but switched to the labor movement. He worked for the Mine, Mill and Smelter Workers, which was a left-wing union. He was a sweet fellow who married a girl off a picket line, a firebrand union girl.

The conference started out being a very broad group of people. Donald Comer, head of Comer Mills, and General John Persons of the First National Bank of Birmingham even came to the meetings. Comer was one of the great industrialists in Alabama, but he had been sort of New Dealish, and General Persons had gotten money for the bank through the New Deal. There was a good deal of support, especially for doing away with the unequal freight rates. But as the conference became controversial and was attacked as Communistic, these supporters all fell away. Alton Lawrence fell away, too. He stopped having anything to do with anyone who'd ever been in the union movement.

I was concerned with the poll tax. The whole group of 1,500 or more people, when they finally met, wanted to get rid of the poll tax. That was the first resolution. There were resolutions on credit and on agriculture and this, that, and the other, but the main concern was the right to vote—to get rid of the poll tax and to get rid of the registration laws. We formed a sub-committee of the Southern Conference for Human Welfare on the poll tax. It was named the Civil Rights Committee, but we worked on getting rid of the poll tax mostly. Maury Maverick, a congressman from Texas, was president of the subcommittee. He became a dear friend of mine and so did his wife. He had severely injured his back in the First World War and was kind of humped over. He was one of the bravest, finest men I have ever known—a real New Dealer. He was a descendant of Matthew Fontaine Maury, a great geographer, and he was very proud of that. We were all so Southern that we bragged about our ancestors. Anyway, Maury was elected president of the anti–poll tax committee and I was elected vice-president. Joe Gelders was secretary.

The last night of the conference, John Temple Graves introduced Hugo. Graves later became one of the most conservative anti–New Deal, anti-Democratic people in the world, but he got up that night and made a per-fectly beautiful introduction of Hugo.

That last night was like a revival meeting. It was like a love meeting. All of a sudden you felt that you were not by yourself. There were all these other people with you. After all, when the wife of the president of the United States and a Supreme Court justice and John L. Lewis are on your side, you have a lot of support. And the Negro people, like Mrs. Bethune, certainly gave me a feeling of support. She was a remarkable character. I was very much impressed with her, and we became friends after that. It was a mar-velous occasion.

Almost everybody who came to that first conference in Birmingham had the same feeling of finally getting together. It was the New Deal come South. Something that young people in the civil rights movement never had as strong as we had in the 1930s was a feeling of support. We knew Eleanor just had to pick up the telephone and call Franklin. We had the feeling of having the power of the government on our side. Bull Connor, in spite of all the police and the black marias, just made us nervous. We never were afraid of him, because we knew he was not going to arrest the wife of the president of the United States and he was not going to arrest a Supreme Court justice.

Hugo made a great speech that last night, quoting from Thomas Jef-ferson. He spoke through Thomas Jefferson as the great Southerner.

Hugo's speech was the end of the meeting, and the whites were all on one side and the blacks were all on the other. I can see that meeting now—one side completely black. It was packed to the roof. I can see it now: white on one side and black on the other and Mrs. Roosevelt and Hugo standing on the platform.

Soon after the Birmingham meeting of the Southern Conference for Human Welfare, Joe Gelders came to Washington to get someone to introduce a bill in Congress to abolish the poll tax. Joe was executive secretary of the poll tax committee and I was vice-president. Lee Geyer, a congressman from California, agreed to introduce the bill, and he agreed to let us use his office as a place to work.

Mr. Geyer was a lovely man and a great student of American history. He was a tremendous believer in free speech and the American Constitution. He thought to deny people the right to vote was a sin and a shame and an outrage. Unfortunately, he had the beginnings of cancer of the throat, so he had difficulty speaking. But he did introduce the bill in late 1939.

Joe then went back down South. I didn't even know how to operate a mimeograph machine, but we decided to get out a newsletter and to arrange the hearings on the bill to abolish the poll tax. The bill was sent to the Judiciary Committee. The head of the Judiciary Committee at that time was Congressman Hatton Sumners from Texas. He was an old gentleman who'd been in the House forever and a day. He was the epitome of the Southern conservative. I believe he even wore a frock coat. He looked like a relic of the past. And he did everything he could to keep the bill from ever coming to a hearing. He used every device and maneuver.

Maury Maverick, the president of the poll tax committee, was still in the Congress at that time. Maury was young and lively and very bright. He was full of vim and vigor and he wasn't scared of anybody, so he got old Hatton Sumners to hold the hearings. Maury testified and so did Clark Foreman and Miss Lucy. We were treated in a very hostile way by the committee, particularly by Hatton Sumners, who was just burning with rage and indignation at the idea of this bunch of upstarts.

The evidence was all there—the fact that not more than 12 percent of the voting population in Virginia voted and 13 percent in Mississippi. The facts were incontrovertible. That is, since the disenfranchising provisions of the 1800s and early 1900s, starting with Mississippi, the number who voted in the South, both blacks and whites, had gone down, down, down. The South in 1939 had an extremely small vote. It was argued that Southerners weren't interested in voting. They just didn't care about it.

Hatton Sumners never printed the hearings. He was a man of so much prestige and power in the House that he wouldn't budge. The Southerners controlled most of the big committees. They had been in office forever and a day because of the small electorate in the South. Many were seventy or eighty and they had been in Congress thirty or forty years. They just ran the show.

The poll tax committee was still working out of Lee Geyer's office. We were a varied group. We'd pick up here, there, and yonder people who came through town. I was the only one who was there more or less on a permanent basis. Wilbur Cohen's wife, Eloise, used to help out. Wilbur helped plan the social security program in its early years and later was tax commissioner of the United States. A lot of volunteers would come in and out, but we were not very well organized. We would send out material and try to interview congressmen, but it was a very amateurish organization. No one was working full-time except Lee Geyer's nephew, who was Lee's secretary. At least he took care of the mail and would answer letters that had to be answered.

What helped us a great deal was that up above us in the building, the old House Office Building, was the Tolan committee office. That was the committee of Congress investigating agriculture and Appalachia and poverty. There were a lot of really brilliant, dedicated young fellows on the Tolan committee staff. They were going to eradicate the poverty of Appalachia. Congressman Tolan himself came from West Virginia. These boys were very bright and they began to take an interest in the poll tax fight, particularly Palmer Webber and David Carliner. Palmer had just graduated from the University of Virginia that summer. He didn't have a job, so he agreed to come in and run the office. He's now a lawyer for the American Civil Liberties Union in Washington. He was a very nice fellow and smart as he could be. But the thing that really helped was that these boys all knew about mimeographing, the technical things that I didn't know from Adam.

Maury was defeated for reelection in 1939 and went back to Texas. Joe Gelders helped when he was in town. He worked and worked and had no money at all. I remember coming into Lee Geyer's office one morning and finding Joe on the front steps. He had been there all night long. He had no money and didn't even have a place to sleep. I took him out and gave him some breakfast. Joe came and went, though, so I really was in charge of the committee. Occasionally we would scrape up a little money and have a party or something, but it was all mighty poor doings.

We began to lobby on the Hill in an effort to get support for the poll tax bill. I was about thirty-six—a good deal younger and better looking than I am now, and I was subjected for the first time to passes from senators and congressmen. To be a senator or congressman you had to have a rather large ego, because it takes an awful lot of work and strength and vitality and vigor. Well, frequently they'd chase you around the desk, literally. You'd see this large mountain of a man rise up and come toward you, and you'd back toward the door. So many of them were men of strong sexual urges, I would say. But you really couldn't take it personally. You didn't feel that you were being particularly distinguished for unusual charms or beauty; it was just that you were female and fair game. It was something you had to get used to. In a way, I was protected more than some of the other girls, who had rather more disastrous experiences, because I was Hugo Black's sister-in-law and Clifford Durr's wife. Cliff was on the RFC and then on the Federal Communications Commission, in both of which positions he could refuse or grant a license to a radio station or a loan of money to a bank. I don't say that every single congressman and senator chased women around the office; but it was just one of the hazards of working on the Hill. Some of the young ladies we would send out to lobby would come back considerably disheveled. It was such a joke, though, because Senator McKellar of Tennessee, who was one of the worst, must have been in his eighties. Senator McKellar was like an old bird dog. He'd just see a woman come in the room and he was right after her.

The poll tax committee was, at that time, part of a Roosevelt coalition. I was in it for the women, but the blacks had stronger feelings. They always said that even when we got the poll tax abolished, they still had registration restrictions to get around. So while they favored abolishing the poll tax, they always realized that they would have to do away with the registration provisions and the property and literacy provisions. In some of the states, if a man was illiterate, he couldn't vote unless he owned three hundred dollars worth of property. The NAACP and the black Elks and all the black organizations supported us.

Abolition of the poll tax would bring more working-class white voters into the Roosevelt coalition, too. The disenfranchising provisions had been aimed at poor whites as well as blacks. The poor whites have continually cut their own throats. They voted for the voting restrictions because they thought it would keep the blacks from voting, but at the same time, it kept *them* from voting, too.

The Southern Conference even joined a 1939 suit in Tennessee to have the poll tax struck down. Our premise was that a money tax was not a voting qualification; it was just a disenfranchising provision. The conference got Crampton Harris, Hugo Black's former law partner, to represent Henry Pirtle, who had brought the suit, and John L. Lewis gave several thousand dollars to finance the case. But the Supreme Court had already ruled in *Breedlove* v. *Suttles* that under the Constitution the states had the right to set qualifications for voters, so Pirtle's suit, *Pirtle* v. *Brown,* failed, too.

Because of the disenfranchisement provisions, the South was ruled by an oligarchy. The planters in the black belt were in alliance with the corporate interests in Birmingham—we called them the "Big Mules." We thought the first step in breaking this oligarchy was to abolish the poll tax, but progress was slow. A bill would be signed out of committee and pass in the House. Then it would be filibustered to death in the Senate. Almost everyone from the South would filibuster, of course. The only support we got from the South was from Claude Pepper of Florida, who introduced the bill to abolish the poll tax several times. Florida had already abolished the poll tax by state action in 1937. Frank Graham helped, of course. He was in the Senate for a while. But I can't remember getting support from any other North Carolina politician. From 1940 until the poll tax committee folded in 1948, we would get a bill to abolish the poll tax introduced, but it never was approved by the whole Congress.

While we were in Congressman Geyer's office we set up a committee and each group that opposed the poll tax had a representative on that committee. Our great support and help with money was John Lewis and the CIO. We had all of labor represented on our committee—the AFL, CIO, Railway Brotherhood. We had the NAACP and the Negro Elks. We had the Methodist church, all the civil liberties and the civil rights groups, the American Civil Liberties Union. Oddly enough, one group that did not support us—which I've always held against them—was the Women's party. They were too sectarian. They believed in women's rights and an equal rights amendment that they were working on back then, but they never supported the anti–poll tax bill. Those were the most rigid, sectarian women I have ever known. They wouldn't talk to you about anything but their own cause. But we did have some support from the American Association of University Women (AAUW).

I keep telling the women today, if you are just going to work for women's rights, you're not going to get anywhere. You have to work for the rights of other people, too. The same is true for civil rights. As long as you work just for the rights of Negroes, you aren't going to get anywhere. You have to appeal to people on a broader basis than just sectarian rights of groups.

As I see it, the discrimination against Negroes and women was all part of the exploitation of human beings by other human beings. Rich Negroes exploited poor Negroes; rich women exploited poor women. I certainly believe in women's rights and black rights, too, but since the beginning of time the haves have exploited the have-nots. People who accumulate money and property and power have always wanted someone else to do all the dirty work—to do the washing and the cleaning up, to nurse the babies and look after the sick. People like to be clean and smell good and live above all the digging of coal and the draining of cesspools. In India the untouchables took care of the outhouse and disposed of the dead animals. The untouchables couldn't drink out of the village well. It's human nature to want somebody else to do the dirty work—whether it is women or blacks or slaves or captured prisoners.

After Lee Geyer died, in 1941, the poll tax committee got an office in the Railway Building through Frances Wheeler, our secretary, who was the daughter of Burton K. Wheeler, the senator from Montana. The head of the railroad union, Mr. Keating, was a great friend of his and so we got the space free. I had met Frances through her sister, Elizabeth, who lived near us. Frances was a brilliant young woman just out of Mount Holyoke. She was an interventionist in foreign affairs and far more radical than her father. She wanted to work for the United Mine Workers, but John L. Lewis had a prohibition in his constitution; not only could no Communists work for the Mine Workers, but no married women could. If you got married, you had to give up your job. He didn't believe in married women working outside the home. Frances had married Allen Saylor, who was in the Federal Communications Commission. Since she couldn't work for the UMW, Frances became secretary of the poll tax committee.

In April 1940 the Southern Conference had its second convention, in Chattanooga. The meeting was dominated by fighting between the people who wanted to go to war against Hitler and the ones who didn't. I was one of the ones who wanted to go to war. I tried to stay out of the fray at the conference, but I was very much on the side of Frank Graham and the people who wanted to pass a strong resolution supporting the Allies.

In 1938, the conference had had the backing of the Roosevelts, but by the time we met in Chattanooga in 1940, Mr. Roosevelt had turned from Dr. New Deal to Dr. Win-the-War. He was cultivating the Southerners to back his war effort. I'm sure he passed the word among the New Dealers not to involve themselves with the conference, because he wanted to keep the support of the Southern congressmen and senators. Not only were they in important positions on the committees, but they were interventionists. They believed in fighting Hitler. Mark Ethridge, editor of the *Louisville Courier-Journal,* and Mrs. Roosevelt attended the conference as Roosevelt's emissaries and to represent the New Deal point of view. We didn't have the big luminaries of the New Deal, but we did have people like Frank Graham, and of course I considered myself a New Dealer, too.

I was one hundred percent interventionist, but I always tried to stay friends with the isolationists. John L. Lewis had become a complete isolationist; he had broken with Roosevelt and was supporting Willkie. Of course, Kathryn Lewis was an isolationist, too. She and I had become good friends and we roomed together at the Chattanooga meeting. Although we supported different points of view, our friendship survived. She went down to that meeting to manipulate the miners, who came pouring in from all over Alabama and Tennessee. They had gotten orders to come and they came. They formed an alliance with the few Communists there to try to get a resolution passed against the Allies. It was certainly a strange partnership.

Mark Ethridge and Frank Graham and Barry Bingham were there trying to get a resolution passed in support of the Allies.

Joe Gelders was also backing the isolationist resolution, and he was relying on the miners' support to get it passed. But the miners were absolutely bored to death. They couldn't have been more bored with all the technicalities: "I amend this section of the constitution" or "I amend this resolution" and amendments to the amendments. All the parliamentary folderol that goes on was just too much. Finally they all just drifted out, and the isolationist resolution lost.

John L. Lewis was the power at that conference. He had upset the whole corporate system in the country with sit-ins. He had become a national, even international, figure and he fought hard in Chattanooga to get the Southern Conference to embark on a pro-Willkie, isolationist, anti-Roosevelt stand. If those miners had only stayed in the hall, they could have gotten anything they wanted.

Frank Graham certainly didn't like the isolationist sentiment in Chattanooga. I was very fond of him and admired him, but he fell into the same trap that others did. Instead of blaming John L. Lewis and the mine workers for the isolationist sentiment and the resolutions to stay out of the war, he blamed the Communists. This is typical of that whole era. There would be three Communists there and three hundred mine workers, but they would blame the Communists rather than the mine workers.

It was at the Chattanooga meeting that I first met Jim Dombrowski. Across the hall, I saw this handsome man with dark brown eyes. Jim looked like Saint Francis of Assisi. He came up and introduced himself. Kathryn was with me. Jim asked if we would like to come up to the Highlander Folk School, which he had helped Myles Horton found in 1932. He would drive us up for a day or so before we returned to Washington. So we went. Jim drove us up and Myles met us. I had never seen the school before and I just loved it. I adored Zilphia, Myles's wife, and the other people there.

On Sunday, people at the school sent out word all over the mountains that Kathryn Lewis was there, John L. Lewis's daughter, and by God, the miners came out again. I bet there were two hundred miners there. They were very silent men, and they all wore black hats. They sat out on the front lawn, and Kathryn had to make a little speech. Myles got them something to eat, but not one of them would take off his hat or come in the house.

Kathryn got along very well with the miners. She knew how to talk to them and so did Jim and Myles. My efforts failed, I can assure you. I would say, "Where are you from?" and "You say your name is Jones? Now, what Jones are you?" I am sure they thought I was an agent of the FBI or something. I got a very poor response. I had to learn that the only way to deal with people like that is to listen. Too much talk makes them suspicious.

I identified with the labor movement, but it took me a long time to realize that the labor movement didn't identify with me. I remember going to one of the CIO conventions. I was considerably younger and prettier then and I was very earnest and lobbying a great deal. All the men wanted to do was take me out and buy me a drink. They wanted to have a good time. I had a terrible shock. I thought all labor men were going to be great. It was going to be just right down the line in our interests. They were going to be just as interested as I was in getting rid of the poll tax and fighting for the rights of labor. I got the biggest shock of my life to see those fat flunkies sitting around guzzling booze and chasing women. That's what they did. That's human, but it was a great disappointment to me. I lost a lot of illusions.

8

Wartime on Seminary Hill

I THOUGHT THE FUROR over foreign policy at the Southern Conference meeting in Chattanooga was an unnecessary diversion from domestic issues like the poll tax fight, but I was also very much interested in foreign policy. I had been concerned with the war in Spain. The Spanish civil war was a tremendously popular war for the democracies, not for the countries but for the people. A democratically elected government was being overthrown by a military usurper, so the cause appealed to me.

I went to a meeting of the Spanish Relief Committee at the home of Mrs. Pinchot, a friend of my sister's, who was the wife of the ex-governor of Pennsylvania, Gifford Pinchot. Mr. Pinchot was a conservationist and a progressive in Teddy Roosevelt's time. Mrs. Pinchot was a rich lady from New York from the Cooper Union family. Her hair was fiery red, just the color of a fire truck except a little more orange, and she had a splendid figure. Her face was pure white and she had big green eyes. She had been a great beauty in her youth, but she was well into her seventies by then and her fiery red hair made her look rather remarkable, to put it mildly. She had a great big house and she gave perfectly marvelous parties for causes.

My life was divided into two or three levels in those days. Part of my life was taken up by the anti–poll tax committee and the labor unions and all the fighting and feuding about them that went on up on Capitol Hill. Then, of course, I had an extremely active and intense family life out on Seminary Hill, surrounded by all kinds of neighbors and the Episcopal church and so on. We had three girls by then—Ann, Lucy, and the baby Tilla, who was born in September 1939. And then, through Sister, I had another life, which was much more official and much more exalted, with famous people and well-known people. My sister always looked out for me and wanted me to meet interesting people. She introduced me to Mrs. Pinchot, and Mrs. Pinchot put us on her list.

We began getting beautiful engraved invitations, "Governor and Mrs. Pinchot invite you to dinner" and to tea and receptions and on and on. She never served any liquor. She thought that was terrible. But she had absolutely marvelous food, the most elaborate you have ever seen. She would serve pheasant with the feathers on. That was the highest I have ever gone in the culinary scale—a beautiful plumed pheasant with the tail feathers all bronzed and green and purple and yellow. The pheasants were cooked and then the whole skin with the feathers was put back on them. The servants would come in with a huge silver platter of pheasants. It was beautiful, but it was a little startling at first. Pheasants are not so grand, really. They are rather dry. But Mrs. Pinchot lived in really elegant style. She had butlers and footmen and maids, but nothing to drink.

There was one catch about Mrs. Pinchot's parties. They were always for a cause. Every time you went, you went for a cause. We once went for the freedom of India. I remember Madame Pandit, Nehru's sister, boiling over with rage about the British imperialists. Oh, it really was something. I went to parties for China, for everything you can imagine. If there was a cause, Mrs. Pinchot had a party for it, but you had to contribute. It was done in a delightful way. Mrs. Pinchot would get up and say, "Now, I know that you dear people want to help our Madame Pandit to overthrow the British Empire. . . ." Or Japan, or whatever. Then you would have to put out the dough. Well, twenty-five dollars was about the least you could get by with—just chickenfeed for most of the guests—and Cliff began to get awfully nervous about getting invitations to these parties. He was still not making a great salary, and twenty-five dollars was mighty expensive for us for an evening out, even if we did have stuffed pheasant! Cliff said we just weren't going anymore. He just couldn't afford it. It was very pleasant meeting all these great and famous people and having a delicious dinner and all, but twenty-five dollars a time—and fifty dollars a month if you went to two parties—was too much. Cliff just refused to go to any more, and when he put his foot down, he put it down.

Right at the end of the Spanish war Mrs. Pinchot invited me to a meeting to start a Spanish Aid Committee. Leon Henderson was to be head of it. Leon later served as chief economist for the National Recovery Administration and director of the Office of Price Administration and was one of the founders of the Americans for Democratic Action. He was a brilliant fellow and very nice. There was also a couple there named Mike and Binny Straight. After we had had tea, I spoke to them. She looked like Alice in Wonderland, about ten or fifteen years old. I found that they lived in Alexandria, and he was running the *New Republic*.

Mike's mother was one of the Whitneys. She had married Willard

Straight, a member of the J. P. Morgan firm. He built railroads in China and made a good deal of money out of them. When Willard Straight died, Mrs. Straight went to England and married a Mr. Elmhirst. Together they ran a famous school, a very progressive school, called Dartington Hall. The Elmhirsts took the side of the Spanish Loyalists.

Binny and her sister had lived in England, too. Binny's father was an American who was over there on business. Mike and Binny met in England and married there.

I can't say that Mike was a member of the Communist party, although I was told he was when he was at Cambridge. In any case, Mike financed people to go to Spain. He was a great advocate of the Spanish Republic. He supported John Cornford, the English poet who was killed in Spain. John Cornford was one of the young men who died for the faith. They were all beautiful, all handsome, all wrote poetry, and all were great romantic heroes. And they died in Spain. The history of the Spanish war is incredibly fascinating. Young people came from all over the world to fight.

Mike Straight had wanted to take out British citizenship and run for Parliament, but the British government wouldn't let him because he had supported these fellows in Spain or had a connection with the Communist party or something. So Mike came over to the United States. His family owned the *New Republic,* and he took it over. His mother was a great liberal benefactor.

Mike was very attractive and nice, about twenty-one, I imagine. Binny was about seventeen and was absolutely beautiful. We became friends because her grandmother, Mrs. Sheridan, came from Georgia. Mrs. Sheridan was a famous Southern lady who lived in New York and instructed Southern girls—kind of like Aunt Mamie, but on a much higher level. A friend of mine stayed with Mrs. Sheridan, which is how I knew about her.

Mike and Binny had a little house on one of the cobblestone streets in Alexandria, and they often had several parties in one week. When Binny married, her mother had insisted on sending her nanny with her. One time we were sitting at the dinner table and Binny was playing the hostess. She had all kinds of interesting and famous people there. It got cold in that little old house and everybody was cold and kind of rubbing themselves. The nanny came in and whispered, "Miss Binny, do you have your woolen drawers on?" Poor Binny nearly fell out of her chair!

Binny called me up one day to invite us to a cocktail party. She wanted us to meet a young English couple who were staying with them. The husband had fought in Spain. Now, Cliff thought a party of more than five or six people should be declared an unlawful assembly. He just hated cocktail parties. But I loved them, and so I went alone.

The young couple I met at the Straights were the Romillys. Esmond was an attractive young man of about twenty who had fought in Spain. He looked like Winston Churchill, with a great jaw and big heavy shoulders. He was very blond and blue-eyed and perfectly brilliant and charming. I thought he was great. He told us about Spain. He was furious at Franco and furious at the United States and furious at the Catholic church and furious at everybody that I was furious with for not supporting Spain. I thought Esmond was the world's most marvelous young man. His wife was a beautiful, slender young girl with great big blue eyes and dark hair and white skin. That was Decca, Jessica Mitford.

When I left the party, I said to Esmond, "Now I want my husband to meet you. I am anxious for him to meet you." So we made a date for dinner, and then I forgot to invite his wife. The next morning I remembered that I hadn't invited her and I had to call up real quick and invite his wife. And of course I invited Binny and Mike. It was a fascinating and marvelous evening. Decca remembered the occasion later in her book *Daughters and Rebels*.

Soon after, the young Romillys went to Florida and bought a bar. Esmond came up from Florida at Christmas on business and came out to see us. At that time England was in the war against Hitler, and Esmond said, "I'll never go to war for England as long as Chamberlain is premier. He is nothing but a Birmingham broker and he is money mad. Those Chamberlains are just money people, tradesmen." It was a very aristocratic sort of looking down on the Chamberlains. Of course, Chamberlain had just sold out England, just acted awful. But Esmond said, "If my uncle, Winston Churchill, gets to be prime minister, I will go to war, because I know that he will fight."

"Why do you know that he'll fight?" I asked.

"Because he and his crowd own England and they will fight for what is theirs. Even if they don't own it, they think they do, so they'll fight."

Sure enough, the next summer, 1940, Esmond appeared again with Decca. He was on his way to Canada to join the Air Force. They stayed with the Straights again. We went to another party at the Straights, and they came to another party at our house, and once again we thought Esmond was fascinating. He came out into the kitchen while I was fixing dinner. "Old Virginny"—he always called me "Old Virginny," from the song, "Carry Me Back to Old Virginny"—"don't you think you could keep dear Decca while I'm gone? You know, the Straights are going up to New York for the weekend and she will be all alone. I am sure that she will be so lonely. If you will just keep her for the weekend, I can't tell you how I would appreciate it."

"Well, Esmond," I said, "I'm terribly sorry, but I'm going to the Democratic Convention in Chicago. I'm leaving almost immediately." "That will be wonderful. Just take Decca with you. We have money and she will be no expense whatsoever. It will take her mind off my leaving and just be great."

Well, I didn't want to take her a bit. One of the young men who worked in Cliff's office, Red James, was going to drive me out and another girl was going, too. I didn't want Decca to go. I was going to appear before the platform committee and make a presentation on the anti–poll tax bill, so I was busy politicking and making dates to see this person and that. But he persuaded me to take her.

We stopped at the Straights' house the morning we left for Chicago and got Decca. Almost immediately she asked us to stop so she could go to a restroom. Thereafter, every fifteen minutes she wanted us to stop again. The boy who was driving said to me, "She's got a weak bladder. We'll never get to Chicago if we have to stop every fifteen minutes." I suspected something else, so I went in the restroom and there she was, throwing up. She was pregnant, you see. She threw up all morning. By the afternoon, she began to get better, and when we got to Chicago, she was fine. She was just sick in the mornings.

We went down to the Sheraton Hotel where all the big doings were, and who did I see the minute that we got there but Lyndon Johnson. By this time, he and I were great friends. Lyndon and Alvin Wirtz, undersecretary of the interior, immediately made us honorary delegates on the Texas delegation. By this time Decca was looking very glamorous and beautiful. We got big hats and lariats and badges to let us in and out. We had the greatest time you can imagine.

They didn't have air-conditioning then, and the coliseum must have been 110 degrees in the shade. It was horribly hot, and the ladies' room was just miles away. So I said to Maury Maverick, "You know, I've got a young English girl with me who throws up all the time. What in the name of God are we going to do?" Maury had on a great big hat, a sombrero, made out of really fine felt. So he went over and swept off his hat like Sir Walter Raleigh and said to Decca, "Madame, use my hat if you need it." Well, Decca said she felt like Queen Elizabeth. She never felt so glamorous and courtly. Fortunately, she didn't throw up in his hat, but she kept it in her lap all the time.

We had a marvelous time at the convention. Henry Wallace was nominated for vice-president, and I was all for him. I marched in his parade and waved my cornstalk. It was great fun.

By the time we got back to Washington, Decca had stopped throwing up so much and she was feeling pretty well. The Straights were still gone, so she came to our house. I asked her what she was going to do. As it turned out, Esmond wasn't going to be back for some time. She said she was going to New York and get a job in a dress shop. I said, "You can't go if you're still throwing up so much. You stay here until you get over being sick." So she agreed.

One day about this time, Cliff got a letter from Oxford University, where he had been a Rhodes scholar, which said the University was trying to send all the dons and their wives over to America because Hitler was threatening to bomb Oxford and Cambridge. There had been a series of what were called the Baedeker Raids, in which the Nazis bombed places like Coventry and just smashed them flat. Now Hitler said he was going to bomb Oxford and Cambridge and destroy everything that was sacred—just as he had destroyed St. Paul's and Coventry cathedrals. The letter from Oxford asked Cliff to take a refugee, a lady named Mrs. Woozley, whose husband was the librarian of Queen's College. Cliff said he thought we had to take her. Then he found out she also would be bringing her baby with her. In my house at that time were Cliff, myself, Ann, Lucy, Tilla, and Decca, who was pregnant; also, my mother and father came to stay very often. That made eight, and then there was this woman—and if she brought her child, that would be ten. Well, ten people are quite a lot to feed, especially if we went on rations, but Cliff said we had to take her.

Mrs. Woozley wrote me and said she didn't want to be any trouble, but she would need, of course, a private room and bath for herself and the baby, and also, would I engage a nanny for her? Can you imagine having to find a nanny? Well, I could see that Mrs. Woozley was going to be a pain in the neck and a lot of trouble and I didn't know if I could manage that or not, but I told Decca to stay until Mrs. Woozley came. Then Mrs. Woozley wrote and said the torpedoing had gotten so bad in the North Atlantic that she believed she would take her chances on staying in England with her husband and being bombed rather than being torpedoed in the Atlantic— which was a very wise decision. Since Mrs. Woozley wasn't coming, Decca said she would be our refugee. And she was, for almost three years.

We had all become devoted to Decca by then and it was all a big joke about her being our refugee. That autumn, Decca's daughter was born. Esmond came down for Christmas to see the baby. Then he flew over to Scotland where he was going to be with the Air Force. The baby was a beautiful child. Her name was Constantia, for the Spanish Revolution, Constantia Romilly. But we called her Dinkydonk because of the way she acted at the Democratic Convention. She was acting like a little donkey. This was just a joke, but the name stuck. We were awfully young in those days and we made jokes about everything.

In November 1941, Cliff had to go to New York to make a speech, and I went with him. Decca was to meet us there the next day, and we were going to see her and Dinky off to Scotland to join Esmond. The night before she was to sail we got a long distance call in New York from one of our neighbors, Mary Walton Livingston. She said Decca had just gotten word that Esmond was lost coming back from a bombing raid over Berlin.

We rushed back to Washington and found Decca absolutely desolate. Decca said she wasn't going to England, but she knew that Esmond was alive. She actually refused at that point to have anything to do with her family, what she called her "fascist family." One sister had married Oswald Mosley, the leader of the Blackshirts in England, and another sister, Unity, had been Hitler's girl friend. A third sister married the duke of Devonshire, a conservative but not a fascist. Her mother and father had been vaguely pro-Hitler, and her father had cut Decca out of his will. When Decca married and ran off to Spain with Esmond to fight, her family had rather disowned her, and she them.

Decca wouldn't believe that Esmond was dead. We made every inquiry that we could through the British embassy and the Air Force. She kept thinking somebody might have rescued him or a submarine had come along.

When the United States entered the war, Winston Churchill came over and stayed at the White House and the first thing he did was to call Decca to ask her to bring the baby over to see him. He told her he would find out about Esmond for her.

Decca went over to the White House and Churchill got in touch with the commandant and the land crew that dispatched Esmond's plane to Berlin and the one that guided the plane back, and there was no doubt that Esmond was dead. He was a navigator and the plane had been over Berlin. It had been shot up and was limping back to England. The plane got within ten miles of the coast of Scotland and went down in the North Sea in bad weather. It was terribly cold and there were huge waves. The next morning rescue teams went out in airplanes and hydroplanes and boats, but they never found anything but a scum of oil. They were sure that Esmond had drowned. Finally Decca accepted the fact that he was dead. She used to wake up at night and I would hear her weeping. I would go in there and she would say, "Oh, the water was so cold. The water was so cold."

Decca makes a joke of everything, and she can be terribly arrogant and upper class and just freeze the marrow of people's bones when she wants to. But she really is a very feeling person and terribly emotional. She keeps it under very tight control, I must say. I suppose I am one of the few people who has ever seen Decca with all her defenses down.

A few weeks after Esmond was killed, the United States entered the war. Up until the attack on Pearl Harbor in December 1941, there was still a terrific fight going on between the isolationists and the interventionists in this country. Cliff and I were totally on the interventionist side. We both were positive the United States would get into the war. We'd either be attacked or we'd have to go to the defense of Great Britain. I was a great reader and I'd read all the history and literature of England, and of course Cliff had gone to school there for three years. We both had great sympathy and love for England. And then, Decca was living with us. But Roosevelt didn't yet feel that he had the country solidly behind him. He would have entered the war earlier if he had felt that Congress would go along, but there was tremendous isolationist sentiment in the country.

Meanwhile, Cliff was trying to spur the construction of defense plants. Many businessmen didn't want to invest in new plants because they were afraid they'd be left with an empty plant and no orders. They were scared they'd lose money. So Cliff's plan was that the government would build the plant for them and guarantee them a profit—cost plus—and buy everything that they made. So in spite of the struggle that was going on politically all over the country between the isolationists and the interventionists, this RFC plan for government financing was already under way and employment was going up.

I belonged to an organization of dear, sweet ladies called the Women's International League for Peace and Freedom. It had been started by Jane Addams, and the members were all Quakers and religious women. They were all for peace. They didn't believe in having war at all. And I must say there were a great many people who had the idea that going to war was terrible. No matter what, no matter how awful Hitler was or how many children died in the gas chambers, we should not go to war.

Pearl Harbor came like a bolt out of the blue. Cliff had been working day and night on the defense plant plan, but on Sundays he always tried to stay at home, and he did on December 7. It was a time of year in Virginia when often there was snow on the ground. We would have extremely cozy Sunday afternoons. If there's one thing Cliff could do, he could make a breakfast and fix tea. He learned to fix tea when he was at Oxford. So he made tea and anchovy toast. It was delicious, too—all full of butter and anchovies. He loved to make tea on Sunday afternoon for the children and me. People would take walks in the woods and drop in for tea. It was just a peaceful, snowy Sunday afternoon. I remember we had an open fire. The children had gone to bed and Cliff and I were sitting by ourselves when the announcement came over the radio that Japan had bombed Pearl Harbor. After that, I can't remember anything but just mad excitement until the president announced the next day that we were going to war.

We had been living in expectation of this for a long time. There'd been a number of interventionist organizations. Mike Straight was head of one called the Committee for Aid to the Allies. When Germany attacked Russia, all the radical groups came over on the interventionist side. That made a big division in the radical and labor groups.

The country rallied immediately when we entered the war. During the war there was very little dissent. There were none of the Vietnam marches and things like that. People really backed the war. Another thing the war did, which sounds awful to say, was to provide employment. Everybody flocked into war work. The WPA and the Civilian Conservation Corps (CCC) and the NYA and the relief organizations were able to close down. Everybody who wanted a job had one—and at good wages.

Until the war began there was still terrible unemployment in this country. The New Deal hadn't been able to solve that at all. But the fascinating thing is how one social issue grows out of another, how the civil rights movement of the sixties really grew out of the employment changes of the forties. The war created jobs and black people began to demand their share of them. They had demanded and gotten fair employment practices in the WPA and the NYA and the CCC under people like Aubrey Williams and Harry Hopkins and Harold Ickes. So when the government financed the private plants to manufacture the materials for war under Cliff's plan, the defense plan, the New Dealers insisted that all this new construction and all these new plants also observe the practices being observed in the WPA and the NYA and the CCC—fair employment, equal hiring between black and white, and equal pay. There was quite a bit of agitation about it.

The Fair Employment Practices Commission (FEPC) was set up to see that the private employers observed fair employment practices. A dear friend of ours, Mike Ross, was made head of the FEPC. He and his wife lived in Alexandria. He looked like an Irish leprechaun. He had a triangular face, vivid eyes, and extremely curly, reddish hair. His well-off upper-class family had sent him to Yale, and he wrote a great book called *The Death of a Yale Man*.

Strangely enough, I don't recall that the FEPC said anything about women. They simply weren't discussed. But when the war finally came and women were needed, thousands of them went into the factories.

Although it was a terrible shock when we entered the war, it was also a terrific relief to us. The stories that came out of Germany were so awful. And that horrible voice of Hitler that came over the radio just kept threatening, threatening, threatening. It looked as though he was going to sweep over the whole of Europe and get England, too. Everywhere the Germans went they killed people indiscriminately. The Jews were killed like so many pigs or sent to concentration camps to be burned up. It was a horror. During the period of Hitler all the horrors that you could imagine happened. He didn't have the atomic bomb, but he did have all the horrors of war and the cruelty. He and his gang committed the most incredible sort of barbarities, like killing everybody in a village, men, women, and children, as they did at Lidice, a village in Czechoslovakia. A sniper apparently shot at a German soldier, so they just killed everybody and burned the village down. The horrors were real. They were actually true.

I think, too, that in my case, the awakening to the horrors of fascism and nazism had come in the Spanish war. That happened to a lot of people. Decca's being with us and Esmond's being in the war gave us a very personal feeling about it. Of course, my nephews and Cliff's nephews and a lot of other people we knew promptly went off to war, as did many of the people who lived in our neighborhood. All during the war we just hung on the radio. We never missed a newscast. I suppose that's why I'm such a news hawk now. You'd just never dream of missing a newscast.

Once we entered the war, Churchill and Roosevelt got along extremely well. They both came from a rich, secure background, except Churchill's family was probably a little older than the Roosevelt family. Churchill didn't have that much money, but they both were men of tremendous security within themselves. I think Roosevelt had more doubt and sensitivity than Churchill.

Roosevelt always said that the great mistake of his life was not helping the Spanish Republic to kill the snake of fascism when it was small in Spain. I've said this before and I'll say it again: I think one of the great reasons he didn't do it was on account of the Catholic church, and Cardinal Spellman in particular. Farley was still head of the Democratic party and he depended a great deal on the Catholics. Practically every Catholic was supporting Franco, including our ambassador to England, Joe Kennedy. The English government had him sent back here because he was so lukewarm on supporting the war. I don't think he was pro-Hitler, but he was certainly pro-Franco, and he didn't believe in going to war against Hitler.

The corporations didn't want to get into the war. Their very reluctance to build plants in preparation for the eventuality of war shows how little they wanted to invest money in a war that might not come. There was no way to order them to do it under the free enterprise system. So what they did was implement what Cliff had worked out, which was to build the plants for the corporations with government money and then give them cost-plus contracts. Cliff had the idea it would be like the TVA. It would be a kind of yardstick and the government would keep these plants after the war. We wouldn't have socialism, but we would have a mixed economy with the government running these few plants. But when Truman came in, he was surrounded by Wall Street people. And of course, the government just gave the plants away. The corporations got it all.

The Seven Sisters by Anthony Sampson describes the interlocking networks between Germany and the seven big oil corporations. Two of them—Exxon and Shell—kept shipping oil to Germany the whole time we were at war. The men who did it were surprised when they were hauled up before Congress. Harry Truman said it was treason. Well, it certainly was going against your own country, but they didn't see it that way at all. They just saw that Germany was a market. There are two moralities: there's the morality that concerns human beings and the morality that businessmen have that concerns profit. These businessmen were understandably not enthusiastic about going to war.

Cliff went over to the Federal Communications Commission in 1941.

When Cliff was sworn in as FCC Commissioner in 1941: *(from left to right)* me, Tilla, Cliff, Lucy, Ann. (Courtesy of Ann Durr Lyon)

All along, Jesse Jones had been opposing Cliff's effort to get the country ready for war. But when the war started, Jesse Jones claimed he had done it all. Cliff was an embarrassment to Jesse, so Jesse told Cliff he'd get him a big job in Wall Street—$100,000 a year. Cliff didn't take it. He went over to the FCC instead, and Jesse Jones emerged as the hero for preparing the country for war when he didn't do a damn thing but stand in the way and try to block it.

Good God, what a household we were during the war! There was Cliff and me and our daughters, Ann, Lucy, and Tilla. Lulah, the youngest, wasn't born until a little later. I brought my mother, who was still suffering from melancholia, to live with us. She wept and wept all the time. Daddy stayed in Birmingham, but he visited us a lot. Then, there were Decca and Dinkydonk. That was nine people, and more were to come.

Lowell Mellett, who had been head of the National Emergency Council, lived right down the road, and he had become a White House aide. He had a Japanese butler, a very elegant butler. When Lowell became a White House aide, the FBI said, "Look, you can't have a Japanese butler who is not even a citizen of the United States in your house when you are on a hot line to the White House." So Lowell came up and asked me if I would take him. I said, "Lowell, I can't take a Japanese butler. He can't cook or wash or nurse children. I don't have the kind of household where you have to have a butler come in and bring you cocktails before dinner." He said, "Well, you could just let him stay there for a while." I had a servant's room downstairs that had a private bath, so Yamasaki came. Nobody had told us, but he had a wife and baby. So here was the Japanese and his wife and baby. That added up to twelve, I think, by that time.

Yamasaki got a job as butler next door with the Siepmans, who lived a more formal life than we did, and Decca hired his wife, Saiko, to be the nanny for her child, Dinkydonk. I must say that Saiko turned out to be an angel, an absolute marvel. She was a Japanese from Hawaii, and she did everything beautifully. There was nothing that she didn't do perfectly. She was a marvelous cook, and she would clean a room so well that it shone. If she washed or ironed, it was perfect, and if she mended clothes, you couldn't see the stitches. Everything she did was perfect, and she was a sweet, kind woman.

Then there was Mrs. Daniels, who came in to help with my mother and the children and to clean and wash. She was a wonderful woman, too. But we had a strange household.

My little girl Tilla and Decca's little girl, Dinkydonk, and the little Japanese boy, Hiroshi, all called Cliff "Daddy." All three of them would just laugh and say, "Daddy this and Daddy that." He had a hard time explaining how he had a Japanese child and an English child and an American child all about the same age.

One of the funniest things that happened was that the FBI came all the time because Yamasaki was living in our house. They had to check on him because he was Japanese and we were at war against Japan. It got so that the children would call up and say, "Mama, the laundry man is here." "Mama, the milkman is here." "Mama, the FBI men are here." They were always two big old dumb goofs who wanted to look around and see if there were any aerials and if we were transmitting messages to the Japanese. Instead of being accused of being a Communist, I was being accused of being pro-Japanese. Well, they went into Saiko and Yamasaki's room one afternoon and they found that his trunk had a false bottom. They knew they had him this time. They knew he was transmitting secrets to the Japanese from this false-bottomed trunk. I thought Yamasaki would die in his tracks. He kept pleading with them that it was just personal things, something very personal. They ripped out the bottom of this trunk and the whole bottom of it was filled with pictures of naked women. And his wife was right there, too. Was he embarrassed! The FBI men weren't embarrassed. They aren't

Lucy, Dinkydonk, Tilla, and Hiroshi, back porch on Seminary Hill. The household was like a League of Nations, and all the children called Cliff "Daddy." (Courtesy of Ann Durr Lyon)

ever embarrassed. They did such stupid things. They made us take Yama-saki's camera for the duration of the war.

Besides the FBI coming out to check on all the diverse people who lived at our house, Decca was being spied on all the time. We didn't know about that until after the war was over. There was a lovely English woman in the neighborhood named Mrs. Walker, a very sweet, attractive woman. Her father had been head of something called the Primrose League, which is a very high Tory group. The British embassy had asked Mrs. Walker to keep her eye on Decca. You see, Decca's husband had fought in Spain and her sister had been a friend of Hitler. Decca was very outspoken and was at that time working for John Kenneth Galbraith at the Office of Price Admin-

The house at Seminary Hill in the summer before the roof was altered, 1936. (Courtesy of Ann Durr Lyon)

istration (OPA). Mrs. Walker, Dee Dee, was always having us up to tea and dropping in to see us. We were very fond of Dee Dee. After the war was over, she said that the British embassy had asked her to keep an eye on Decca, to see that she didn't consort with the wrong people, I suppose.

Decca's family kept begging her to come home to England, but she wouldn't. Whenever her aristocratic relatives were in this country, they would come out and beg Decca to go back to England with them. One English gentleman who was at the British embassy came out. I remember he had his handkerchief tucked into his sleeve. I forget his name—two or three different names, Montague Foreshire Berkshire, or whatever it was. He was just the epitome of the British upper class. He and Decca practically had knock-down, drag-out fights about her going home to England. One day

Jessica Romilly with Constantia ("Dinkydonk"), aged eight months. (Courtesy of Jessica Mitford)

I remember their fighting and screaming and yelling. I went in to try to make peace. I brought in tea to calm the raging fight. Decca was all huffing and puffing and mad, and he was flushed and as hot as an aristocratic young Englishman could be with the handkerchief stuck in his cuff. Well, I knew one girl at the British embassy whom I'd been to Wellesley with. Just to try to bring some new note into the conversation, I said to him, "I wonder if you know my friend so-and-so whom I went to school with. She's married to an attaché at the British embassy."

"Oh, yes. I know her well. We have a number of Americans at the embassy who are married to Englishmen."

"She's an awfully nice girl," I said, "such a brilliant girl."

"She is indeed. She would be very nice indeed if she would just wash her neck and clean her fingernails." Can you imagine a more total insult than that? He was furious at Decca and was taking it out on me.

Decca was quite a storm center. She would go into Washington with the car pool to her job at the OPA. The car pool consisted of Cliff; Bill Livingston, who was a lawyer with Cliff at RFC; Kenneth Galbraith, the New Deal economist; Charlie Kendelberger, who was with some New Deal agency; and Charles Siepman, who was with the FCC. Decca would have to sit on someone's knees because the car was so full. There was no alternative to car pooling: gas was rationed and the bus didn't run more than once a day. So Decca found a young man named Kenneth somebody who went into Washington at an earlier time, which was more convenient for her. He was a very nice, stiff sort of Wall Streeter, who later became head of the New York Stock Exchange. He would pick her up every morning and they would ride into town together having furious fights about capitalism and socialism the whole way in and out.

It was a very mixed group around Seminary Hill. Lowell Mellett, Thurmond Arnold and his wife, Sister and Hugo, Supreme Court Justice William O. Douglas, Congressman Tom Eliot from Massachusetts, and the Washington correspondent for the BBC, Leonard Miall, and his wife, Lorna, all lived there. We all got to know each other well and to depend on one another because of the car pool.

Eric Sevareid and his wife, Lois, lived on Seminary Hill. Poor Lois had a nervous breakdown, which created a good deal of excitement. She would go raving crazy and come running into your house, just as wild as she could be. She was not violent and dangerous. She was just mad. Eric was awfully good to her. They had two little boys about the ages of my children and I saw a lot of them. The curious thing was that Lois regained her reason and then he left her and married somebody else. And she never did go crazy again. She stayed sane for the rest of her life.

We used to have square dances in the neighborhood because we couldn't get into Washington to do anything. We didn't have gas, so we were thrown on each other. And we all became extremely good friends. We were all caught in the same situation, worrying about closing the black shades at night because we thought the Germans were going to bomb us. You can imagine what trouble that was—every single night having to close all the shades. Every neighborhood had a warden. If he saw a crack of light, he warned you. And then we'd have trouble with ration stamps. If anybody got sick, everybody else helped. The Galbraith's boy died during that period, and all the neighbors stood by them. If you live close that way, ideological differences don't mean so much. We were all trying to win the war. We were all united on that, but there were differences of opinion and a lot of arguments.

The poll tax committee was in abeyance at this time. I had a hard time getting to town. If I went in with the car pool in the morning, I would sit on somebody's knees, usually Kenneth Galbraith's, which were very boney, I must say. He was always very nice about it. He was the biggest, and I was rather large and heavy. And we were always crowded. It was a very interdependent life.

Kenneth Galbraith had a perfectly lovely wife named Kitty whom we all adored and still do, but Kenneth and I would have frightful arguments. About everything. But I really have a great deal of affection for him and certainly for his wife.

You see, the marvelous thing about this country—which we have preserved up to this point—is that people can live together and disagree and yet keep a personal relationship. Whether that's going to continue in this country or not, I just don't know. The lines are getting more definite.

9

Poll Tax Politics

DESPITE THE SPLIT over foreign policy at the Chattanooga convention of the Southern Conference for Human Welfare, the poll tax committee continued getting support. Officially, it was called the Civil Rights Committee, but our main concern at this point was to abolish the poll tax. John L. Lewis, the CIO unions, Sidney Hillman, who was head of the CIO's Political Action Committee, and Joe Curran, who was head of the National Maritime Union, all supported us and gave us money. John Abt got the Amalgamated Clothing Workers, of which he was chief counsel, to contribute. The AFL unions hated Lewis so much that whatever he supported they wouldn't support, although they did give us a little money. David Dubinsky, head of the ILGWU, wouldn't give us one damn dime, because we didn't bar Communists from the committee.

After Lee Geyer died, in 1941, we had to find someone to sponsor the bill to abolish the poll tax. By this time we had a board composed of the labor unions, the NAACP, the Negro Elks, and a lot of the Christian organizations, the church organizations, the Methodists and the Baptists and Mrs. Mary McLeod Bethune's organization, the Council of Negro Women. The newspapermen were our great allies and help, too. A lot of us would have lunch together every day. Capitol Hill was a very lively place in those days and lots of fun. Izzy Stone helped us, of course. Izzy was absolutely wonderful. He was working for *PM* then. I. F. Stone was a long-time Washington newspaperman, a political analyst and critic.

In August 1941 we decided to separate the committee from the Southern Conference and call it the National Committee to Abolish the Poll Tax. The Southern Conference would be a member of the committee, and we would no longer be the poll tax committee of the Southern Conference.

George Norris of Nebraska had become our great champion in the

Senate. He was one of the most wonderful characters that ever lived, a perfectly angelic man and just a monument of integrity. He was a great advocate of the Tennessee Valley Authority, which was one reason he was so interested in getting rid of the poll tax—he felt the people in the TVA area should have the right to vote, but the poll tax and the people's poverty prevented it. Maury Maverick had lost his seat in the House and was mayor of San Antonio, so we were trying to get someone to take Maury's place and carry our effort in the House.

By this time the anti-Communist crusade had started, but we didn't separate from the Southern Conference for Human Welfare because of the Communist issue. The poll tax committee had simply gotten bigger than the Southern Conference. The labor unions realized that they were not going to get anywhere in the South until they got their people voting, and the church people thought it was the right thing to do. The NAACP and the Negro organizations had joined us too.

A lot of women's organizations helped us some. The AAUW didn't give us much help because it was always a very cautious organization and had to have meetings and pass ten resolutions before doing anything. The League of Women Voters was the same way. The league believed in our cause, but it didn't want to take action until it had held the next meeting. The help we got came from the Roosevelt coalition—the unions, the civil rights and civil liberties organizations, and the churches. And we got an awful lot of support from the White House itself—for a while anyway.

I was vice-chairman of the NCAPT, but I was also still involved with the Southern Conference, especially the D.C. committee, of which I was chairman. The D. C. committee was started as a political organization and was not tax-exempt. The idea was to start state committees that would be actively engaged in trying to get people to run for office. The Democratic party at that time was such an oligarchy in the South. We were trying very hard to broaden the base and get more people to come in and take part in politics.

I was vice-chairman of the National Committee to Abolish the Poll Tax and chairman of the Washington Committee of the Southern Conference. The Washington Committee was organized in 1944 and it became one of the most active local chapters of the Southern Conference. The emphasis in the Southern Conference had gone from labor to the war and then to race. One of the biggest things we did was to have a dinner for Hugo and by doing so to integrate the Washington hotels. Bill Douglas arranged to get the Statler Hotel for us through his brother, who was the head of the chain. Hugo's colleagues on the Supreme Court were all invited. Cliff and I went, of course. Poor Cliff was really caught between a rock and a hard place there. His mother was mad at him for attending an integrated dinner. She wrote him that she had lived for many years under the shadow of his grandfather's brief defection to the Republicans during Reconstruction and she couldn't bear another cloud over her sunset years. "The South has a tradition to preserve," she wrote, "and preserve it we shall with bloodshed if necessary." Cliff went despite his mother's plea. The dinner was the first big breakthrough on the hotels in Washington. Of course, we were all red-baited and there was a lot of hoorah about it, but it went off very successfully.

By the time of the Nashville convention of the Southern Conference in 1942, the United States was already in the war, so foreign policy was no longer divisive. Everybody was united behind the war effort. But the race issue was beginning to play a larger part.

We met at a leading hotel in Nashville. I had just gotten in when Jim Dombrowski said, "Virginia, we are having a meeting of the board." We went to the elevator and in the group there was Mrs. Roosevelt and Mrs. Mary McLeod Bethune, Jim Dombrowski, Dr. Charles Johnson of Fisk University, and me. The elevator operator, a young black boy, said to Mrs. Bethune, "I'm sorry, but you can't ride this elevator. You will have to ride the freight elevator." Well, Mrs. Bethune drew herself up in all her majesty and said, "Young man, Mrs. Mary McLeod Bethune is not freight." So with that, she began to climb the stairs and the rest of us climbed with her. The meeting was on the fifth floor, and Mrs. Bethune had awful asthma. She would pause at every landing and gasp. We were scared to death. Mrs. Bethune was a consummate actress, so we never could be sure just how much of it was asthma and how much of it was acting. When we finally got to the fifth floor, Mrs. Bethune said in a raspy voice, "Call the doctor. Call the doctor." Oh, God, we called the doctor and we called the manager and we called the ambulance and everything we could think of. Everybody was scared to death. She kept on wheezing and trying to catch her breath. Finally, the doctor came and gave her a shot. He wanted to take her to the hospital, but she wouldn't go to the hospital. She wouldn't do anything but stay there and make that hotel manager feel guilty. She had that manager scared out of his mind. Everyone could imagine the headlines: "Mrs. Mary McLeod Bethune Dies in the Presence of Mrs. Roosevelt Because She Wasn't Allowed to Use the Elevator." She scared the living daylights out of that manager. He apologized and carried on, and for that moment, segregation was forgotten in the Hermitage Hotel.

Louis Burnham, who was head of the Negro Youth Conference, had arrived at the hotel the day before and had run into the wall of segregation. He responded the way educated black people sometimes did. He put a towel around his head and said he was from India. The clerk registered him right off, a bellboy took his bags up to his room, and nobody minded at all.

Paul Robeson came down to Nashville in all his magnificence. Not only was he very handsome, but he had an overpowering dignity and presence.

When he sang, people rose up out of their seats. It was marvelous, just terrific.

The Nashville meeting went off pretty well, except for the fight I had with Frank McCallister. He was still going around red-baiting everybody, telling people that others were Communists and spreading suspicions. There was a fellow from the textile workers, Roy Lawrence, who was always saying to me, "Well, Mrs. Durr, I suppose that you want to know what the 'workers' think." He thought that was a really great blow to me to tell everybody that Mrs. Durr had to know what the "workers" think. When these red-baiters get out to mow you down and destroy you, a lot of them may be dumb, but they really make a concerted effort. There is no doubt about that.

The Southern Conference and the National Committee were both red-baited constantly. Morris Ernst was a lawyer from New York and an extremely brilliant fellow who had a reputation as a civil liberties lawyer. I had never met him, but he called me one day and said he knew a Wellesley friend of mine, named Jane Hellman. So he asked me out to lunch. He was a charming fellow and he'd come from Demopolis, Alabama.

Morris Ernst came to warn me against infiltration of the Communists and to tell me that NCAPT would never get anywhere unless we got rid of them. Oh my Lord, he had a list. Of course Joe Gelders was on the list. If we had anything to do with Joe Gelders, we were ruined. Joe was in the Army at that time, I believe, but in any case Morris was absolutely livid on the subject of Joe Gelders. The Fur and Leather Workers Union had contributed a little money to us, and they were an out-and-out Communist group. The head of it was a Communist. Many of them spoke with very strong accents and had learned their trade in Europe. They just gave us a little money, maybe twenty-five dollars a month, because they thought it was a good cause. But the head of it was a Communist, and Morris Ernst couldn't have anything to do with them. Then there was a union called the Marine Cooks and Stewards. I had never heard of it. But they were dangerous, and Morris Ernst had to get rid of them. In fact, we had to get rid of about half the people on the board to suit him.

I said to Mr. Ernst, "Look, we've only got one rule, and that is that everybody who supports the anti–poll tax bill can send a representative to the board. That's our rule, and that's the only rule we've got. So we're going to stick by it." Then he said the ILGWU, headed by David Dubinsky, would give us a lot of money if we'd get rid of these other people. Dubinsky had never given us any money before. Well, of course, he was dealing with somebody who was pretty dumb about all the distinctions in the unions in New York. I really wasn't up on the latest factions, and it irritated me considerably. We never did get any money from Dubinsky, I suppose because we were hobnobbing with Communists. The head of the Fur and Leather

Workers Union was a Communist. And I believe the head of the Marine Cooks and Stewards was. And then in the Maritime Union a West Indian named Ferdinand Smith was a union official and a Communist. They threw him out later on when all the big splits came.

The smaller unions didn't give us a whole lot of money. They would give us maybe twenty-five or fifty dollars a month. John L. Lewis was the one who gave us the most money. He was smart enough to see that the Southern oligarchy was ruining all the unions by keeping them from organizing. He wasn't bothered, at this point, about the Communists. Even though Communists were not allowed in the Mine Workers Union, he was using them to organize unions in the South. He was cynical enough just to send them South and let them be the shock troops, let them be killed and beat up and put in jail and do all the dirty work.

One of the things that saved me from being involved in all the factional fights was that my life was lived on so many different levels. My personal life was based on a neighborhood and a group of people who couldn't have been less radical in any way, shape, or form. They were lovely, sweet people, but they were not engaged in any issues. The New Deal was still radical to them. And of course there were no Negroes on Seminary Hill, except for servants. Then through Cliff's position with the RFC and the FCC, he was always in a position to do people big favors or not do them big favors. He had the power to give loans and radio frequencies or not. That, too, was a protection. And the issues were so split up. Burton Wheeler, who was an isolationist, was head of the Senate committee on communications, which controlled the FCC and transportation and communication of all kinds. And his daughter, who was at odds with her father, was secretary of the poll tax committee. Things in those days were pretty mixed up.

The poll tax committee was in the Railway Building then, and railway union people would print out sheets for us. They were behind the anti–poll tax bill and they couldn't have been any nicer to us. But trouble developed. When the railroads changed to diesel engines, there was a big fight in the unions about getting rid of the Negro firemen who had been shoveling the coal. A lot of the railway men, particularly the Southern ones, would come into our office and see Negroes working at typewriters and working on the anti–poll tax bill, and they didn't like it. They complained about their using the bathrooms—same old thing, you know. They didn't like that. So we had to move out.

We rented an office on Capitol Hill and moved up there. Mr. Roosevelt had been helping us all he could through Mrs. Roosevelt. Senator George Norris had introduced an anti–poll tax bill in the Senate, but he lost the election in 1943. We wanted Claude Pepper to take over as sponsor of the bill. Mrs. Roosevelt had a luncheon for him at the White House and invited Mark Ethridge and all the big shots. The food at the White House was never very good, but it was a nice lunch. There were beautiful flowers and all. She was just wonderful to us.

Frances Wheeler had gotten a job with the United Electrical Workers by 1941, and Sarah Hartman D'Avile had become secretary of the National Committee to Abolish the Poll Tax. She came from Pennsylvania from a very upper class family. She had been to Vassar and had then been a social worker in Memphis and Richmond. She became extremely radical, and I think she joined the Communist party for a while. In any case, she was a wonderful secretary and was there until the committee was finally dissolved in 1948.

In the poll tax fight, we were working to get legislation passed through the Senate and the House to remove the poll tax requirement for federal elections. Congress had the right in federal elections to do away with things like that, we thought. We tried to organize grass-roots support. We sent out letters and newsletters and had meetings and speakers all over the country. The unions and all other organizations that were part of the committee took up the cause. It became a tremendous issue.

Though I had a pretty large family by that time, I did some speaking but not a lot. I lobbied and raised money and went to meetings and just worked and worked. Cliff thought it became an obsession with me. The children would say, "Oh, poll tax!" I was reading *Bleak House,* about Mrs. Jellaby and her African project. I often wondered if my children didn't feel the same way hers did. They hated it so. But I was in contact with a tremendously broad sweep of people. We knew that we were backed by the White House and that was quite a support.

What organized opposition we had came from the socialists. They formed the Southern Electoral Reform League just to hurt the poll tax committee. They had put Mrs. Roosevelt on the list of people supporting the Southern Electoral Reform League, so she went down to the meeting and repudiated the organization. They said they were trying to abolish the poll tax on the state level, but they weren't trying to do anything but make trouble for us as far as I could see. Mrs. Roosevelt agreed. She wrote a long letter to me and said they were just organizing to hurt us.

I went along with the Southern Electoral League because I took the position that I would support anything that was against the poll tax. I didn't red-bait them. I was on their committee and I went to the meetings when they had them, but it didn't amount to a hill of beans. Very few of the states were ready to abolish the poll tax. The action was in Washington because the poll tax was becoming a national issue.

Now what was going on in the Southern Conference outside of the poll tax fight I really don't know. I had a very single-track mind. I thought the Southern Conference existed for the poll tax. I didn't have much of an impression of other issues at the time. I felt that unless people got the right to vote in the South, nothing would ever change.

Late in 1941, Sarah D'Avile and I went to see Mrs. Roosevelt to discuss our plans for the coming session. She was perfectly lovely. She had us out for tea on the south portico overlooking the Washington Monument and she couldn't have been more gracious and sweet and kind. She discussed what we should do and what she could do to help us. Then she said, "Before we go any further, I think I had better speak to Franklin and see what his ideas are." While she went in to speak with Franklin, the White House butler came out and served tea.

Mrs. Roosevelt was gone about fifteen minutes. When she came back she looked very upset. This was before she took voice lessons, and when she got upset her voice went very high and almost squeaked. She said that as far as Franklin was concerned he wasn't going to touch the poll tax with a ten-foot pole and she couldn't have any open part in it either. That's when he changed from Dr. New Deal to Dr. Win-the-War. Roosevelt needed the Southern senators so badly for his foreign policy that he decided he couldn't offend them on such issues as the poll tax. Mrs. Roosevelt said that whatever we did from now on, we would just have to do on our own.

But Mrs. Roosevelt remained concerned about the poll tax issue. I went to see her later and she and I together cooked up an idea that we would get a federal bill through to remove the poll tax for soldiers. She got together Tom Corcoran, Ed Prichard, and Ben Cohen, all big shots in the White House, William Hastie, who was dean of Howard Law School, and Dr. Nabrit, who was a professor at the Howard Law School. Mrs. Roosevelt rattled all the big guns. And we did have a bill drawn up to abolish the poll tax for people in the armed forces, for federal elections only. The Soldier Vote Act passed in September 1942, but the Southerners fought it tooth and toenail. They said it was the nose of the camel under the tent. That was the first victory we won.

The National Committee to Abolish the Poll Tax continued to get support from labor and black groups. The NAACP couldn't have been nicer. Mrs. Bethune was the representative of the National Council for Negro Women and was a tremendous help to us because of her close ties with the Roosevelts.

Mrs. Mary Church Terrell, who was head of the National Association of Colored Women, also helped NCAPT. She was a very light Negro and had lived in Washington for years. I first met her when she was on the NCAPT board. She was in her eighties then, a remarkable woman. Mrs. Terrell was the person who first broke segregation in Washington. She went into a chain restaurant and was arrested. Mrs. Terrell looked old and she dressed old. She wore high boned collars. My mother used to wear them. They were made out of net and whalebone. Their purpose was to hold up your double chin, I guess, or your sagging chin. They had little frills on top. Old ladies used to wear them all the time. You see, when people got to the age I am now, in those days, they dressed like old ladies. They didn't put a henna rinse on their hair. They wore black dresses and white frills and these high collars with whalebone. And it was very attractive really. Now everybody wants to be young, but then everybody just accepted the fact that they got old and so they dressed old and looked old. Mrs. Terrell wore a little bonnet and always wore black and always had on white gloves and pearls and earrings. She was a very handsome woman and very charming and intelligent.

Mrs. Terrell and I were very friendly. One day she said to me something about coming from Memphis, Tennessee, and I told her my mother's family came from Memphis.

"What was your mother's family name?" she asked.

"Patterson."

"You couldn't be the granddaughter of Josiah Patterson, could you?"

"Yes."

"Well," she said, "he was my guardian."

"My grandfather was your guardian?" This really gave me a turn.

"Yes, yes. I have a great many letters from him and from your uncle, Governor Patterson. If you will come to my house one day, I'll show them to you." She lived in one of the brownstones in Washington on an avenue with beautiful old trees. It was a nice old Victorian house with Victorian furniture. Her husband had been a municipal judge in Washington, one of the first black judges in the country. She showed me the letters from my grandfather and my uncle, and she told me the story of her family and mine.

My grandfather lived in Memphis and was a lawyer. He went off to the Civil War and one of his best friends was Colonel Church. He was a great soldier in the Confederate Army. As so many of them did in those days, Colonel Church had both his black family and his white family. His white family was very rich and fashionable. He also had his black family. He had a son whom he gave his name to, a black son called Bob Church, Jr. This was really unusual. This son was half black and he gave him his name and said, "Now look, you are my son. I have claimed you and given you my name and I don't want you to ever let a white man treat you like a nigger."

Well, Bob Church, Jr., became the black political boss of Memphis. He formed an alliance with Ed Crump and he provided the black vote for Crump. They would bring voters in from Arkansas by the truckload to vote in the Memphis elections. They controlled the city for years and years. And Mary Church Terrell was Bob Church's daughter. She had been sent to Oberlin College in Ohio, one of the first integrated schools. After Bob Church, Jr., died, his son broke with Ed Crump. He went to Chicago and became a political power in the Republican party. She told me the story and had the letters to prove it.

In his will, Colonel Church left some of his property to his black children and named my grandfather the executor and their guardian. That was the first time I had realized that all these relationships had existed. Some of the white men did protect their black children and educate them. In Alabama when Governor Oates was running for governor, men got up in the legislature and said, "Well, what about all those nigger children you've got in the backyard?" And the governor got up and said, "What about them? I feed them. I clothe them. I house them and I educate them. What do you do about yours?" He got elected.

Claude Pepper of Florida introduced the bill to abolish the poll tax in the Senate in 1941, and he did so year after year after year. But we had trouble finding someone to introduce it in the House. We had a meeting and Clifford McAvoy represented the CIO. He was a very nice fellow indeed, but I remember one of the things that people had against him was that he wore a derby. That was supposed to be a tremendous sign of swank in those days and they thought for a lobbyist for the CIO to wear a derby was too much. The CIO, through Clifford McAvoy, suggested we get a fellow named Joseph Clark Baldwin, who had just been elected to the House, to introduce the anti–poll tax bill. He was from a silk stocking district in New York, and he was a Republican.

By that time the House was not so heavily Democratic and the Republicans were helping us a great deal. Of course, a lot of Republicans backed us in order to create friction within the Democratic party, because the poll tax issue always split the Southern Democrats from the rest of the party. Republican support of our bill wasn't all pure idealism. Still, the bill would always be filibustered to death in the Senate. Baldwin wore a derby, too, and he carried a rolled umbrella. He was very gentlemanly and had been to all the best schools. We all thought he would be a great fellow to represent the anti–poll tax bill because he was just coming into the House and had made no enemies. So he was selected.

Then we heard that another congressman from New York, Vito Marcantonio, had a bill. He represented the Democratic party, the Republican party, and the American Labor party. He was elected on all three slates. So we went to see him, to tell him that we had met and decided to back Congressman Baldwin's bill and to ask him if he would withdraw his bill. Congressman George Bender from Ohio had a bill, too. Bender had already said he would withdraw his bill if we would all concentrate on Baldwin's bill.

When we went to Marcantonio's office we were met by his secretary, Miss Johnson, who was a very austere New England old-maid type. She looked as though she had been carved out of granite, but she was a very nice woman. I had taken along Miss Eleanor Bontecou. She had been dean at Bryn Mawr for a while and was working with us in the anti–poll tax fight. She later was in the civil rights division of the Justice Department.

We sat down and said in a very nice ladylike way, "Congressman Marcantonio, we have come to see you because the board of the National Committee to Abolish the Poll Tax has decided to back Congressman Baldwin's bill. We wondered if you would withdraw your bill so that we could all concentrate on Congressman Baldwin's bill. We are backing his bill because he is a Republican and we are trying to get more conservative support." Oh, my Lord, Vesuvius erupted! Whew! He sprang up and you never heard such a tirade in your life. "I withdraw my bill and let that Park Avenue fancypants . . ." He just raved on and on. He would not withdraw his bill. His bill was going to be the bill that got through and was going to be the bill that the House backed and as far as we were concerned, we could just go and drown ourselves. He didn't give a damn whether we supported him or not. Oh, he was mad, just furious!

We went back and had a meeting of the committee and reported what he had said. Well, Marcantonio was elected on the American Labor party ticket, the Democratic ticket, and the Republican ticket, and he got the Republican leadership to back his bill, he got the Democratic leadership to back his bill, and of course he was the only American Labor party person in the Congress so he got the American Labor party to back it. He even got Baldwin to withdraw his bill. We were faced with the choice of supporting Marcantonio's bill or having no bill. We either had to eat crow or we had to get out of the business.

We went to see Marcantonio again. He had won, so he was very nice to us this time. Any help that we could give him, he would be very glad to have. He was very pleasant. He had licked us good, too. We had to eat humble pie, I am telling you. From then on, we worked together very closely and he couldn't have been nicer or more helpful.

Marcantonio's wife and I became great friends, too. She was a New England blue blood who was about two feet taller than he was and had done social work. She had met him in Harlem. She was a charming woman and a wonderful person.

Marcantonio was the son of Italian immigrants, and he was the most perfect Jeffersonian I have ever known. He would work with anybody, but he was a Jeffersonian if there ever was one. He believed in freedom of speech and he believed in free voting and he believed in the Constitution and the Bill of Rights. And you could always believe Marcantonio; he never told you a lie. He was one of the most trustworthy men I have ever worked with. But the Catholic church refused to bury him when he died. He wasn't a Communist, but at that time you could have an organization of three thousand people and if three were Communists, the organization was a Communist front. So the Catholic church refused to bury him when he died because he was a member of some organizations that were said to be Communist fronts. They wouldn't give him the last rites or anything.

Marcantonio would get that anti–poll tax bill out of the House every time, but it always failed in the Senate. The Southerners filibustered it over and over again, but we did make it a national issue and we did abolish the poll tax for veterans. The poll tax was finally abolished by Constitutional amendment, but that didn't happen until 1964. Ironically, the amendment finally passed because of the cold war. This country was the great apostle of freedom opposing the Russians because they were totalitarian dictators, and it was awfully hard to explain to people why we had a poll tax that prevented citizens from voting.

I was friendly with both Senator Sparkman and Lister Hill during the effort to pass the poll tax bill, but they never would support us, of course. I knew that, but I was friendly with them anyway. I remember Lister Hill's telling me, "If you guarantee that this thing is going to pass, I'll support it, because the kind of folks that we'll get from abolishing the poll tax are the ones that will vote for me." But he knew we couldn't get it through because of the opposition. Lister Hill and John Sparkman were New Dealers. They never were really vicious. They filibustered civil rights bills, but they didn't race-bait and they didn't red-bait. In the South besides Claude Pepper, the other great friend we had for the poll tax fight was Estes Kefauver from Tennessee. Claude and Estes could support us because Tennessee and Florida had abolished the poll tax by state action. We really didn't expect to get Southern support. When we got Claude Pepper and Estes Kefauver, we thought we were terribly lucky.

When Jim Folsom got elected governor of Alabama he supported us, but he couldn't do much. He was trying to abolish the poll tax through the state. Ellis Arnall came later. He was for us, I believe, but I never knew him. Of course, Senator Byrd in Virginia was absolutely against us, as were Carter Glass and Howard Smith. I lived in Smith's district. I thought he was like an old buzzard picking over carrion. He was against the whole New Deal. He was against everything.

Almost all the Southerners filibustered the poll tax bill. I was the subject of one of Mr. McKellar's famous filibusters. He was a powerful and very conservative senator from Tennessee. And racist, oh my! My uncle had been governor of Tennessee and Kenneth McKellar had been a friend of his and a friend of my grandfather's. When I first met him he was so polite and nice to me. You would have thought he was just full of old-fashioned Southern courtesy. Well, McKellar got up on the Senate floor and you never heard such carrying on about me. Here I was a flower of the old South and my grandfather had been the congressman from Memphis and my uncle had been Ham Patterson, the governor of Tennessee, and why in the world would a woman like that turn into a—I think he called me a Communist, a nigger-loving Communist. It was just a horrible speech. His Southern courtesy certainly dropped away from him very promptly indeed. But the idea of old McKellar's calling me a tool of the Communist conspiracy didn't bother me in the least.

I was accustomed to having unpopular views, of course, and getting some opposition. My interventionist views before the war created some problems, particularly with the Lewises, but I really think the fact that I was inconsequential eased the tension. The real power lay in the unions, in the big organizations. I was a key figure, and I think I did a lot of good. All the different factions would come to me. But I myself had no power, no organizational power. I had no money and no power but I got along with the disparate groups who were backing the anti–poll tax bill. I didn't get mad at them.

I never could have any power through Hugo because the last thing Supreme Court justices' relatives can do is speak to them about a case. They recuse themselves immediately if that happens. If you were ever known to speak to Hugo about a case, that would be the worst thing that could happen. In fact, Hugo and Sister's dinner parties were pretty dull because nobody could talk about anything very much. They were always so afraid it would come before the Supreme Court. We usually talked about roses and tennis. And sometimes Bill Douglas would sing hymns. He was raised very strictly in the church and he knew the most marvelous array of hymns.

The one group of people I did get mad at were the red-baiters. Trying to abolish the poll tax was about as American a thing as you could do. The people who began to red-bait and put everything on that basis made me sore. In the thirties being a Communist wasn't equated with being a traitor or being a subversive or trying to overthrow the government by force and by violence. The big split came at the time of the Soviet-Nazi pact. Then when the Communists began to talk about the phony war, I got mad at them, too. But there were a lot of people who talked that way. Joe Gelders, for instance, swallowed that line whole. He thought that France and England were trying to get Germany to fight Russia and leave them alone.

At that point, the true Communists believed that Russia was like holy Russia, that everything had to be done to protect holy Russia. It was a religion. Russia was the first Communist country, or socialist country, and everything had to be sacrificed to it. I wasn't a part of all that. It was peripheral to my life. I was a New Dealer and I was for getting in the war and defeating Hitler.

Maxim Litvinov had been trying to get the democracies to combine against Hitler with Russia, but his idea was defeated time after time. Now Litvinov was a perfectly lovely man. I knew his wife, Ivy, who was a sister of David Lowe, the great cartoonist. She was English and Litvinov had met her when he was in exile in London. The way we met her was through some neighbors, Charles and Janie Siepman. Janie had been a student of Basic English, and when Ivy was married to Maxim Litvinov and living in Moscow, she was a great expert on Basic English. When Janie Siepman went to China to visit the Owen Lattimores, who were living in China at that time, she stopped by Moscow and got in touch with Madame Litvinov and took some lessons from her in Basic English. She and Madame Litvinov struck up a very warm friendship, so when Madame Litvinov came to Washington as the wife of Ambassador Litvinov, Janie renewed the acquaintance and they became devoted friends.

I first met Madame Litvinov in our car pool during the war. One day a white-haired middle-aged lady was in the car. It was in the summer and she had on a pair of sandals and no stockings and a cotton housedress and no bra and no girdle. It was about a hundred degrees. Washington can be the hottest place in the world, like a soup kettle, just steam. She looked like a nice lady and she spoke with an English accent. Since Charles Siepman was English, we thought she might be a friend of his. We never did get her name very well, you see. We were driving out to Seminary Hill and she was chatting away and then we passed a subdivision going up. It was called "Revolutionary Homes," and the lady remarked "Well, I don't think I see anything revolutionary about that."

We all thought that was very funny and someone said, "Well, what do you know about revolutions?"

"I know quite a bit about revolutions."

"Why?"

"Because I'm Maxim Litvinov's wife." That did make her sort of an expert, although she hadn't been through the revolution.

She was really a delightful woman and it is her son, Pavel Litvinov, who has been fighting for civil liberties in Russia and has now been expelled. He is in this country. He was one of the fighters with Andrei Sakharov for free speech in Russia.

I liked Ambassador Litvinov very much the few times I met him. In Washington you rose in the social hierarchy according to your husband's job. By this time Cliff was on the FCC and we got invited to the embassies.

I had read about Litvinov's fights in Geneva trying to get the democracies to stop Hitler, but I had come from almost perfect ignorance of politics. I knew Democrats and Republicans but that's all. I have always been more personal than ideological. I like people for themselves more than I do for their ideas. Sometimes they change their opinions and take on what I think are crazy ideas, but I don't throw them off and say they're heretics. I like to agree with people, but I don't mind disagreeing with them. I believe this is a Southern trait, a trait of loyalty. You don't just wipe people out because you disagree with them. So some of the Communists I liked and some of them I didn't.

One Communist we knew had been a professor at Johns Hopkins. He was an extremely sweet fellow, but he was always giving me great heavy books to read by Immanuel Kant. Well, I never could read them. They just didn't make sense to me. He was trying to win me over to the cause of Marxism, but he started me out on Kant. I can tell you, starting out on Kant is mighty difficult. I never got much out of it. But he was a very sweet fellow, and I had him out to dinner. Cliff and he got in several arguments, but we didn't feel threatened.

I felt absolutely safe. I was an American. It was my country. I had my administration in the White House. The wife of the president was my friend. I went to the White House for receptions. My husband was in the government. My brother-in-law was on the Supreme Court of the United States. I felt perfectly safe. Who in the world could accuse me of anything illegal or underhanded? Everything was perfectly open. People had different ideas, but that was all right. The United States was built on diversity and diverse views. I was either too ignorant or too safe, I suppose. I don't believe the country's ever felt that safe since McCarthy began that crazy business of accusing everybody of being a traitor.

I was raised in the church and, good God almighty, when I was a little girl the preachers used to sit around the table at my father's house and argue way into the reaches of the night about things that seemed to me to be utterly insane, absolutely ridiculous. They called the Catholic church the whore of Rome, for instance. I didn't know what that meant, so I looked it up, and I was quite confused, as you can imagine, but I grew to feel that those arguments were about as silly as those I was hearing between socialists and Communists. I wasn't afraid of different ideas or of the people who held them; I just thought it was silly to split hairs when it didn't get people fed or get them the right to vote.

We had some hints of the fear that was coming through Martin Dies. As soon as the La Follette committee got under way, Dies then started up the House Un-American Activities Committee. Dies then started the business of calling people Communists. He even called Shirley Temple a Communist. The WPA had a drama section for unemployed actors to put on free plays. Hallie Farmer was directing them here in Alabama. She was a Bryn Mawr sort of lady, very cultured. She told a congressman from Alabama who was on the Un-American Activities Committee that they had put on a play by Marlowe. Well, his first reply was, is he a Communist? We didn't take the Un-American Committee too seriously. It was just so stupid. The idea of its ever striking close to me was absurd.

Roosevelt gave people a tremendous sense of security, in spite of his getting sick and being crippled. He was always laughing and telling jokes.

Every time he'd be on the news reels he'd have that cigarette perched in the corner of his mouth. And if you'd go to the White House to a reception, he'd be standing up. I don't know how he was supported, but he was standing and smiling and shaking hands. It was a feeling of security. The depression was ending. We had a man in the White House who was doing something. And he got elected and reelected and reelected. The people were behind him. It was a great period. Unions were being formed and coming South. We felt we were making progress in the anti–poll tax struggle. The National Committee to Abolish the Poll Tax hadn't been hurt badly by the red-baiting yet. The country was at war, but we were winning it. Up until 1945, until Roosevelt's death, the country had a feeling of hope. We were going forward.

All the accusations of communism were just an irritating diversion. I hate to put on record how provincial I was. I had come from Alabama, but I'd gone to Wellesley and I'd gone to the National Cathedral School. Yet I'd had so little education in the real world. For a bunch of unions in New York to be fighting each other over socialism and Trotskyism and Lovestoneism and communism—well, it meant exactly as much to me as whether you got saved by total immersion or dipping. I thought it was just as silly.

Here we were booming along on the poll tax fight and it finally just ground to a halt over red-baiting. I took that very hard. We had Claude Pepper in the Senate and Vito Marcantonio in the House. We'd gotten support by then from around the country. We were really making the poll tax a major issue. Newspapers published editorials saying, How can you worry about Eastern Europe when in Alabama they can't vote? or How can you worry about the democracy of Greece when Mississippi can't vote? They were comparing the South to countries that had no democratic privileges or rights.

Now, I had been unequivocally for fighting Hitler from the very beginning. I knew it would put the poll tax issue on the back burner, but what good would it do to have the right to vote if Hitler took over the country? By this time I had read about children being burned up in furnaces and the death of millions of people and the terrible Jewish persecution. Hitler seemed to be a monster who had to be fought. I didn't blame the Russians for making the deal with Hitler at all. I thought that was an expedient thing to do to gain a little time to prepare. They must have known the Germans were going to attack. I did think it was awfully silly for the Communists over here to say the war was a phony war. I still think that was just crazy. And I'll argue with anybody today about that. Everybody knew the pact was phony. But there was nothing phony about Hitler's war.

We had a house full of people living with us during the war, as I've said, but the Japanese woman who lived with us and took care of Decca's child, Dinkydonk, finally left us. Half of her relatives were killed in Hiroshima and Nagasaki and she left us soon after that. She came to me weeping. She said she thought we were very nice people and she had been very happy with us but she could not work for Americans for a while. Her relatives in Japan were just obliterated. I wonder why she didn't murder us in our beds.

I thought the Japanese detention camps were terrible, but Hugo Black had voted to uphold them when they were challenged in the Supreme Court. I never argued with Hugo about his cases. He never liked to discuss his work on the Court at home. He may have discussed it with Cliff, but he never discussed it with me. If he was later sorry that he had voted to sustain the detention camps, I never heard it. Hugo was a very public man. All of his life he had been a public man. From the time he was a boy he wanted to be an orator. And he was a great public man. He could divine the public interest. He did make mistakes, I'm sure, and I think the Japanese detention camps decision was one of them, but he had a feeling for what the public wanted and needed. That's why he was so passionate about the First Amendment. He felt that when people couldn't discuss issues, then nobody could be free. That's one reason I always had such a feeling of safety around him.

When you grew up, didn't you feel safe? I was scared of snakes and runaway horses, but there really was nothing to be scared of in those days that I can remember—except hell. And my mother dispelled hell for me—told me that it didn't exist and it was ridiculous to pay any attention to it. I'm sure there was a great deal of fear in the world, but I wasn't aware of it. In the circumstances that I lived in I certainly wasn't afraid of black people, because they took care of me and nursed me and fed me and were my protectors. In fact, they were the people I depended on to look after me. I was only fourteen or fifteen during the First World War, and it was a long way off. No bombs fell on Alabama or New York. To me that war was a lot of good-looking young men with bars on their shoulders and learning how to dance and knitting sweaters.

Maybe we were protected from fear because we didn't have television then. The horrors of the world came to you through the newspapers and if you didn't read the newspapers for a week, you wouldn't know there'd been an explosion somewhere or that a thousand people had been killed by a volcano or whatever. The world was very much more restricted. Now TV shows people being killed and slaughtered every day, whole cities being blown up. It makes the world a pretty terrifying place. I don't know what it's going to do to young people unless they take it casually. They don't seem to know the difference between the ads and the news sometimes. My two-and-a-half-year-old grandson likes "Sesame Street" with its funny-looking monsters, and he thinks they're cute as they can be. If he sees somebody on the news that looks peculiar he says that's the Cookie Monster. What he sees on the news he relates to "Sesame Street." What this is going to do to people, I don't know. Art Buchwald had a marvelous editorial about the problem of telling the difference between the ads and the news. Well, how can a little two-and-a-half-year-old boy tell the difference between "Sesame Street" and the news? He thinks it's all the same thing. The play monsters and the real monsters are the same.

When I grew up, there was not so much danger from automobiles. You could play outside on the streets and skate and ride bicycles on the streets. The streets were ours. The streets were the province of the children. There were some cars, but you were not terrified for your life every minute. And the trains were a delightful way to travel. We just loved to go on a train ride. There weren't any airplanes. Maybe a few balloons. The world seemed safer in those days. I'm sure underneath all this there was fear. There were terrible things going on in Jefferson County—the convicts and the mines and the unions being broken up. But in the middle-class world I lived in you were protected, you felt safe.

When I went to Washington, I always felt absolutely safe. I would walk through the streets at night and come home on the bus at ten o'clock and walk from the bus, which was half a mile from our house. I wasn't scared. Cliff and I both had grown up in an era when we were not frightened. There was nothing much to be frightened of. Both our families had come over here in the early 1700s and had fought in the Revolutionary War. We had a sense—which I still have—that we owned the country. This may be an arrogant way to feel. I own it. It's mine. There may be things that make me mad and that I want to change, but it's my country. And this is my state. This is my county. As Cliff used to say, this is my side of the street. In other words, you felt you had a solid base. You didn't have a feeling of floating in mid-air. You had a solid base of reality to stand on—which may or may not have been the real reality, but that was the base you stood on.

When I got to Washington and began to deal with all these people who were at odds over various political ideas—communism or Trotskyism or Lovestoneism or socialism or Fabianism—it didn't affect me very much at all. It meant very little. It made me mad if they interfered with what I was trying to do, but otherwise I didn't pay too much attention to them.

I used to enjoy Marcantonio because he had the same feeling—that they all were so funny and a bunch of—well, I won't repeat all his words. If Martin Dies went on the floor of the House of Congress to make a violent anti-Communist speech, Marcantonio would arrange to have him called to the telephone as a joke. Marcantonio came from New York City and had lived on East 116th Street in an Italian community all his life. If he was ever scared of anything I never saw it. He felt perfectly safe, too. Of course, in the end the Catholic church wouldn't bury him in consecrated ground and wouldn't give him the last rites, but I don't think that bothered him very much. He had a marvelous sense of humor, and all of these fights over ideology were extremely funny to him.

Vito Marcantonio was a super politician. The people in the House liked Marc. They may have called him a red and a wop, but they liked him. He'd take the poll tax girls to lunch and he'd introduce us to everybody. There would be a lot of joking.

We had Marc and his wife to dinner one time, and I decided, since he was Italian, to have spaghetti—like somebody having me to dinner and having fried chicken. Well, he was so funny. I thought it was pretty good spaghetti. He ate it. Then he said, "Now, Virginia, that was fairly good spaghetti. But that spaghetti was not as good as it should be. You come out here and I will tell you how to cook spaghetti." And you know he took an hour to tell me how to cook spaghetti. You boil a huge pot of water—it would have to be like a washtub practically. And you don't put a whole lot of spaghetti in it, because it will stick together. It has to be all separate. Then you dip it out and you immediately put butter on it or something to keep it from sticking. Then the sauce, instead of being cooked from four o'clock to six o'clock as I had done, has to be cooked two days. And he explained to me in detail how to make the sauce—putting the little bit of sugar in and all. He was such a human man and he really wanted me to learn how to make spaghetti.

Marcantonio was a very straitlaced person in many ways. If he ever caught anybody in a lie, that was the end of them. He had a very, very strict sense of honor. Everybody knew that Marc's word could be depended on.

Marc's wife, Miriam, was a lovely woman. She had worked in a settlement house in New York and she had met him there on the Upper East Side. It was the strangest combination. She was a tall, slender, handsome New England aristocrat who came from one of the bluest of the blue-blooded families, and he was a short, fiery Italian. They were absolutely devoted to each other. I used to stay with them in New York, and we'd have such a good time. We would go out for dinner and everybody knew Marc and would greet him. We would eat in little Italian restaurants where the laundry was hanging overhead and the food was delicious. Then they would have the most marvelous breakfasts with Italian sausage and all. They were a very happy couple. They loved each other and seemed to have a great respect for each other. I became extremely fond of her.

After Marc died I went up to see Miriam. What a hell of a time she had after he died. She couldn't find a job. McCarthyism was in full stride. She finally took a job in Bellevue Hospital under another name. By that time she was terribly thin, and she had Marc's mother with her. Marc had a retarded brother, and his mother had never sent him to an institution. Eventually they had to put him in an institution after Marc died. Miriam then took care of Marc's mother, who had never learned to speak English. Finally she had to send her to a Catholic home because she cried all the time, just wept, wept, wept, and wailed. When she wasn't crying she was praying—both for the son who had been sent to the institution for the retarded and for the son who had died and not been buried in consecrated ground. She was either crying all the time or praying all the time. Poor Miriam was trying to make a living in Bellevue Hospital and keep them going, because Marc never had any money. He just gave it away. Congressmen made relatively little then, and Marc was very generous. He gave money away and helped people out. There was none left for Miriam when Marc died.

Miriam took me to see Marc's grave. He was buried near Fiorello La Guardia. He and La Guardia had been great friends and they had started out together. That was a painful morning. Marc's mother went with us and became hysterical. She tore her hair and screamed and cried and threw herself on the grave. It was awful. Shortly thereafter Miriam had to put her in a Catholic home where they spoke Italian. Miriam didn't live very long after that.

Southern Politicians

NOT ALL THE POLITICIANS we dealt with during the poll tax struggle had Marcantonio's sense of honor, as you can imagine. Jim Eastland certainly didn't. I had to take some sweet Southern ladies with the Women's Society for Christian Service of the Methodist church to see Eastland one day. The WSCS was one of the poll tax committee's greatest supporters, and these were very fine church women. A Mrs. Arrington from Mississippi was head of the WSCS. She came to Washington with eight or nine other women, and they stopped by the poll tax office. It was hot summer and they were all dressed like the ladies in Mississippi and Alabama dress, which I think is very pretty—light voile dresses, white shoes, white gloves, white beads, and white hats with flowers on them. They looked very lovely, I thought—very Women's Society.

They wanted to go to the Methodist Building for lunch. We tried to find some Negro women to take with us because the ladies from Mississippi wanted to integrate the building. They thought it was terrible that the Methodist Building wasn't integrated, and it wasn't for years and years. These were really remarkable women. And they wanted to go to see Jim Eastland, their senator.

Now this is an absolutely true story, a nasty story, but a true story. We went to Jim Eastland's office. Of course, I didn't want to go with them. By that time I had come to hate him, but they insisted that I go because they didn't know how to get around in Washington. So we walked into Jim Eastland's office, and his secretary saw these nice ladies from Mississippi all dressed up and ushered us right in to Jim Eastland. There he was, sitting at his desk. He rose when they came in and he shook their hands. Mrs. Eastland's sister-in-law was a great worker in the Women's Society for Christian Service of Mississippi. In fact, she was the secretary. There was something said about Mrs. Eastland's sister-in-law being a great friend and so forth. Everything started off very pleasantly until they came to the poll tax. And then do you know what he did? He jumped up. His face turned red. He's got these heavy jowls like a turkey and they began to turn purple. And he screamed out, "I know what you women want—black men laying on you!" That's exactly what he said.

We left very promptly and went to the Methodist Building for lunch. It was so embarrassing to these ladies that their senator had said such a thing. They tried to apologize to me. "Well, now, Mrs. Durr, you know the Eastlands. I don't know whether you know it, but they don't come from southern Mississippi. They come from northern Mississippi." That didn't mean anything to me, so I said, "What do you mean?" They said, "They come from the hill country, not the delta, you see. And they are not really, well, ah, they have made their money quite recently." What they were saying was the Eastlands were poor white trash who had only recently made money, that Jim Eastland was common as pig tracks and that was just the kind of remark he would make. They were so embarrassed for him and kept apologizing to me. They couldn't imagine that a Mississippi senator would say what he did.

Mississippi had a strange mixture of men who were almost insane on the subject of race, men like Congressman John Rankin and Senator Theodore Bilbo, who ranted and raved. They never stopped. But they were fairly liberal on economic issues. Rankin, for instance, always supported the TVA, and Bilbo, as horrible as he was, supported almost all the liberal economic issues of the New Deal. But they never ceased to rant and rave on race. I can't remember a single liberal congressman or senator coming up from Mississippi the whole time I was in Washington. They were all just as reactionary as they could be. Of course, Jim Eastland was the worst. I never thought John Stennis was anything but a reactionary either. He had better manners and was more of an aristocrat, but he certainly was as reactionary as the others.

In Alabama, we had a very liberal delegation in the 1930s, because my brother-in-law Hugo Black was a senator. Of course, John Bankhead was a senator, too, and he was no liberal, either on race or economics. The Bankheads were very conservative people. John Bankhead did support legislation to help the farmers, because he had a big farm himself. John's brother Will was Speaker of the House before Sam Rayburn. He was very powerful and an extremely attractive man. He was Tallulah Bankhead's father. Everybody called him Mr. Will. He was conservative and had a lot of charm and wit, but you never got anywhere with him at all. He'd act as though you were his best friend and he loved you to death and knew all about you, but then he'd keep on voting conservative.

John and Will Bankhead's grandfather had been warden of the prison.

That's how they got started in politics. At that time, the state rented out convicts. Of course, the convicts wouldn't get any money. Planters or mine owners would pay the state ten or fifteen dollars a month for each convict and they were supposed to feed them and look after them. Cliff's uncle had four hundred of them once in a stockade. He was paying the state for them, and they burned his house down one night. These were white convicts. But in any case, the convict lease system was one of the bases of the Bankheads' power. The old man finally got to be senator. They moved up to Jasper and had coal mines up there in which they worked convict labor. The convict lease system was just a substitute for slavery, but the convicts were treated worse than slaves. *Gone with the Wind* has the best description of the convict lease system that I ever read. The convicts were treated terribly. They were starved and beaten. I don't remember the exact date the system was abolished, but I remember that Hugo Black was one of the great opponents of it. I think it continued until the twenties. And it was in Georgia, too, all over the South. It was a terrible, terrible system.

Lister Hill was in the House from Alabama. Lister was liberal on everything but the race issue. He voted very well in the House, and then he came to the Senate and was a good New Dealer in the Senate. He never would tackle the race issue, and he got caught between the two opposing forces. The reactionaries didn't think he was enough of a racist and the liberals thought he was too much of one. So Lister got caught in the cross-fire in the sixties. Lister was a very good senator in every way except on the race issue. John Sparkman was also a good senator from Alabama. He and Lister and Hugo all fought very hard for the TVA, which at that time seemed a great step forward. And there was Congressman Luther Patrick from Birmingham, a very good man. So Alabama had a surprisingly liberal delegation.

In Texas, there was old Senator Connally. He wore long hair that fell down over his shoulders. He was head of the Foreign Relations Committee and was one of the most powerful men in the Senate. He was a pleasant fellow and had charming manners, but he was just as old-fashioned as he could possibly be. Sam Rayburn was more liberal than Connally by far and he upheld the New Deal, but he was never liberal on the race issue. His protégé, Lyndon Johnson, was liberal on economic issues. Of course, he was also liberal to the oil men, too, in Texas, but Lyndon always voted right on the New Deal economic issues. During the early years of the poll tax fight, Lyndon would put his arm around me—Lyndon put his arm around all the girls—and say, "Honey, I know you're right. I'm for you. I know the poll tax ought to be abolished, but we haven't got the votes. As soon as we get the votes I'll see that we do it." And he did. That was the surprising thing about Lyndon—when we got the votes, he did abolish the poll tax. But Lyndon's credo was "You can't get anything done until you get the votes." Young people think Lyndon was a perfect monster because of the

Vietnam War, but Lyndon was not a reactionary on economic issues and he was not a racist.

In Louisiana there was Huey Long. Huey ranted and raved, too, but not on the race issue. He would make the most outlandish speeches you ever heard, but he wasn't a racist. Huey actually believed in doing something for the people of Louisiana. He voted for every measure that would help them in any way, schooling or roads or anything that would help Louisiana or the people of Louisiana. And they all just adored him.

Huey Long was a strange man. I saw him make speeches on the floor of the Senate and I would be so embarrassed by his behavior. He was always scratching himself and getting wax out of his ears and picking his nose and picking his teeth. He was just vulgar. I could not believe he was so uncouth as to behave that way on the floor of the Senate. I think he thought that identified him with the common man. I heard him make a speech in the Supreme Court and he was well mannered and well spoken. He reminded me of a chameleon. He could be so many different things. But mostly he was loud and wore loud suits and red ties. I can remember his making raving speeches on Roosevelt. He was a great enemy of Roosevelt. Like George Wallace, he kept proclaiming that every man was a king. And he was fighting the big corporations of Louisiana. But the difference between him and Wallace is that he actually did something for the people of Louisiana.

Senator Walter George, from Georgia, was the epitome of the Southern gentleman. He had white hair and nice manners and was extremely powerful. His wife, Miss Lucy, always called him Mr. George. She was a cute little thing. She'd go everywhere with him. He was a right handsome man, but I never knew him to run around any or have any affairs. But she certainly did stick closer than a boa to him. If she wasn't with him, she was singing his praises, Mr. George said this and Mr. George said that. My sister belonged to a sewing club that Miss Lucy belonged to—for wives of Southern senators. I went there once or twice and Miss Lucy talked all the time about Mr. George this and Mr. George that.

Senator George was extremely conservative and was the first one that Roosevelt attacked in his purge in 1936–1937. That was the beginning of the fight against the poll tax, because Roosevelt realized after the failure of the purge that as long as his supporters—the poor whites and blacks and some of the small businessmen—were disenfranchised, he couldn't get enough support.

The other senator from Georgia, Richard Russell, was a very powerful man. He was a complete enigma to me. I met him a number of times, and he was always courteous and polite. He never married and he lived alone in a little apartment. As far as I knew he had no vices of any kind—except a love of power. And he was extremely reactionary and racist. But he had such nice manners and was pleasant to people, very popular with the men in the Senate. I met him once or twice at dinner at the Lister Hills'. He came from Winder, Georgia, and was one of eleven or twelve children. Dr. Jeb Russell, his brother, was the preacher at the Trinity Presbyterian Church in Montgomery when I came back to Alabama. The two brothers were exactly alike. They were always pleasant, always polite. They seemed to agree with everybody, but underneath it all they were as reactionary and racist as they could be.

Cotton Ed Smith was a senator from South Carolina. He was just a great mass of blubber and talked race all the time. "No nigger was ever worth more than fifty cents," he would say. He couldn't have been worse. I used to get embarrassed by him because he would always go on about the sex thing. If anything happened to change the Southern system, the white women would just rush to get a black man. We'd have a race of mulattoes. He and others like him seemed maniacal on the subject of sex. It used to embarrass me because I felt it was a terrible reflection on the Southern white man, that he was such a poor lover or husband or impotent or weak that the white Southern women just couldn't wait to get a black man. All the white men I had known had seemed to me to be pretty strong, potent men.

I also thought it was an awful reflection on Southern white women. These men who claimed to be Southern gentlemen would get up and make vile speeches about white women of the South and how they were protecting them. Every black man wanted to rape a white woman and every white woman apparently wanted to be raped. If you read those speeches today you really would be shocked by them, because they showed a kind of sickness, a Freudian illness. I really think those fears came from the fact that the white men of the South had had so many sexual affairs with black women. And they just turned it around. It's the only thing I can figure out that made them so crazy on the subject. Cotton Ed Smith was one of the worst.

The other senator from South Carolina was Olin Johnston. He came from up in the hills where the cotton mills were, and he had worked in a cotton mill. We thought he was going to be a liberal, because he was pretty liberal on economic issues—but talk about a racist! He was one of the worst racists I ever heard. He came out of a cotton mill and he was just nigger, nigger, nigger all the time.

Bob Reynolds came from North Carolina. He wasn't the millionaire Reynolds; he was the senator. He lived a very high life in Washington— wine, women, and song. When he was fifty-seven he married one of the richest girls in Washington. Her mother was Mrs. Evelyn Walsh McLean. She was only about seventeen or eighteen and she soon committed suicide, but he lived on. He seemed to thrive on his sins. The more liquor he drank, the healthier he was. The more women he seduced, the better off he seemed to be. He was most reactionary, always nigger-baiting and race-baiting and red-baiting. He would go back down to North Carolina and tell the people that his opponent ate Russian fish eggs. That was one of his great lines. These characters you couldn't imagine unless you saw them in action. Here he was dressed up in a three hundred dollar suit, married to the daughter of Evelyn Walsh McLean, who owned the Hope diamond, living a life of luxury, wine, women, and song, being just a man about town, and he could go back down to North Carolina and fool those people that he was their friend. He was the poor man's friend and the other man ate Russian fish eggs. Well, you can't blame him, but why in the world would those people down in North Carolina believe him? Maybe it's because he was so entertaining.

The Senate is supposed to be a gentleman's club. However they may have felt about each other in private—and I can tell you they had very strong feelings about each other in private—as a member of the gentleman's club, they would never say it in public. They would always say, the honorable gentleman or my dear friend from so-and-so. They would have had fist fights, I suppose, if they'd gotten up there and said, he's a low-down son-of-a-bitch and paid by the power company. They really couldn't have gotten along at all. So it was always, my honorable friend. But you could catch on pretty quickly as to who hated whom.

Hugo thought it was extremely important that Sister make friends with all the senators' wives, because he thought the social life in the Senate was where you got the real information. And she did. She made friends with all the senators' wives. She was about thirty when she went to Washington, and she was regarded as the prettiest wife in the Senate. Then when Henrietta Hill came up, *she* was regarded as the prettiest wife in the Senate, not only the prettiest but the youngest. They were very popular. All the senators were crazy about Sister and Henrietta and the wives liked them, too.

Hugo and Lister were powerful in the Senate and they worked with Roosevelt. At that time Roosevelt counted on them for his economic measures. They were very close to the White House, the sources of power. Then, after all, they were Southerners, too. Hugo and Lister didn't take any open stands on race. I don't think either one of them was really racist, but they certainly never took any open stands against racism. Hugo encouraged me all he could to do what I was doing, trying to get rid of the poll tax and work with the Democratic Women's Committee, but publicly he never took a stand.

Now, I lived in Virginia, the most reactionary state. Compared with Virginia, all the other Southern states were citadels of democracy, because at least they did elect poor men sometimes, even though they were racist—like Olin Johnston or Bilbo or Huey Long. But in Virginia they elected gentlemen, so-called. The vote in Virginia was the smallest vote of all, less than 12 percent of the electorate.

During the war, I was elected president of the northern Virginia PTA.

The PTA ladies said that I had to become a Virginia citizen in order to testify for the Virginia PTA before the congressional committee that was considering the bill to give federal aid to education. So I agreed to become a citizen of Virginia. I really liked the state. Cliff was an Alabamian from start to finish and never even thought about being a citizen of Virginia.

My neighbor across the way was Mary Walton Livingston. She was from the McCandlish family, who were prominent in Virginia. Her uncle was undersecretary of state. I asked her how I would go about getting to vote. She said, "Well, the first thing you have to do is get registered."

"Who is the registrar?"

"I will find out from the courthouse." She knew everybody at the courthouse, so she called up and found out who the registrar was and where he lived.

"Does he have a telephone?" I asked.

"No."

"How will I know he's going to be there?"

"You'll just have to take your chances." Now, this was during the war and gasoline was rationed, but I was allowed five gallons to go to register to vote.

I drove out an old road and came to an old country farmhouse. I asked the old lady who answered my knock on the door if I could see the registrar. I said I wanted to register to vote. She said he wasn't there and she didn't know when he would be back. I waited and waited, but dark came on and I had to go home. I went back a second time and he wasn't there. The third time, he was in and said he would be delighted to register me. Like most Virginians, he had nice manners.

He said to his wife, "Mamie, where is the poll book?"

"I think we've got it in a trunk in the attic."

"Well, you see if you can find it." So she went up in the attic and rustled around for a while, and finally she came back with the poll book. She thought no one would come to register during the war, because it was so hard to get gasoline and they lived way up there in the country. The registrar asked me for identification and then he asked me to sign the book.

"Do you have a pen?" I asked.

"No. Don't you?"

"No, I don't. I have a pencil."

"You can't register with a pencil."

"Well, let's see if we can't find a pen," I said. So the old lady began looking around, and she finally found an old rusty pen.

Then he said, "We don't have any ink."

"You don't have a pen and you don't have ink?"

"Well, I thought certainly you would have brought your own."

I told him that I certainly thought he would have a pen and ink. I said,

"You know, this is the third time I have been here trying to find you at home so I could register. I've spent fifteen gallons of gas coming here."

"Lady, that's just too bad. I don't have any ink."

I asked his wife if she knew of anything we could use for ink. She said, "Well, I've got some Mercurochrome. Let's mix it up with a little soot and see if we can't make ink out of it." And she did. She got the Mercurochrome and mixed it up with some soot, and it made a kind of pale red-blue ink. I signed the book and got my receipt to show I had registered.

When I came back home, I went to Mary Walton again and said, "Now, what do I do next?" She said, "You have to go up to the Fairfax County Courthouse and pay your poll tax." That was about twelve or fifteen miles away so I had to scrounge around for some more gas. Virginia required two years' back poll taxes plus the current year. The tax was $1.50 a year, so I paid $4.50. I thought, Thank God, this is over. I am registered. I've got my registration receipt and the receipt for my poll tax.

The next election, I went to the polling place down the hill from us. Mr. Donaldson, who ran the polling place, told me my name wasn't in the book. I said, "Mr. Donaldson, here is my poll tax receipt and here is my registration receipt. I must be on the book."

"You are not," he insisted.

"I just don't see how that is possible. What in the world could make me not be on the book?"

"Did you pay your interest?"

"My interest?"

"You know, when you pay your back poll taxes, you have to pay interest on them." I hadn't paid the interest because the people at the courthouse hadn't asked for any. They simply didn't want me to vote. If I had been a member of the courthouse ring, or somebody they knew, then they might have told me about the interest, but I was an outsider, a stranger. Now, I went to Wellesley for two years, and I had been working on the anti–poll tax legislation for five or six years. I was keenly interested in events and did my best to inform myself. But I still had a terribly hard time figuring out how to get registered to vote in Virginia. I had to go back to the Fairfax County Courthouse and pay twenty-seven cents before I finally got my name on the poll book.

Virginia was really the hardest state I've ever seen to get anything done in because the people in Virginia seemed to be so satisfied to be governed by the aristocrats. Virginia was interlocked by upper class that was all interconnected and had been for a long time. While a lot of them had lost their money, they still had the feeling that they were pure-blooded. There were great discussions of aristocracy and who was kin to whom.

Virginia had been modeled on the English landed gentry system, and the politics reflected this. Only a small number of people voted, and they

were controlled completely by the Byrd machine. Byrd was a very gentlemanly fellow, too, at least in his manners, and so was Carter Glass. Stirring
up the people of Virginia was very difficult indeed. The black people of
Virginia had lovely manners, too. Of course, they were the first people who
did begin to stir things up, trying to get the vote. They really worked hard
at it. There were several Negro professors at some of the Negro colleges
who led the struggle for the vote in Virginia. And they were Virginia gentlemen, too. Black Virginians and white Virginians seemed to me to be very
much alike.

The worst man of all in Virginia in my opinion was Howard Wirth
Smith. He was head of the Rules Committee in the House. He represented
my district. Smith was like a rock of ages standing there refusing to let any
liberal legislation through at all. Howard Wirth Smith looked like an old
buzzard, flapping his wings over the House. He was the most powerful
man in the House and one of the most powerful men in Congress. He'd
been there for a long time. Strangely enough, he was not an aristocrat. He
was just somebody the aristocrats used, but he was certainly their faithful
servant. I think he hoped that by being their servant he would rise into the
class of the aristocracy. He bought a big estate, and I understand that his
daughter or son married into the aristocracy.

Some may laugh at my use of the word aristocracy, but in the South
that I grew up in, that was a very common expression. It's now considered
to be bad form to talk in terms of class, but the South was absolutely class-
ridden, even in the black community.

Many of the Southern congressmen, after they got over the first flush
of enthusiasm for Roosevelt, formed a coalition with reactionary Republicans, which was really a third party in the Senate. The Democratic-
Republican alliance sometimes voted Republican and sometimes voted
Democratic—but always on the conservative side.

The Southern congressmen were just terrified of the race issue. They
immediately translated the fight against the poll tax into the race issue. The
Negro had no rights, couldn't vote, had no power whatever. The unions
were coming South and some of them were integrated. White Southerners
thought that getting rid of the poll tax would give all these people the right
to vote—the unions and the Negroes and all these new labor people. The
world would turn over. Cheap labor was the great selling point of the South.
Every Southern state, every chamber of commerce, and every corporation
thought the way to make the South prosperous was cheap labor. They also
were willing to take anything the United States government gave them.

George Wallace took every dime he could get out of the federal government, and the people who followed him took every dime they could get
out of the federal government. At least twice as much money goes to Alabama from the federal government as Alabama ever sends to it in taxes. And

of course New York and Chicago and other big cities in the North complain bitterly. The tax money comes South. Everybody who can get a federal grant in the South gets one, whether it's medicaid or medicare or unemployment or commodities. All the highways are built with 10 percent state money and 90 percent federal money. Alabama fought, bled, and died for all the federal military installations it could get. Montgomery alone has two or three. The thing that makes the South so schizophrenic is that it fights for federal benefits all the time and everybody who's elected is going to get them something, a new school or something for them. Then George Wallace runs for office complaining of interference by the federal government. The federal government's becoming your master. The federal government is your enemy. The federal government has made you bus.

Generation after generation the Southern people seem to think in terms that make no sense at all. When I get up and run for office—which I have done twice now for minor offices—I try to tell the voters that if they follow George Wallace they want commodities cut off, they want food stamps cut off, medicaid, social security, veterans' benefits, all cut off. That's their privilege, if that's what they want, but they can't have it both ways. But they do want it both ways and they won't listen. They'll go ahead and vote for George Wallace and for Ford and for Nixon, who are claiming that the federal government is just a monster, but they'll grab for every federal benefit they can get.

I suppose the thing in my life that has been the hardest to accept and to rationalize and to be cheerful about—though I try to make the best of it—is the fact that after all the struggles we had to get the vote and after all the struggles we had to get women to vote, we got Lurleen Wallace and George Wallace. The people of the South were freed. They got the right to vote. The black people got the right to vote, the white people got the right to vote. Even illiterates got the right to vote, under the federal laws. And whom do they elect? I hate to think the Southern people are just naturally stupid, but it seems to me that for generations they have just cut their own throats. They march off to the Civil War not owning a slave, and thousands of them get killed. For what? So somebody else could own slaves and have a big white plantation and be rich. And what was it to them? Not a damn thing, yet they went off and died for it. They're doing the same thing now. They get the vote; they're free. And whom do they vote for? They vote for George Wallace.

Of course people vote for pretty lousy characters in the North, East, and West, too, but it seems to me we Southerners can pick some of the worst. Look at Jim Eastland. He got elected year after year in Mississippi after so many more people in Mississippi got the vote. There must be some reason for it. If the rich voted for one group and the poor another, it would make some sense, but it's not that at all. The poor vote for the rich. This is what makes the South so puzzling: the poor man will vote for the guy who's representing the rich man and fooling him by saying he's for them when he's not for them at all.

There are millions and millions and millions of people in the South. Now they're free. The poll tax is gone. The literacy tests are gone. The women are free to vote and the men are free to vote. The blacks are free to vote. Eighteen-year-olds are free to vote. I think people are confused and maybe they're ignorant. And I think people have lost faith in democratic government. I think they no longer believe that it makes any difference whom they elect, that a few rich men will still control everything anyway.

We're living in an age when people just want a decent life. They want a house and an automobile and good medical service and good education. But they don't think politics has anything to do with that, because they hear promises and promises and in the end they don't get anything.

I haven't lost faith, because I think people will eventually wake up. It's going to get much worse before it gets better. And my fear is we're going to become a corporate state with tremendous repressions. How long that will last, I don't know.

Cliff had much more faith in people. He had faith in their intrinsic goodness, their intrinsic worth. He knew that I wanted to help people, that I really hated to see people suffering. But he also thought I really still believed that some people were a whole lot better than other people. He thought I was a snob. He didn't think it was so much on a class basis—money or clothes or social position. But he thought I was a snob about ignorant people, people I thought acted in a dumb way. He had more faith in people than I do. And he had much more tolerance of them. I'd say, "Well, why in the name of God would he do anything as stupid as that? To go and vote for that Republican masquerading as a Democrat, somebody who's absolutely nothing, a tool of whoever pays him, whether it's corporate interests or whatever." And Cliff would say, "Well, what can you expect of the fellow? What does he know any different? Who ever told him any different? What has he ever learned? What does he get?" He had much more tolerance. I get mad. I want to shake people and say, "Stop being so dumb and cutting your own throat. It didn't do you any good to go off and fight for the slave civilization. What good is it going to do you to fight for the corporate civilization?"

Cliff thought you had to be very gentle with people—you couldn't antagonize them, make them mad. I find the people in Elmore County, where I now live, as nice as any people I have ever known in my life. They are pleasant. They are courteous. They are gentle. And they'll help you out. When Cliff died, they came around in droves. They are nice people. On a personal basis, I like them very much. And I like living here because it's so pleasant. And yet they'll vote for George Wallace. This is something I just can't explain. It's beyond me. Or they'll vote for Richard Nixon. Richard Nixon made them believe that he was for the little man. How could he have made them believe that?

II

The Beginning of the Cold War
and the End of the
Poll Tax Committee

THERE WAS A GREAT feeling of victory in Washington when the war ended, but the overwhelming emotional outburst came at the death of Roosevelt. His death really marked the end of the New Deal. I can remember the day of the funeral. We took the children and went into town to see the funeral cortege. People lined the streets by the thousands, many of them in tears.

The people on the inside of the White House knew that Roosevelt had had a stroke and was ill, but the public at large, of which I was one, thought he was just as happy and healthy and cheerful as always. Up until the war, we would be invited at least once a year to the White House, and the president always looked just the picture of health. But those public social events were canceled during the war, so most of us hadn't had a chance to see him face to face for a long time.

Mrs. Roosevelt always looked well, too. She and I never became real friends, although she did write me some very warm letters. She often called me Virginia, but of course, I always called her Mrs. Roosevelt, so there was never really an intimate relationship.

Mrs. Roosevelt was a very intense person. Whatever she was interested in, whatever she was talking to you about, was the most important thing in the world. She made you feel that her whole being was concentrated on getting rid of the poll tax or helping the sharecroppers or coming South and doing what she could. She would often be repetitive and tell the same little tale over with the same little laugh. She told all the Southerners repeatedly that her grandmother came from Georgia and was a Bullock. Well, that's the family that Bullock County is named for, where my family came from down below Tuskegee, so I knew all about the Bullocks and Bullock County and Colonel Bullock. But I bet she told that tale fifty times. She was trying to identify with the Southerners.

Mrs. Roosevelt was particularly friendly with the young people who were in the Southern Conference Youth Committee and the Southern Negro Youth Conference. She kind of adopted some of these idealistic young people. She would invite them to the White House and give them the best guest rooms. Of course it was a thrill for a boy from Tennessee or Texas or a country boy like Howard Lee, an Arkansas sharecropper's son who became executive secretary of the Southern Conference for Human Welfare in 1939, to sleep in the White House. Mrs. Roosevelt defended many of these youths against accusations of being reds or radicals, but the Soviet-Nazi pact of 1939 changed all that.

Ambassador Litvinov had failed to get the Western democracies to unite with Russia against Hitler. Litvinov's overwhelming mission for the Russians and for the new Russian revolution was to get the West to join with Russia to fight Hitler, who had pledged to wipe them all out and reduce them to serfs.

The Russians would hold big cocktail parties at the embassy, and I would sometimes go. They would just put on the dog. They would have great swans carved in ice and the whole middle would be full of fresh caviar. People would go to these parties for the caviar whether they liked the Russians or not. The greediness of people was just beyond belief. They'd eat enough caviar to fill up a tank.

The people at the Russian embassy parties were interesting. One man that I met there had a beard and spoke fairly good English. He was rather a famous figure, a world diplomat of that time, from Bulgaria. I said, in my usual Southern chit-chat, "Oh, you're from Bulgaria? How fascinating. What part of Bulgaria are you from?" He was from the South. "So you're a native?" No, he wasn't a native of Bulgaria. He was a native of Montenegro, I believe. I said, "So you grew up in Monte. . . ." "No, no. I grew up in Athens." By this time I'd given up. I had this Southern instinct to place people, to ask who their grandfather was and had they lived in Montenegro long. Finally he said to me, "Madame, just say I am a salad. I am a salad," he said, "like I come from every country."

The Russian parties were a barometer of United States–Soviet relations. When relations were bad, a third secretary would come from the State Department, some lowly character. If relations were good, then the secretary of state would come with all his entourage. You could always judge how things were going by whom the various countries sent.

After Litvinov failed to get Western support, the Russian line changed. The Russians are not very gentle about shifting gears. They threw out Litvinov and put in Molotov. This was just before the European war broke out, before Germany marched into Poland.

But in 1939, before the war broke out, Russia and Germany signed a nonaggression pact, and it really split the United States. Leftists in this country had generally been anti-Hitler, and now they were asked to defend Russia's apparent alliance with Hitler. Organizations with political interests soon split into those who defended Russia's pact with Germany and those who condemned it. The pact broke up all kinds of organizations.

The Communist party of the United States was regarded as having allied itself with Hitler. People wouldn't speak to each other and would refuse to sit in the same room. In the poll tax committee I would have to say, "Now look, we came here to get rid of the poll tax. If you're going to fight about the Stalin pact, you're going to have to do it outside." I wasn't on any side, because I thought the pact was sensible from the Russian standpoint. Hitler had been saying for twelve years he was going to smash the Russians flat and make them serfs of the Germans, who were the superior race. I thought the Russians were just buying time to build the country's defenses. The pact affected me primarily because I had to keep the poll tax committee from launching off into a destructive fight, but I was not really interested in the pact itself. I was just interested in getting rid of the poll tax so people could vote.

Many of the young people that Mrs. Roosevelt had been nurturing, like the Young Southerners and the Southern Negro Youth Conference, split up over the Hitler-Stalin pact. The pact supporters had a big rally on the White House south lawn. President Roosevelt came out with Mrs. Roosevelt and he gave them holy hell. He said it was awful for them to say that this Hitler-Stalin pact should be supported. He told Mrs. Roosevelt not to have them in the house any more. At that point, she said that they had fooled her. All the time she's been so kind and nice to them and had them staying there at the White House, they had been underground Communists and fooled her. Now that they had come out in their true lights, she repudiated them.

Now, I knew many of these people, but I never turned on them. We had raging fights, but I never got so mad at them that I wouldn't let them spend the night if they didn't have a place to stay. Cliff would get mad at them, too. He thought these young people had been terribly misled.

These kids, like so many young people today, had a sense of disillusionment about their own country. The New Deal hadn't filled them with hope and glory. They still felt that the country was not their country because the capitalists owned it. They had become radicalized, but they were not violent at all. They took it all out in fighting each other, having different organizations and accusing people of being Trotskyites and Lovestoneites. But when this country finally did enter the war, these young Southerners—people like Howard Lee, who had supported the American Peace Mobilization, an anti-interventionist group—went off to war and fought. They didn't escape to Canada or go to Mexico. They believed in the war finally, particularly after Germany attacked Russia and they thought Russia was in danger.

By the mid-forties, the world was changing, and so were the Southern Conference for Human Welfare and the National Committee to Abolish the Poll Tax. Roosevelt died in 1945, the same year the war ended. The National Committee to Abolish the Poll Tax closed its doors in the summer of 1948, and the Southern Conference for Human Welfare did the same in November of that year. The poll tax committee died the same way the Roosevelt coalition died, the way the whole liberal movement of the United States died. It became exclusively anti-communistic. The red-baiting had been happening from the beginning of the conference in 1938, but it got worse and worse.

In February 1946 a terrible incident happened near Nashville, in Columbia, Tennessee. State guardsmen and police rode through the black community shooting at houses. The black people stayed in their homes with the shades down, scared to go out to get a loaf of bread or a bottle of milk. Dozens of blacks were arrested and beaten up, and two of them were shot and killed while being questioned. The whole episode had started because of a fight between a black soldier who had just returned from World War II and a white man.

Jim Dombrowski had set up a national office for the Southern Conference for Human Welfare in Nashville, and after the shooting he and some other people started a committee to protect the people in Columbia. I was a member of that committee and we met in Washington at the YWCA. There were lots of people there, left-wing union people, right-wing union people, and so forth. The day after the meeting, I got a call from Walter White in New York. He was a black Southerner who went to work in the national office of the NAACP in 1918 and became something of an expert on lynching investigations.

"Mrs. Durr," he said, "we are forming a committee to protect the people in Columbia and I want you to join."

"Well, Mr. White, I have already joined the committee."

"Mrs. Durr, if you join *that* committee, you are going to be sorry. It has Communists in it." This was so typical: two committees were formed and the New York committee wouldn't have anything to do with the Washington committee because New York said there were two Communists on the Washington committee. I can't even remember who they were talking about.

There was also a lot of tension between Dombrowski and Clark Foreman, who were the main leaders of the Southern Conference during the forties. Some said I acted as a bridge between the two, but it was more like walking a tightrope. You couldn't have had two more different people. Jim was the most meticulous human being I have ever known. There wasn't a cent that was spent that wasn't duly noted. He was very slow because he was so meticulous. Every dime was accounted for. Everything had to go through the proper channels. Everything had to be certified and checked and rechecked. Clark was an impetuous, quick person. He would have a bright idea and would want to get the money for it and put it into action right that minute. He would run here and run there until he got it done. Of course, Jim always wanted vouchers and inventories and receipts. It would drive Clark crazy. He and Jim were constantly at odds. They both had great qualities, but they got on each other's nerves. We just tried to keep them going together and not flying apart.

Don't ask me how we kept them together. It seems to me that I spent hours and days in my life trying to make peace between them. It was really difficult. There was no competition between them about the leadership role. Jim was perfectly satisfied being the secretary and had no desire to be director. They just had completely different personalities. It was a very trying period.

The Southern Conference did hold together, for a while anyway. Once, during this time, the executive board met in Greensboro, North Carolina, and we had permission to meet in the local hotel. When lunchtime came, though, Jim got up and in the sweetest way said, "Now I'm terribly sorry, but the hotel won't serve any of our black members, so we have arranged for you to be carried over to the Negro school for lunch." Well, Mrs. Bethune got up and let out a real diatribe. She said, "Now look, Jim Dombrowski, when you arrange a meeting, you arrange for us to eat together. We are not going to be shunted off this way." She got very upset about it and refused to go over to the black school to eat. I said, "Mrs.Bethune, you come on up to my room and I will get you a sandwich." I wanted her to lie down because she was an old lady and I was worried about her. She didn't have an asthma attack that time, but she was pretty agitated, and she got everybody else pretty agitated, too.

I took her up to my room and she lay down on the bed. I called down to the dining room and asked if I could have lunch sent up to the room. They said yes. I asked for two chicken sandwiches and two glasses of iced tea. Well, in about five minutes here came in three black waiters, not one but three. They set up a table, put on a white cloth, and set the table beautifully. Then they brought up the sandwiches and iced tea and they stayed and served Mrs. Bethune and me, one behind each chair and one to serve. This was their way of showing Mrs. Bethune honor, and she sat there like a queen and ate her sandwich and drank her iced tea with these three black waiters just bowing and scraping. She was a powerful woman. She broke segregation in that hotel, too. That's the second time she did it. She didn't let anybody fool around with her.

This was at the beginning of the cold war. Roosevelt had died and

Truman was now president. Arthur Goldberg was counsel for Phillip Murray's CIO then. Lee Pressman, who had been general counsel for the CIO and had helped get the whole CIO started, had been fired because he was too red. He later became an informer and told who all his Communist friends were, but he was a brilliant lawyer and had done a lot of good.

There were a few Communists around the poll tax committee. There was the young professor at Johns Hopkins who was always trying to get me to read Kant, but after the red-baiting got bad, he stopped coming around to the office.

You see, we were surrounded by the FBI. We were always having strange young men come in saying that they wanted to be volunteers—saying their name was Joe Smith and they worked in the Post Office Department but they had a few days off and wanted to do volunteer work. As soon as they left, I would call the post office and find that no Joe Smith ever worked for the post office. We knew they were FBI people. The first thing they would always want to do when they came in was to get hold of the mailing list. We would not only give it to them, but we'd say that we would appreciate their making several hundred copies of it because we needed more copies to send out all over the country. This was in the days before photocopying machines, of course, so these young men would work for hours on end cranking out mimeograph copies. Then they would say, "Now we would like to see the list of donors." And we would give that to them. They would have complete run of the files. It was all open and aboveboard. We would say, "If you don't mind, we need about five hundred copies of the donor list." They would grind them out and almost drop in their tracks.

The only active Communist that I know of who was working in the office at that time was an old lady. She wasn't really so old, I suppose, but she seemed old to me at the time. Her name was Sarah Rosenbaum, and she was Eugene and Walt Rostow's aunt. The Rostow brothers became prominent for their work in the Kennedy administration. Sarah's family came over here from Russia around 1900 and her father was some sort of religious leader. They had been helped by a Jewish committee that rescued people from the pogroms in Russia, and the family settled on a big farm near New Haven, Connecticut. Her mother got some cows and kept the family alive. The children would milk the cows before they went to school and then they would distribute the milk in the afternoon. They worked awfully hard. And the old gentleman, her father, would sit by the fire reading the Torah with his yarmulke on his head. He was a religious man and wasn't supposed to work. But the old lady and his children worked mighty hard.

Now Sarah Rosenbaum was an out-and-out Communist. She was the cutest thing. She used to make cocoa on the radiator. She was perfectly delightful. She later opened a Marxist bookstore in Washington. Many people were sent to jail and lost their jobs because they belonged to Sarah's Marxist bookshop. She finally went to California to live with her daughter, who lives out there now. I got a card from Sarah's daughter after Cliff died. Sarah would send me copies of letters she wrote Gene and Walt Rostow, her nephews. They were supporting the Vietnam War, and she would just tear the skin off them. You never read such letters in your life, how they were betraying the family and disgracing the Jews.

The FBI people would try to get Sarah, but she was perfectly open and frank with them. The FBI never really got anything on the committee because it was open to everybody. It was a completely open organization. They always wanted our contributors' list to see how much gold we were getting from Moscow, but nobody ever gave us much except the unions. They were the only big contributors.

The war was over and the National Committee to Abolish the Poll Tax still existed, but the labor movement had changed. During the war, the CIO had formed from unions that split off from the AFL, and the AFL refused to come to the poll tax committee as long as the CIO was there. This is the way the groups just doomed the causes they really believed in. The AFL was in a power fight with the CIO, and the AFL leaders sent word that unless we got rid of the CIO they wouldn't come to the meeting. We had an absolute rule that anybody could come to the meetings, any organization that supported the anti–poll tax bill, so we couldn't very well exclude the CIO just because the AFL was feuding with them.

When the AFL got mad at the CIO, our main source of support was threatened, and that was the beginning of the end of the NCAPT. Then John L. Lewis got mad at Phil Murray and pulled his mine workers out of the CIO. Lewis had given us a lot of money and been wonderful to us. He sent word that if we didn't get rid of those leftist CIO unions, he couldn't support us any more—and he didn't. Then the CIO split right open. We had lost the Railway Brotherhood on the race issue, we had lost the AFL on account of the CIO, we lost the mine workers on account of the CIO, and then, by God, the CIO split! That was the fatal blow. They kept together during the war, but when the war was over and Truman came in, the red-baiting just overwhelmed us.

We had a meeting and Hoyt Haddock was there from Joe Curran's Maritime Union. Joe Curran had been a Communist or was supposed to have been one and then he flipped over and became an anti-Communist. Keeping up with these people was almost impossible. Haddock was a great big fellow from Texas who worked for Curran. He used to appear before committees and we used to write his speeches for him, because he wasn't very literate. We found out later that he represented the ship owners *and* the Maritime Union. He was playing both sides of the street. We went to his house once or twice for dinner and wondered where he got his money.

He was living in luxury, serving Napoleon brandy and all. As it turned out, the ship owners were paying him about $35,000 a year while he was working for the union. We didn't know anything about it at the time. We still thought Hoyt was our friend. He said, "Now look, I've been talking to Phil. He says to tell you girls that we will support you and get you money and do everything we can for you, but you have got to get rid of some of these unions you've got in there."

By that time, the CIO was having a purge. They got rid of Harry Bridges's union, the International Longshoremen's and Warehousemen's Union, and the United Electrical Workers Union and the Mine, Mill and Smelter Workers Union and the Fur and Leather Workers Union. And they got rid of the Marine Cooks and Stewards. They got rid of all the left-wing unions whether or not they had any Communists in them. If a union didn't bar Communists, the CIO got rid of it. We sent word that we were not going to purge and were going to stand by our principles, so Phil Murray sent word back that that was the end of CIO participation in the poll tax committee. At this point, we were down to the left-wing unions, the civil rights organizations, and some of the religious organizations. The last meeting we had took place about 1947.

As I look back now, I don't think that the poll tax committee ended in a blaze of glory. Just two years after the war was over, a representative of the Jewish Anti-Defamation League, which was on the committee, asked us to meet at his office. We didn't have offices at this time. Money was running out and we were having a hard time, so we met this man in his office. He said that the Anti-Defamation League and some other Jewish organizations were going to be very helpful. They would raise money for us and would do all they could to help us. There was just one proviso. He had the attorney general's list of subversive organizations and he wanted to be sure that nobody in the committee was on the list. He picked on the National Lawyers' Guild and two or three other organizations. He said they would all have to get out. I asked him why. He said they were all on the attorney general's list.

"You mean to say you are going to use the attorney general's list to decide who can be on this committee?"

"Now, Mrs. Durr," he said, "you have got to be realistic. The United States government is starting to purge all leftists and Communists and radicals of all sorts, and we have to do the same thing or we won't get any support."

I was pretty tired of that line by then. I looked at this man and said, "You know, you are the kind of Jew that brought on Hitler." I didn't mean that Jews were for Hitler. I just meant that if you didn't fight fascism from the start, it ate you up.

That was the end of the poll tax committee. It was a pretty bad ending,

I'm afraid. We stood by our principles, but people didn't stand by us. Everybody began to purge. The NAACP purged, the unions purged, everybody purged. NCAPT just fell apart. Nobody supported it. We didn't have backers who had money and we couldn't rent an office. The backbone of the New Deal and of the poll tax committee and of most of the liberal organizations in the country was the unions. When they broke up, we didn't have any solid support at all.

Still, the poll tax finally was abolished, so we did feel that we had done some good. It took a long time, but a constitutional amendment finally abolished the tax for federal elections. Then Lyndon Johnson abolished it for state elections in the Voting Rights Act. So Lyndon did what he said he would do. His Voting Rights Act got rid of impediments to the vote.

During the war, the relationship between the United States and Russia had been pretty close. There were Russian and American concerts to raise money for the wounded or the Red Cross. People like Mrs. Daisy Harriman and Mrs. Eisenhower would be chairmen. Constitution Hall would be draped with the Red flag and the United States flag. The Russians would sing and dance, and the Americans would sing and dance. Russia was very popular, and all the fashionable people would attend. Mrs. Marjorie Post, the heiress of the Post Toasties fortune, would open her house to Russian-American parties.

When World War II ended, we felt we were on top of the world. We had defeated Hitler, and Henry Wallace was talking about the brave new world and milk for the starving. Wendell Willkie was going around the world making speeches saying we were all in one world. There was a period of euphoria when the Russians and Americans met on the Elbe and shook hands. The Russians were going to be more democratic, and we were going to be more socialistic. The two countries would be great friends and keep peace in the world.

As a result of the building of industry during the war, this country had the biggest industrial plant in the world, completely untouched. The German industrial plant had been bombed by the British and the Americans. The French industrial plant had been pretty well ruined during the war. Italy was a shambles. Spain was a shambles. The only other industrial base left in the world except ours was what the Russians had moved behind the Urals. We had lost a good many men in the war, but compared with Britain or France or Russia or Germany, we'd lost only a handful. We were the richest and most powerful nation in the world.

Truman abolished the lend-lease program a couple of months after the war. All the devastated countries of Europe that had depended on us to rehabilitate them had to pay for what they got. In 1947 the Marshall Plan went into effect. The Marshall Plan was an effort to refinance the foreign governments, but Russia didn't join in because if it had, it would have had to become capitalistic. It would have had to allow American companies into Russia, as I understand it. Of course, the Russians didn't like that a bit. That's when the cold war really started, when Russia began to close its borders and be anti-American.

Almost overnight, the attitude toward Russia changed. Anybody who had ever sympathized with communism or had belonged to an organization that did was now suspect. And this attitude affected everything.

Molotov came over to the United Nations, and Truman insulted him, gave him absolute hell. They had a tremendous fight, and Truman eventually became a great anti-Communist. He really believed that communism was godless and anti-Christian. He became terrified that communism would sweep the world.

Cliff went to Russia in 1946 for the FCC in an effort to reestablish communications connections, and he said he didn't think the Russians would sweep anywhere because the Russian people were so exhausted. The country had lost twenty-five million people. When he flew from Berlin to Moscow, he saw hardly a house standing. People were living in caves. The Germans had killed all the animals. It was a desolated country. They kept the thermostats in public buildings around thirty-five degrees just to keep the pipes from freezing. Everybody was huddled in overcoats and gloves and scarves. The only thing that kept Cliff from freezing to death was the tea, and of course that was served in glasses that burnt your hand.

The fear was that since the Russians had won, Communists would take over the world. In all the European countries there had been strong underground Communist movements. I don't say everyone in these movements was a Communist by any means, but there had been a very strong underground movement that included Communists. Many of them were elected to government offices just after the war. The United States feared that they would take over and the countries would go Communist. So the deal was that we would give the countries money if they got rid of the Communists.

Our government would only deal with the conservative factions in these countries. That's what happened in Greece. The Greeks had a very strong underground during the war, and the underground had fought against the Germans. When the Germans were defeated, the underground expected to take over the country, and they were mostly Communists. But then the English came in to prevent a Communist takeover, and the English called on us for help. We sent in people to keep the guerrillas from setting up a government. Greece had a civil war and we took the side of the anti-Communists.

In Turkey something similar happened, so our country decided to promise to keep the Communists out of Greece and Turkey. That was the first anti-Communist pact. After that we made them right and left. There wasn't any mystery behind it—we were scared to death that communism would sweep the world.

People weren't afraid of the American Communist party. By that time the American Communists were so anxious to get money for Russia to rebuild that they had dissolved the party. They had a meeting and declared themselves out of business. This was when Earl Browder was the party's secretary. They wanted to form a united front again, all of the leftists together—mainly in hopes of getting loans to help rebuild Russia. The Russians never did think the American Communist party amounted to much anyway.

All this time, some men were trying to keep the wartime alliance going— United States, England, France, and Russia. After the Allies divided up Germany, the countries stopped collaborating pretty quickly. And anti-Communist sentiment in this country kept growing and growing. Henry Wallace got fired from Truman's cabinet because he made a speech in Madison Square Garden about keeping the Alliance going. Even Claude Pepper was making speeches supporting the Alliance, but the mood of the country was headed in the opposite direction.

Truman and the people around him were so convinced that Russia was poised to take over Europe that they let their fear of Russia and communism rule their thinking about all our foreign policy. As a private man, Truman was a very decent fellow, but he was very limited in his concept of the world. No sooner had he gotten in the White House than he was surrounded by cold warrior types like John Foster Dulles and Dean Acheson. These eastern sophisticates and brilliant international lawyers formed an enclave around Truman and came to dominate his thinking—especially on foreign policy.

All Washington was splitting up into cold war and anti–cold war people. The cold war people were gathered around Truman and Dean Acheson and all those people who said Russia was going to sweep to the sea and take over western Europe. The idea was that we would have to fight the Russians sometime and the quicker the better. A lot of Army and Navy people lived near us on Seminary Hill, and they were always talking about preventive war, getting there before the Russians got strong again and before they got the atomic bomb. It was a touchy period.

The House Un-American Activities Committee had been in business all during the war, and after the war was over, Truman instituted the loyalty order. Everybody who worked for the United States government had to be examined. If the investigators found anything in your past or your present that made you suspect at all, you came up before the committee, which was composed of leading citizens. But you were accused by nameless people. The committee wouldn't say John Jones who lives at 1727 Oak Street saw you at a meeting of the Spanish War Relief back in 1936 and what do you say to that. If you'd ever been *for* Republican Spain, you were tainted. They would say, T-17, a confidential informant of the FBI in whom we have the utmost trust, says that you were at this meeting. You never knew who the informant was. It was like fighting ghosts. A lot of people were scared to death, and many of them committed suicide.

Cliff and I were not called up before the loyalty board. Cliff eventually got his own FBI report, and everybody they'd interviewed about Cliff said he was just perfect, that he went to church and was honest and clean and paid his bills and was a lovely young man. There was nothing on Cliff at all. What they had on me was that I had worked on the poll tax committee and had once presented a petition to Congress for the abolition of the poll tax. That had been reported in the *Daily Worker*, so of course it had been reported to the FBI. The fact that we had friends who were Communists— or I did, like Joe Gelders and Tex Dobbs and Alton Lawrence—made us suspect to some degree, but nobody called us on it.

Now you've got to understand my position, which still is strange. While I was not a Communist, as long as the Communists were doing what I believed in, which was fighting the war against Hitler or fighting the poll tax, then I accepted their help. I thought that red-baiting was horrible. It ruined everything. It certainly killed the National Committee to Abolish the Poll Tax.

Clark Foreman and I weren't scared, mainly because we never had been members of the Communist party. We had nothing to conceal as far as that was concerned. During the time that Communists were active in the union fights—when they were organizing the sharecroppers and all—members of the Communist party had to promise that if they didn't agree with the party line they wouldn't say anything about it. They had to go along with the line until the next meeting, when the line changed. Well, for Clark and for me that was absolutely impossible. We weren't going along with a line we didn't agree with. No one ever strongly urged me to join the Communist party, I must add, because I didn't have the reputation for being discreet or keeping my mouth shut. Nobody just really begged me to join, and I never did.

12

Campaigning for Henry Wallace

I GOT INVOLVED WITH Henry Wallace originally through the Washington committee of the Southern Conference for Human Welfare. We invited Henry to speak at the Watergate auditorium in June 1947 and he impressed me. He promoted cooperation between the United States and Russia and warned against war talk.

Henry traveled all over the country and the rest of the world making speeches. Finally, the political action committee of the CIO supported him. He got enormous crowds. People had just been through one war and they didn't want to go through another one. So Henry's message of peace and one world was welcome.

A group called the Progressive Citizens of America was formed in 1947 to back Henry Wallace as the party's presidential candidate. I became a member of the northern Virginia branch because the Democratic party in Virginia was so hopeless. It never crossed my mind that the Progressive party would win, but I agreed with many of Henry Wallace's ideas. A lot of military people in our neighborhood were constantly talking about a preventive war with Russia, and I was against getting into war again.

I had met Wallace at the Hills' one Sunday at lunch when he was still secretary of agriculture. A woman at the table with us said, "Oh, Mr. Wallace, I have just longed to meet you. You know, I am a great believer in blood. I think the important thing is good blood. Of course, I am from the South, and we believe it is very important to have good blood. I know that you are a geneticist so I am sure you must agree with me." He said, "Well, you know, I'll tell you. It's very easy to raise pure-bred chickens. You can put a wire around them and separate them. It's simple. It is a little more difficult with hogs, but you can do it if you get the wire strong enough. And with cattle. Of course with corn, you have to put cheesecloth over the tassels so the wind won't blow the pollen. But the trouble is, they haven't found a fence high enough or strong enough to keep the human male from straying." He was perfectly serious about it, and I thought he was delightful.

Henry was so sweet and so serious. He tried to help us in the poll tax fight. He was a horrible politician, but I just adored him. Sister and Henry were very fond of each other. They loved to talk about mysticism. He believed in revelations and that people could have contact with the other world.

Beanie Baldwin became head of Wallace's Progressive Citizens of America, and he was one of the reasons I joined Wallace's campaign. I had known Beanie during our years in Washington, and he and I shared many New Deal dreams. He was Calvin Benham Baldwin, but everybody called him Beanie. He had been one of Henry Wallace's assistants when Henry was secretary of agriculture in the 1930s. There seemed to be no other choice for me. I lived in Virginia. There was no Republican party to speak of in Virginia. There may have been ten or twelve Republicans, but I never met any. And the Democratic party of Virginia was absolutely controlled by Harry Byrd. It was a machine that was impossible to break.

Sister could not support Henry because Hugo would have had a fit. Cliff was very nice about my working for Henry, but Hugo just gave it to me up and down. He thought I was a total idiot to leave the Democratic party and vote for Henry Wallace. Hugo was a yellow-dog Democrat. He thought you had to stick by the party, even though he didn't think much of Harry Truman.

I was the only one in the entire family who was for Henry Wallace. It was mighty lonesome, I'm telling you. I even went to the Progressive Citizens of America convention in Philadelphia in 1948. Wallace, of course, won the nomination. Pete Seeger and Paul Robeson sang and it was thrilling.

After the Progressive party convention, Cliff and I went on a trip to Poland sponsored by the One-World Award people. The organization annually made an award to someone in science, or art, or music who represented the idea of one world. Previous awards had been made to such people as Arturo Toscanini and John Huston, director of *The Treasure of the Sierra Madre*. This time they chose Fiorello La Guardia, who was then head of the United Nations Relief and Rehabilitation Administration, the agency that was trying to give money and livestock and grain to needy nations. La Guardia had cancer and was about to die, so he couldn't make the trip. The committee chose about eight or ten people, including Norman Corwin and Cliff. Einstein was asked to go but he couldn't, so he sent his great friend Dr. Otto Nathan. I never had been out of the United States, so Cliff took me along. By this time our daughter Ann was old enough to take care of her younger sisters. The trip was to Poland because that's where an international peace conference was being held—right in the ruins of Europe to show how terrible war is.

We first went to Gydnia in Poland, and then we were flown down to Wroclaw. We went to a peace meeting held in a big hall. Lots of intellectuals were there from all over the world. The Russians were changing their line toward the United States, and they began calling us hyenas and rattlesnakes and wolves. They were trying to arouse sentiment against the United States by telling everyone that America was the danger, that America was the new imperialist power that was going to conquer the world. Ilya Ehrenburg, who was a Russian journalist, kept bearing down on Alabama lynchings and we got into an argument. I told him that I was for Henry Wallace. I had a big Wallace button on. He was very scornful. "And what is Wallace? Nothing. Who does Wallace represent? Nobody. Do you think the great USSR can make its policy on the basis of a handful of liberals for Wallace?" Joe Starobin, a writer for the *Daily Worker,* interrupted the argument and said, "Mrs. Durr is a liberal. She is for Wallace, but I am a Communist." And Ehrenburg said to him, "Ha! An American Communist! And what do you amount to? Nothing. What power do you have? None. Do you think the great USSR is going to plan its programs on the basis of a handful of powerless people in the United States?"

We went to another big meeting in Paris. It was a big Communist meeting advertised in the paper, and I wanted to hear what they were saying. Cliff wanted to go to the Folies Bergère, but we couldn't get tickets. The Communist meeting was at La Place Stalingrad, in the red ring around Paris. There were a lot of fish trade people at La Place, and the place stank of fish. Everybody there had on an apron bloodied from fish guts.

The big shots were up front, and one of them was named Jacques Duclos. I couldn't understand them. I just heard them say, "A bas America. A bas America." I was still wearing my Wallace button and one of the young men came up to me and said he wanted to introduce me to Duclos and the other people on the platform because I was for Wallace. So Cliff went up with me on the stage and the young man said to the assembled dignitaries. "This lady is for Wallace." Duclos said exactly the same thing that Ehrenburg had said, "And what is Wallace? Nothing. Who does he represent? Nobody. Do you think we can plan the future world revolution on the basis of a handful of liberals in America?"

These incidents in Poland and France made me mad. After all, here we were trying to keep people from dropping atomic bombs on them, and I thought they might at least have said, "Well, we appreciate your efforts, even if you don't succeed."

Cliff and I got back home in September, and I immediately plunged into Henry Wallace's campaign. Wallace went all through the South with Clark Foreman and Aubrey Williams's son and a lot of other people we knew, and he refused to speak to segregated audiences. They got tomatoes and other things thrown at them because of it. He struck a great blow against segregation right then and there.

A typical episode of the campaign occurred in Norfolk. We were going to have a rally in the city auditorium on Sunday afternoon, and Clark Foreman had gone ahead to make preparations. We got a very firm commitment from the city that the auditorium would not be segregated. We spoke on the radio and got a good deal of publicity.

When we went down to the auditorium on Sunday, we found the place surrounded by the police. They said we had to obey the segregation ordinance. The place had already filled up with blacks and whites, so they said we were all going to be arrested. Clark stood there with me arguing with the police. He turned to me and said, "Look, let's just run down the aisle and start the meeting and hold them off as long as possible. Maybe by that time, Wallace will be here. I don't think they are going to arrest us with him here." So we ran down the central aisle and Clark jumped up on the platform and he said, "The meeting will come to order. Mrs. Durr, who is chairman of the Virginia Committee, will preside." I stood up there not knowing what to do and Clark said, "Get somebody to pray." Oh, we prayed and we prayed. And then Clark said, "Sing 'The Star-spangled Banner'." So we sang all four or five verses. It got very weak toward the end. The police were on either side of the stage and were just about to swoop in and arrest us when Henry Wallace appeared. He walked down the aisle to the platform and made his speech, completely oblivious to everything.

We had broken segregation in Norfolk with the police there, and we were pretty pleased about it. Henry always went to bed early, so we didn't see him that night, but the next morning he invited us all to have breakfast with him. There were headlines in all the Norfolk papers about how segregation was broken at the city auditorium. Henry Wallace never even acknowledged it and he never thanked us. He never said, "What a good job you did," or "What a great event this is." He was so wound up in himself and in what he was doing that he wasn't even aware of what had happened. He could be sweet, but as a politician Henry was absolutely hopeless. He could never remember anybody's name, and he completely ignored everyone around him.

Wallace never took an active part in his own party. I was on the board of the Progressive party, and at meetings, Henry would get up and walk out. He didn't want to be troubled with details. He just wanted to get up and make his speech. He was possessed with the idea he was leading a crusade for peace. He didn't actually think he could be elected, but he thought he could get about ten million votes. Later, he thought it would be fifteen million, but he ended up getting less than a million.

One day during the campaign a busload of young people, black and white, from a Yiddish theater in New York arrived at my house unannounced. I had heard a vague rumor they might appear, and so I fed them and put them up. They gave skits supporting Henry in shopping centers. I arranged for them to perform at a Negro Baptist church, and a lot of Negroes attended. The actors were sincere and earnest and dedicated, but I was glad to see them go. People in northern Virginia were just not used to skits in Yiddish.

The campaign was really difficult. In the first place, the meetings were frustrating. A Wallace rally would start at seven-thirty or eight o'clock with singing, and then there'd be money-raising speeches and then local people would speak. By ten-thirty or eleven o'clock when everybody was exhausted and had to go home, they'd bring on poor Henry. By that time Henry would be tired, too, and he was never a great orator.

Right in the middle of Henry Wallace's campaign, his chief backer, Mike Straight, who had encouraged him to get into the campaign, withdrew his support. He said there were too many Communists in the Progressive party.

The press completely ignored Henry. They scarcely mentioned his name, and when they did it was "Henry Wallace, the Communist-backed candidate." The Wallace people decided to run local candidates on the Progressive ticket to get some local newspaper publicity. We knew we wouldn't get many votes, but I agreed to run for the U.S. Senate. I made some speeches. I got some audiences—mostly blacks. They knew me from the effort I'd made to upgrade the black schools in Fairfax County and to abolish the poll tax.

Even the blacks who supported Henry got awfully queasy about communism. They didn't know what it was exactly, but they knew it was bad to be regarded as a Communist and they wanted to avoid it as much as possible. I remember a black fellow in Norfolk who had arranged a meeting at which I had spoken. I saw him several years afterward at the Democratic Convention, and he said, "Mrs. Durr, you sure got me in a lot of trouble. After that meeting in Norfolk, the FBI visited me every week. I nearly lost my job."

Then Henry began to be an anti-Communist, too, and eventually became a real red-baiter. I always thought his wife and his family were the reason. They were very conservative. His wife apparently hated being allied with people like Paul Robeson, black radicals. I'm sure Henry caught hell from her.

Later Henry blamed his own followers and supporters for having ruined his campaign. He met my daughter at Radcliffe one time when he was making a speech there. Lucy went up to him and said, "Mr. Wallace, my mother supported you in the Progressive party. She's Virginia Durr and she thought so much of you." He said, "Well, all I can say about your mother is that she gave me very bad advice." *I* gave Henry Wallace bad advice! Vice-president of the United States and secretary of agriculture, and it was all my fault that he ran. He blamed everybody but himself. I lost all my respect and affection for him.

An amazing thing happened to me shortly after the election, though, that made me feel it was all worthwhile, that Henry's campaign had done some good. I was traveling by train on my way to Alabama just after Christmas. I always rode the day coach. Flying was too expensive and so was a Pullman. It was about eight o'clock at night, and it was raining very hard. A well-dressed man got on. He had pigskin luggage and an English raincoat and he just looked rich. He evidently thought I looked respectable enough, so he sat down by me and immediately began to explain why he was riding the day coach. He was going to some fashionable place where they played polo, but his plane had been canceled on account of the weather and it was too late to get a Pullman. He said he hadn't been on a day coach since he was a boy, and he asked why I was on it. I said, "Well, it was the only ticket I could get." I didn't say it was the only ticket I could afford, which was true. He asked me where I was from, and he told me he was from North Carolina. So we began that old Southern game of "Do you know so-and-so." I knew at least the names of all the people he asked me about, because I had been to the Cathedral School in Washington with many of the girls he mentioned. Since I seemed to know all the right people, he put me down as being kosher. He knew I was safe. He could trust me to be a good conservative Democrat.

This fellow sat by me until he got off to change trains. He had been in the State Department and was now lobbying for the international oil companies. He went on to talk about the danger of Communists and how difficult it was to fight them. Then he said, "Mrs. Durr, I am going to tell you something that I know you won't believe, but it is the truth. You know, when the war ended, the United States was the only country in the world that had a viable industrial system except the Japanese in Manchuria and the Russians behind the Urals. If we could have destroyed those two systems, the United States would have been in control of the entire world. We would have been the only people in the world that had the industrial machinery to provide the goods that people needed. And we had just about persuaded Truman to have a preventive war."

"Why didn't he do it?" I asked.

"Now, I know you won't believe this, Mrs. Durr, but I am telling you the truth—he got scared of Henry Wallace. I don't know if you know of Henry Wallace." I told him that I did know of Henry Wallace, and he said, "Well, you know, he collected around himself a bunch of scum, pinks, reds, you know, that type. None of them amounted to a hill of beans, just absolutely no power. But it scared Harry Truman and he wouldn't consider a preventive war as long as Henry Wallace was running that campaign. Not only that, but Truman went out and made a campaign on peace." He added, "We lost the best opportunity the United States ever had."

"Well, that's just awful, isn't it?" That's an absolutely true story. You see, this man thought I was just a sweet Southern girl and that surely I agreed with him, so he felt free to confide in me.

One of the great miscalculations of the Wallace campaign was that we were absolutely sure we were going to get the Negro vote. It was the first race for president where a candidate had taken a firm position and said he would not address a segregated meeting. We were terribly proud of Henry and very pleased. There were Negroes in the Progressive party, and in Virginia some of the party leaders were black. But the blacks didn't vote for us.

I was so surprised and shocked by that that I went up to Howard University and took a course under Franklin Frazier to try to understand what had gone wrong. The Negroes voted for Truman. I found out that black people react just like white folks. They thought Truman would win and we wouldn't, and they wanted to be on the winning side. The fact was that Truman had made some gestures toward integrating the military, so they went right along with Truman like the other people did.

I never wavered on supporting Henry at all, but the Southern Conference was divided in its support. After the campaign, the Southern Conference split up. Jim Dombrowski formed the Southern Conference Educational Fund, which was going to be the tax-exempt propaganda wing of the Southern Conference for Human Welfare. He went back to New Orleans and began to work on that. Aubrey Williams agreed to be president of the fund. The Progressive party just faded out after a year or two. Even Henry turned on it.

You can see how lightly everybody took my supporting the Progressive party by the fact that Harry Truman decided to reappoint Cliff to the FCC in 1948. Truman even told Cliff he was sure to be confirmed by the Senate. And the people on the Senate committee said that Cliff would be confirmed. They just thought Cliff's wife had a slight aberration to support Henry Wallace. Cliff had stuck by the Democratic party, and that's what counted. In those days women were not regarded as being very important. I was Cliff's wife and Hugo's sister-in-law. On my own maybe I was a little too radical, but I had no power.

In a place like Washington, it's power that counts. All the articles written about how some beautiful woman lured somebody to do something are just crazy. Sex in Washington is secondary to power. There were very few men I ever knew in Washington who didn't put power above sex.

None of my closest, most beloved friends thought I did right in joining Henry Wallace's campaign. They thought Henry was a fiasco. And they thought I had made a mistake by joining up with such a crazy lot of people. But I don't think I was wrong. I still think that Henry was right and that Harry Truman was wrong, and I believe it to this day and hour.

13

The Anti-Communist Crowd

IN THE WALLACE CAMPAIGN race-baiting was a problem, but the red-baiting was worse. It happened everywhere. You couldn't go to a church meeting or to Sunday school that somebody didn't get up and denounce godless communism. It was really a hysterical period. McCarthy was the epitome of it later on. But before McCarthy, Richard Nixon had become the great anti-Communist.

Life is so strange and so interesting. Nixon, the greatest anti-Communist of them all, a man who built his reputation on the Hiss case, was the one who later extended the hand of friendship to Russia and China. A Democrat would have been torn limb from limb and been denounced as a Soviet spy and a Communist traitor and a subversive. But Nixon was so much an anti-Communist that he could make overtures to China and Russia. Of course, when he did so a recession was beginning and we needed new markets, which must have been part of his thinking.

Nixon was elected to the House in 1946. As usual I knew a good deal about him primarily through personal connections. Cliff's assistant at RFC and one of his best friends was Bill Livingston from Iowa. Bill's sister, Louise, was married to Jerry Voorhis, a young congressman from California. Jerry and Louise lived across the road from us, near her brother's place. Their daughter, Alice, became a good friend of my daughters, and we saw a great deal of the Voorhises. Jerry was a devout Episcopalian and was against communism because he thought communism was godless. I remember that he and Esmond Romilly had had a great debate on Spain one night at our house before the war. Jerry had been terribly upset that Spain had let the Communists in. In economics, he was quite liberal. He was a great believer in cooperatives, and later became head of the whole cooperative league of the United States.

In 1946, Jerry went back to California to run for reelection. A lot of the rich business people thought Jerry was too liberal, so they financed Richard Nixon to run against him on the Communist issue, saying Jerry was connected with communism because he got the support of the labor unions. Jerry did what most people did when attacked like that. He was so outraged and astonished at being called a Communist that he became defensive. Instead of fighting the campaign on the issues, he began to deny that he was for the CIO or Harry Bridges, and so he cut off a lot of his support. He fell back on a refrain that became quite common. "I am more of an anti-Communist than he is because my anti-Communism is based on principle and religion." He was defeated on the pure, unadulterated lie that he was connected with the Communists. That was my first realization that Mr. Nixon was coming to town and that he was coming to town based on a big lie. I disliked him immediately.

Nixon became the leader of the anti-Communist bloc in the House. He built his whole reputation on being an anti-Communist. He certainly came on the scene before McCarthy, but he didn't become a national figure until the Hiss case.

Alger Hiss was an attractive and charming fellow. His wife, Priscilla, was a Quaker from someplace near Philadelphia. She'd been married before and had one son, and then she and Alger had a son. I did not know them intimately, because they moved in the Dean Acheson–Georgetown–State Department crowd, which was far more fashionable than the Seminary Hill–New Deal crowd, although we had some mutual friends and sometimes went to the same parties. Washington society, even in the New Deal days, was organized on a class basis and the really fashionable New Dealers lived in Georgetown and were connected in some way with the State Department. Dean Acheson and Alice were the ruling authorities. Anyone invited to the Achesons' had really made it. Of course, we felt that if we were invited to the Brandeises' we had made it.

We knew the Hisses through Marney and Henry Abbott. Henry Abbott's great-grandfather was one of the Adamses of Massachusetts. Abbott and Hiss were great friends, and we would occasionally have dinner with the Hisses at the Abbotts' or vice-versa. Alger Hiss was in the State Department at that time, working for Dean Acheson. When Whittaker Chambers accused Alger of being a Russian spy and produced the famous pumpkin papers, we just didn't believe a word of it. A lot of people in Washington didn't believe it. They thought it was a frame-up even then. I still think it was a frame-up.

The story in Washington at that time was that Priscilla was always taking in stray people, and she invited Chambers and his wife to stay with them. Chambers made homosexual overtures to Priscilla's older son, and Alger got furious with him and drove him out of the house. Now I don't know whether there's any truth to that story. Alger says in his book he knew Chambers only casually.

The strange thing that happened about Alger—which is still a mystery to me—is what happened to his marriage. All the time Alger was in jail, Priscilla, his wife, went to see him every weekend or whenever she was allowed to. The Hiss case was well publicized, and pictures of her appeared in newspapers and magazines. Priscilla always looked sweet and pretty, and it was sad to see her going in or coming out of the prison. She'd take the boys with her sometimes. But within a year or so after Alger got out of jail, they separated. I was never so surprised in my life.

I saw Priscilla Hiss some years later in New York at the wedding of Clark Foreman's oldest daughter, Shelagh. A small, white-haired woman came up to me and said, "Virginia, you don't seem to remember me." And I didn't.

I was terribly embarrassed and I said, "Well, I'm afraid I don't."

"This is Priscilla Hiss." I was absolutely astonished, because she looked so much older and her hair had turned white. She looked much too old.

I didn't know that she was separated from Alger so I asked her, "Where is Alger?"

"Well, as soon as Alger got out of jail, he became a hero to a lot of people. He became a symbolic hero, particularly to a lot of rich women here in New York. And they just took him away from me. They surrounded him and made him a hero and became worshippers, formed a cult almost." That was a strange remark, because Alger never seemed to me to be that kind of person. Priscilla was terribly bitter. She felt Alger had treated her very badly. The whole episode was very unpleasant because she was desolate and she looked so old and so unhappy.

That's the last time I ever saw Priscilla Hiss. I understand she's still just terribly bitter about Alger. I saw Alger in Princeton in the early 1970s. He was there at Hugh Wilson's invitation to speak to Hugh's class. I was at Princeton at the time visiting my daughter and son-in-law Lucy and Sheldon Hackney. Sheldon was provost at Princeton then, and he and Lucy knew that I had known Alger in Washington, so they invited him to dinner. I didn't dare ask Alger about Priscilla because he was accompanied by the woman with whom he'd been living for some time.

Joan Baez sang at Shelagh Foreman's wedding, where I last saw Priscilla Hiss. Hugh Foreman, Clark's son, was a great friend of all the folk singers. I remember Joan Baez sang like an angel and looked beautiful, but afterward she just lay down on the floor and went to sleep. Everybody had to step over her.

The next morning I went by to tell the Foremans good-bye, and Joan Baez and a whole crowd of folk singers were there. I asked one of the boys if he would be good enough to get me a package of cigarettes. Somebody had some cigarettes and offered me one, the kind that doesn't have a filter, and I said, "Oh, I can't smoke those. Please get me a package of cigarettes."

Joan Baez spoke up and said, "I suppose you're used to ordering black people around all your life, so you think you can order us around."

"My Lord," I said, "I don't know why it's such a terrible request to ask a young boy to go out and get a package of cigarettes."

"Well, you just bring that Southern arrogance with you and think you can order people around because you've been ordering black people around all your life."

I was absolutely astonished at such rudeness and I said, "Well, evidently you don't approve of anybody from the South." Then she got on a long diatribe about the South and the way we were treating the blacks and all.

"You don't approve of me either, do you?" she said finally.

"Well, no, actually I don't." By this time I was furious.

"Why don't you approve of me?"

"Well, in the first place," I said, "I thought your behavior yesterday at the wedding was extremely odd and very rude. I think if you want to take a nap you don't have to lie down in the middle of the floor and go to sleep and make everybody step around you. You just made yourself conspicuous and you certainly caused other people a great deal of inconvenience. I think it was pure exhibitionism." Oh, she practically bared her teeth at that.

"I think I have a right to rest when I want to. That's what makes us so different, the conventionality—if I was tired, I had a right to lie down on the floor and rest."

"Well, you might have, but you certainly caused a lot of inconvenience and I thought it was very bad manners."

Then she asked, "What else do you think is wrong with me?"

"I think the way you're dressed is absolutely disgraceful. You just told me you're going on a train to Boston, and look what you've got on. You've got on a bikini and a brassiere and you're barefoot. I think your costume is extremely inappropriate. To my mind, it's just not the way to dress to go on a train to Boston." Oh, she got furious at that.

It was a miserable episode because the poor Foremans had just taken her in and had been good friends to her. Of course, they were embarrassed by my rudeness too. But I didn't see why I should be insulted for asking a boy to go out and get me a package of cigarettes. Poor boy—he was scared to death. I think he finally did go out and get it for me, but he slipped it to me surreptitiously so Joan wouldn't get mad at him.

In the 1940s, we didn't think Richard Nixon was like Dies and Eastland. We didn't think he was as much of a blatherskite as they were. He was more subtle, and he operated through other people. For instance, in the

Hiss case, Chambers was the one in the papers, but Nixon was pulling the strings. We despised Nixon because we knew he had lied about Jerry Voorhis, and we assumed he was lying about Alger Hiss. We despised him because he was causing so much uproar and pain and trouble on the anti-Communist issue. By that time the hysteria was getting bad.

It was so ridiculous. Someone would find himself in a loyalty hearing if he had a phonograph record by Paul Robeson or if he read the *New Republic* or the *Nation*. People could be caught up in a loyalty hearing if they had been to a meeting of the Spanish War Relief ten years before. And there was always danger they would lose their jobs. Just the fact that a person had been in a loyalty hearing frightened everybody around him. It was a reign of terror.

When McCarthy first came on the scene in 1950, we all thought he was crazy as a bedbug—just a wild-eyed demagogue. Even Dean Acheson had stood by Alger Hiss in 1947. He'd known Alger for years and he said he wouldn't turn his back on him, which we thought was a very admirable statement. But as the red hysteria got worse, the State Department gave in to it more and more, and when McCarthy said there were fifty-seven Communists in its ranks, everyone immediately went on the defensive. Instead of saying, "Why, he's just a liar, a hick," they gave in to him. McCarthy had no sense. As my mother used to say, he was common as pig's tracks, and he was. But the trouble was, he scared the administration and it went on the defensive. He scared the United States out of its wits.

I know that young people won't take my word for it, but the person who got rid of McCarthy was Lyndon Johnson. He was majority leader during the Eisenhower administration. Working behind the scenes, he maneuvered to get a resolution through the Senate that finally got rid of McCarthy. After his facade was stripped away and he ceased to be the terrifying figure, McCarthy was just a pure old drunk.

The anti-Communist crowd, including Nixon and J. Edgar Hoover, had thought McCarthy was useful. You didn't have to be a Communist to be suspect. If you weren't an ardent anti-Communist, you were in trouble. When I look back on the period, it is hard to believe the country was going through such frightful turmoil. I despised them all. I thought they were a bunch of liars and opportunists and common. I suppose I shouldn't use those terms. But they were such common, vulgar people, people you would never associate with if you could help it. And the people around them were all such common, vicious, vulgar opportunists.

Many of the people I'd been with in the New Deal became anti-Communist liberals and I had trouble with some of them. I would still see them at parties and I was still very fond of them. They wouldn't defend McCarthy, but they wouldn't oppose him either. The Americans for Democratic Action, ADA, even had a loyalty oath. It was people like Kenneth

Galbraith and Arthur Schlesinger that I argued with. They were so big in the ADA. Now I'm still devoted to Kenneth Galbraith and to his wife. I still have some hard feelings about Arthur Schlesinger, but Arthur's a whole lot better than he used to be.

Nobody thought I was a Communist. Even Jim Eastland didn't think I was a Communist. He thought I was a "fellow-traveler," which was even more dangerous. The sin that Cliff and I committed in those days was that we were not such *anti*-Communists. We didn't think the Communists were going to try to kill us. The whole red scare was based on the notion that the Russian hordes were going to sweep over Europe to the English Channel and sweep over Asia. The Russian hordes were going to kill everybody. We just didn't believe that. Cliff had been to Russia, and we'd both been in Poland in 1948 and we had seen the devastation. In the first place, we didn't think the Russians wanted to sweep over Europe and Asia. And in the second place, we didn't think they were able to do it even if they had wanted to, because they'd been so terribly hurt by the war. We'd been there.

I actually tried to make friends with some of the Russians at the embassy, but Cliff and I were invited to the embassy only for the great big caviar and champagne events, where there were thousands of other people. I did meet a lot of people from communistic countries though. I met a lot of Czechs through my friend Emily Condon. These Czechs were the last people you would suspect of being revolutionary Communists. They were pleasant, middle-class people. I mean middle class in the sense of not being extravagant, although many of them invited us to marvelous dinners.

Have you ever had a Czech dinner? They would always have goose. It was so good, especially stuffed with chestnuts. When I'd been in Prague on the peace tour with Cliff, all I had to eat was that horrible coffee and bread made out of bran. But the Czech embassy and the Czechs who lived here had marvelous food, wonderful cakes with whipped cream between the layers—tortes. You'd come away from one of those dinners and you could barely walk. Between the food and the vodka, you were barely able to get home.

Through the Czechs, I met a lot of Poles. I became great friends with Ambassador Winiewicz. He wasn't a Communist as I recall. Anyway, he didn't act like one. He and his wife were very social. Madame Winiewicz wore French dresses and French hats and spoke French. She had been a Polish noblewoman and had taken a lot of Jews into her home during the war. She never learned much English, but she was very expressive with her hands. Winiewicz himself was a brilliant, attractive diplomat and spoke beautiful English. I remember having dinner at the embassy one time with Walter Lippmann and his wife. The Winiewiczes went in for society. They invited fashionable people to the embassy and had musicales with great pianists, and they served marvelous French food.

I adored the Poles. The Poles were like the Southerners in that they made people feel welcome. They were very warm and cordial, and they believed in dressing up. They laid a great deal of stress on delicious food. They were just charming people, and I was very fond of the Winiewiczes.

I got to know some Russians, too. They were extremely suspicious, even before the cold war. I met one young Russian man at the Polish embassy. He was very attractive and said he wanted to bring his wife and baby out to meet us. He seemed extremely anxious to be pleasant. His little girl was about two or three years old, and her head had been completely shaved. He told me they did that in Russia to avoid head lice. That took me aback. I said, "Well, there are no lice in your apartment, are there?" He said no. He gave the usual story about how he'd been a poor boy living in the country, and they did have lice, and now he was with the great Soviet. The state had educated him, and now he was an engineer and in the diplomatic service.

I suppose other people were suspicious of us for socializing with Russians, but I didn't think about it at the time. I mean, I didn't pay any attention to it. I was so interested to see what they were up to or thinking about, what their ideas were. And of course you got very different points of view, because they came from all different classes of society. The Winiewiczes were very upper class; the Czechs were middle class; and this man from the Russian embassy was evidently a peasant who had been brought up through the ranks. He may even have been a member of the KGB. I have no idea. The day he came out to our house, he called beforehand and wanted to know exactly who was going to be there. And nobody was there that I remember except maybe some of the young mothers in the neighborhood who had children the same age as mine. The Russians seemed to live in a state of fear and suspicion.

There were a lot of Russians on the ship when we went to Poland, and they kept entirely to themselves. They never spoke to anybody else. One of the young Russian couples had a little boy, six or seven years old. It was very rough one day, and the ship was going this way and that. The little boy climbed up on the railing and was clinging to a post. The ship was going so far over that it scared me to death and I rushed toward him and seized him. Well, the Russians came up and seized him away from me. They looked exactly as if they thought I was trying to kidnap him.

It was difficult to make friends with any of the Russians after the war because they were always sure, I suppose, that you were a member of the CIA or FBI or whatever. So eventually I gave up trying.

I think Hugo thought I was very foolish to take up with strange foreigners in Washington, but he never said anything to me about it or to Cliff either. As the cold war heated up, many people became as frightened of the red-scare movement in this country as the anti-Communists were frightened of Russia, but Hugo never criticized me or Cliff for associating with foreigners.

Cliff and I felt safe and secure, physically safe and ideologically safe. We were Americans. We had a feeling of complete safety, of complete devotion to our country. It was ours and if it made mistakes, it was up to us to fight to correct those mistakes.

The people I've known who were Communists felt great devotion to the party. They thought it was the hope of the world. I never had that feeling. I never was caught up in that. But I never was caught up in all the anti-Communist hysteria either.

Cliff and I didn't take the anti-Communist hysteria very seriously at first. We deplored it, because we thought it was unnecessary and it interfered with the important work that needed to be done in this country—things like getting the right to vote for everybody. But we never thought the anti-Communist hysteria would touch us.

14

Cliff

THERE were few things Cliff Durr was scared of. He had grown up in a stable family with a very firm set of beliefs, although he later came to disagree with a good many of those beliefs. He was utterly protected. As a child he had a black nurse named Henrietta, whom he adored. She looked after him until he was five or six years old. His aunt, Little Auntie, and his mother and his sister were crazy about him. Cliff was the youngest of several children and he sometimes felt left out. He strongly resented being asked to do small favors. If we were in the garden I'd say, "Cliff, would you mind handing me my trowel?" And he'd say, "You sound like Aunt Sally." Aunt Sally was a great-aunt who was always asking him to run down to the store for a spool of thread. He said he was just the errand boy in the house, but he was brought up in an extremely loving and protected atmosphere.

Cliff's grandfather Judkins was the greatest influence on his life. He was a strong, stable man, who owned the farm that we eventually lived on— Pea Level, in Elmore County, just north of Montgomery County in central Alabama. His grandfather always taught Cliff to look for explanations of what he saw or heard. He would talk to him about the Civil War, and he would say to Cliff, "Maybe the South wasn't right." Or he'd say, "Maybe a Confederate couldn't kill ten Yankees. Those Yankees were pretty straight fellows." He had his own philosophy. Cliff loved to tell a story about a ghost, which pretty well shows that philosophy.

[My playmates up here [at Pea Level] . . . were all black and never went to school a day in their lives. There weren't any schools to go to and ignorance and superstition were rife. Never having any TV to watch at night, we amused ourselves after supper by telling ghost stories. The existence of ghosts was never in doubt, because always some older folks would come along and join in the stories and would actually have seen ghosts or swore positively that they had. So I had no doubts on the subject of their existence. I just had never seen one. If you had had the experience of seeing one, that gave you a certain amount of prestige.

Well, Grandpa sent me to Wetumpka one day to deliver a message to a man he wanted to do some work for him. So I bridled up this favorite mare and rode into town and delivered the message. But then I hung around for the rest of the day at the grist mill and the saw mill and other exciting places till the day was pretty well spent. When I started back home it was getting dark and before getting on very far complete darkness overtook us—but I wasn't concerned about it. The mare knew the road better than I did even. We were going along a particularly lonely stretch of the road when this mare, who was known for a particularly calm disposition, suddenly shied and almost threw me. I looked hurriedly over my shoulder to see what had frightened her, and there it was tall and skinny among the blackberry bushes, the muscadine vines, and it had an eerie glow that was just out of this world. So I gave the old mare a kick in the flanks, which was involuntary and not at all necessary because she had the same idea I did—to get out of there. So notwithstanding the ruts in the road and boulders, we covered the remaining miles back home in something like Kentucky Derby time. So I got back to the house and soon discovered that I had not only achieved safety but a certain amount of prestige. I had actually seen a ghost. Now if I had just said that I had seen a ghost, there would have been some question about it, but the foam on the old mare's flanks and her obvious nervousness confirmed it, since she had a reputation of being a pretty level-headed beast. So some of the old Negroes came around and even identified my ghost for me. There was an old fellow in a long tattered overcoat that was murdered about fifty years ago in these hills. He'd come out from time to time at night with a spectral lantern looking for his murderer.

Well, I was enjoying the attention tremendously when Grandpa came along, and he was not impressed. He said, "Now, boy, you go back down there to that rock. You put the bridle back on that mare, and you and the mare both go back down and take another look at that ghost. And I want to be sure that the mare sees that ghost, too." Well, Grandpa was kindly, but he could get a pretty stern look on his face, so he was a clear and present danger.

So I got back on the mare, and we went on back. There was no Kentucky Derby time this time—we just walked. We got about a hundred yards from the ghost, and I got off and tied the reins to a little blackjack oak sapling. I wasn't quite sure whether a ghost could see through things or not. I wasn't quite sure about their eyesight, but I hoped that maybe they couldn't. I thought that maybe if I got down and crawled behind the bushes till I got real close, I could see the ghost before the ghost saw me—which

I did. And I finally got right up to the ghost and had a good look at it. Then I turned around and got the mare. She was in a terrible state of excitement, trembling all over, raring up. She almost jerked the reins out of my hands several times. But Grandpa said the mare had to see that ghost, too. Well, finally I succeeded somehow in getting her right up to the ghost. She let out a snort of disgust and immediately stopped trembling. It was a blaze on an old pine tree that had been struck by lightning. The gray cloak was Spanish moss hanging from a blackjack oak right behind. And this eerie glow came from a quarter moon that peeked out from the clouds. It was a cloudy night, and you'd get a reflection back.

But I can remember still coming back home again. I was really embarrassed, and the mare was, too. She generally had her head up, but her head was down. I found a tremendous resentment against Grandpa building up in me. Just a short time ago I'd been a hero, and now I was just a stupid kid—and it was all Grandpa's fault. But he knew how to deal with kids. So I got back and found he was in a different mood. He let me know that it took a lot for a kid to go back and face that again. He let me know that he thought I'd acted very fine.

Then he started giving me a little dissertation on horses. He prided himself on the good manners of his horses; as he said—they were well-behaved. He said that when a horse sees something and shies from it, it's very important to ride or lead the horse back to whatever scared him and make him see it, see that there was nothing to be scared of. He said, "If you don't do that, they'll get so they shy at everything that's the least bit unfamiliar. That can ruin a horse, and they can get dangerous because a shying horse can get to be a runaway horse, and a runaway horse can be dangerous to horse and rider, too." He said, "You know, people are not too different from horses. They see things that are a little bit different, and they tend to shy away from them instead of taking a look at them. And so they get in the habit of shying away from anything that's a little bit different until they get irrational with fear." He said, "It's true—there are dangers in the world, but generally if you take a look at what frightens you, you'll find there's nothing to be scared of at all. But even if there is a real danger there, it's best to take a good look at it and then you'll know how to deal with it." And I've often thought of that.]¹

Cliff was always the leading boy at school. One reason was that Professor Starke beat them on the hands. Cliff didn't like the idea of anybody's hitting him. His grandfather had told Cliff that if Professor Starke ever hit him, Cliff should come home and his grandfather would go up there and

¹"The Reminiscences of Clifford J. Durr," Columbia University Oral History Collection, New York, 1976, part 3, pp. 20–24.

beat the hell out of him. So Cliff wasn't afraid that he'd be disgraced if Professor Starke beat him. He just didn't want it to happen.

Nobody was very rich in Montgomery in those days, but the white people in Cliff's neighborhood all lived comfortably. And he accepted the black people as his protectors. When Cliff would come up to Pea Level in the summer, he'd play with the black boys. He knew the little black boys couldn't read and write, but they'd go fishing and play together the whole summer.

Cliff went to the University of Alabama fairly young and did extremely well. He was president of the senior class and of the Sigma Alpha Epsilon fraternity, he was a Phi Beta Kappa, and he got a Rhodes scholarship. He wasn't a particularly convivial or popular boy, because he had very little money, about thirty-five dollars a month. He was very attracted to girls, but he couldn't afford to take them on dates. He was shy, too, and he never did learn to dance. He'd been brought up in a family where the women were all very modest.

Cliff never got much advice about sex. Professor Starke told the boys that if they were overcome by any sexual urges they felt they couldn't conquer, they should sit in a marble tub and pour ice water down their backs. The only other sex instruction he got was from his father. He took Cliff out to the cemetery one Sunday afternoon and told him that the Durrs had always been honorable men, and the Judkinses, too. He said if Cliff felt an overwhelming sexual urge, he should go to a whorehouse rather than get a nice girl in trouble. Now whorehouses just didn't appeal to Cliff, nor did the black prostitutes that the university boys would bring down from Birmingham by the carload. He thought that was pretty disgusting. He was very romantic. When he fell in love, it had to be special.

When Cliff went to Oxford as a Rhodes scholar, he took trips all over Europe and read a great deal and studied Roman law and English law. He had romances, but they were only romances. He had pictures in his album of girls sitting in boats with big hats on and fluffy dresses. He was in love with romance.

After Oxford Cliff went into the firm of Ray Rushton, a conservative lawyer in Montgomery. This was in 1921. His father had told Mr. Rushton, who was a great friend of his, "There's not a bit of use in your paying Cliff more than twenty-five dollars a month, because he lives at home and I pay his country club dues and he can use my car when he wants to. If you just take him on, twenty-five dollars a month will be plenty." Cliff didn't see much prospect for advancement at that.

Living at home didn't give Cliff much privacy, and that's one of the reasons he left Montgomery. He went out with Sara Mayfield some when he was living in Montgomery. She later became a writer. She and Cliff would ride bicycles out to the Alabama River and read poetry together and go swimming. One day Cliff's aunt found out he'd taken his bathing suit and Sara's mother found out she'd taken her bathing suit. Cliff said he and Sara were sitting on the banks of the Alabama River eating sandwiches and discussing the beauties of poetry when suddenly his old-maid aunt descended on him from one side and Sara's mother descended on her from the other. They said they'd found that their bathing suits were gone and they were afraid Cliff and Sara were going to drown in the Alabama River. I don't think that was exactly what they were worried about, but that's what they said.

Cliff decided that having his old-maid aunt watching after him was too much, so he went to Milwaukee. His sister's roommate, Dorothy Thigpen, had married a young lawyer from there named Shea. While visiting in Montgomery, he offered Cliff a job. Cliff always looked back on that period with great pleasure. The firm paid him only $75 or $100 a month, but he got good experience and he liked his work. He said he nearly froze to death. He learned to ice skate, which he enjoyed, but it was just too cold. He decided to come back to Alabama, but to Birmingham, not Montgomery.

Cliff moved to Birmingham about 1924 and got a job with Martin, Thompson, Stern, the firm that represented the Alabama Power Company. He started out at $200 a month, which was quite a raise. His older brother John had moved to Birmingham in the meantime, so Cliff lived with John and John's wife, Annie Paul. They even bought a Ford. The Fords were high up and rattling, but they were awfully cheap.

Cliff had been with the Birmingham law firm for about two years when we were married in 1926. He stayed there until 1933, when he became assistant counsel for the Reconstruction Finance Corporation in Washington. Originally the RFC was concerned with saving the banks, but more and more it became involved with preparing the country for war. As I said earlier, Cliff worked night and day on his defense plant project, trying to get the country ready for war. Then, in 1941, he went to the Federal Communications Commission.

The way Cliff got on the FCC in the first place was very political. Fritz Thompson from Mobile, a newspaper editor, had been appointed to the FCC largely through the influence of Lister Hill. Lister at that time was extremely powerful in the Senate and was a great friend and supporter of Roosevelt. The president had to depend on Southern congressmen to support his preparedness effort. The Southern congressmen and senators were the balance against the Midwesterners and isolationists who didn't want to go to war. The president didn't want to reappoint Thompson, but he didn't want it to seem that he was repudiating one of Lister's supporters. It was all a bit of political face-saving. Cliff was suggested because he and Lister grew up together in the same town, went to college together, and their fathers were friends. If Cliff got the job on FCC, it wouldn't seem any repudiation of Lister. It would be just a succession of Lister's supporters.

At first, Cliff was reluctant to take the FCC position. He didn't know anything in the world about broadcasting. We had one little radio in the house that we listened to occasionally for news, but Cliff had no idea at all about radio and television. He did see the possibilities, though, and after he took the job he became extremely interested in the field. The developments that were being made, particularly in television, fascinated him.

Cliff was given an early TV set because he was on the FCC. Not many television sets were on the market yet, but the industry wanted him to watch the progress of the new medium. "Howdy Doody" was on, which the children adored, but the main attraction was women wrestling in mud. Don't ask me why that attracted people, but it did. Television was absolutely new and the neighbors would come rushing over to see women wrestling in mud. There was also a little news on. TV programming in the early days was pretty awful.

The TV lobbyists were always inviting me to lunch and dinners. Ah, the boredom. It seems to me that the big shots in the broadcasting industry always divorced their faithful old wives and married their secretaries, because the young women who were the hostesses for these men were always silly little girls. They were pretty, but they didn't know anything. They were just silly and frightfully boring. Again I asked Cliff if his future depended on my going to these luncheons and he said no, so I was relieved of that. I would say one of the children had a cold.

I think the major achievement while Cliff was a commissioner on the FCC was public television and public radio. Cliff was really responsible for setting aside the channel for educational and public television. There was some educational radio at the various universities, particularly at the University of Wisconsin, and he was very much impressed with what they did there.

Alabama had the first statewide public television network. Cliff and Gordon Persons were friends, and Gordon was the governor of the state, so Cliff got Gordon interested in it.

People don't realize even today that the television channels are owned by the public. In other words, the air is still owned by the United States, by the people. The commercial television stations are licensed by the government to use certain channels. Of course, if the government wanted to charge tremendous fees they could make a lot of money, but they don't. They charge a moderate fee because the channels are a public utility. The air still is owned by the people.

TV and radio were being used more and more by the advertising medium, and it was distressing to Cliff to see this great instrument of radio and the beginnings of television being used to sell deodorants. It bothered him terrifically. So he and Ed Brecher and some other young men who were in the FCC got the presidents of land grant colleges to come to Washington to testify about the need for educational channels.

Cliff and Ed Brecher and Dallas Smythe and Red James and others wrote speeches for the land grant college presidents to give to persuade Congress to set aside the educational channels, but the main reason the channels were set aside is that the big commercial stations couldn't get the necessary material to build towers for the new frequencies because everything was frozen for the war. The commercial stations just weren't able to take over the additional space, but they made a big effort to block public channels. They brought in all kinds of arguments about government censorship. As it turned out, of course, the commercial channels have become almost entirely advertising mediums.

Cliff did his best to ensure quality control with the Blue Book. The Blue Book set up voluntary standards for radio and television stations, but it didn't do much good. You just have to accept the fact that commercial stations are set up to make money. They don't think about educating the public. They are just giving the public as much as they think they want and selling advertisements.

Frankly, I can't watch television any more. I watch the news, but I have given up entirely watching the other programs because of the advertising. The only channel I ever watch for pleasure is public television. Recently *Catch 22* was on television, and it was interrupted so often by commercials that I just couldn't watch it.

I think television confuses people's sense of what's right and what's wrong or what's true and what's false. The networks stop in the middle of the most compassionate program to advertise a deodorant or toilet paper. It fractures the mind of the American public.

Toward the end of Cliff's term on the FCC, Henry Wallace asked Cliff to be head of the RFC. They'd gotten rid of Jesse Jones and put Wallace in as secretary of commerce, which included authority over the RFC. Several people told us that just before Roosevelt died, he had on his desk the nomination to make Cliff head of the RFC, and it's in the Hyde Park papers. Of course, he died before it was acted on.

By the late forties the cold war began to affect the FCC and Cliff's work there. J. Edgar Hoover would send over FBI reports on people who wanted radio stations: Mr. So-and-so had been identified by T-19 as having had connections with So-and-so, who was seen by agent T-17 at a Communist meeting. The FCC began refusing people radio licenses on the word of faceless FBI informants. Cliff and Hoover got in a terrible fight then, because Cliff thought that to deny a man a license on the basis of anonymous T-17 information was terrible.

Cliff was a great believer in face-to-face confrontation. He was a very unselfconscious person. He just did what came naturally. If it was wrong, it was wrong. If it was right, it was right. He'd have some arguments with himself occasionally about things to do or not to do, but typically he was very unselfconscious. I think this quality came out of the tradition of the principled, honorable Southern gentleman. The idea of honor and truth had been driven into him—by his grandfather Judkins, among others. And his own father had been a man of utmost honor and trust. The Durrs had the reputation of paying their bills on time, of being upright and morally upstanding. Even today I can go any place in Alabama or into east Georgia and if I say my name is Durr I can get a check cashed, because all the druggists know the Durr Drug Company. They've been dealing with the Durrs for generations.

Cliff and I didn't take the anti-Communist hysteria too seriously until Truman issued the order requiring the loyalty oath. Suddenly the government had sanctioned the whole anti-Communist hysteria. The government of the United States had said, yes, the government is in danger of Communists, of subversion, of being overthrown. Maybe there is a tremendous number of spies in Washington, and we've got to weed every one of them out. What shocked and sickened Cliff was that the information used against people was from nameless informers. It was like fighting shadows, and it went against everything that Cliff's ancestors and my ancestors fought for in Scotland and Ireland and in this country—to have an open trial. The whole system of English and American law was destroyed by letting a man lose his job and be named as a spy or a traitor on the word of some nameless FBI informer. Cliff just said he refused to carry out such a law, that it was unconstitutional. It was against everything he believed in.

Cliff had studied law in England. He had a great reverence for English common law. He had a great reverence for the Constitution. He had a tremendous belief in law. My generation and his generation had seen the law as beneficent, a protection to the people. So often young people today see the law as an enemy, but we in our lives saw the law as the protector of the people, and particularly the Constitution of the United States as the protector.

So when Truman asked Cliff to accept reappointment to the FCC in 1948, he refused. As a member of the commission, he would have been responsible for the inquisition of all the people who worked for the FCC, so he refused reappointment.

Cliff went to see Truman and told him that he could not accept reappointment to the FCC and that he was against the loyalty oath. Truman told him that he was just trying to get ahead of Parnell Thomas, who was then head of the Un-American Activities Committee. Parnell Thomas was holding meetings in Hollywood and everywhere. Of course, he later went to the penitentiary for stealing from his own employees, or making them divvy up with him. Truman told Cliff to give the loyalty hearings a fair chance. Well, how did the hearings give a man a fair chance when his loyalty had been questioned by T-17 or T-18 and he never knew who that was?

Cliff's dislike of Truman was surprising to people who think Harry Truman's such a great American, but Cliff felt that Truman inaugurated the program. As long as it was Joe McCarthy or crazy Dies or some other idiot doing these things, it didn't carry so much weight. But when the government, when the president inaugurated the loyalty program and had people called up and accused by informants, faceless informants, at that point he felt that things were getting bad.

Very few people in Washington in 1948 held the same convictions that Cliff did—very few would turn down an appointment because they refused to support the loyalty order. Most people rationalized. Cliff thought that was terrible, which is why he always said, "I was so glad to get back to Alabama because here in Alabama I know who the sons-of-bitches are, but in Washington I so often got fooled. I trusted somebody and it turned out they rationalized."

Cliff had several offers to go to New York when he left the FCC. They wanted him to come with them to use the expertise he had learned in the FCC to fight the FCC. A lot of Washington lawyers would get experience in government and then they would go and join a New York law firm and return to Washington as the advocate of the corporations—using what they'd learned when they were in government to oppose the government. Cliff wouldn't do that.

I can remember a man who came down from New York. I can't even remember his name now, but he was an extremely nice, well-dressed man who had a big firm in Wall Street that dealt in communications matters. He was so nice to us and had such a nice wife. They took us out to dinner and told Cliff that they'd pay him fifty thousand dollars. Oh, everything just sounded grand. But Cliff and I both realized that he was buying Cliff's reputation for being a man of integrity.

The idea of Cliff's going back on his principles is just unthinkable. It never was a question. It was something he never even thought about. Cliff was a man of absolute principle, and he never cared much about money. He was terribly anxious to pay his debts, but clothes and big cars and fine furniture and all that didn't mean anything to him. He was not brought up with a whole lot of money, so it never had any great temptation for him. Ten thousand dollars was the highest salary he ever made in his life, and he never made that much after he got out into private practice.

There were people Cliff admired in Washington during this time. George Norris, for example, whom everybody admired and thought was a monument of integrity. And Cliff had the greatest devotion to Hugo. He and Hugo were like brothers. He had tremendous love for Bill Douglas and for

Lowell Mellett. He had complete confidence in Harry Plotkin and Ed Brecher and Larry Fly, all of whom worked with him at the FCC, and in Wayne Coy, who was its head. He thought Ben Cohen was a fine fellow and he always trusted him. He liked Tom Corcoran, but Tom was more of a politician and was apt to change without notice. Of course he had a tremendous admiration for Roosevelt. He thought Roosevelt was shifty, too, sometimes, but he always thought he was going toward the right ends. And he had a tremendous admiration for Ickes, whom he thought was a great fellow and as honest as he could be. Cliff was devoted to Henry Wallace and admired him very much. They had a good relationship. He always felt Lister Hill dealt with him in a very honest way, and John Sparkman, too. John and Lister were politicians, but he trusted them. And he liked Claude Pepper.

Seminary Hill was still a refuge for us. I remember going to a church meeting and one of the old gentlemen who taught at the seminary came up to me and said, "I'm glad to see that Cliff's taken a stand against these faceless informers." That was what made Seminary Hill a delight, because it was cut off from the mainstream of Washington politics. You could go back to Seminary Hill and have a pleasant, quiet neighborly life. I don't believe that the terror started in this country until McCarthyism started, when people got fired from the government. As long as crazy people like Dies were accusing people of being Communists because they read Marlowe, people didn't take it seriously.

Cliff's term on the FCC ended in 1948. He was forty-nine and I was forty-five. The poll tax committee had fallen apart, the Southern Conference was dead, the labor movement was moving to the right, and Cliff had refused reappointment to the FCC. We didn't know what we were going to do.

Our youngest daughter, Lulah, was less than two years old. I had Lulah when I was forty-three—great surprise. The Negroes always said, "Miss Virginia, you caught her on the change"—which meant the change of life. "Miss Lulah, she's gonna be a fine girl 'cause you caught her on the change." I never had heard that expression before, but I must say, she turned out very well.

We had no inkling at the time Cliff turned down reappointment to the FCC that the next years were going to be as hard as they turned out to be. Cliff had been offered a job at Yale earlier, but he had refused it at the time because he wanted to finish out his term on the FCC. Cliff thought that when we got back from Poland he would be going to Yale, but the offer never was renewed.

We were still not scared, even though we didn't know what we were going to do. We thought surely we'd land on our feet. It's curious that we weren't scared, but we really never were. We were naive, I suppose. We weren't Communists. We'd had friends who were Communists, but we certainly had had many friends who were anti-Communist, too. So we didn't feel threatened in the least.

15

The Loyalty Oath Cases

CLIFF OPENED HIS LAW office in Washington in 1948. He went in with Nathan David, who had worked for the FCC. They weren't partners, but they shared offices. Nathan was a very bright fellow from Boston. Cliff had high hopes about his law practice. Oh, high hopes indeed. While on the FCC he had made an extremely good reputation for being fair. Scoop Russell was the lobbyist at that time for NBC, and he had urged Cliff to accept reappointment. He said CBS and NBC and all the big chains would support him because they knew that while he might not rule with them all the time—which he certainly did not—he was so fair he never would prefer one over the other. They really wanted him to stay on. Cliff thought he would do very well in private practice because he knew so many people and they all seemed to think highly of him.

Cliff's first client was Roy Patterson, who had been fired for disloyalty. He was a country boy from Texas. He'd been in the war and been decorated for valor and bravery. He'd been wounded and had a metal plate in his back. In Washington, he'd worked in some government department and had been found disloyal because he belonged to the Washington Book Shop.

The Washington Book Shop was the Marxist bookshop run by Sarah Rosenbaum, whom I had known at the poll tax committee office. Sarah had coffees at the bookshop, and I used to go in there to talk with her. It was very open. I never saw anything concealed about it at all. She sold a lot of books about Marxism, and of course during the war that was okay. It was only after the war when the red-baiting started that belonging to the Washington Book Shop was disloyal.

Roy Patterson came to Cliff and asked him to take his case, and Cliff agreed. Cliff took him to the hearing. Roy Patterson said he had joined the bookshop because the books were cheaper there and it sold good records.

He also said it was the first place he'd ever been where Negroes and whites drank coffee together. He thought that was quite an asset. A member of the committee asked, "Why in the world would you, a Texas boy, want to drink coffee with Negroes?" He said he felt it was a very broadening experience. In the war he fought beside Negroes and he had come to realize that they're just like everybody else, human beings. And he enjoyed the experience.

I believe Cliff got him off the first time, but then they accused him again and he lost his job. He was such a nice boy and had such a nice wife. It just stirred Cliff up terribly. This boy came back with honors from the war, fighting for his country so bravely, and wounded, and then got fired from the government on the charge of being disloyal because he'd belonged to the Washington Book Shop. That's all they had against him.

The Patterson case got a great deal of publicity. It was one of the first loyalty cases. All the big corporations and radio networks that were going to give Cliff their business never came near him. After the publicity about Roy Patterson, he was dropped like a ton of bricks by everybody who had money to pay. Of course, the poor guys in the loyalty oath cases, when they got fired, were taken off the payroll. If they ever got reinstated, they had to pay a whole lot of bills. They'd finally get to the lawyer and frequently ask him if he'd knock off fifty dollars or a hundred. So our income began to go down, down, down. That was when I started teaching English.

When I took the course at Howard University after the Wallace campaign, I learned that through Howard I could teach foreigners English for three dollars an hour. Cliff was having a hard time in his law practice. He wasn't getting anything but loyalty oath cases. Three dollars an hour sounded like pretty good income. For four hours a day, I could make twelve dollars. One day's work was enough to pay the maid's salary. So I taught English to the Rumanian ambassador and his wife and to some Czechs and Poles.

At first, only two other lawyers, Dave Ryan and Joe Forer, would take loyalty oath cases, and they were regarded as left-wingers themselves. They were the ones who took Mary Church Terrell's case when she integrated one of the Washington restaurants. More people took the loyalty oath cases later on, but at first there were only those two lawyers and Cliff in all Washington who would defend people on loyalty cases.

Thurmond Arnold and Abe Fortas and Paul Porter had a big law firm, and they would defend people who'd been accused of being Communists who were not, but if they ever found anybody who had actually been a Communist or had even joined a Marxist study group, they'd send him over to Cliff. They wouldn't touch anybody who had actually been a Communist. Thurmond had once asked Cliff to go in to his firm and Cliff had turned him down because he had wanted to stay on the FCC. So Thurmond had formed his firm with Abe and Paul. They were all for civil liberties for people who had been accused of being Communists, but they wouldn't defend the civil liberties of people who actually had been Communists or even had had any association with Communists.

So the kind of clients Cliff got were people who were or had been Communists or had some connection with a Marxist study group—like Dave Boehm, for instance. He was a brilliant physicist at Princeton and was considered a second Einstein. But he had been a member of a Marxist study group, and Princeton fired him. He admitted he'd been a member of a Marxist study group, but he never had joined the Communist party, as I recall. He finally went to Brazil and then to Israel, but he ended up in London. He's now in the Physics Department at the University of London.

One of the worst cases Cliff had was that of a very bright black woman. She had been made head of a division in the War Department, and then she had been accused of disloyalty and of being pro-Communist and had been fired. Out on Seminary Hill, one of the men who was on the War Department Loyalty Board went to the same little Episcopal church we did. He and Cliff discussed the case, and Cliff said the impossibility of these cases was not knowing who the accuser was. This man agreed. He said he thought it was terrible to fire people on the basis of faceless informers.

When her case came up, the people who accused her were revealed: two women from the South, one from Texas and one from Arkansas. They were little old maids who'd been in the government for years and years and years. They had typed and filed—and dried up. They were pitiful old creatures who were furious because a Negro woman had been put over them as head of their department. These old-fashioned Southerners just couldn't stand working for a Negro. They said they had seen Communist literature on her desk and that's when they'd gone to the FBI.

As it turned out, the woman had been taking a course at George Washington University, a course in comparative politics that covered democracy and dictatorship and monarchy. She would go to her class from her office, so she would bring her books or whatever she was studying with her. These two little women had seen on her desk some books about communism, and they'd gone to the FBI. They broke down and cried and wept and wailed at the hearing. They said the FBI had promised them that they would never, never, never be revealed. But this man we knew who was on the Loyalty Board had demanded to know who they were, so they had to face the person they were accusing. And it turned out that the whole thing was absurd. The man that Cliff had talked to had thought it was just as wrong as Cliff did for people not to know who was accusing them. Cliff always thought that fellow was a very brave man, but that case did not set a precedent. No indeed.

When McCarthyism started, when innocent people, people who'd done absolutely nothing, were accused of crimes which were not crimes when they did them, the fear began. But Cliff fought against it. He'd come home from loyalty hearings where some old lady was called up and accused of being a Russian agent because she was taking a course in Russian literature. Somebody had informed on her, had said that they'd seen her reading Russian literature. Cliff would come home and throw up and have sick headaches. It made him not only furious but also sick.

You can't imagine how disillusioning it was to him to see people he admired and revered and thought were great friends fail to stick by him. Jim Rowe and Tom Corcoran and Abe Fortas and Paul Porter wouldn't touch these loyalty cases with a ten-foot pole, and Cliff didn't know Dave Ryan and Joe Forer very well. Cliff felt that he had no support at all. Hugo and Bill Douglas dissented in the cases that went to the Supreme Court, but all the cases were confirmed anyway. Even the great liberal Felix Frankfurter went along. The Court upheld faceless informers; it upheld loyalty orders; it upheld people being fired because some FBI agent, whose name wasn't revealed, said they had been at a meeting of the Spanish War Relief. It just got worse and worse.

At this point Cliff wanted very much to go back to Alabama and get out of Washington. Cliff's former assistant at the FCC, Red James, had opened a law office in Alabama with Cliff's nephew, Nesbitt Elmore, and they wanted Cliff to go into the law office with them, but we didn't go.

I'm sorry to say that I was the one who asked him not to. We had many friends in Washington, and I didn't want to go back to Alabama. I was much more afraid of the race issue than I was of the Communist issue. I'd been involved in the race issue. I'd been insulted up on the Hill. I'd had all these old men attack me. I knew what Southern politics was, and I knew how the people in the family felt—Cliff's family and my family. They all disagreed with us one hundred percent on the race issue, and that would be so painful. So I convinced Cliff that it would be better to stay in Washington. And I made a mistake.

The hardest thing Cliff ever had to face and the thing that tore him up the most was that he and his family disagreed so completely on the race issue. He hated to do things he knew they disapproved of. But the family stuck by him in spite of it. They didn't agree with him, but they still stuck by him.

Cliff also taught at Princeton on the weekends after he went into private practice. George Graham, who was head of the politics department at Princeton, had been our neighbor on the hill. He arranged for Cliff to teach Friday and Saturday mornings. George admired Cliff and hoped to get him on the Princeton faculty. But Cliff was not invited to return, because he made a speech at a peace meeting in 1948 at the Waldorf Astoria. Some of the alumni at Princeton had fits about that. They also objected to Cliff's involvement with the Lawyers Guild. Tom Emerson had been president of the Lawyers Guild, but since he was teaching at Yale he asked Cliff to become head of it. Cliff accepted, although he had never been a member. The guild's members were nice fellows and took a strong stand on the cold war, but there were some Communists in the guild and they drove Cliff crazy. They were always bringing up things like Albania and Montenegro and Inner Mongolia and passing a resolution on the Gobi Desert or something like that. He was so glad when that year was over. You can't imagine the foolishness of some of the right-wingers, and the left-wingers, too.

Cliff met Robert Oppenheimer at Princeton. Oppenheimer was the shining light of the Institute for Advanced Studies. Then Cliff spoke with Oppenheimer at a scientific meeting in Washington that Ed Condon organized. Ed was head of the Bureau of Standards. I remember the chief concern was to have the meeting someplace that wasn't segregated. Ed Condon got Cliff to speak about freedom of communication, and Oppenheimer spoke on the atomic bomb. That's when I first met him. He had a beautiful face. He was tall and slender and he had remarkable eyes—very penetrating, brooding eyes.

Robert Oppenheimer came down to Washington one time to see if Cliff would take the case of his brother Frank, who'd been accused before the Un-American Activities Committee. Robert Oppenheimer told Cliff that he had asked some lawyers in New York to defend Frank—some great liberal lawyers—and they had refused. When Frank was at the University of California, he had been a member of a Marxist study group for about six months, and this was apparently the problem with the Un-American Activities Committee.

Cliff agreed to take the case of Frank Oppenheimer. Robert and Frank arrived in Washington on Friday or Saturday. The hearing was on Monday or Tuesday. Cliff met with them at the office on Saturday and then he called me up. He said, "Look, Virginia, I'm going to bring Robert and Frank and Frank's wife out to spend the night. They're all so nervous, I think I really ought to bring them out in the country. Maybe it'll quiet them down. They're scared to death. They're the most nervous trio I've ever seen."

Frank was bright and very nice looking. His wife, Jackie, was a very funny and attractive Irish woman. That night Frank was in a state of panic, scared to death. He paced constantly. We fed him everything we could to quiet him down, but I don't think he slept at all. We found out later that he was terrified that he was going to involve his brother Robert. Now, I never knew whether the Marxist study group was an offshoot of the Communist party or really part of it, but Frank said that he began to study Marx at the University of California. He'd dropped out after a few months because he got bored with it. Have you ever tried to read Marx?

Robert Oppenheimer came down and had dinner one night, but he didn't stay over for the hearing. Of course, Robert was tried not very long after that, but I think he should have stayed, because Frank was scared to death. Robert, as I understand the situation, was never a member of the Communist party, but his wife had been married to a Communist who had been killed in Spain. Steve Nelson, a big Communist, was the one who had told her about her husband's death and had arranged for her to come home. I didn't know her and I don't know whether she was a Communist or not. I don't think Robert was ever a Communist, but whenever Steve Nelson would come out to San Francisco, Robert and his wife would always have him to dinner because they felt so grateful for the way he'd helped Mrs. Oppenheimer.

When the red hunt got even worse, Robert was called up. They were really after him because he opposed the development of the hydrogen bomb. Robert didn't think we ought to build it, and Edward Teller did. The account of the Oppenheimer hearings is an incredible document. They sealed him off from his own discoveries. He couldn't get access to the things he'd invented.

The Oppenheimers became friends of ours. After the hearing Frank Oppenheimer couldn't get a job. He'd lied about belonging to the Marxist study group because he was scared of involving his brother. He never went to jail, but he couldn't find a job. He had been fired from the university right away, so he went to a ranch near Denver, way in the mountains. When we went out to Denver with the Farmers' Union in 1950, Frank came up to see us. We found out later he was being followed by the FBI then all the time.

A man came to see us years later when we were living in Montgomery. He walked in and shook my hand. He said, "Why, Mrs. Durr, I'm so glad to see you again"—I'd never seen him before in my life—"How is Mr. Durr?"

"Fine."

"How are the children?"

"Fine."

"Well, how do you like living in Alabama? Do you miss Denver?"

"Not at all," I said. "I hated Denver. But how do you know so much about me?"

"I was the FBI agent who was assigned to follow Frank Oppenheimer, and every time Mr. and Mrs. Oppenheimer came to your house, I was always right behind them. When you and Mrs. Oppenheimer took the children out to the park, I was right there. I got to be real fond of you-all." I don't know whether he was still with the FBI or not, but it was the oddest thing to have this man walk in and say, "Oh, I know you well. I used to follow you every time the Oppenheimers would come to see you." It was really crazy.

Frank now has a scientific museum in San Francisco that is quite something. He wasn't as great a scientist as his brother, but he certainly was a lovely character. And he just adored his brother. I think he suffered more over his brother than he did over himself.

Before Frank Oppenheimer's hearing, during the two or three days he stayed with us, Ed Condon called up. The committee had been after him, too, because he'd been to Russia for two or three scientific meetings and his wife was a Czech. But Ed wasn't afraid to stand by Frank and help him. Ed's wife, Emily, was in the peace movement, the International Women's League for Peace and Freedom, which is where I first met her. The league was made up of marvelous, determined ladies who all wore health shoes and dressed in sturdy tweeds. I had parted with them on the issue of the Second World War. I had been in favor of fighting and they hadn't. But after the war was over, they took me back in. They were women of great integrity. They really believed in no war at all.

I was a member of the Women's International League for Peace and Freedom for years. When I returned to live in Montgomery the league tried to form a group here. It never got off the ground, but the women would come and stay with me—Anna Lee Steward and Mildred Olmstead. Oh, it was a remarkable group. Of course, the league took part in the civil rights fight, too. Cliff would have to go down to the bus station or the airport to meet the ladies. They usually came by bus because they never had much money. He never failed to pick them out because of their health shoes and the big bags of material they carried with them. He said he could tell them by the way they looked, and they did tend to look alike—solid, good, usually middle-aged women.

We were in London in the fall of 1967 when there was a great peace demonstration against the Vietnam War. It took place the same day as the big demonstration at the Pentagon that Norman Mailer wrote about in *The Armies of the Night*. Our daughter Lulah at that time was an au pair girl in Cambridge, so she came up to be with us. I was dying to go to the peace meeting in Trafalgar Square. Cliff wouldn't go. He had back trouble and he hated to stand around. He said he'd seen all the peace meetings he ever wanted to see in his life right in his own house with those International League people. He said they'd talk all night long and then leave him to wash the dishes. He never cared much for them. They were just such determined women. They were like the suffragettes.

In any case, Lulah and I went to the demonstration. And it was the strangest thing you have ever seen. It was at the height of the hippie movement and the whole of Trafalgar Square was filled. I never saw such a queer lot of people in my life. There were monks with brown habits on and cowls over their faces. I thought, "My God, the whole Catholic monastery must have turned out." Then I noticed they had little girls by the hands, little girls with short dresses on, miniskirts. Well, these were the miniest miniskirts I had ever seen. And they all had long hair. I thought it was awfully strange for a lot of monks to be leading these little girls around hand-in-hand, arms around each other, hugging and kissing. It seems a monk's habit was one of the hippie costumes of the time. Another group wore big hats with plumes, like the three musketeers. I thought I'd gone to a fancy dress party. And they were all fighting for the platform. I never did get it straight. It was like an old Trotskyite /Lovestoneite/Communist struggle. They were all fighting each other for the platform. It was just turmoil and uproar.

Then I saw a woman standing not far from me. She had on health shoes, tweed suit, felt hat, and an umbrella. I said to Lulah, "I'll bet you she is a member of the International League for Peace and Freedom." And Lulah said, "Mama, for God's sake, don't go over there and ask a strange woman if she's a member of the International League for Peace and Freedom." But I just knew she was, so I walked over, and of course I had on a felt hat and a tweed suit and health shoes. I said, "I wonder if by chance you're a member of the International League for Peace and Freedom." "Why, yes, I am," she replied, "I've been a member all my life." So she introduced herself, and I came back and introduced her to Lulah. Lulah was so embarrassed at that point that she disappeared. She went home. She said she didn't know what I'd do after that. I'd go up to any strange person.

I remarked to this woman about the strange assemblage. She said, "Well, this is a hippie gathering. The people that you would want to be with are meeting someplace else." She told me that she had come to the demonstration to invite these young people to join in a march that night. But she never got their attention.

In any case, she got me in a bus to go to the International Women's Peace and Freedom meeting. I rode for ages. Finally I got off in some distant part of London. Everybody around me was Pakistani or Indian. I'd go up and ask them where the town hall was and they'd reply in Bengali or Hindi. They couldn't understand me and I couldn't understand them. I was completely lost. I didn't know how to get to the town hall. Nobody could tell me. Finally I saw a police car with two policemen. I stood in the middle of the street and waved them down. They thought somebody had been molesting me or had seized my purse. But everybody had been very polite; it's just that I couldn't understand them. I asked the policemen where the town hall was. They tried to give me directions. I said, "I'll never find it. I don't know this street or that street. I'm a total stranger." So the policemen took me to the peace meeting in their police car.

There were a few people standing out front when I arrived. I think they thought I was a police spy or something. Anyway I went in and sure enough there was the whole International League for Peace and Freedom, just this enormous crowd of people—all my kind of people, tweeds and health shoes and cups of tea. They didn't know me from Adam, but they recognized me right away as a member of the Women's International League for Peace and Freedom.

The group had met all day and was going to meet all night. The speakers were members of Parliament and were following the events in Washington by international telephone. I got in with the solid citizens, as it were. Finally I had to leave. Some of the ladies took me out to supper and then somebody took me home. They were just as nice as they could be.

And that's how I met Emily Condon—in the Women's International League for Peace and Freedom, and that's how we met Ed Condon and got to know all these young scientists. Robert Oppenheimer had asked Cliff to represent his brother, but Cliff represented a lot of young scientists who were friends of Ed.

PART THREE

DENVER

1950–1951

16

Cliff's Back and Virginia's Petition

IN 1950, CLIFF got an offer to go to Denver with the Farmers' Union. It was the only acceptable offer he received. The lobbyist for the Farmers' Union was our friend Russell Smith from Alabama. He had introduced us to Jim Patton, the union president. Jim was a great liberal at that time, and he thought the cold war and the loyalty program were terrible. He asked Cliff if he would come out to Denver and represent the Farmers' Union.

The Farmers' Union was still an extremely liberal organization. It had taken a strong stand against the cold war and against red-baiting and the loyalty order. Cliff admired Jim Patton as a man who stood on principles.

By that time, we knew we had to sell our house, because we couldn't keep it up. Ann was out of college then and was working in Chicago at Hull House as a social worker. Lucy was in high school and Tilla was in late grade school. Our youngest daughter, Lulah, was born in 1947, so she was just three years old. The choice was between Alabama and Denver. Cliff wanted to go back to Alabama, but I didn't want to, so he took the job in Denver.

We moved to Denver in the summer of 1950, and we sold our house on Seminary Hill. That was a great trauma, selling the house we had loved. We drove out to Denver with all the kids, and Cliff became general counsel of the Farmers' Union Insurance Corporation, working with a man named Huff. We bought a little house, because it was cheaper to buy than to rent, and started to settle into a new life.

Cliff had had back trouble for quite a while before this, and the long trip across the country aggravated it. His back started just giving him hell, and he could hardly walk. Cliff finally had to have an operation. He was in the hospital in terrible pain for a month or so. Everything we'd gotten on the Seminary Hill house, we had to pay out in hospital bills and doctor bills and nurses' bills. I can't remember how much it came to, but it was terribly expensive.

The operation and trying to get settled took up the whole fall. It was a dismal time. Denver was cold and terribly dry, and we knew practically no one. We had stayed with Hugo's former Birmingham law partner, Barney Whatley, and his wife, Gertrude, when we first arrived. Barney had made a great fortune in molybdenum, and they were very nice to us. And we made one really good friend, Rudy Gilbert, who was the Unitarian preacher. He and his wife lived not too far from us, and they tried to make us feel at home. We went to the Unitarian Church because we liked Rudy so much.

While Cliff was in the hospital, I got a postcard in the mail, a double postcard, which said, "Do you believe in bombing above the Yalu River?" It was signed by Linus Pauling and Phillip Morrison and some other scientists. This was during the Korean War, and MacArthur was trying to bomb beyond the Yalu and get us into a war with China. It seemed to me that no one who had any sense would want to bomb above the Yalu and get in a war with China. I wrote on the answering card that I did not believe in bombing above the Yalu and signed my name and sent the card off. I never thought anything more about it. I never even told Cliff about it.

Cliff had been back to the office–still on crutches and in a cast—scarcely a week when the *Denver Post* came out with a huge headline saying, "Wife of General Counsel of Farmers' Union Insurance Corporation Signs Red Petition." That was me. Rudy Gilbert saw the paper and came over and stayed with me for a while.

The phone rang and it was Mr. Huff, head of the Farmers' Union Insurance Corporation.

"Mrs. Durr, have you seen the morning paper?"

"Yes, I have."

"Well this is serious business, a very serious affair. Now, we have a man in the office from the *Denver Post* who has written a letter for you to sign. He will publish it and all this will be cleared up—the thing about your signing a red petition."

"Well, what does the letter say?"

"He'll read it to you." The reporter read something like the following:

Dear Sir,
In reply to the article which was published this morning in the paper, I want to say that I have been duped by Reds. And I am sorry, and I beg your pardon. I did not know it was a Red petition. Please forgive me. I'm just a poor weak woman and my husband's been sick. If you'll just realize that I'm an idiot and a fool, and I'm just crawling on my hands and knees, everything will be all right—I hope.

"Mr. Huff," I said, "I couldn't possibly sign a letter like that."

"Mrs. Durr, I see you think you have a conscience. I'm a Quaker, and I also have a conscience. And my conscience tells me if you don't sign the letter, your husband's job ends at six o'clock this afternoon."

"Well, let me speak to Cliff."

"I'm sorry. You can't get through to Cliff."

"Well, Mr. Huff, you won't let me even speak to my husband?"

"No. We can't get through to Cliff."

"Has Cliff seen this letter?" I asked.

"No."

"Mr. Huff, I can't possibly sign it until I see Cliff."

"Well, I'm sorry, Mrs. Durr. We feel that this is your responsibility, not Cliff's."

"I'll think about it and call you back."

By that time I was about ready to go through the ceiling. Here we were out in this cold country with no friends and Cliff on crutches. Rudy agreed with me that it was a terrible letter, but he also said he just didn't know what in the world we'd do. The only other person who had signed that petition whose name was also in the paper was the chief justice of the Utah Supreme Court, a man named Wolfe.

I put in a long-distance call to the chief justice of the Utah Supreme Court. I told him apparently he and I were the only two people in the Rocky Mountain states who had signed this petition that was sent out by Linus Pauling, and that my husband was being fired by the Farmers' Union because I had signed it. I asked, "What do you think I ought to do?"

He was an awfully nice man, and he said, "Mrs. Durr, I think you're in a terrible fix. Are you people of wealth?"

"No."

He asked, "Do you have any money?"

"Hardly any." We didn't, except Cliff's salary.

"What can you do if you have no money to live on? Do you have any children?"

"Yes, three of them at home."

"Well," he said, "I think you will just have to do what people do when they are forced to do things that they don't believe in. You'll just have to do it. You'll just have to do it and say you are doing it under duress."

"But I don't see how I could keep my self-respect if I signed a letter like that."

"Well, sometimes you have to give up your self-respect. You have three children and no money and a sick husband."

The chief justice of the Utah Supreme Court was advising me to sign the letter. He was awfully nice about it, but he just didn't see anything else we could do. I was really in a fit. Poor Rudy was walking up and down and making coffee and trying to quiet me down. I tried again to get hold of Cliff, but the operator wouldn't let me go through. I happened to look out the window and there he was, hobbling up the walk on his crutches. Rudy and I rushed out and helped him up the walk and into the house.

"What in the world are you doing home?" I asked.

"I've been fired. They called me into the office and showed me this letter they wanted you to sign and said that you wouldn't sign it. They said you would have to sign it or I would be fired."

"Well, what did you say to them?"

"I told them I would never allow you to sign a letter like that." Then he had walked out of the office and called a taxi and come home. There we had been worrying and wondering and figuring—and Cliff just immediately knew what we had to do. When Cliff told me that, I fell into his arms. We had each other. That's about all we had.

The man who was head of the Denver paper was named Palmer Hoyt, I believe. Cliff wrote him a real hot letter—or I did, I forget which—but they never published it.

The day after Cliff was fired, Jim Patton came around and told him to wait until they had a board meeting. Then, of all crazy things, the union called Cliff and said, "Mr. Durr, you'll have to come back to the office." The Utah AFL-CIO had called the Farmers' Union a bunch of Communists, so they were defending themselves against the charge of communism. Poor Cliff had to go back and defend the Farmers' Union against the charge of communism.

A short while later Cliff had to go in the hospital again for his back. At that point Cliff's mother and his sister came out to see us. His mother was about four feet high, and she had never really approved of me entirely. She'd always thought I had led Cliff astray as far as Southern positions were concerned. But she was just wonderful. She said there was nothing to do but to go back to her house until Cliff got well. So that's what we agreed to do.

The Farmers' Union had made a big switch just a few weeks before my name was in the paper. Jim Patton had been very good about fighting the cold war, fighting the loyalty order, fighting the witch hunt. But then Truman had gotten him to Washington and taken the union into the fold, and the union liked being on the political inside and having an edge over the Farm Bureau. The whole Farmers' Union just switched over to the cold war and witch hunt and began to throw people out. Aubrey Williams and the union in Alabama were thrown out. The union said it was because there were not enough members, but the real reason was that the Alabama union was too radical.

Every union and every organization was just cleaning out, as it was called. Everybody who they thought might be under suspicion or might

Durr Blames Firing On Denver Post Story

Clifford J. Durr, former member of the federal communications commission who was dismissed recently as attorney for the National Farmers Union in Denver, said Saturday he was not dismissed "because either Mrs. Durr or I ever was a Communist."

Durr's dismissal by the union came after it was disclosed in The Denver Post on Feb. 21 that Mrs. Durr was a member of the Independent Action Committee of Denver, an organization that circulated ballots asking reaction to the question "Shall we bring our boys home from Korea and make peace with China?"

"No question was ever raised about my competence (by the union)," said Durr. "I was fired because the Farmers Union thought it could placate The Post and forestall possible attacks upon itself by firing me."

REFUSED TO RENOUNCE A. D. C.

Mrs. Durr's affiliation with the Independence Action Committee of Denver, Durr said, was not renounced by her and she was unwilling to say that she had been "tricked, deceived or duped" into joining the organization because "that would have been untrue. She joined it with a sincere desire for peace and a conviction that negotiation is a sounder basis for real peace than is endless death and destruction."

After disclosure that Mrs. Durr was a member of the committee, according to Durr, his wife offered to resign from the committee if "her membership embarrassed the Farmers Union." The union, however, said that "mere resignation" wasn't sufficient and that she would have to "publicly confess" or admit she had joined the association not knowing its purposes or background, Durr said.

"The choice offered was the surrender of her self-respect and intellectual integrity or the termination of my employment" (by the union), Durr said.

SCORES POST STORY.

Durr charged that The Denver Post story about Mrs. Durr's membership in the action committee indicated by "indirection and innuendo that one or the other of us are Communist."

He said his dismissal by the Farmers Union did not stop the union from having him appear as its attorney in a pretrial conference in Salt Lake City after the disclosure that Mrs. Durr was a sponsor of the action committee in Denver.

C. E. Huff, who is chief of the union's insurance operations, informed Durr that his "usefulness" to the organization was at an end but did request that he continue to represent the union in a libel suit against the Farm Bureau Federation in Utah brought because the Utah organization charged the "Farmers Union is Communist-dominated," Durr explained.

REQUESTED BY HUFF.

Durr added: "I attended this conference at the specific request of Mr. Huff who evidently assumed my knowledge of the facts and law involved would more than offset any embarrassment (to the union) from my identification with the case.

He said that he was sent to the Utah trial conference because "lawsuits are tried in courts and not in the newspapers" and that the Utah courts were not concerned over "my indirect identification by matrimony" with the action committee.

Durr, who lives at 2555 Ash street, is going to Washington for a visit and then intends to live in Alabama. For several weeks he has been incapacitated by trouble with his back and this week his physician told him he would be able to travel to the east without jeopardizing his health.

Denver Post, May 31, 1951. (Courtesy of the *Denver Post*) get them in trouble had to go. It was a kind of save-yourself time. Those who got fired were looked on as traitors, as being in the service of a foreign government; they were disloyal to their country and they were blacklisted. They were made complete pariahs. You can't imagine how terrified people were.

There was a big military hospital at Denver, where a lot of men wounded in Korea were sent. I rode the bus a lot in Denver because it was so hard to drive in the snow, and I would often talk to these mutilated young men. They hated the war in Korea. They would tell me what a dreadful war it was and how miserable they were and how they despised it. It was really a bad year, I can tell you. To me it was just a terrible, terrible year. I was so glad to get back to Alabama I didn't know what to do.

Before we went to Alabama, though, we went back to Washington for Ann's wedding. She came out to Denver at Christmastime and got engaged to Walter Lyon. Her father was still recovering from the bad back operation, but we had a Christmas tree and Walter came. It was a very happy time. They planned to get married in Denver, but then Cliff got fired and they got married earlier.

We went back to Washington that spring. The flowers were blooming. My sister was in New Mexico with her son Sterling, whose wife was having a baby, so we stayed with Emily and Ed Condon. They paid no more attention to the accusations of our being subversive than a fly on the wall.

Ann and Walter had a perfectly beautiful wedding in the Unitarian church. Everybody brought flowers. The church was just full of flowers.

We hadn't sent out formal invitations, but we had telephoned our friends and everybody we'd ever known in Washington and Virginia came. Hugo, of course, came, and Bill Douglas came. The Condons had a perfectly lovely reception at their house afterward. It was a very happy occasion. Walter was Nancy and Mike Straus's cousin, so the Strauses had a big party for them, too. Mike was head of the Public Power Division of the Interior Department, and we had known them when we lived in Washington. The hysteria in Washington by that time was pretty high, but our old Washington friends seemed not to be scared of us. They all came, anyway. Right after that, we drove down to Alabama.

PART FOUR

MONTGOMERY

1951–1976

17

Family and Friends

CLIFF'S MOTHER WAS a beautiful woman. She had been a great beauty in her youth, and she was a true Southern lady. She believed in the Confederacy and she believed in the Civil War and she believed the black people were our responsibility. We had to be kind to them and look after them. She also believed in segregation. In fact, she was just about the most typical Southern lady of the old school you can possibly imagine. She did not approve of my ideas at all. I don't know that she even approved of Cliff's ideas. Cliff's family would say, "Well, you know, if he hadn't married Virginia he wouldn't have changed." Nevertheless, Cliff's mother took Cliff, me, and our three daughters who were still at home into her house in Montgomery. Cliff was in bed there for more than a year. Her love for her son and her loyalty to her son overcame all the disapproval she may have felt about his ideas. The rest of the family was just as loyal.

When we came to Montgomery in 1951, the civil rights struggle hadn't started yet. At first we were well received and everybody was extremely nice to us. They knew that Cliff had been in Washington, but they really didn't know what he had done. As one of his uncles said, "I declare, if Cliff had just stayed in Alabama, he probably would have amounted to something. But going up there and working for the government—here he is flat on his back and broke, too." They were very frank about it. They thought Cliff had made a great mistake to leave Alabama.

After Cliff got well, in 1952, he opened his law office in Montgomery. Cliff shared offices with Red James, and Cliff's nephew Nesbitt Elmore was also in the office from time to time. But then Red James got a job in Texas in the law firm of Roy Hofheinz, who had a radio station in Houston and who eventually built the Astrodome. Red is down there now and is a judge in Houston.

Cliff's mother, Lucy Judkins Durr, with flowers in her garden in Montgomery. She did not entirely approve of me or of many of the views Cliff and I held after our years in Washington, but she took us into her home when we had no place else to go.

Cliff got involved in a number of civil rights cases that his nephew Nesbitt Elmore had taken. Then, through Mr. E. D. Nixon, the head of the NAACP in Montgomery, and Aubrey Williams, who had become the editor of the *Southern Farmer,* he began getting cases from people who had been beaten up in jail and people who had been charged 500 percent interest on loans. Cliff also represented the Durr Drug Company, of which his brother James was the head, and he represented Fanny May, which was a federal mortgage agency.

We were starting quite a nice little law business, and I was Cliff's secretary. Not that he wanted me. While he was sick I had taken a course in typing and shorthand and had gotten a job in the insurance department of the state government. I made $125 a month, which is hardly enough to live on, but it helped. Then when Cliff opened his law office he could not find anybody who could spell. The secretaries he tried were whizzes on the typewriter, but they couldn't spell, and Cliff was a great purist as far as the English language is concerned. With a great deal of reluctance Cliff allowed me to come in and help out for a while, and I just stayed on.

I loved working in the office with Cliff. We had the three children who were in school and it meant that Cliff's hours and mine were the same. It really worked out very well. I worked for him from the time he opened his office in 1952 until he closed the office in 1965, but he protested every day. He said that I wasn't a proper secretary because I was too interested in the cases. I asked him a lot of questions. It is a marvel that we got along as well as we did because I was dying to get in on the cases, and he just wanted me to be a proper secretary.

When we came back to Montgomery, I resigned from all the organizations in which I had been active in Washington—the Women's Division of the Democratic party, the Southern Conference, the ACLU. I realized that we were going to have a terrible struggle just to get by. We had three children at home, and we were living with my mother-in-law, who as I've said, was a perfect example of the traditional Southern lady. She certainly didn't believe in mixing up the races or getting involved in anything like that. For several years we just lived in Montgomery very quietly.

The only time that I was active in anything was when Mrs. Rutledge asked me to do something. Mrs. Irvin Rutledge, Clara, belonged to the First Presbyterian Church. The Rutledge family was a very great family from South Carolina, so Mrs. Rutledge had a great deal of assurance. She had been fighting the battle of equal rights for blacks for a long time. Whenever there was a rape case or lynching or anything like that she would get a group of church women together and go to see the judge or sit in the front row in the courtroom. She was in the Southern Conference for a while, which is where I met her first. But she was also in the First Presbyterian Church in Montgomery, and that's where I saw her most.

I hadn't said anything controversial to anybody for two or three years, quite a long period for me to stay silent. Then Mrs. Rutledge called me up one afternoon and said, "Virginia, you have got to take me out to the YWCA campground at Grandview."

"Well, Clara," I said, "I'm right in the middle of doing something for Cliff."

"Well, I'm sorry, but you have to go. I'm going to take supper to Mrs. Cooper." I think that was her name. She was the wife of the Negro bishop of the AME Zion Church and she was on the national board of the United Church Women. The United Church Women were having a meeting out at Camp Grandview, and Mrs. Cooper had been invited to speak to them. The YWCA camp told the United Church Women that she could come but she couldn't eat dinner there, because she was black.

Mrs. Rutledge was an imposing woman. Her call was like the voice of the daughter of God. Cliff said, "You've got to go with Mrs. Rutledge. You know, you can't fool around with Mrs. Rutledge." She's ninety years old now and still full of spirit. She still is God's spokesman. So I went and got her and went out to Camp Grandview.

We heard Mrs. Cooper and all the other ladies speak. They were lovely, the brotherhood of man and all. Then the time came for supper and the lady who ran the camp came up and told Mrs. Cooper that she was terribly sorry but the rules of the camp were such that she could not be served. So Mrs. Rutledge stepped forward and said she had brought this lady's supper with her. Well, like Mrs. Bethune, Mrs. Rutledge was also putting the ladies to the test, I think, because several ladies caught up their suppers and said, "We will go outside and eat with Mrs. Cooper." But the camp director said, "I am sorry but you can't eat on the grounds of Grandview. It's against the law, against the rules." So we had to go off the grounds of the camp and sit down and eat our supper. By this time Mrs. Cooper and some of the other ladies were crying, and nobody ate much. We told Mrs. Cooper we would take her home, but she said, "No. You are not going to take me home. I'm going back there and I am going to stay till the very end." She dried her eyes and we took her back and stayed until eleven o'clock that night.

It was a very embarrassing evening for everybody concerned. One lady got up and said, "Mrs. Cooper, I don't want you to think we are prejudiced on account of color. We want to stay separate, but you see I am almost as black as you are, so it's not color." She rolled up her sleeve and she was very sunburned. "It's just that you-all have such different church services," she explained. "Your services are so emotional—people screaming and hollering and throwing themselves around in church. We don't like those kind of services." Mrs. Cooper said, "Well, many black churches don't have those kind of services and some white churches do."

The meeting finally ended, and we took Mrs. Cooper home. It was a very upsetting evening for the white ladies, and for the black ladies, too. In time, when the United Church Women here finally integrated, Mrs. Cooper forgave us.

The church was the first organization that integrated in Montgomery, and that came about through a long process. When I came here, there were two groups of United Church Women, one black and one white. It was sometimes rather absurd. The white United Church Women would have a black woman from Africa to speak about the missionaries in Africa, and the black African woman would eat lunch with us. She was received as an honored guest. Meanwhile, the black United Church Women would be meeting on the other side of town because they were not allowed to come to the white United Church Women's meeting.

A group of people in town decided to integrate the two groups: Mrs. Fletcher McLeod, whose husband was a Methodist preacher; Mrs. Andrews, who was very active in the Presbyterian church; Tom Thrasher, who was then the director of the Church of the Ascension, an Episcopal church; Mrs. Moreland Smith, who was a very active member of the Church of the Ascension; Mrs. Irene West, a black woman, and her sister Mrs. Campbell; Mrs. Lee Simpson; and Mrs. Rutledge. They got together and formed an integrated prayer group. We used to meet and pray and sing and hold hands and have a cup of tea afterward. We always met in Negro churches. Mrs. King lived in Montgomery then, Mrs. Coretta King, and she and Mrs. Abernathy came. We grew to be about a hundred women, black and white, from all over the state.

The group stayed together all during the bad times until the last meeting—at St. Jude's. The head of the United Church Women in the South, Mrs. M. E. Tilly from Atlanta, came to our meeting that day. We had brought box lunches and we ate together. During this period, John Crommelin had a group of people in Montgomery who were fighting integration, and they took all the license numbers of our cars at the meeting. Crommelin was a retired admiral from Montgomery who was known for his right-wing and anti-Semitic views. He published the names and telephone numbers and addresses of everybody at the United Church Women meeting in his paper, *Sheet Lightning*. The women began to get terrible calls at night and were harassed in other ways. That broke the group up. We never met after that.

The women became frightened when their names were publicized. Even their husbands began getting phone calls from people who threatened to stop doing business with them if their wives went to any more integrated meetings. Several husbands took out notices in the papers disassociating themselves from their own wives. One man disassociated himself from his aunt, and another disassociated himself from his daughter. They were scared of the repercussions of their business. I was lucky—Cliff stayed by me.

Except for the United Church Women, I wasn't involved in any integrationist group—or any other kind of group—for a long time. I was busy working for Cliff in his law office and busy with our family. We had a few friends, but our life centered around our girls and Cliff's family.

There was a particular time, until they left Montgomery, that Aubrey and Anita Williams were intimate parts of our life. After the war was over, President Roosevelt had nominated Aubrey for appointment to the Rural Electrification Administration. Aubrey had made quite a name for himself in Washington, particularly for his work on the National Youth Administration, and he was very well thought of by the New Dealers. Of course, the reactionaries thought he was terrible.

When the Senate held hearings on Aubrey's nomination as head of REA, he was opposed not only by some of the Yankee reactionaries, but by Southerners like John Bankhead of his own state. John said Aubrey was a radical and he couldn't support him. Lister Hill supported Aubrey, as I recall, but John Bankhead did not. Aubrey never got the job. He was turned down by the Senate of the United States.

In the meantime, Aubrey and Marshall Field had become friends. Marshall Field, of the Chicago Field family, was a supporter of the New Deal. He was so outraged by the Senate's rejection of Aubrey that he gave him $500,000 to go anywhere in the United States and buy anything he wanted and start up any business he wanted to. I suppose it was a loan. Aubrey came straight down to Montgomery, Alabama, and bought a farm paper called the *Southern Farmer*, which was owned at that time by William Baldwin, a nice enough fellow but very conservative.

Aubrey hired Gould Beech as editor of the *Southern Farmer*. Gould was a brilliant fellow who had been editor of the *Montgomery Advertiser*. He and Aubrey built the *Southern Farmer* up with baking advertisements and baking contests and all sorts of things. Cliff represented the *Southern Farmer* and got a retainer from Aubrey. I forget how much it was, but it certainly was a big help. Aubrey had a big building and the latest printing machinery. Among all the farm talk about how to make cookies and fertilize corn, Aubrey would slip in some editorials and bits of news that he thought would show the Southern people how to get out of the fix they were in, how to overcome racism and poverty.

Aubrey was a fascinating man. I don't think I ever knew a man whom both men and women loved to the degree they loved Aubrey. His father's family had had a plantation in Eutaw, in Greene County. They had owned slaves, but they lost everything during the Civil War and settled in Springville, just north of Birmingham. His father, who had been raised on a plantation, owning slaves and all, became a carriage maker. I don't know whether he owned his shop or whether he worked for somebody, but Aubrey was proud of him. He was a great craftsman. Aubrey remembered his grandmother, his father's mother, who had been the mistress of the plantation.

His grandmother had saved a few linen sheets and a few pieces of silver and china, and as poor as they were, she always slept on linen sheets and ate with silver and off of china. She lived the life of a martyr, somebody who'd lost everything. She must have been a very depressing woman—always weeping for the past.

Aubrey's father married a Miss Taylor who came from Jefferson County. The Taylors were real pioneer types. They had come down the Appalachians and ended up in Jones Valley, where Birmingham and Springville are, and started farming. They were the frontier type. They could do anything. Aubrey was terribly proud of that side of his family, because he thought they were first-class, hardworking people. He'd go on for hours telling stories about his uncles. He told of one uncle who raised everything they ate and everything they wore. His wife made his suits out of linsey-woolsey that she had spun. Aubrey said that this uncle of his, his mother's brother, was a fine old man but a real country fellow. He would go in to Birmingham on the East Lake streetcar with a load of eggs and fresh vegetables and buttermilk and sell them. Aubrey's sister was getting to be a young lady and she was extremely prissy and very ashamed of this uncle who looked so countrified and wore an untailored suit that his wife had made for him. His sister used to hide so she wouldn't be recognized by her uncle. One day she and Aubrey were riding to town on the streetcar when their uncle got on in the linsey-woolsey suit. He saw his niece and nephew and began in a loud voice to tell them about his wife. "Well, my wife's doing all right, but she's got the runs. Between the bedroom and the backyard, we just had a terrible time cleaning up the mess." Aubrey said his sister blushed and tried to crawl down in the seat.

Aubrey loved to talk about his country kin and the mules they had. Aubrey had a wonderful sense of humor. He knew I was a woman's libber—or at least I thought I was—so he would tell me about what the women did on the farm. They'd get up and go downstairs and build a fire and cook breakfast—hot biscuits, bacon, eggs, grits, and ham, and everything you can think of. Then the men went out in the fields while the women washed the dishes and straightened up the house. Then the women went out in the fields and they hoed until twelve o'clock. Then they came in and cooked up this great big dinner for the men—fried chicken and corn bread and lots of vegetables. And the men came in and ate. Then the men went outside and sat under the tree for fifteen minutes or half an hour while the women washed the dishes and straightened up. Then the women went back with the men to the fields and hoed all afternoon. At night, they'd come in, and the men would sit on the front porch because by that time their day's work was done. But the women had to go in and warm up whatever was left over to give the men for supper. That was their day. And on Saturday they had to do the washing. That was a pretty rough job itself, with iron pots of water.

Aubrey was always teasing me about what an easy life I had—how his aunts and cousins just took their lot in life for granted and didn't feel put upon. They'd go out in the fields and hoe even when they were pregnant, up until the last few months.

Aubrey's family was very poor. His mother was a fine woman, but she had six or seven children. And his father drank. Aubrey went to work when he was five years old. He worked with the laundry man and would run in and deliver the packages of laundry. Then he went to work at a department store in Birmingham as a cash boy. Aubrey didn't learn to read and write until he was fourteen years old.

Aubrey's mother had belonged to the Cumberland Presbyterian Church, which was a rural Presbyterian church. In the Southern Presbyterian Church you had to have a theological degree to preach, but in the Cumberland Presbyterian Church you could preach if you'd been called. Of course, you had to be called if you were in the Southern Presbyterian Church, too, but you also had to go to school and have a degree. Aubrey went to the Cumberland Presbyterian Church with his mother, and he attracted the attention of the preacher's wife because he was such a bright boy. He always was such a charming, engaging kind of fellow, had a wonderful sense of humor and laughed a lot. He made people happy just to be around him. The preacher's wife began to teach Aubrey to read and write.

Aubrey's mother and father thought it was the most awful thing in the world to take charity, that it would ruin their self-respect. That's one reason Aubrey was so emphatic about having jobs in the WPA. He said there were times when literally all he and his family had to eat was peas. Their neighbors would let them pick pea fields. They'd go out and pick black-eyed peas and live on that until his father made a little money.

Aubrey was very proud of his family, but he used to complain that some of his relatives became poor white trash. He would tell about the women with snuff dripping down and men spitting tobacco juice all the time and having pellagra and hookworm. He didn't blame them for being poor white trash, but they were. But his own people were not poor white trash; they were good, hardworking, plain people who had to scramble for a living. But they were very poor.

While Aubrey was working in the department store, Loveman, Joseph and Loeb, one of the managers was so taken with him—he was fourteen or fifteen then—that he came to him and said he and his wife had no children and they would like to adopt Aubrey as their own son. He would be able to go to school and everything would be given to him. I said, "Well, what was your reaction?" And he said, "It was one of absolute, total fury. The idea of a man coming to me and asking me if I wanted to be adopted away from my own family." When he went home and told his mother and father that the man wanted to adopt him, they got furious, too. His father wanted to go and cuss him out.

Aubrey went off to Cumberland College—now it's Maryville College—and he got an education there. Then he went to the theological seminary in Cincinnati. During the First World War he went to France as an ambulance driver for the YMCA, then joined the French Foreign Legion, and finally enlisted in the U.S. Army.

There's a story that a black man rescued Aubrey during the war and that Aubrey then lost his Southern prejudice about blacks. He said that that wasn't strictly true. Aubrey and a black fellow were pinned down in a trench under German fire. They had to crawl I don't know how many miles, and both of them were wounded. They helped each other out trying to get to a safe place. It was no dramatic rescue by one or the other. He said it was just a question of both trying to get out of the German fire and save each other. But that experience in the Army did break down a lot of his Southern prejudice, I'm sure, because he didn't get a bit of that up at Maryville College. He was up there with all those people around the Smoky Mountains, and they were just as racist as they could be.

Anita, Aubrey's wife, was the beauty queen of Cincinnati. She was from a German family, but she used to laugh and say she had some Aztec blood in her, Mexican or something. Whatever she was, she was a beautiful woman. She had dark hair and was very shy, a timid kind of woman. It was strange that anybody as beautiful as she was was as shy as she was. And she adored Aubrey. They had four boys, Winston, Aubrey, Jr., Morrison, and Jerry. Anita didn't really like Montgomery. She made a few friends, but she wasn't very happy.

When we first came to Montgomery, Aubrey was really enjoying his life here. He was trying to form a farmers' union, an integrated farmers' union, and was already being accused of being a radical and a red. He had remained active in the Southern Conference for Human Welfare, until the conference split up over Henry Wallace.

Aubrey had a lot of visitors, all kinds of people—people who were studying the South and people who were making surveys, foreign newsmen—the same kinds of people who in later years came to our house. Aubrey's house was always the center of things, a lovely place to go. Anita was a delightful hostess and a marvelous cook. They had wonderful parties in the backyard. Aubrey would invite anybody he thought might possibly see the light.

Aubrey was a very popular man, although people thought he was rather dangerous because he was too radical. Whatever he did, he did it with everything in him. He was the most enthusiastic person I've ever known. He made every day exciting. He'd come running up the steps to our office and burst in with a new discovery. He bought a farm in the country that Morrison was running. He was trying all kinds of new experiments—and he had just discovered that if you put a whole lot of earthworms in sawdust, it would in time turn into just marvelously rich dirt. Well, it's true; it does, in a matter of years. Aubrey was going to buy up all the sawdust in the country and get all the earthworms to transform the soil. He was just thrilled over the idea. Then the pig parlors came along. Aubrey burst in one day and he was all full of pig parlors. He wanted Cliff to put pigs all over the place, pig parlors. And that's what Aubrey did up in Autauga County. He and Morry raised a lot of pigs. Whatever he did, he did it with every ounce that was in him. He loved baseball. Baseball bored me to death and always did, but Aubrey went to every baseball game the Montgomery baseball team had. You'd think it was the Giants or something. He'd scream and yell and cheer as though it was the greatest team ever. He loved to play cards. He would make a card game seem like the most important thing in the world.

I remember one time a very conservative real estate man said to Cliff, "Cliff, you know that friend of yours, Aubrey Williams, is the most striking man I ever met in my life. I wish I had courage enough to see more of him, but he's got such a reputation for being a red and radical that I'm scared to do it." He admitted it. Aubrey was more or less shunned by a great many people who thought he was red and a radical, particularly after he'd been opposed by John Bankhead.

Aubrey would come up almost every day to our office and bring coffee. He was very gregarious. He loved to be with people. He'd come downtown and walk up and down Commerce Street and see who he could see. I don't think anybody ever asked him in to coffee very much, because they were scared to be seen with him. So he'd buy the coffee and bring it up to our office and we'd sit around. That's when he would tell us about the earthworms and the pig parlors, or whatever he had on his mind. But he kept up with politics, too. He was highly interested in politics. He had lent Mr. Nixon the money to keep the NAACP going, and he was trying to organize an integrated farmers' union. He was really doing very well.

I think when he came down to Montgomery Aubrey intended to run for office, but then he saw how impossible it was. He was a great friend of Jim Folsom, and he was behind Jim in a lot of things. Jim Folsom, drunk as he used to get, was probably the best governor Alabama had as far as race relations was concerned, so Aubrey did all he possibly could, and this was still the period before the *Brown* decision.

During this time, the early fifties, Cliff was trying to get his law practice started, but he kept getting police brutality and loan shark cases. Cliff was awfully glad to be back home. He was devoted to his family. He loved his brothers and sisters and his mother and his aunt. And he loved the First Presbyterian Church. Well, he didn't exactly love it, but he went back into it and became a deacon. He really wanted to settle back into Montgomery and be a part of it, but he had broadened out a great deal, and things like the loan shark cases really got to him. The people who were charging the Negroes tremendous rates of interest were some of the best people in Montgomery. That shocked him and made him ashamed. He thought it was shameful for white men who had a good background and were gentlemen to take advantage of Negroes. He felt the same way about some of the insurance cases he had—where some poor black person would pay on an insurance policy for years and years and get sick and find that the fine print said the policy didn't apply. He took one of those cases all the way to the Supreme Court of the United States and got twenty-five dollars for it. We always had to take the cases up as paupers because our clients never had any money. I had to type the cases on the typewriter and then we'd have them photocopied. We never had the money for printing.

You see, even after Cliff got the reputation for representing blacks, the Negroes who had money never came to us. They didn't believe that they would ever get justice, so the only thing they could do was to get the most powerful lawyer in town who was willing to take their case and pay a good sum to him. So they would go to some powerful white lawyer and they would accept the most awful kind of treatment. The lawyer would say to them, "Well, Joe, you old black scum, what are you doing here now? You been fightin' with Mamie again?" Or something like that. Putting them down and treating them like children. "Yessuh, Mr. Hill, I reckon I'm a little troubled now and I hope you can get me out." It would make you sick to see a Negro being willing to accept this position and a white man treating him that way. But that's the way they survived and that's the way they got off in court. If they hired one of the Hills, a prominent and politically active family of lawyers in Montgomery, the jury would usually let them off, but if they hired Cliff, they were not sure they'd get off at all. So the only ones who ever came to us were the ones that didn't have any money, who couldn't pay Mr. Hill, who couldn't pay the lawyers who were the big shots in town.

Cliff was brought up to believe that a Southern gentleman never took advantage of a black man. The black man had his place, and *he* had *his* place. But to cheat a black man or to take advantage of his ignorance was common. It shocked Cliff when he found that white men in Montgomery were taking advantage of poor, ignorant Negroes who couldn't even sign their names. It made him ashamed that they acted the way they did, and he felt a slight contempt for them.

Cliff hadn't changed as much on the racial issue as I had, during the years we were in Washington. He hadn't had the same experiences I had. He thought segregation was wrong, but he had never come in contact with the race issue the way I had. Cliff had worked in Washington on a high level. He was up there with the big shots—Jesse Jones and Tom Corcoran and Ben Cohen, the people in Washington who were at the top. He was in a position of great power—first in the Reconstruction Finance Corporation and then on the FCC. Cliff was the one who decided whether or not the RFC would lend people money, which meant their banks were saved or not saved or a defense plant was built or was not built. So he was in a position of great power in the RFC. On his decision rested the fate, say, of a man whose bank was failing or somebody who wanted to start a defense plant or even giants like the armaments companies. Then when he went to the FCC, his decision determined whether someone got a radio channel, which meant money or no money. He was always being courted or wooed by big shots, by the lobbyists for CBS and NBC and ABC.

While Cliff was at the FCC, presents would start arriving a month before Christmas—big crates of oranges and wonderful pears from Oregon. Cliff had a rule that if it was edible, we'd keep it. Lyndon Johnson used to send us a great big turkey from Texas, a broad-breasted turkey. And we'd get hams and boxes of candy and delicious fruit. Presents would just come rolling in. I remember when the children had scarlet fever during one Christmas how thrilled they were because I let them open all the presents as they came in. When Cliff got off the FCC, all that stopped. The next Christmas we got one box of crackers.

Cliff was at the higher levels of government in Washington, but when he went into private practice in Montgomery, he came into closer contact with blacks and their problems. Mr. Ed Nixon, who was head of the NAACP in Montgomery, brought Cliff a lot of cases. Of course, they didn't pay much, but still he brought them to us. Mr. Nixon was a very nice man and we liked him a lot. He was an honest, forthright kind of fellow. I got to know his wife very well, too—the sweetest, prettiest thing you ever saw, just a lovely woman. If you ever want to meet a real Southern lady, meet Mrs. Nixon.

I had known Mr. Nixon for two or three years and I'd always called him Mr. Nixon and he called me Mrs. Durr. One day I saw him at the post office. I said, "Why, hello, Ed." People called him Ed Nixon. He didn't say anything. I held out my hand and said, "Hello, Ed," and he didn't take my hand. I went on back to the office with the mail and in about fifteen minutes, he came up and sat down.

"Now Mrs. Durr, I want to get something straight with you."

"Well, what in the world?"

"Look, don't you ever call me Ed again. If I called you Virginia, I'd be lynched. Suppose in the post office you said, 'Hello, Ed,' and I said, 'Hello, Virginia.' You got me in trouble right then and there. And to shake my hand in public that way, that's going to get me in trouble. Now when I can call you Virginia, you can call me Ed. And I'll shake your hand in public when it's safe. You ought to have better sense than to come up to a black man in the public post office and say 'Hello, Ed' and put out your hand."

Now this was different from most Negro men, if you know what I mean. He was really trying to educate me into the proper etiquette, which he thought I had lost, I suppose, living in Washington. It wasn't that he was mad at me. It was that I was putting him in danger. He didn't think they were going to do anything to *me*, but he thought they might do something to him.

Mrs. Parks, who started the bus boycott in 1955 by refusing to give up her seat to a white man, was different, too. I couldn't call her Rosa until she could call me Virginia. Now she finally does, and that took twenty-odd years. I had to call them Mrs. or Mr. until they could call me by my first name.

We were all caught in this same terrible segregated situation. Segregation in Montgomery was just as tight as it could possibly be. One of the things that struck me particularly was the situation on the buses. It was terrible to have the driver yell, "Move back, nigger!" I didn't ride the bus very often, but I did sometimes. The city had a mobile library. I remember one time when it stopped by the fountain at Court Square. A black boy and girl got on it and tried to get a book, and the librarian wouldn't let them. Actually the whole idea of segregation was based on the idea that blacks were diseased—usually venereal disease was what people suspected the blacks of having. You couldn't drink from the same water fountain or use the same bathroom because they were diseased. You couldn't sit by them on the bus because they smelled bad. You couldn't eat with them in the drugstore or restaurant because they were offensive, smelled bad, and were diseased.

The Negroes had to suffer under the most painful thing in the world— the feeling of being unattractive. When somebody says to you, "I think your ideas are crazy and I think for you to support Mr. So-and-so is idiotic and as far as I'm concerned you're crazy," it makes you mad. But the white people were telling the black people that in their own person they were unattractive, that they were ugly and black and smelled bad and were probably diseased. That's a terrible burden for people to bear.

We were caught up in the system of segregation in Montgomery just like everybody else, and it began to affect the way we felt about living in Alabama. Cliff had such mixed emotions. Alabama was home, and we were near his family. But our ideas—our ideas about race especially—were painfully different from those of Cliff's family. The loan shark cases and the police brutality cases brought home to us that some white Southern gentlemen, so-called, were perverting the tradition of protecting the Southern Negro and were exploiting him instead.

Those early years of law practice here, 1952, 1953, were disillusioning and financially difficult. I often wondered how we would make it.

18

The Eastland Hearing

STRANGELY ENOUGH, THE COMMUNIST witch hunt never came South until Jim Eastland held his big hearing in 1954. The idea of calling people Communists just because you didn't agree with them doesn't work so well when people know each other, and people in the South knew each other. People in Montgomery knew Cliff and me. They might not agree with us, but they knew we weren't Communists and they knew we weren't about to try to overthrow the government by force and violence.

By early 1954 we knew the Supreme Court would soon decide *Brown* v. *Board of Education*. Nobody knew when, but it was already a topic of conversation. Jim Eastland was running for reelection to the Senate in Mississippi on the platform that if the Supreme Court voted to desegregate the public schools, it would show that the court was clearly an arm of the Communist conspiracy. Eastland was on the Judiciary Committee and head of what was called the Internal Security Subcommittee. The Internal Security Subcommittee corresponded to the Un-American Activities Committee in the House.

We went down to the office one morning in March and there was Aubrey Williams sitting on the doorstep clutching a subpoena. He was being called down to New Orleans to appear before the Senate Internal Security Subcommittee. He wanted Cliff to represent him. Cliff had been sick for two years and he was just getting on his feet again. He'd had a little heart trouble—a little angina, the doctors said—so I was worried about his going to New Orleans and getting into another loyalty fight. He'd been in so many in Washington. I didn't want him to get mixed up in anything that would make him sick again, so I called the doctor, and the doctor said under no condition should Cliff go to New Orleans and represent Aubrey or anybody else in a controversial case like that. It might kill him. I kept telling him over the weekend that he just couldn't do it.

Then on the following Monday morning we went to the office and found a marshal waiting for me with a subpoena. I was called to New Orleans to appear before the Internal Security Subcommittee. With that, Cliff said he was going. He called the doctor and told him that staying in Montgomery while I was in New Orleans would be more of a strain on him than going to the hearing.

We walked out to get some coffee and on the way we met John Kohn, a very conservative lawyer but a lovely man. Cliff had known him all his life, but I didn't know him well at all.

[He came up to Virginia and said, "Virginia, who's going to represent you down in New Orleans?" Virginia said, "Well, I reckon Cliff will. He's gone to these things up in Washington. He knows how they operate." John's reply to that was, "A man doesn't have any more business representing his wife in a situation of this kind than a surgeon would have performing a delicate brain operation on his wife." He said, "Virginia, unless you tell me I'm intruding, I'm going to New Orleans as your lawyer, and I'm going at my own expense." Which he did.][1]

Myles Horton of the Highlander Folk School was also subpoenaed, and he came to Montgomery to see us before the hearing. Cliff put us through some practice hearings. He'd act the part of Jim Eastland and he'd make us all so mad we'd want to kill him.

As Cliff put us through rehearsals of what we could expect in New Orleans, I got madder and madder. Jim Eastland had gone to the University of Alabama and was almost my age. He came from the hill country. He was no Southern aristocrat at all. The nice girls wouldn't have anything to do with him, but he married a very nice woman. Her sister was active in the Women's Society for Christian Service of the Methodist Church. If Jim Eastland's name ever came up, these nice, sweet Southern ladies who belonged to the Women's Society for Christian Service would all say, "Poor Mrs. Eastland." That was the way of the Southern ladies. They'd never say, "Her husband's a no good so-and-so." They'd say, "Poor Mrs. Eastland. Now, her sister's a lovely woman. You know, she's in the Women's Society for Christian Service. And Mrs. Eastland is really a nice woman. I declare, she has such a hard time." They'd never say exactly what it was, but you got the idea.

[1]Cliff's comments during the interviewing of Virginia for the Columbia University Oral History Collection, New York, 1976, part 3, p. 153.

The idea of Jim Eastland, just as common as pig tracks as they used to say, trying to call me to account—it made me so angry my adrenalin began to rise. I wasn't scared. I was just as mad as hops.

Before we went to the hearing, Aubrey and Cliff's attitude was one of outrage. Here they had been faithful servants of the United States government, and they knew so many people in Washington. The idea that no one had risen to stop the hearing and support them made them furious. But they wouldn't call anybody and ask for help. They absolutely refused. I said, "Look, you may stand on being a Southern gentleman and being so proud, but I'm not going to be so proud. I'm going to call up the people in Washington and tell them what I think about this."

The first person I called was Lyndon Johnson. By that time, Lyndon was majority leader in the Senate. He'd been a friend of Aubrey's, too. Aubrey gave him his first job down there in Texas and really got him started on his career. I called him all day long. He was busy. He was on the floor. He was in a conference. I never did get him. That night I kept calling at the house and finally got hold of Bird about ten o'clock. I was a great friend of Bird's, so I said, "Bird, I've got to speak to Lyndon." "Well, Lyndon's already in bed asleep," she said.

"Bird, you know, Jim Eastland has called Aubrey and me down to New Orleans, and we're going to be put on the hot seat in one of those inquisitions. I've got to speak to Lyndon."

Bird said in that sweet way, "Virginia, I don't know what it's all about, but I know you and Aubrey are good people, so I'll wake up Lyndon."

Lyndon got on the phone and I said, "Lyndon, what are you doing sending these bloodhounds down here after Aubrey and me?"

"Why, honey, I don't know a thing about it."

"Here you are the majority leader of the Senate and you don't even know that we're going to be hauled up before the Senate Internal Security Subcommittee."

"Why, baby, I don't know a thing about it. That's terrible. What can I do for you?"

"Can you stop it?" I asked.

"I'm afraid I can't stop it now," he said.

"Well, if you can just see that no other Democrats come, that will help a lot." I knew that if Eastland brought enough committee members with him there'd be hell to pay. He could claim the sanctity of the Senate and all that.

"Well," he said, "I can't promise anything, but I'll do the best I can." And he did, because no Democrats came with Jim.

On Sunday afternoon I got hold of George Bender of Ohio. He'd been a great supporter of the anti–poll tax fight because he was trying to get the black vote. George Bender was considerably to the right of Bob Taft, but he was a great Taft supporter, and he let the poll tax committee use his mimeograph machine and his frank. We'd send out things all over his district and put his name on them. It really did him a lot of good. He was elected congressman-at-large from Ohio.

I called up George in a little place called Chagrin Falls. I said, "George, this is Virginia Durr."

"Sweetheart," he said, "are you as beautiful as ever? What can I do for you?" He was the biggest flatterer you ever knew.

"George, I've been called up before the Internal Security Subcommittee down in New Orleans and I just think it's terrible."

"Oh, honey," he said, "you don't have to worry. You never did anything wrong. A sweet girl like you, all you have to do is just tell the truth."

"Yes, George, that's exactly what I'm going to do, but they're investigating the Southern Conference, which started the fight on the poll tax. If I'm going to tell the truth, I'm going to have to tell how we used your frank and your mimeograph."

"Now, Virginia," he said hastily, "there's a provision in the Constitution that you don't have to tell everything you know."

"Oh, no, George, there's no Fifth Amendment for me. I'm not a Communist, never have been a Communist. I'm not going to invoke the Fifth."

"Well, Virginia, what can I do for you?"

"George, if you'll just see that no Republicans come to New Orleans with Jim Eastland, that will help a lot."

I never could write to Lyndon and George and thank them, but I know that they did work behind the scenes to keep anybody from going to New Orleans with Eastland. Nobody was there but Jim Eastland and a horrible character named Richard Arens, who was lawyer for the subcommittee. Oh, what a character he was!

Another curious thing happened about our trip to New Orleans for Eastland's hearing. A Mrs. Ethel Clyde was a great friend of Myles Horton and Jim Dombrowski. Her husband had owned the Clyde Steamship Company and she was quite rich. She must have been about ninety years old or well into her eighties. When we arrived in New Orleans we found that she had reserved a whole floor of the St.Charles Hotel for us and paid all the bills.

By that time John Kohn had arrived, and John was looking very grand in a white linen suit and very handsome and Southern. Mrs. Clyde took us all out to dinner that first night, and she put John Kohn on her right at dinner. During the evening I thought I heard Mrs. Clyde say to him, "Mr. Kohn, are you a Communist?"

"Well, uh, no, uh, I never have been."

"Oh, Mr. Kohn, you should be one. I have been one for years and it's done me a world of good. I owe all my present good health"—I thought I heard her say—"to being a Communist."

I thought, oh, my God, John's going to get scared to death and run right out. So after dinner was over I said, "John, did Mrs. Clyde ask you if you were a Communist?"

John said, "Do you know what that old lady said to me? She turned to me and said, 'Mr. Kohn, are you a *nudist?*' She said, 'I owe all my good health to it. I've been a nudist for years.' She must have had about five petticoats on and one of those high Victorian dresses. The idea of Mrs. Clyde being a nudist was just too much." Mrs. Clyde stayed with us at the hearing the whole time and paid all the bills.

[That night everybody said that they weren't going to invoke the Fifth Amendment, that they'd answer any questions about themselves but they weren't going to feed Eastland any names. I had to tell them that the Fifth Amendment was for you and not anybody else. You can't invoke it to protect anyone else. After you refuse to answer questions about other people, you're in contempt.][2]

The first day they took two men from Miami Beach who were not members of the Southern Conference, who had never been. One was Leo Scheiner, who was a lawyer. The other was a Mr. Shlafrock, who'd been a contractor in Miami. Their only contact with the Southern Conference had occurred during an outbreak of anti-Semitism in Miami. Swastikas had been painted on the synagogues and temples, a lot of nasty anti-Jewish literature had been passed out, and a synagogue had been bombed. Jim Dombrowski of the Southern Conference Educational Fund had gone down there to write about it for the paper and also to see if he could help in any way, and that is why these men from Miami were called up before Eastland. They both pled the Fifth Amendment.

Then Paul Crouch got on the stand. He was an informer for the Justice Department at that time. He'd been a Communist and had been sent to Alcatraz for trying to foment a revolution in the Army. He got out in three years, but then he went back into the Communist party. I understood that he'd gotten out of prison because he'd promised to be an informer. He had become a professional informer and was paid twenty-five dollars a day. He was crazy as a bat. He said that the Russian Navy was going to land at Miami Beach because there were so many Jews there. Can you imagine anything crazier than that?

[2]Cliff's comments during the interviewing of Virginia for the Columbia University Oral History Collection, New York, 1976, part 3, p. 160.

That night I just couldn't sleep. I was in a state of anger and rage. So I wrote a statement.

[I woke up in the middle of the night. Virginia had gotten a typewriter in the room. I heard the typewriter pounding away, and I said, "What are you doing?"

She said, "I'm getting up a statement."

I said, "Why are you doing that? I told you you're going to jail, but you said that's all right. You'll tell them all they want to know about you, but you're not going to feed them names."

She said, "I know, but from what I saw today, I'm not going to have anything to do with that committee whatsoever."

So I read the statement in which she started off by saying, "I have the highest respect for the investigatory powers of the Congress. I think that's an important function. But from what I saw going on yesterday, this is not a proper exercise of Congressional powers—this is nothing but a Kangaroo Court.". . . And she ended the statement: "I stand in utter and complete contempt of this committee."][3]

I told John Kohn that I wasn't going to testify, that I refused to say anything, and he said that was all right, that I could stand mute. But in my statement I would have to say I wasn't a Communist, which I did put in. When John got back to Montgomery, everybody teased him. They said John was the only man who had ever made me stand mute. He shut me up completely.

When I got on the stand, I wouldn't take the witness seat, because I refused to admit I was a witness. I was being persecuted. I took the attitude that I was a victim, not a witness, so I wouldn't even take the witness fee they paid.

[Well, of course, they put Virginia on the stand the next day, and she wanted to read her statement. Eastland wouldn't let her, but she handed it to the press.

Virginia didn't invoke the First Amendment or the Fifth Amendment or anything else. She said in answer to the first question, "My name is Virginia Durr. I'm the wife of Cliff Durr. That's all. From here on out, I'm standing mute. That's all the questions I'm going to answer. I'm not going to have anything to do with the committee." The TV camera was grinding away. When they asked questions of Virginia she just remained silent. Every

[3]"The Reminiscences of Clifford J. Durr," Columbia University Oral History Collection, New York, 1976, part 3, pp. 294–95.

now and then she'd take out a compact and powder her nose. It drove them into a rage.]⁴

Eastland began asking all these crazy questions. It was the maddest thing you have ever known in your life. They asked me about somebody named Tony Ambatielos. Did I ever know Tony Ambatielos? I couldn't think. I racked my brain. I couldn't remember to save my life, but I just kept saying, "I stand mute."

The main person they kept asking about was this Tony Ambatielos and Betty Ambatielos. For the life of me I couldn't remember if I had ever even heard their names. Years later when I was in London one summer, I picked up the *London Times* and there it was: "Mrs. Betty Ambatielos Pleads for Her Husband Who Is Confined on an Island in the Aegean Sea." Then it came back to me. I remembered the names. Right after World War II, when the Greek revolution was being quashed, I got a call from the first Mrs. Edgar Snow, whom I had met but didn't know. She wrote under the name of Nyna Wales. "Mrs. Durr," she said, "I understand you're a great friend of John L. Lewis."

"Well," I replied, "yes, I am. He helped us in the anti–poll tax fight. I got to know the whole family quite well."

"Well, Mrs. Ambatielos is here and her husband is on an island in the Aegean Sea. They're being starved and his condition is awful. Would you call Mr. Lewis to see if he can help free her husband?"

Tony Ambatielos was head of the Seaman's Union, and I don't doubt that he was a Communist. I didn't know him or his wife, but I knew Mrs. Edgar Snow. Snow had two or three wives after that, but this was the first Mrs. Snow. I did call Mr. Lewis. I said that Mrs. Ambatielos was trying to get her husband out of the terrible situation he was in, in the Aegean Sea on this rocky island. Mr. Lewis said in that Shakespearean voice he had, "Mrs. Durr, I am very sorry that Mr. Ambatielos is suffering, but I think I have my hands full without going to the defense of Mr. Ambatielos." That was all there was to it. Then I had to call up Mrs. Snow and tell them that Mr. Lewis wouldn't see her. That was the extent of my involvement with Mrs. Ambatielos.

I'm sure at that time that my phone wasn't tapped. I wasn't a big enough prize. But I'm sure Mr. Lewis's phone was tapped, because it was the only possible way they could have known about this, through a tapped telephone.

It's odd how these things follow you. Recently, one August when I was at Martha's Vineyard, I picked up the *New York Times*, and there was a picture of Mr. Tony Ambatielos who had been sprung from prison on an

⁴"The Reminiscences of Clifford J. Durr," Columbia University Oral History Collection, New York, 1976, part 3, p. 295.

island in the Aegean Sea. My life's been haunted by this man I never met. But there it was. It was the craziest thing.

[When the hearing started, John Kohn and another lawyer who was representing Jim Dombrowski, Ben Smith of New Orleans, said, "We can't find out what the rules for a Senate committee are. We've written to Washington and we can't find them. We wish you'd let us know what the rules are so we can behave accordingly." And Eastland said, "Sit down. I know dilatory tactics when I see them. I'll let you know what the rules are as we go along." Then John asked if he had the right to cross-examination. Again, pounding the gavel, Eastland said, "Mr. Kohn, you're supposed to be a lawyer. You should know that never in history has the right of cross-examination been permitted before a Congressional committee. Sit down."

They got through with Virginia and they went ahead with their inquisition of Aubrey Williams. When Aubrey got through, Eastland leaned over and said, "Mr. Williams, in view of the fact that you've been such a cooperative witness"—which he hadn't been; he'd said, "I'll tell you about me," but he refused to involve anybody else—"I'll waive the rules and permit your lawyer to cross-examine Mr. Crouch."

Well, I was taken aback. I knew nothing about the man. But in qualifying him on opening day, they put Crouch on the stand and he had told how he had been in Alcatraz and confined to the military barracks for three years for subversion in the ranks. It was supposed to be forty years, but after three years he was turned loose and he'd become very active in the Communist Party. Then he moved to Russia. Here's a guy who had one year in the U.S. Army as a private and the Russians had him lecturing at their military college which was the equivalent of our West Point. And they let him in on their plans against the Panama Canal. These were the yarns Crouch would spin. This was all I knew about him. He said he spent five thousand hours telling the FBI what he knew about Communist activities and he wasn't through yet. You asked him a question and it was like putting a dime in a jukebox. He just played a record. With all the other witnesses, he was well rehearsed. He had met Aubrey Williams after a speech. . . . He referred to Aubrey as "Comrade Williams" and gave all the dates, times, and so on.

During my cross-examination, I didn't know what to do except to let the press see this guy with all of his paranoia—not paranoia; he was a psychopath. So I just asked him questions to let him brag about his Communist activities. He began to brag that he was a greater menace to the country in his heyday than Russia and the hydrogen bomb combined. He told how he was trained to blow up planes. I said, "You were trained to lie, too." "Oh yes," he said, "we were trained to lie."

After I got a lot of this out, I asked him why he left the Communist

Party. I suspected that he had been an agent or informer all the time. I said, "Why did you leave the Communist Party?" He said, "I left the Communist Party, Mr. Durr, to save the lives of my children and yours if you have any. I saw some of our top scientists handing out atomic secrets from the laboratories in California to members of the Communist spy ring and at last I saw this thing that I had been connected with in all of its horror. I got out to save the lives of my children and yours if you have any."

I said, "When was this that you saw atomic secrets being handed out?" "1941." I said, "You mean the lives of your children and my children were in danger all this time and you waited seven years before you reported it to the government?"

I finally had about gotten through. Then I said, "Mr. Crouch, are you still a Communist?" All I got was a speech. Then I said, "Can you prove you're not a Communist?" At that point, Arens, the counsel, leaned over and said, "Mr. Crouch, is Mr. Durr a Communist?" Crouch said, "I don't know if he still is, but I saw him at meetings of the top Communist echelons in New York."

Eastland got a little uneasy then and said, "Let's have another witness." But I said, "Let's get all this on the record." So I began to ask him when it was. He'd been very specific about everybody else. He'd rehearsed his testimony. He said, "Between 1939 and 1941." I said, "Let's be a little more specific." I kept trying to pin him down to a specific time or date of the month, day of the week, whether it was winter or fall or summer. He couldn't remember anything more than it was between '39 and '41. I asked what place, where at least one meeting was held. "Well, we changed meeting halls so often because we didn't want to meet at the same place all the time." He kept getting vaguer and vaguer. I asked him who was present at any of these meetings. He mentioned Browder and Foster and all the big shots of the Communist Party. "Well, what went on there?" "There were a lot of speeches made." "Who made the speeches?" "Browder and Foster and others." He, Crouch, had made some speeches. "Did I ever make any speeches?" "No." "What did I do?" "You just sat there." "Were you ever introduced to me?" "No." "Didn't anybody ever tell you what my name was?" "No, but you're one of those distinctive looking people like Dr. Robert Oppenheimer. Once you see their face, you never forget it."

At that point, I asked Mr. Eastland to put me under oath, and I was sworn in. I said, "Now, Senator, every word that he has said about my attending these meetings of the top Communist echelon is an absolute and complete lie. I've never been to a Communist Party meeting. I've never been a member of the Party. I've never even thought about being a member of the Party. Now, both of us are under oath, and it's your responsibility as chairman of this committee to see that one or the other of us is indicted for perjury." Well, of course, nothing was ever done about it.][5]

 I was so shocked at the conduct of the hearing that I called up Senator Langer, who was head of the Judiciary Committee. He was an old fellow from North Dakota who smoked a cigar. I had known him because he'd been a supporter of the anti–poll tax bill. I told him what was happening at Eastland's hearing—Jim Eastland harassing people and this crazy Crouch telling all these wild tales. So Langer requested that the U.S. attorney attend the sessions and he sat there the whole time.

 We got an awfully good press, too. There was a young man down there from the *Montgomery Advertiser* named Fred Anderson. We didn't know what he would write, but one of his stories ended, "All day today, reporters at the press table could listen to the Eastland hearings and see out the window where an American Flag fluttered gently." He was showing how shocked the reporters were that such an inquisition could occur in this country.

 The hearings went on all week. On Thursday or Friday I had come out to go to the ladies' room, and when I came back Cliff was lying on a bench in the Federal Building white as a sheet. Jennings Perry had come to the hearing to help us out. He had been president of the poll tax committee at one time and editor of the *Nashville Tennessean*. He was a dear friend and a wonderful fellow. He still is. He had come down to see what he could do to help us with the press, and I'm sure he did help us. Jennings was leaning over Cliff, and I thought he'd had a heart attack. Everybody was running around scared to death.

[Virginia was out when this happened. Crouch was put on the stand again. He began to tell about Virginia, how Mrs. Roosevelt would pass cabinet secrets to Virginia and Virginia would pass them on to the Communist spy ring. I get angry very slowly and very seldom, but when I do, I sort of blow up. I found myself tensing up during the testimony. Jennings Perry was sitting behind me and I must have given some evidence of this, because he patted me on the shoulder as if to say, "Don't let him get your goat. Don't get worked up about this idiot. Nobody's going to take him seriously." I thought I'd relaxed, but something happened to me when he got up to leave the witness stand. For a while I blacked out. What I know is what I read in the papers later. I guess my hands were white and I was gripping the jury rail, and as he got up to leave I vaulted over the jury rail and blurted: "You goddam son of a bitch, lying about my wife that way—I'm going to kill

[5]Cliff's comments during the interviewing of Virginia for the Columbia University Oral History Collection, New York, 1976, part 3, pp. 164, 166–70.

you!" Maybe I did say it, but I don't remember. I do remember a couple of marshals grabbing me. I didn't get within ten feet of Crouch. The marshals were holding me firmly but, I have a feeling, rather gently as if to say, "Look here, we don't blame you, but we can't let this kind of thing go on in the federal courtroom." They escorted me out.

Well, I was all right, but Jennings threw me down on that bench. We got up off the bench finally and I said I was all right. I said to Virginia and Aubrey, "Let's go out and walk around." We walked around the park outside the federal building for about ten or fifteen minutes. There's a little coffee shop nearby and we went in and had a cup of coffee. Then we started back to the federal building, and outside the federal building I saw an ambulance parked. I looked around and saw no signs of an accident. I was wondering about the stupidity of an ambulance running out of gas.

The hearing room was on the third floor of the federal building and the elevators were so far that we walked up the three flights of stairs. I was going down the hallway toward the hearing room when a young doctor came up to me with his stethoscope. He examined me and then said he was going to write me a prescription for a sedative. Then came an older doctor down the hall, and the younger one turned to him and said, "Well, doctor, I think he's going to be all right. I've written him a prescription for a sedative." The older one said, "Weren't you in my class in heart at Tulane Medical School?" "Yes sir." He said, "Didn't I teach you a damn thing? Here's a man with a history of heart condition—he blows up like this, and you're going to dismiss him with a sedative?" He turned to me and he said, "You're going to the hospital with me right now. I've got an ambulance waiting for you downstairs."

I was completely baffled. I began arguing with him and finally I said, "You let me go in the courtroom just for three minutes and I'll come on out and get in that ambulance and go to the hospital with you." He said, "Why do you want to go back in there?" I said, "I just want them to see me walking in there with my own two feet to let them know they haven't gotten me down." He said, "Does that mean a lot to you?" I said, "Yes, it does." He hesitated a moment. He said, "No. I'm not going to let you do that because you'll go in there and blow your top again and we'll be hauling you away in a hearse instead of an ambulance." We negotiated awhile. Finally I said, "Well, if you send that ambulance on, I'll get a taxi and go to a hospital with you."

He took me over to the hospital and put me in a very nice room. Mrs. Clyde must have put up the money for that, too—I don't know—but they started giving me electrocardiograms and all kinds of tests. I picked up the afternoon paper and while I was lying up there in the hospital, this guy Paul Crouch had demanded that a police guard be assigned to him to protect him from me—three policemen assigned to protect Paul Crouch from me

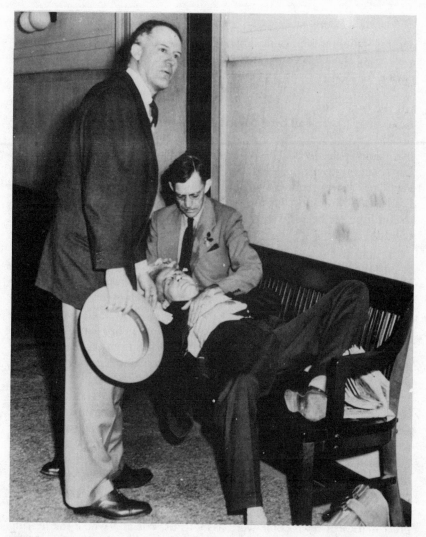

Cliff, in a state of near collapse at the Eastland hearing, with Aubrey Williams and Jennings Perry. (Courtesy of Wide World Photos)

while I'm lying up in the hospital. And damned if one of the policemen didn't drop dead of a heart attack that night. They kept me in the hospital about a week and then let me go some place on the coast for about two weeks.][6]

[6]Cliff's comments during the interviewing of Virginia for the Columbia University Oral History Collection, New York, 1976, part 3, pp. 171–74.

We went to Gulfport after Cliff had been in the hospital about a week, and my daughter Ann came down. Cliff was not terribly sick, but he was sick, so we stayed in Gulfport two or three weeks. I think Mrs. Clyde was paying for all this.

[At the conclusion of the hearings, Anderson took a poll of all the newspaper people who had been covering the hearings throughout. The question, as I recall, was: "From what you've seen of these proceedings, which of the principals involved do you regard as the greatest menace to the American form of government and way of life?" Jim Eastland was number one, Paul Crouch was number two, and Arens, his counsel, was number three. Eastland had announced at the beginning of the hearings that he was going to continue the hearings in Birmingham in a few weeks. He decided he'd call that off.][7]

Eastland held these hearings in the South to get Hugo Black. Eastland was running for reelection to the Senate and he was running against the prospect of a decision like *Brown*. He wanted to convince people in the South that the Supreme Court was communistic. Young Hugo Black, Jr., was a representative of the AFL-CIO then. And John Sparkman had run as the vice-presidential nominee in 1952 with Adlai Stevenson. Eastland was going to blast John and draw Hugo Black, Jr., into it because he represented the AFL-CIO, which was supposed to be communistic, too.

One of the advantages of living in Cliff's hometown is that nobody believed Cliff and I had the talent to overthrow the government by force and violence. Even the people of Montgomery thought that was silly. In Montgomery everybody's grandfather had tried to overthrow the government by force and violence in the Civil War. My grandfather tried to overthrow the government by force and violence for four years. There was hardly anybody we knew in Montgomery whose grandfather hadn't tried to overthrow the government by force and violence, and they still were revered as great heroes. A few people were nasty to us, but as a whole the hearing didn't cause as much of a ripple as you might think. The fact that John Kohn defended me and the *Advertiser* reporter who came down wrote such good things about us helped.

This was 1954, and the McCarthy furor was at its very height, but we got hundreds of letters and telegrams in our support. Still, Cliff worried about his family because the Durrs had been very conservative people. They had never been involved in politics in any way, and we just hadn't discussed anything controversial. That's one reason I was so unhappy. I was impris-

[7]Cliff's comments during the interviewing of Virginia for the Columbia University Oral History Collection, New York, 1976, part 3, pp. 174–75.

oned in a wall of conformity. We couldn't say anything about anything. We just went along being pleasant because Cliff was sick and his family was so kind to us. We couldn't very well stay in their house and then argue with them about segregation and McCarthyism.

I don't think McCarthyism really had much impact at that time in the South. They hadn't had any of the hearings here until ours came along. But the threat of integration did have impact. Southerners were very, very much opposed to it.

When we got back to Montgomery, Cliff stayed in bed for a few days because the journey had tired him. We were still living at the Durrs' house. Cliff's mother and his aunt and his sister met the situation by not referring to it. Cliff's illness they referred to a great deal. They worried about him. But they just didn't refer to the hearing. It was as though it had never happened. That's the way Southern women have so often met a difficult situation—just acted as though it hadn't happened.

But more than anything else, Cliff was worried about his brother James. James had stood up for him in the face of criticism and had given him the job as counsel for the Durr Drug Company. Cliff knew that some of the people on the board thought that was an ill-advised move, so he was terribly anxious to see how James took the hearing. We hadn't heard a word from James except for a check that he sent. After we got back to Montgomery, James called up one day and said he was coming by on his way back from lunch to see Cliff.

There was a bathroom next door to the bedroom, so when I heard James coming up the stairs, I went into the bathroom, leaving the door open just a crack so I could hear. James sat down by Cliff and he said, "Cliff, you sure did make a damn fool of yourself down in New Orleans." My heart just sank. I thought, this is the end. This really will do Cliff in if James feels this way and all the family feels this way. Then James went on to say, "Now look, Cliff, if you want to kill a man, why in the world did you try to do it in the federal courtroom with the marshals sitting all around? If you want to kill a man, you ought to take that son-of-a-bitch and wait until he gets out on the street. Get him in an alley or on the street and then kill him. That's the only way to handle a son-of-a-bitch like that. To try to kill him in a federal courtroom, I think that's the silliest thing I've ever heard of. I think you were very foolish." Well, I rushed in and flung my arms around James and kissed him.

The commissioner of police in Montgomery at that time was Dave Birmingham, who had come from Birmingham, Alabama. He'd known my father and me as well. He came up to me in the post office and said, "Virginia, do you and Cliff need any protection?"

"What do you mean?" I asked.

"Well, have you had any bad telephone calls?"

"Yes, but not many and not very bad."

"Well," he said, "if you feel that you need any protection, I'll stake some policemen out there."

"I don't think we need any because we haven't had any serious threats or anything like that. Mostly people just call up and breathe heavily and hang up the phone."

"I don't think you're going to have any trouble anyway because the Durrs are known as killers."

"The Durrs are known as killers?" I was absolutely taken aback.

"Why, yes," he said. "You know, Cliff's grandfather tried to kill that fellow down on Court Square, and then Cliff tried to kill that fellow in the courtroom in New Orleans. The Durrs have the reputation of being killers, so I think you're going to be perfectly safe."

I couldn't wait to get home to ask Cliff how the Durrs got a reputation of being killers—all Presbyterian elders and deacons, conservative people. Cliff said in a perfectly matter-of-fact way, "Well, yes, my grandfather did try to kill a man one time." He said his grandfather Durr was very slow to anger. A man had come into the Lehman-Durr cotton business about ten o'clock in the morning one day and said something to him and he didn't get mad until about three o'clock that afternoon. It took him all that time. But then he got mad because he realized the man had impugned his honor. He had a gun in his desk drawer that he hadn't used in years. He got his gun out and walked up Commerce Street, which was the main merchant street of Montgomery in those days. He told everybody he met that he was going up to the square to kill this Mr. So-and-so. By the time he got to the fountain, there must have been three hundred people there to watch him kill that man. Nobody interfered at all. They just came up to see the killing.

Grandfather Durr was a dignified-looking man. He looked like the Presbyterian deacon that he was. He went up to this man and said, "Mr. So-and-so, you've impugned my honor as a gentleman and I'm going to kill you." And he drew out his gun and fired at him seven times. But the gun hadn't been used for many years and it misfired every time, so he didn't hurt him at all. He salvaged his honor by the attempt, at any rate.

Cliff told me all this very calmly. I asked him, "Wasn't Grandfather Durr ever brought up before the Grand Jury for attempted murder?"

"Oh, no," he said.

"Why not?" I asked.

"Well, the people in Montgomery knew my grandfather, and they knew that he was an honorable man. They figured that if Mr. Durr thought the man needed killing, he probably needed killing."

Cliff and I spent the summer of 1954 in New England. Some people named Wilcox invited us up because they knew Cliff had been sick. They admired our stand in New Orleans and sent us some money—five hundred or a thousand dollars. We went and visited the Strauses, too. They were related through marriage to our son-in-law Walter Lyon. Then we visited Miss Florence Luscomb up in Massachusetts. What a great lady she is. She is now in her eighties and she comes from a long line of Massachusetts Supreme Court justices. She's like Mrs. Rutledge; she's been in some cause all her life. We visited the Grays, too. John Chipman Gray and his wife were friends of ours in Washington. His grandfather was the famous John Chipman Gray of Harvard. They were descendants of the old abolitionists, and they were helping the civil rights fight in the South as much as they possibly could. Then we visited our daughter Ann. And we visited Willard Uphaus, who ran something called the World Fellowship. We had a lot of support from friends in the North and that helped a great deal.

It was a month or six weeks before Cliff took up his law practice again. A lot of people who had been coming to us about wills and deeds dropped away. We had never had a big practice, but what we had began to slide away. I don't believe very many people thought Cliff and I were trying to over-throw the government by force and violence or that we were revolutionaries or Communists. They just didn't want to be touched by all the bad publicity.

The same thing happened to Aubrey. The American Legion wrote to every single advertiser in the *Southern Farmer* and told them that Aubrey Williams, the publisher, had been accused by Jim Eastland of being sub-versive, and that by advertising in his paper they were encouraging a man who was spreading subversive doctrine. Aubrey began to lose all his adver-tisers, and the paper just dried up. Aubrey finally moved to Washington because he'd had two cancer operations by then and he thought his end was coming.

The situation was hard on the children. Lucy had had some flack about the hearing while we were gone. She was very much embarrassed by it. And our daughter Tilla had had some embarrassing experiences in the school. Southerners knew instinctively that Eastland's attack on me was aimed at the Supreme Court and the *Brown* decision and Hugo Black, and that's what they were worried about. One of Tilla's teachers told her in front of the class, "You just tell your uncle I'm not going to teach any nigger children. I don't care how many laws they pass." Well, that was a hard thing for a child of twelve or thirteen to take. Tilla, from that point on, hated the school and wanted to get out of it. It got worse, of course, after the decision came down in May 1954. We finally had to send Tilla out of the South to school.

Lulah was little, but even Lulah suffered. I think one of the most pain-ful moments in my life was when Lulah had just started school. She was in the first grade. The *Brown* decision came down in May of 1954. Lulah was invited to a birthday party. I'd gotten her all dressed up in a little white ruffled dress with a big sash. She tied up her present, but she couldn't re-member whether the party was at three-thirty or four. It was right around the corner, so I called up and the husband answered the telephone. I said, "I'm Mrs. Clifford Durr, Lulah Durr's mother, and Lulah has been invited to your little girls' birthday party"—two little twins—"and she doesn't know whether the party's at three-thirty or four."

"Now, what is the name you said you were?" he asked.

"Mrs. Clifford Durr."

"You're Hugo Black's sister?"

"No," I said, "I'm Hugo Black's sister-in-law. He married my sister." I still didn't note any hostility in his voice at all. I thought he was just trying to place me or identify me.

"Well, I don't know myself," he said, "but I'll ask my wife." I waited and waited. I heard them talking in the background and I waited and waited. Finally he came back to the phone and said, "Mrs. Durr, there will be no party this afternoon as far as your daughter is concerned because I wouldn't have a child of yours in my house."

Well, that was pretty insulting, and it was terribly painful to Lulah. She couldn't understand at the age of six why they'd withdrawn the invitation. At this particular point, the children suffered because they were Hugo Black's nieces.

That's why I'm always standing up for Cornelia Wallace. She had lived in the governor's mansion with Jim Folsom and Rachel, Folsom's oldest daughter, during Folsom's first administration. Folsom's first wife had died, so Cornelia's mother (Folsom's sister) served as first lady. And of course Jim refused to condemn the *Brown* decision when it came down, so Cornelia and Rachel suffered, too. They were not invited to join a high school sorority and were treated badly. Rachel Folsom told me years later when she moved here that she hated to come back to Montgomery because she had such bad memories.

The whole time of the Eastland hearing had a surreal quality of craziness, insanity. And it got crazier as it went on. Paul Crouch, the informer, went to Hawaii. Finally he was exposed as a liar. A lot of the things he said were not true. He was just trying to earn that twenty-five dollars a day or however much the FBI was paying him to be an informer. He had cancer and his wife wrote Aubrey Williams a letter from Hawaii, if you can believe this. Mrs. Crouch wrote Aubrey Williams a letter from Hawaii that her husband was sick and dying of cancer and that he had had nothing personal against Aubrey. She said he'd always admired Aubrey very much and thought he was a fine person and he was glad to have it cleared up that Aubrey had never been a Communist. She asked if Aubrey would send some money because her husband was in such bad shape and they needed money. I think Aubrey sent twenty-five dollars or so. Aubrey's attitude was, the poor devil. He was a strange man, Aubrey was. Cliff got angry, but Aubrey just had a tremendous pity for people.

Cliff got so mad sometimes. The White Citizens' Council was formed during this time to resist the *Brown* decision and stand up for white supremacy, and Jim Eastland came over to Montgomery to speak to the council. About twelve thousand people gathered to hear him speak. We came home from the office at lunchtime, and I saw Cliff put his pistol in his pocket. I said, "Cliff, what in the world are you doing with your pistol in your pocket?"

He said, "I'm going to give it away."

"Why?"

"I'm afraid I'll kill Jim Eastland. If I have an available pistol, I'm afraid I'll go out there to the coliseum and kill him." Now this is something that I haven't told many people, but it actually happened. He took that pistol and gave it away.

Dr. Gomillion at Tuskegee told me that he never would keep a knife in the house because he was scared he'd kill somebody. That's the thing about the South that makes it so unlike other places. Underneath the quiet, serene, come-back-and-see-us-sometime and love and kisses, is this violent passion. A rage and a violent passion. That's what makes the South so scary sometimes. A man like Cliff, who believed in law and order and was a lawyer, had to fight this instinct and rage and desire to kill a man. But Aubrey would just say, the poor devils. He was like Judge Rives, who always said, "I may feel contempt for them, but I can't be quite scared of them. I can't hate them."

On the last day of the hearing Eastland had vowed that he was going to cite us all for contempt and have us jailed, but when he got to Washington, he never did a thing. He didn't even print the hearing for a year or so. We had thought about a suit for defamation of character, but I didn't want Cliff to get involved in any more turmoil. He had had a heart attack and my main concern was to keep him from having another. During those years, I was just trying to keep things going—the house, the children, and Cliff.

Our lives changed drastically as a result of the Eastland hearing. Cliff's family was very kind to us, but we moved into an apartment of our own because we didn't know what the effect of the hearing might be. We didn't know whether we would be attacked or whether there'd be crosses burned. So we moved right close by them in an apartment of our own. That, too, was a great release because I had been living a very artificial life, not my own life at all. You know, you can be grateful for kindness; at the same time, kindness can be a prison. You can't say or do or be anything that you really are because you don't want to offend anybody or hurt their feelings or cause them embarrassment.

In a way, I was grateful that my cover as a nice, proper Southern lady was blown by the hearing, because then I could begin to say what I really thought. After we moved, I started going to the Council on Human Relations, the only interracial group in the city. I had been scared to join that before, but it became an outlet for me after the hearing. It was part of the Southern Regional Council, and it did a great deal at that time to bring black and white together. It was a tremendous relief to me to be able to join something like that, where I was with people who were against segregation.

The local United Church Women then formed an integrated group. I began to know the Negro community. In fact, one of the first telegrams we got in New Orleans was from the Women's Democratic Club of Montgomery. I didn't know whether it was white or black. It was a strange telegram. "We are with you and our prayers are with you and we are proud of you." It was full of glowing praise and signed by lots of people I didn't know. As soon as I got back to Montgomery I asked Mr. Nixon who they were, and he said it was a black women's Democratic club. Then I got to know them all quite well. A lot of them were teachers at Alabama State College and they later became prominent in Martin Luther King's struggle.

One of the women in the club was Mrs. West, the grand dowager of the black community. Her husband had been a dentist and her son was a dentist. She was a well-educated woman of tremendous spirit. I called her and told her how grateful I was for the telegram, and she invited me to a meeting of her club. The women at the meeting were all nice-looking, well-dressed, and educated. I said, "Before I say anything, I would like to know why you, without knowing me, having never met me even, took my side and sent me that wonderful telegram and invited me here this afternoon."

They laughed and said, "Well, you ought to know the reason for that."

"No. I really don't."

They explained, "We knew if Jim Eastland was after you, you were pretty good." In other words, they had judged me by my enemies.

It's ironic that, by and large, political people were very quiet during the fifties, either because there was nothing to be active in or because they just had to watch themselves, as I had been doing earlier. The hearing changed all that for me. It put me into the fray, and I loved it. I felt freed.

The Eastland hearing had an effect on Cliff, too. When the *Brown* decision came down in 1954, all hell broke loose. There was no choice. You either had to stand up and be counted or move. We didn't move. A lot of people just got out, but Cliff never thought about moving, although he got several offers of jobs in other places at that time. He felt that Alabama was his and that the United States and Elmore County and Pea Level were his. He was a very rooted man. He loved the country and he particularly loved Elmore County. He felt that he belonged there. He wanted to be buried at Pea Level, but of course we couldn't do it.

One political consequence of the Eastland hearing was that George Wallace tried to start a committee like the Un-American Activities Committee. But the legislators wouldn't vote him subpoena power. They realized how dangerous the subpoena power could be when we could be hauled down to New Orleans and treated the way we were. They were afraid Wallace might use it on some of the legislators. They voted him the money for a state committee called the Sovereignty Commission, but they never voted him the subpoena power, so it never was much of a threat.

Bobby Shelton, who was head of the Ku Klux Klan, referred to Cliff in all of his speeches. This was the only thing that scared Cliff a little bit; he thought it might stir up the crazies. A crowd of them did shoot into Aubrey's office building one day, but nothing more happened.

Just before Aubrey left Alabama, he hired two or three men, Alabama country boys, to fix his furnace. Aubrey was a country boy, too, and he liked these fellows. He insisted that they eat lunch with him and Anita every day. Anita was a wonderful cook and she'd cook up a wonderful big dinner. Aubrey would tell us, "I've got the finest lot of boys fixing my furnace. They're so smart, and they know so much." It turned out that they were the very ones who were caught trying to blow up Dr. King's house. It was the most awful shock to Aubrey.

Fear is not the reason Aubrey left Montgomery. He stayed for ten years, but he was a sick man. He had heard they were going to call him up before the State Sovereignty Commission. Aubrey could talk to Cliff more than he could talk to me about his personal feelings. With me, he was always joking and laughing, making fun of me. But he said to Cliff, "You know, Cliff, if they get me up before a committee, I'm old and I'm sick. It doesn't frighten me, but I know I might start crying."

Cliff said, "Why, Aubrey, you'd never do that."

"Well," he explained, "I'd be crying for Alabama. I'd be crying for my own country. I'd be crying for those boys that tried to blow up Dr. King's house. Just the idea of my own people acting this way is more than I can stand."

19

Brown, Buses, and Bombs

WHEN THE *BROWN* decision came down in May of 1954, it was regarded by the black people I knew here in Montgomery as the second Emancipation Proclamation. There was rejoicing in all the churches. They had singings and meetings. It was thrilling to see the joy that came over them. For the first time since Reconstruction they felt the federal government was actually on their side. They had had a brief period of eleven years at the end of the Civil War when they had had equality. They could go to the theaters and they could ride the trains and the buses. They'd had Negro representation in the legislature. Then by 1876 the government had withdrawn the federal troops, and the Bourbon Democrats came in. Little by little all of the black people's rights were taken away.

The white reaction to desegregation was painful to the blacks. Many of them really believed that when the segregation laws changed, they would be received with joy. Of course, it was only a false hope. Every step toward desegregation was a hard battle.

When the schools opened, the first black pupils were met with a great deal of hostility from the teachers and the white pupils. Before they ever got into the school, there were lawsuits and other obstacles. Here in Alabama, George Wallace made school segregation his great crusade. He'd send the troopers in to close the schools. He did that over in Tuskegee, in Macon County. He stood in the door at the university. He was going to see that the law was not obeyed. It was only the force of the federal government that made him give in.

Now this is something that I saw with my own eyes—the last-ditch struggle to keep segregation. And I do not believe, as some people do, that there has been a great change in the Southern people. I believe that the only reason white Southerners accepted integration was that it was backed up by the federal government. They knew if they did not follow the Supreme Court and the law as laid down by the Supreme Court, they would be punished. The federal judges of the South, the ones I knew, and the lawyers who brought the cases up before the federal courts have been the heroes of the segregation fight. I do not mean by that to take away from the struggle and suffering of the Negroes and the young people who fought for them. Four young men were murdered in Mississippi, and many civil rights workers were jailed. All of that made the struggle for racial equality a nationwide struggle. When a couple in Wisconsin had a daughter living in Mississippi, all of a sudden what happened in Mississippi was very important to them. When the NAACP brought a case, the whole country was alerted to it. It became a national issue. It was no longer a Southern issue. It had the backing of the nation. But the important thing was that it had the authority of the federal courts and the federal judges.

The very next fall after the *Brown* decision a few black children actually began going to white schools in Montgomery. Mrs. Johnny Carr's son Arlam was one. Mrs. Carr and I had been friends from the prayer group and United Church Women and also from the Council on Human Relations. The black students were selected not by the parents but by the board of education. They were not the best and the brightest but a cross section of young Negroes. I think there were only eight or ten, and they went to Sidney Lanier High School, which was right across the street from where we were living at that time.

Arlam Carr was a very bright boy, and his mother was a very bright woman. Her business is insurance, and she is now head of the Montgomery Improvement Association, the largely black group that formed to support the bus boycott in 1955. Mrs. Parks and Mrs. King were friends of hers.

The Negro community made certain that the children who were going to the white school had nice clothes to wear and money for their books. Then they arranged a car pool. The children were taken to school and they were met afterward because there was fear of some disturbance after or before school. In Little Rock, where they'd had so much trouble, the disturbance had happened outside the school rather than in the school.

Since I lived right across the street from the school, Mrs. Carr said, "Mrs. Durr, is it all right if I tell Arlam if I'm late or his pick-up is late that he can come over to your house?" She didn't say if there was any danger, or if he got frightened. She just said, if they were late. So one afternoon Arlam did come over. And he brought a young black girl with him. I said, "Arlam, is there anything wrong?"

"No, no. Nothing at all except Mamma's late picking us up," he said.

"Are you sure? Are you okay? Nobody is giving you any trouble?"

"No," he said, "Everything's fine."

He never admitted there was any trouble. He was an extremely proud, bright boy. But I met by chance just the other day the young girl who had been with him. She said, "You don't remember me, Mrs. Durr, but I came to your house with Arlam Carr when we were surrounded by a lot of white kids. We didn't want to stay there waiting for the car pool." They never told me that at the time. They denied it completely, which I always thought showed a very brave spirit.

There were some things that happened that were nasty. Arlam was very bright, but some of the black kids could hardly read and write. They'd been very badly prepared. Some of the white teachers were very mean. They would take those children's papers, particularly the ones that were badly written and badly spelled, and pass them around and have them mimeographed to show what they had to teach. It's hard to believe that a teacher would be that mean. They were trying to prove that these black children were so stupid and so illiterate that it was ridiculous to try to teach them.

Except for these few incidents, there was no violence that I can recall when the schools first integrated. The black children were very brave. They were heroes in their own community, whereas my children, like Tilla and Lulah, were anything but heroes. They were pariahs and outcasts for being the nieces of Hugo Black and the daughters of Virginia and Clifford Durr. It was very different, indeed, from the way the black children were treated. Of course, the support from their community got the black children through a very hard period. They'd be introduced at church services, and benefits would be given for them. They were treated as heroes, and they *were* heroes, because it was pretty tough.

After 1954, there was increasing bitterness and defiance in Montgomery. I remember the case of a Jewish fellow here named Victor Kerns. He was a teacher at the high school. The board of education had a meeting at Lanier High School, and Victor was the only one who stood up and said he would teach black children. The teachers then gave up their own tenure so the board of education could fire any teacher who didn't go along with resistance to the *Brown* decision.

Victor wasn't fired, but he did leave and went to Auburn University to get his Ph.D. A scary episode happened before he left. He and his family lived in the southern part of Montgomery. His wife, Ann, was a high-strung young woman, very nervous and sensitive and fearful. She and her mother, Mrs. Rosenbaum, had taken in a great many of the Jewish refugees from Germany. Mrs. Rosenbaum was an extremely strict Orthodox Jew and she had taken in a lot of Jews who were Orthodox. Victor was from Brooklyn and he was a very brave fellow, but one day somebody knocked on the door and two big men with guns on their hip swaggered in. Ann took the children to the backyard. The men told Victor if he didn't stop this nigger talk something would happen to him. It was a direct threat from the Klan.

Jimmy's Restaurant down on Commerce Street had white waitresses, and when the restaurants were about to be integrated, Jimmy fired them all and put in black waiters, because he didn't think white waitresses should wait on black men. One of the waitresses he fired was the sweetheart or the mistress of a big Ku Kluxer who worked for the power company as a lineman. He and Jimmy got into a quarrel about the girl's being fired, and it got terribly bitter. The Klan was going to picket the restaurant. The Klansman's father arranged a meeting for them out at Normandale about ten o'clock one night to see if they couldn't work it out. Instead, they had a shoot-out, and Jimmy killed the fellow. The tension in the whole town built up on so many stupid little incidents. This killing really stemmed from a fear that the restaurants were going to integrate.

By the time of the bus boycott in December of 1955, I had gotten to know many of the black leaders in Montgomery. I had met Mrs. King before the boycott at a black funeral at which she sang. Dr. King had just taken over as pastor of Dexter Avenue Baptist Church, and they were new in Montgomery. Mrs. King was a very young girl then, slender with long, pretty hair. I thought she was a very pretty young girl and sang very well. We were introduced to each other, and afterward she sometimes came to the Council on Human Relations.

Dr. King spoke at the council once or twice. One night that he spoke the White Citizens Council infiltrated the meeting. Dr. King gave that famous speech he gave so often about how we don't want to be loved but we want to be respected. He used the Greek word he used so often, *agape*, which means human love, not love in the sense of sexual love but love in the sense of human beings loving each other. That was the night Juliet Morgan, who was a librarian, turned to me and saw a White Citizens Council member there. She said, "You know, I feel like somebody is pointing a gun at me." She was afraid she was going to lose her job, and she did later on.

I knew the Kings, but I never had any personal contact with them until Tilla applied to go to Antioch College, where Mrs. King had been. We got a letter from Antioch saying that Tilla would have to have a personal interview with a graduate of Antioch. They said the only graduate they had in Montgomery was Mrs. Martin Luther King. Tilla didn't want me to go with her. Tilla never wanted me to speak for her. She thought if I went, I'd do all the talking, so she took a taxi over there. When she came back she told me the taxi driver had said, "What you doing, white girl, going in that nigger neighborhood?"

Not long after that one of the many visitors we had during that period said she was very eager to meet Mrs. King. I called her up and told her I was Tilla's mother. She remembered me, so we went over in late afternoon. Mrs. King was dressed in a very pretty light summer dress and her hair was piled on top of her head. She served us delicious Southern tea, iced tea and cookies. She was a gracious hostess and her house was decorated very tastefully. They had one child then, a little girl named Yolanda. Mrs. King was a perfect Southern lady.

After that Mrs. King and I became friendly. I stayed at her house in Atlanta once or twice later on. The Kings didn't attend the Human Relations Council meetings regularly, because he traveled a great deal and she was home with their daughter. She had some speaking engagements of her own, but she didn't become the great public speaker she is today until after he died. She led a very domestic life.

By the time of the boycott I'd met the Kings, but that was about all. We had developed a very strong relationship with Mr. E. D. Nixon and with Mrs. Parks, however. We knew through them what was going on in the NAACP in Montgomery. As I recall, it was the summer of 1955 that Mrs. Parks went to the Highlander Folk School. Myles Horton had written to me to say they had a scholarship for somebody at the Highlander Folk School for two weeks. They wanted me to find somebody in Montgomery, preferably somebody black, to come and take the scholarship. I immediately thought of Mrs. Parks. It was the summer before the boycott.

During 1954 and 1955, Mrs. Parks had been one of the people who helped the black schoolchildren; she tutored them and saw that they were properly dressed and that they got their school books. She didn't have an automobile, so she rode the bus. She made only twenty-three dollars a week as a seamstress at the Montgomery Fair, as I recall. The Montgomery Fair was a big department store here. Mrs. Parks's husband worked as a barber and he was sometimes sick and unemployed. They lived in a housing project with her mother, who kept house for them.

When Myles called from Highlander, I immediately went over and asked Mrs. Parks if she would like to go. She said she would but she didn't have any money. You can imagine under what straitened circumstances they lived, even doing extra sewing, which she never charged enough for. I used to be embarrassed at the amount she charged to make a dress. She'd charge, say, three dollars, which was absurd. I'd have to just beat her down to make her charge twice as much, which was still very little. But in any case, she said she didn't have any money, so I said, "If I can get you some money, can you go?" She said yes. I went over and got the money from Aubrey Williams, who had more money than we did at that time. The round-trip bus fare to Highlander and back was no more than twelve or fifteen dollars.

Mrs. Parks also didn't have a bathing suit. I told her about all the swimming at Highlander. One of my girls had a bathing suit they gave her. She didn't have a suitcase, so one of the girls lent her that. Rosa Parks is one of the proudest people I've ever known in my life. She hated to admit she didn't have a suitcase or a bathing suit or money. It was painful for her. She was a very proud woman, so all of this had to be accomplished with a great deal of tact, which I am not noted for. But Mrs. Parks was very fond of

Aubrey Williams. By that time she'd gotten fond of me, too, and she really wanted to go. She had heard about the Highlander Folk School. She had never lived in an integrated situation in her life except the time she went to Miss White's School, a private school for blacks in Montgomery where they had white teachers. So she went to the Highlander Folk School and she had a wonderful time.

Now Myles always has taken great pride in the fact that he thought Mrs. Parks's stay at Highlander encouraged her in the boycott. Having known Mrs. Parks, I think it gave her a great lift. She loved it. She liked Myles so much and she loved being in a completely natural integrated situation where there was no discussion of it. She didn't like the Council on Human Relations because she always felt so black there. All they talked about was race. She said, "You know, every time I went to one of those meetings, I came away blacker than I was before, because everything was discussed in terms of race."

When Mrs. Parks came back from the Highlander, she still had her job at the Montgomery Fair as seamstress. It was during the Christmas rush and the room where she worked was little and hot. The heavy pressing irons added to the heat. She had bursitis in her shoulder, which pained her very much. One afternoon she stopped to buy a big bag of groceries after work. Her arm was very painful, and she was exhausted from her day spent in that hot little room. She had complained about the bus to me and discussed it many times. She had told me how she'd pay her money and then have to run around to the back door to get in, and the driver would slam the door and ride off leaving her standing on the curb after she'd paid her money. She had resented this for years. She resented having to get up and give her seat to white people. The buses had been a very hot issue in Montgomery. The local NAACP had had many cases they'd tried to take into the courts about it. Mr. Nixon was very angry about it, although he had his own car. He never rode the bus. Mrs. Parks had to ride the bus twice a day.

This particular afternoon, Mrs. Parks later told me, she was exhausted. The bus she took went out to the housing project and was full of blacks, but some white men got on. The bus driver turned around and said, the way they always said, "Niggers, move back." And she just sat. The driver stopped the bus and came up to her. He said, "Did you hear me say to move back?" She said yes. He said, "Are you going to move back?" She said no. He called the police, and they came and arrested her and took her to jail. She was booked and put behind bars.

We got home about five o'clock from the office. Only Lulah was at home then, and she always had coffee ready for us. Lucy had graduated from high school and had gone to college, and we had sent Tilla north to school. Lulah was pretty lonesome because she didn't have any friends in the neighborhood, so we always tried to get home on time. We had just walked in and poured some coffee when the telephone rang. It was Mr. Nixon. He said, "Mr. Durr, will you call the jail and see why Mrs. Parks has been arrested?" The police recognized his voice as being that of a black man, and they wouldn't tell him anything. They treated him with the utmost disdain. Cliff called the jail and said he was Clifford J. Durr and he was a lawyer. They knew who he was, I think. He asked why Mrs. Parks was in jail. They told him she'd been booked on the city segregation ordinance. So Cliff called Mr. Nixon back. Mr. Nixon asked if Cliff would go down with him to make bail. Cliff said, "Mr. Nixon, I don't have anything to make bail with." We didn't own any property at that time, and we only had three or four hundred dollars a month to live on. Mr. Nixon said, "That's all right. I can make bail, if you'll just go with me." He was afraid they wouldn't let him make bail. I was determined to go, too, so I put on my coat and came running out.

I waited for them while they made bail. Everything went very smoothly. They brought Mrs. Parks out from behind the bars. That was a terrible sight to me to see this gentle, lovely, sweet woman, whom I knew and was so fond of, being brought down by a matron. She wasn't in handcuffs, but they had to unlock two or three doors that grated loudly. She was very calm. I asked her how they had treated her and she said, "Very nicely." Just at that moment her husband arrived. He was very excited and upset. She went home with him in the car some friend had brought. We told her we would follow her home in Mr. Nixon's car and would discuss the case in her apartment.

We all went to her apartment, and after she had freshened up and had a little supper, Cliff and Mr. Nixon and Mrs. Parks and her husband and her mother and I discussed the case. Of course, Mr. Nixon wanted her to make a test case of it. Mr. Nixon remembers her as being extremely reluctant to do so, but I remember that it was her husband who was so reluctant. He kept saying over and over again, "Rosa, the white folks will kill you. Rosa, the white folks will kill you." It was like a background chorus, to hear the poor man, who was as white as he could be himself, for a black man, saying, "Rosa, the white folks will kill you." I don't remember her being reluctant.

Part of the city bus ordinance said that the white people got on in the front and sat from the front back; the black people got on in the back and sat from the back toward the front. No signs were posted and the center was always a no-man's land. When more whites got on, the bus driver would make the blacks get up and go stand up in the back. But the city ordinance included a phrase that said the bus driver couldn't order a black to give up a seat unless there was another seat available farther back in the black section. In other words, he couldn't just say, "Nigger, get back." Cliff asked Mrs. Parks if she wanted to test the constitutionality of the law itself or if she wanted him to try to get her off on the fact that the bus driver hadn't been following the law. She said she wanted to test the constitutionality of the law.

Cliff told Mrs. Parks he thought he could get the charges dropped, if that's what she wanted, to prevent her going through a long court session. Cliff told her, "Now if you're going to fight this on a constitutional basis, you will have to get the NAACP to finance it because it's going to cost you a fortune. It'll have to go all the way up to the Supreme Court of the United States and it's going to cost a lot of money. You don't have it and of course we don't have it." Certainly the Montgomery NAACP or even the Alabama NAACP didn't have it, but Fred Gray, a lawyer for the NAACP in Montgomery, had connections with the NAACP Legal Defense Fund in New York. So that night it was decided that Mrs. Parks would challenge the bus ordinance on constitutional grounds, and Fred Gray would represent her. It would be an NAACP case and Cliff would do all he could to help Fred, but Cliff would not be the lawyer of record.

Mrs. Parks was brought up to trial on the Monday after her arrest. In the meantime, Mr. Nixon had organized a boycott of the buses on the day of her trial. It was supposed to be just a one-day boycott. I can very well remember going to a meeting Mr. Nixon had that Sunday afternoon at a black church. It was an NAACP meeting and Mr. Nixon asked me to come. I remember that he was very emotional. He said to the people, "I'm a Pullman porter and every time I go on my job, I put on an apron or a jacket." He said, "You know, we've been wearing aprons for three hundred years. It's time we took off our aprons." I always thought that was a vivid phrase. He asked them not to get on the bus the next day. He had spread the word to all the preachers and they all told their congregations to stay off the buses on that Monday, the day of Mrs. Parks's trial. They announced they would have a meeting at the Holt Street Baptist Church on Monday night.

Fred Gray represented Mrs. Parks in the courtroom. She was found guilty and fined. Then he announced they were going to appeal the case.

That night I left the house to go to the mass meeting. Mr. Nixon had had to go off on his run as a Pullman car porter, and Martin Luther King was selected to be the speaker. There must have been ten or fifteen thousand black people crowding in and around that church. At that time I felt on very friendly terms with all the black community. I hadn't the slightest feeling of fear being the only white person, but I couldn't get into the church because of the crowd. King made a magnificent speech that electrified the black people. He became their undoubted leader that night.

The Parks case went on and on, and so did the boycott. The black people formed car pools, and the city tried cracking down on them by arresting the drivers for going two miles an hour over the speed limit. The police were harassing them. So Cliff got in touch with Fred Gray, and they decided to transfer the case to federal court. It came before a three-judge panel: Judge Rives and Judge Johnson declared the ordinance unconstitutional; Judge Lynne dissented, saying the panel shouldn't declare the ordinance unconstitutional until a higher court had ruled in that area of the law. Then the case went to the Fifth Circuit Court of Appeals and then to the Supreme Court. Finally the Supreme Court declared the ordinance unconstitutional, and the Negroes began to ride the buses again.

The boycott lasted the entire year, December 1955 until December 1956. I would see the black women walking to work every morning and walking back at night. It was like the black tides would come up out of the black section of town and go to work and then sweep back again. We would offer the women rides when we saw them walking, particularly out in the country club area where the distances were rather great. I would say to a complete stranger, "Would you like a ride?" They'd say, "Yes, thank you very much." They'd get in the car, and I'd ask them where they lived. They always lived on the west part of town. I'd say, "I'm glad to see that you're supporting the boycott." "No, ma'am. I hadn't nothing to do with that boycott. The lady I work for, she wasn't feelin' so good this afternoon, so that's why I was walkin' home." "No, ma'am, I don't have nothin' to do with that boycott. It's just that her little girl's sick." One reason after another, but they wouldn't admit they were supporting the boycott.

Then the policemen began giving tickets to the white women who were taking black women home. I had a washwoman who came once a week, an older lady who belonged to the Church of Christ. She admired Dr. King greatly. She said she had seen the angels come down and stand on his shoulders every Monday night. In everything he said he was speaking with the voice of God. Now, everything she did was also dictated by the voice of God. She got so she talked to God so much that she didn't do much ironing. She was really a sweet old lady, but she was a religious fanatic. I was taking her home one afternoon and we were stopped. I knew positively I had stopped at the stop sign, but a policeman came roaring up to me. He said that I had stopped too late. I'd gone two or three feet over the line. I knew there was no use in arguing, so I told him I was sorry and got my ticket and took this old lady home. I had to pay five dollars. This incident was typical of what happened over and over again all over town.

The mayor of the city, Tacky Gayle, issued a plea for the white women of Montgomery to stop taking their black maids home. He said they could break the boycott if the white women would stop taking their black maids home, or even stop hiring them. Well, you have never heard such a roar of indignation in your life as came from the white women of Montgomery. They were just furious at Tacky Gayle. They said, okay, if Tacky Gayle wants to come out here and do my washing and ironing and cleaning and cooking and look after my children, he can do it, but unless he does, I'm going to get Mary or Sally or Suzy. And they said, "Sally has never had a thing to do with that boycott in the first place. She told me she only stays off the buses because she's scared of those hoodlums that might hurt her."

A vast deceit went on. Everybody knew everybody else was lying, but to save face, they had to lie. The black women had to say they weren't taking any part in the boycott. The white women had to say that their maids didn't take any part in the boycott. We had a good example of that in Mary, Mrs. Durr's old cook who came from Hardaway, in Macon Couty. She'd been with the Durrs for years and now was Mrs. Durr's nurse. Mrs. Durr by that time was quite old and feeble and had to stay in bed, but a lot of people would drop by in the afternoons. Mary would sit in the room.

Mrs. Durr was a beautiful old woman, all propped up in bed, with a pink bed jacket and a pink ribbon in her hair and looking so pretty. Her mind was failing her, but she was still able to carry on a conversation. One afternoon when I was in the room somebody said to Mary, "Mary, I hope you don't have anything to do with that boycott." Mary said, "No, ma'am, I hadn't had nothing to do with that boycott. There's my sister Olla. She don't live very far from her job so she just walks to work. And my brother, he's got a job at the cotton mill and he just goes to work with some other men who are driving a car. And my other sister she just walks to work cause it's so close. No, ma'am, none of us has a thing to do with that boycott. We just stays off the buses." The white people really believed that. They didn't see through it at all.

In truth, Mary was a passionate advocate of the boycott. She'd meet us as we came in the driveway to ask how the bus boycott was getting on, how Dr. King was. She couldn't read and write, but she listened to the radio. That afternoon after the guests had left and Mary was fixing supper, Cliff and I said to her, "Mary, you are the biggest storyteller in the world. You know very well you're supporting the boycott and all of your family are. Why in the world did you make up that tale about how none of you were, and you were all walking just because you wanted to?" She laughed and she said, "Well, I tell you, Mr. Cliff, I tell you, I learned one thing in my life and that is, when your hand's in the lion's mouth, it's just better to pat it on the head." That expressed the feeling in the black community. The black women needed those jobs. They weren't paid very much, but that's all the income many of them had. They couldn't afford to say, "I'm supporting the boycott." So the white women lied and the black women lied. And the maids kept coming and the white women kept driving them back and forth to work.

There was phenomenal support for the boycott. Absolutely phenomenal. The unity of the black people was the most amazing thing I have ever seen in my life. Because of segregation the blacks had their own churches and clubs and neighborhoods. There were two black lawyers, Fred Gray and one other, and there were several black doctors and a black hospital. So the black community was complete in and of itself.

The Supreme Court of the United States held that segregation on the buses was unconstitutional, and the black people felt they had won that decision by all their walking. I spoke at the Dexter Avenue Baptist Church and I said that I felt the law had won black people the right to integrated buses. I didn't get much of a hand on that. Not that anybody said anything against it, but they wanted to believe they had won the victory themselves, that they had done it through their own united strength. And they really had done so, for the first time.

Now, I believe the Supreme Court is made up of men, not idols, and that they do sense what is going on in the country. The *Brown* decision came absolutely in the middle of the cold war and McCarthyism. Here we were blaming Russia for being a totalitarian dictatorship. We had fought nazism and fascism and the persecution of the Jews. Well, we put ourselves in the forked stick. The whole basis of the cold war was that communism meant dictatorship and capitalism meant democracy. How could anyone say that capitalism was the best system in the world when the whole Southern part of the United States was segregated and Negroes had no rights at all? It created a great dilemma for the United States.

Dr. King came on the scene at a moment of history. That's why we here in the South didn't get that feeling of total terror and failure that so many people in the North got during the McCarthy days—the feeling that there was no use trying. The civil rights movement *was* working. I always thought King was a great politician. He started the movement in the churches, so when the people started trying to red-bait the Negro movement, they had to go into churches and red-bait Jesus Christ—pretty difficult to do.

All this time, of course, the Alabama Legislature was passing crazy resolutions. They were going to dissolve the public school system and give money to private schools. But Judge Johnson and Judge Rives in the federal court showed that they were not going to give in to these threats. A cross was burned on Judge Johnson's lawn. Somebody bombed his mother's house later. Two federal marshals guarded him all the time. Even his son, Johnny, was guarded.

Now Judge Rives was from an old Montgomery family and he never had any guards. He got threats, and that worried him because his wife was more or less an invalid, but he always felt that anybody who was cowardly enough to make a threat anonymously was too cowardly to act out the threat. Judge Rives had a great deal of confidence. He was a brave man.

When people finally began to give up segregation, the favorite phrase was, "Well, I'm doing it because I don't want to go to Atlanta," which meant they didn't want to be put in the federal penitentiary. The threat of the federal penitentiary in Atlanta and Judge Rives and Judge Johnson standing there so completely resolute, not giving one single inch, changed the whole climate of opinion. Judge Rives and Judge Johnson were going to carry out the law.

In February of 1956, during the bus boycott, Autherine Lucy went to the University of Alabama. Folsom was governor then. Robert Shelton was head of the Ku Klux Klan in Tuscaloosa and a lot of the rubber workers there were Ku Kluxers. The opposition to Autherine Lucy was organized and fomented by a crazy young student at the university named Leonard Wilson, the Ku Klux Klan, Bobby Shelton, and the rubber workers. They were the ones that filled up the campus the day Autherine Lucy was to start school.

The president of the university at that time was O. C. Carmichael, whom I had known very well because he had been one of my teachers in Central High School in Birmingham. He'd been a Rhodes scholar, one of the first in Alabama. He came from a big family up in northern Alabama. He began teaching Spanish at the high school just after he returned from being a Rhodes scholar. I was about fourteen or fifteen, and the class had about two boys and eighteen girls. The eighteen girls all fell simultaneously and madly in love with him. We would do anything to stay after school just to have a few minutes more with our god. There wasn't a girl in his class who failed to fall for him. He was very handsome, with reddish blond hair and blue eyes. He had to be extremely proper and stiff and dignified or the girls would have mobbed him. We didn't learn much Spanish, but we certainly did suffer the pangs of love.

At the time of Autherine Lucy's admission to the university, Dr. Carmichael said that he was going to obey the law. We didn't think he was as encouraging or as brave as he should have been, but he was too encouraging and too brave to suit the trustees of the university and the legislature, so he had to leave. Cliff and I felt he could have been more forward and prevented some of the disruption, but all he would say was, "I will obey the law." He did obey the law, and the university made him leave because it didn't think he put up any fight.

That's why George Wallace got to be so popular—he always lost, but he put up a fight. That appealed to the Southern spirit: we're going to resist the Yankees and we're not going to let them tell us what to do. The fact that the law prevailed at that time is a remarkable thing. And I must say that I think the firm stand taken by such people as Hugo Black and Cliff and Judge Rives and Judge Johnson kept events from breaking out in open violence.

Cliff's brother James was under terrific pressure at this time, but he still stood by Cliff, even though he didn't agree with him, and kept him on as lawyer for the Durr Drug Company. If it hadn't been for Uncle Jimmy, I doubt if we could have stayed here. Uncle Jimmy was one of the unsung saints.

James Durr also stood behind the people who worked for him. A Negro employee, Eli Judkins, drove one of the car pool cars at night in the boycott. Some of the Ku Klux Klan or White Citizen's Council over in Selma read in the paper that this man had been arrested for taking part in the boycott, and one night a druggist called James and said, "Mr. Jimmy, we see where this man got arrested for being a part of the boycott. We want you to know until you fire that man, you'll never get another order from us." And James said, "Well, now look, if you want to come over here and do my hiring and firing and run my business for me, come over and do it, but as long as I am head of the Durr Drug Company, I will do my own hiring and firing." And he didn't fire Eli even though he was against the boycott.

In 1956 or 1957, James bought a big block of tickets for the Chamber of Commerce dinner and invited Cliff and me to go. The commissioner of police, L. B. Sullivan, was at the head table, and all of a sudden in the middle of the evening I saw a policeman come around and speak to him. He got up and went out and I said to Cliff, "I bet there's trouble." We went out into the hall and there was a Negro waiter whom Cliff knew, and he said Martin Luther King's house had been bombed. Cliff and I got in our car and drove up to see what had happened.

When we got there, there were just hundreds—it seemed to me thousands—of people around the house, all black. King's house had been bombed, and his wife and child had been there but, purely by chance, had not been hurt.

We parked the car and walked through a great crowd of Negroes. We knew some of them, and they all shook our hands and led us right up to the porch of the house that had been bombed. There was a feeling of friendship and rapport. And King came out. His wife and Rev. Ralph Abernathy and all his supporters were there. At that moment, if King had said "Burn the town down," I really believe they would have done it, because this bombing was the first act of overt violence. But King stood on the steps and said, "Now you have got to realize that if you respond to this hatred with hatred, you're putting yourself exactly on the same plane with these people. This is as low an act as a person can do, to bomb a man's house with his wife and child in it." That was what he said. He talked some more and then every one went home. King at that point, I thought—like Judge Rives and Cliff and Judge Johnson—prevented terrible violence.

The next bombing took place in 1957 while we were still living in town, before we moved out to Cliff's grandfather's old place at Pea Level. The planes from Maxwell Air Force Base would often break the sound barrier but seldom at night. You'd hear a terrific shattering noise above your head.

One night about two or three o'clock in the morning, we heard the same sort of noise. It seemed to be all over town, all over. Of course, it woke us up, and my first thought was what in the name of God was Maxwell Air Force Base doing breaking the sound barrier at three o'clock in the morning. Then the telephone rang and it was Mr. E. D. Nixon. He said, "Mrs. Durr, they have bombed Reverend Abernathy's house and his church. They've bombed two or three more black churches and they've bombed Reverend Graetz's house." Graetz was a white Lutheran minister who was active in the MIA, the Montgomery Improvement Association.

"Did they bomb you?" I asked.

"No," he said, "they didn't bomb me because I was sitting here with my shotgun. They came by here and threw their light on me and when they saw that shotgun, they went on. You know, I'm not a non-violent nigger." He meant he was going to protect his house.

Later on I asked Mr. Nixon how he had happened to be up so early. They bombed his house once when he was out of town; the bomb had barely grazed the sidewalk, but it frightened his wife a great deal. He said when he heard the first noise, he realized immediately what it was, and he went out and got the shotgun and sat there with his shotgun ready to fire. He said that two or three cars came up and the lights fell on him and then went on. He would have shot at them, no doubt about it.

The Graetz family had four or five children at the time of these bombings. They were a young couple in their late twenties. He'd come down as a missionary and had a Negro Lutheran church on Holt Street. We went over and invited them to come and stay with us. Their house was pretty well blasted. Windows were broken. There was a hole in the yard. It was cold. I borrowed extra blankets and put up cots. Jeannie Graetz called me the next day and said, "Virginia, I'm sorry, but I'd rather just take a chance on staying in this house than moving all these kids. I just can't face it." She was pretty shaken up. Later their house was totally wrecked by a bigger bomb, but they weren't there.

The First Baptist Church, which was Abernathy's church, had been completely bombed out. That bombing was solved, but in a strange way. The man in a filling station across the street from Martin Luther King's house remembered some men who had stopped there for gas. I don't know how in the world he did, but he remembered the cars and had taken down the license numbers. Ever since King's first bombing, he had been noticing cars that came out late at night. The police got the numbers of the cars, and caught these men cold. They were the men who had been working at Aubrey Williams's house.

The bombers were not convicted. The only thing John Blue Hill, who was their lawyer, asked Martin Luther King was whether he'd ever proposed to a white woman and dated white women. The judge kept ruling him out of order. You see, when you got down to the roots of the thing, you always got back to the white woman and the black man. This was the mystique. I call it the cesspool of the South.

Cliff always said that John Blue Hill stopped the bombing, because he charged the bombers so much to defend them. He charged each one of them five thousand dollars. There were seven of them, so they had to raise thirty-five thousand dollars. It was very much the technique Cliff used on the policemen in the police brutality cases. He knew they weren't going to get a conviction on any police brutality, but when they had to come into court and hire a lawyer and get bad publicity and pay out so much money, beating up blacks on Saturday night just became too expensive.

But the thing that struck me again, as it had struck me so often in the old days of the Klan when as a child I had seen them marching, was how poor these Ku Kluxers were, how emaciated, how scrawny they looked. They looked as if they had never had proper food. You couldn't help but feel that they had been deprived all their lives.

The Montgomery city officials closed the zoo and the park that surrounded it in the late fifties rather than integrate it. I wrote a letter to the editor about that and came home and found my whole yard littered with obscene pamphlets. Children would go into the park and play on the abandoned merry-go-rounds, and one three-year-old child got her head crushed in one. The city even took the chairs out of the library so no one could sit down. The idea was that if libraries had to be integrated, everybody had to stand up. Vertical integration apparently was more tolerable.

We never felt we were in any real danger during this time in spite of our identification with Mrs. Parks and Mr. Nixon and the Council on Human Relations. But it wasn't an easy time, and it was especially hard on the children. Our second daughter, Lucy, had made a circle of friends before the civil rights movement started and she had a lot of boyfriends. She was extremely popular, and her friends didn't care whether her father or mother committed murder. But the two younger girls, Tilla and Lulah, had a rough time of it. The teachers singled them out in class and embarrassed them, and the children said their father was a nigger-lover and a Communist. Finally, they just wouldn't go to school, so we had to send them to boarding schools. Tilla went to the Cambridge School outside of Boston, and Lulah went to Windsor Mountain School in Lenox, Massachusetts.

There were times still when I thought we should leave Alabama. Cliff kept getting offers from other places in the country, but he never really considered them. He felt that we were at home here.

20

Civil Rights in the Courts
and on the Streets

BY THE 1960S THERE WAS even more pressure for Negro rights in Montgomery, and Cliff was involved in some of those cases. One was the Gasch
case. Mr. Gasch was a student at Auburn University taking pharmacology,
and Mrs. Gasch was working on the *Montgomery Advertiser* as a
typographer to help her husband through school. They had gone downtown on a Saturday morning to pay bills or do some shopping, and they
had run into the Freedom Rider mob. They tried to protect some of the
Freedom Riders from being beaten, and the police promptly arrested them
and put them in jail. She called her father, who called a preacher here in
Montgomery, who in turn called Cliff. Cliff got them out on bail and brought
them to our house. Mrs. Gasch was terrified. We began to try to get the
typographical union to support her, but it was a segregated union and it
refused to help. In fact, she lost her job right then and there.

Mr. Gasch had been a Marine. He had waded into the mob to protect
the victims. When he was interviewed by out-of-town newspapers, he said,
"I just did what any man would do, protected the people who were being
beaten up." Cliff wanted to be prepared to appeal the case, because he knew
they'd be found guilty in the state court of obstructing the police or standing on the sidewalk or something. But Mrs. Gasch had been so upset by the
night she'd spent in jail that she said she wasn't going to take any chance of
going back. So they paid a twenty-five-dollar fine for breaking the peace
and then went to Texas. She never came back to Alabama. She was an extremely sensitive girl, a girl who'd been brought up in the church, and she
was very shaken by this whole experience.

The biggest case we were involved in was the Regal Cafe case. That
was one of the biggest cases Cliff ever had. Ralph Abernathy called the office

one day and said, "Mr. Durr, a lot of young Methodist students, white Methodist students, have been arrested and are in jail. We think you'd better come over here, because we think a white lawyer would do us more good than Fred Gray." Fred Gray usually took the black defense and Cliff took the white defense.

Cliff and I went over to the jail and Cliff went in to meet the dean of a Methodist college at Jacksonville, Illinois. The dean was an associate professor of sociology and he was touring with a group of students during the spring holidays. He had taken students one spring to the West and they had studied the Indians, the electric power dams, and so forth. Then one year he had taken them East and they had studied New England. This spring vacation, he brought them South—not only to study the civil rights conditions but also to look at the cotton plantations. They were a very respectable group of people. Usually the governors and the Methodist churches would receive them and they'd stay at the YWCA or YMCA or at Methodist churches.

This particular morning they had arrived in Montgomery very early. They had just come from Arkansas where they'd been received by the governor. They went to Alabama State Teachers' College, a black college, and began a discussion with the students about what had happened in Montgomery. When lunchtime came, the black students suggested that they all adjourn to the Regal Cafe, a very good black cafe. They engaged a private dining room, which couldn't even be seen from the street.

The police learned of this mixed group somehow, probably from an informer who had seen them going into the Regal Cafe. Now, the city could no longer say that integration was against the law, so it had passed an ordinance that if anyone did anything that was *likely* to provoke a breach of the peace, that person would be arrested on a criminal offense. The peace was certainly disturbed, because the chief of police drove up with police wagons and motorcycles. Then a fire engine drove up. I never did find out why the fire engine was there. Everybody in the neighborhood came out to see what was going on.

The witnesses that we had in the case said they didn't know that the black and white young people had gone into the Regal Cafe; they just gathered around to find out what was going on. There certainly was a terrific disturbance, but the police were the ones who created it by coming there in full force. They created a decidedly nonpeaceful situation.

The young people were just sitting in the cafe with the dean and his wife and their three-year-old daughter. All of a sudden the police walked in and arrested every one of them for disturbing the peace under the new ordinance.

Cliff and I went to the jail. We couldn't make bail for the students, because there were so many of them. I believe Fred Gray was able to make bond for the black students, because he had the support of the black community, but we didn't have that kind of support from the white community for the white students. Cliff did manage to get the dean and his wife out. Their child had been taken away from them by the police. They had no idea where their three-year-old girl was, and they were just wild with worry.

Cliff brought the dean and his wife back to the house, and we all immediately began trying to find their child. We called young Wiley Hill, who was head of the court of domestic relations and was a terribly sweet guy. Cliff had gone to the university with him and was very fond of him. Judge Rives had studied law with Wiley's father. The Hills were known as hard-boiled, ruthless people, but this particular Hill was an extremely kind fellow. We had heard that he suffered from epilepsy, and, sadly, he later committed suicide. He was as upset as Cliff was about this little three-year-old girl being taken from her parents. He finally learned that the police had turned the child over to one of the foster homes. Cliff called the lady who ran this foster home, and she said the child was there and was asleep. She'd washed her clothes and she would have her in court in the morning. Cliff said, "The mother and father are here and they want her right now." The woman said, "I'm sorry, but I can't go running all around town, and her clothes are not even dry yet." Cliff said, "We'll come out and get her and bring her a blanket." He finally had to call Wiley Hill again, and he had to order the woman to turn over the child to her mother and father. We went out to the foster home, and the child and her parents stayed with us that night.

The next morning, the president of the college called up and said he'd make bond to get all the students out of jail. Aubrey Williams offered to make bond for them, too. There were ten or twelve of them, and they got out on bond. They were tried in police court that afternoon by Judge Lowe, one of the most vicious, anti-black persons I've ever known. He found them all guilty and fined them.

In their appeal to the state circuit court, they were all found not guilty except the dean. The court decided that the dean had led these students into a situation where they were likely to provoke a breach of the peace. Cliff appealed the case to the Fifth Circuit Court of Appeals in New Orleans, and the dean's conviction was overturned in *Nesmith* v. *Alford*.

The trials and the appeals lasted for two years and cost I don't know how much. Of course, we didn't get much out of it. I think we got $2,500, but that was all. There is a terrific amount of work to an appeal, especially the typing. I got a terrible crick in my neck and had to go to the hospital and be put in traction because I typed so much. But the Fifth Circuit Court of Appeals did find the ordinance unconstitutional. I am a profound admirer of the law, when the law works. And the law, in these cases, did work.

One of the leading citizens of Montgomery at that time was Billy Bowman. He was chairman of the board of the First National Bank and was a very powerful man. He also had the honorary title of French consul, so the French embassy called him and asked if he would go to court and appear as a witness for a young French girl who was among the students. Mr. Bowman was a great witness because he was Mr. Big in Montgomery. He didn't know much about the case, but he could see that this beautiful French girl was being persecuted. He was extremely angry about it, and he told Dave Crossland, who was the district attorney, "I don't think you know anything about the law and I don't think you want to see justice done."

By the time of the Regal Cafe case, living in Montgomery was like living in the midst of a storm: You never knew what was going to happen. We worried for the black people and for ourselves, but mostly we worried for our children. Lucy was at Radcliffe. She had had a triumphant career in high school and had gotten a scholarship to Radcliffe for her tuition, but not for her board and room. Kenneth Galbraith and his wife, Kitty, who'd been neighbors and friends of ours on Seminary Hill, wrote and said that they would get Lucy a job with one of their friends as a live-in maid, which they did.

Tilla seemed to draw the eye of everybody, the teachers particularly. She didn't do well in school and was miserable, and she began to get fat. She finally flatly refused to go to school, so we were in a quandary. Then some other friends of ours from Boston, the John Chipman Grays, got Tilla a scholarship to Cambridge School.

Lulah was in the Bellingrath School in Montgomery, and she too was doing very badly and was very unhappy. The Brechers got her a scholarship to the Windsor Mountain School. So Tilla went to the Cambridge School, Lucy went to Radcliffe, and Lulah went to the Windsor Mountain School, all through the efforts of our friends in the North. That support made a tremendous difference to us.

Cliff's mother became totally senile in the late 1950s. The house was rented, and she went to live with her daughter in Birmingham. The only family that was left in Montgomery was James, whose wife had died, and Cliff and me. The girls were all off at school. After finishing at the Cambridge School, Tilla went to Brandeis for a year and then she came back to Montgomery and took a business course.

Tilla was here when Nat Hentoff and Dan Wakefield interviewed us. Nat was writing for the *New Yorker*, and Dan was editor of *Nation*. Wakefield and Tilla went down to a meeting at the city auditorium in honor of the policemen who had stood so bravely against the tide of integration. Tilla was recognized, and when they left, their car was attacked and Dan Wakefield's coat was torn off him. I remember that Telford Taylor was here at the time. He was working on one of his books at Maxwell Air Force Base. He'd been a general and he'd also been one of the prosecutors at the

Nuremberg trials. Telford was rather shocked and surprised to see Tilla and Dan Wakefield return looking so bad. They were terrified. They had been physically attacked, the first time any of us had been.

During this time, I got to know Ralph Abernathy and his wife, Juanita, very well. He's a jolly fellow. I always told him he was just a typical Alabama black-belt politician, kissing all the ladies and kissing all the babies and telling jokes. When King moved away from Montgomery, Abernathy was left with the responsibility on his back. I often asked him why he wasn't frightened. His house had been bombed and his church had been bombed and he had been threatened, and still he wasn't afraid. I asked him why and he said, "Well, Mrs. Durr, I'll tell you." His father owned a good-sized farm in rural Alabama and they grew practically everything they had to eat on the farm. He had eight or ten brothers and sisters and they all worked on the farm. I think they lived near Livingston or Demopolis. He said,

My father would go in to town on Saturday to buy what we had to have, like coffee or sugar. That's all we ever bought. And he told me never to speak to a white man under any circumstances. Not to say yes or no or yes sir or no sir. Just never speak to them. A man would ask me something and I'd just shake my head, so I got the reputation of being dumb. Nobody would bother me because I was dumb. That was my father's way of protecting me when he'd take me into town. I would sit in the wagon and hold the reins, but if a white man said anything to me, I'd just be dumb. So I never had any contact with white people at all. I went to a black school. I went to a black church. I was surrounded by black people. The first time I ever came in contact with white people was when I was drafted. Fortunately, I was put in a company with a lot of Swedes from Minnesota, and they didn't care if I was black or white or red or green or what. As long as I did my share of the work, I was okay. So my first contact with white people was with people who seemed to me to be completely free of prejudice about my being black. I didn't have the fear drilled into me that other people had.

Dr. King told me very much the same thing. I'd been up to visit Hugo during the time of all the rioting and sit-ins and marches. Hugo was opposed to the marches. He thought they were terrible. So when I got back, I told Dr. King, "My brother-in-law Justice Black thinks those marches that you have are terrible things. They create a lot of trouble and may cause rioting." He said, "Well, Mrs. Durr, I'm sorry to disagree with the distinguished justice, but what I am doing and what I have to do, is to get the fear out of these black people. They've been scared for three hundred years and I have to get the fear out of them before they'll ever be able to do anything."

Martin Luther King was trying to develop a sense of pride in the blacks.

He felt that pride was something they had to have. Pride in their own courage and pride in their own being. I used to hear him speak quite often. Our house all during the period was constantly being visited by foreign newspapermen and Harkness students to whom we were playing host and hostess—Englishmen and Frenchmen and Germans and Italians. The Harkness students were like Rhodes scholars, only they were European students who came to this country to study instead of the other way around. They were financed by the Harkness family, an American family of some wealth. These visiting Europeans always wanted to go and meet Martin Luther King or hear him speak, so I heard many of King's speeches and sermons. Sometimes I felt he would carry things to rather childish extremes—about black is beautiful, for example. He would chant, "Black is beautiful."

Dr. King would have a meeting every Monday night at one of the churches in Montgomery. I remember going one night with Ruth Glass, who was a distinguished sociologist in England. She was at the London School of Economics and had written a book about the immigrants who'd come to London. She was terribly eager to hear what King had to say. We went to a Negro church on the west side of town. It was jammed. All of King's meetings were. Those churches were always hotter than the hinges of hell, packed with people and not air-conditioned. Dr. King was getting ready to go to Washington for the big march—where he made the famous "I have a dream" speech. They had engaged a lot of buses to take crowds of people up to the march, and this was the last meeting before they left. He told them, "Now look, when you go to Washington, you are going to represent the black people of Alabama. I want to tell you-all that we've got to be awfully careful." He said, "You've got to present an image that we can all be proud of, so don't eat fried chicken and throw the bones out of the window." Mrs. Glass thought that was very patronizing. Dr. King said, "I know you'll take your lunches with you, but don't eat fried chicken and throw the bones down. Be sure you find a garbage can to dispose of the remains of your lunch. We don't want to leave the Lincoln Memorial and the green just littered with chicken bones." Then he said, "When you go into the bathrooms, be sure that you wash your hands carefully and make yourself look as neat as possible even if you've had to sleep on the bus." Mrs. Glass thought *that* was patronizing. He said, "Now don't talk loud. Don't let's have the impression of a lot of loud black people, eating chicken and throwing the bones down and whooping and hollering. We want to represent the black people of the South, and we've got to make a good impression. We've got to show them we've got pride in ourselves, in the way we look and the way we eat and the way we talk."

I just thought Dr. King was trying to prepare them. Here were a lot of black people who'd never been to Washington, and he was trying to instruct them in how to behave in a big city so they'd make a good impression. I didn't see anything in it that was so patronizing. Mrs. Glass said he was talking to them as though they were children. I thought he was talking to them as you would talk to any small-town person who was going to a big city—telling them how to act.

I came to have a great respect for Dr. King. I felt his wife and I were friends, but Dr. King never let down his dignity and reserve for a minute. Now Abernathy was different. Every time he'd see me in a public place, he'd come up and kiss me. He knew as well as I did that that was absolutely taboo, but I was an old lady by then, and that was his way of showing that he liked me. He was an old Southern politician—he kissed all the ladies, both black and white. Underneath that clownish manner, he is a very brave man.

Cliff was no longer teaching Sunday school at the First Presbyterian Church. When he got back from the Eastland hearing in New Orleans, he went to his class one Sunday morning and nobody was there. And they never came back. That was a gentle way of letting him know that they didn't care to have him as a teacher any more.

The church had a young preacher named Dr. Patterson, a very great preacher and one of the most brilliant men I've ever met. He taught a Bible study class on Wednesday, which I was very interested in. Privately he began to have some contact with Dr. King. He tried to keep it all within the framework of Christianity, but word got out that he was sympathetic to the blacks. The Southern Presbyterian Church passed a resolution favoring an open church—in other words, the church would not be barred to anybody, because it was God's house. Dr. Patterson voted for the open church resolution at synod meeting, and he soon got in trouble for it when he got back to Montgomery. He developed a terrible ulcer, and when he got well, he went to a big church in Atlanta. Finally he left the church entirely. He's in some form of welfare work now. Dr. Patterson was a man who knew what was right and was a brilliant preacher, but he just couldn't bring himself to take a stand publicly. Of course, remaining quiet didn't do him any good—he had to leave town anyway.

Dr. Patterson and Cliff were never very close because Cliff was such a marked man by then. We went to church every Sunday, and Cliff had been elected a deacon. He was John W. Durr's son and James Durr's brother, so it was very hard for the people of the church to turn us away. But after Dr. Patterson left, the church doors were barred on Sunday and you couldn't get in until someone had looked at you and seen you were white. That's when we stopped going to the Presbyterian church. Cliff had been about the fifth generation of Durrs that had sat in the same pew. The whole church experience probably hurt him worse than anything that happened to him, because he felt that was real repudiation. Cliff never had been to another church, and he never joined another one.

A few years ago the First Presbyterian Church of Montgomery again had trouble with their preacher. A black man came and sat in the back of the church and the preacher welcomed him. After that the preacher and the choir director and the religious education director all left. I don't know whether they left voluntarily or were asked to leave. In any case, the church leaders called Maxwell Air Force Base and said they needed a temporary preacher. The field commander didn't have anybody to send but a Catholic priest and a Jewish rabbi and an Episcopal priest, so they took the Episcopalian. He arrived and he was as black as the ace of spades. It caused a great shock, but as I understand it, nobody got up and left. They sat through it. Ten years ago the whole church would have walked out en masse.

As bad as things got here in Montgomery during the civil rights movement, the worst time of all, to me, was 1961, the year of the Freedom Riders. Decca was visiting us and doing an article for *Esquire Magazine* on the you-alls and the non-you-alls. It was a take-off on her sister's book in England about the yous and the non-yous—how to tell the upper class from the lower class. It was supposed to be a rather light piece. She'd been pursuing rather frivolous aspects of Southern life that whole week.

We decided we'd go up to Pea Level and have a pleasant, quiet weekend, without any interruptions. Cliff went up on Friday night because he wanted to put the place in order before Decca saw it. He was always so proud of it. He wanted it to look its best.

We had two cars at that time, an old Buick that Aubrey Williams had given us and an old Jeep we'd had for years. Cliff took the Buick up on Friday night and Decca and I got up on Saturday morning and got ready to go, but we decided to go by the office first and pick up the mail. As we got closer to the office, which was at 17 Moulton Street, we saw an enormous crowd of people. Of course, I knew immediately that the Freedom Riders had arrived. They had been expected all week. This was Saturday, May 20, 1961.

Decca, with her journalist's instinct, hopped out of the car and said, "Oh, I want to get to the bus station." We were about a block from the station and you couldn't park. Cars were parked in every direction. So I was left with the car, loaded with a lot of junk to take to Pea Level for the weekend. I drove around until I finally spied a used-car lot. I parked there, illegally, but there was no place else to park. Everything was just jammed.

I went up to our office through this great crowd. From the second floor, I had a box seat. I could see exactly what was going on at the bus station. The Freedom Riders had come in on the bus. They had been escorted to the city limits by the state troopers, who at that time were headed by Floyd Mann, in my opinion the best appointment Gov. John Patterson ever made. He is a remarkably brave, fine man and has my real admiration. When the Freedom Riders got to the borders of Montgomery, the city police were supposed to take over. But the city police hadn't the slightest idea of stopping the Ku Kluxers or whoever did the beating up.

What I saw from our office window was a vast concourse of people. I saw the Negroes being frisked by the police. They made each Negro hold his hands up and then they'd take his shoes off—maybe to keep him from running away; I don't know. And they would systematically proceed to frisk him. The crowd was yelling, "Go get the niggers! Go get the niggers! Go get the niggers! Go get the niggers!" It was the most horrible thing that I have ever seen.

Then I saw a white boy stagger up to a black cab. He was bleeding badly. At that time a black cab driver couldn't take a white passenger, and a white cab driver couldn't take a black passenger. I heard later that he asked the driver to take him to the hospital. The black cab driver said he couldn't do it. He finally staggered over to a white cab driver, who did take him.

I felt absolute stark terror. I'd lived in Montgomery for ten years. We'd gone through the bus boycott and the *Brown* decision and all the things that had happened after the *Brown* decision. We'd gone through the Eastland hearing. What terrified me so was that the people who were shouting and holding up their babies to "see the niggers run" were just ordinary Montgomery people who had come downtown on Saturday as they usually do, to shop. And they had turned into a raving mob. It was a terrifying sight. It destroyed the confidence I'd been building up for ten years. I had been telling myself, "You can come home again. The South has good people, and Montgomery has a lot of fine people, and the people here are not terrible, brutal, racial bigots." I'd begun defending the South, and Montgomery in particular, because of the many kindnesses we had received. We had met with unkindnesses, too, but we had met with enough kindness that I was beginning to feel that Montgomery was my home. These were my people and all they needed was the right leadership. But all of a sudden I was terrified. These were the people I was living among and they were really crazy. They were full of hatred and they were full of bigotry and meanness. They were enjoying the sight of these Negroes and these few white students being beat up. I didn't face the mob, because I was on the second story of the building across the street. But it was pretty terrifying all the same.

I was also terrified for Decca because she was in the midst of this mob. With that English accent of hers, I thought if she opened her mouth, she'd be attacked. I didn't know what would happen to her. But Decca is brave and takes terrific chances. She was after her story, and she wanted to be right in the middle of what was going on.

At that moment, some young ministerial students from Huntingdon College came into the office led by Bob Zellner, who had become a great friend of ours. The president of Huntingdon had threatened to expel Bob because of his civil rights activities. Cliff had taken the case and had persuaded the boys to wait until they graduated before they began doing civil rights work. In the meantime Bob had become a very dear friend, a member of the family almost.

One of the students who came into the office with Bob had become hysterical and was insisting that he was going over to the bus station to have a prayer session. They were all terribly upset by what they saw, but this one particular boy had gone past the bounds of reason and he was determined to go over to the bus station. If he got killed then he would have died for Jesus. We didn't think he was going to do any good by trying to hold a prayer session and getting beaten up. We had to restrain him to keep him from going.

Bob has a very adventurous spirit himself, so I told him I was terrified that Decca was over there in the middle of the mob. He had never met her, but he said, "I'll go and get her and bring her back to the office." I gave him a good description of her, and he went and got her. And, oh, she was furious. She wanted to stay right where the action was.

Then she told us the things she had seen, like a Negro being beaten so badly and Floyd Mann coming and standing over him, putting his legs on either side of him to protect him. He either drew his gun or put his hand on his gun and said, "Anybody that touches this man, I'll kill them"—defending the Negro. The young Gasches, whom Cliff defended later, had been arrested and put in jail for trying to defend some of them. John Siegenthaler, whom Robert Kennedy sent down to observe the whole thing, had been knocked unconscious and was lying in the middle of the street.

Then I saw Judge Walter B. Jones drive up in a great big black automobile with the attorney general of the state, MacDonald Gallion, one of the worst white supremacists and segregationists in the state. They got out and just stood there watching, just rubbing their hands—just enjoying it, apparently, and thinking this was exactly what these people deserved.

Finally, Police Commissioner Sullivan and the Montgomery police appeared on the scene. But they protected the people who had been doing the beating. After half an hour, the Freedom Riders had either been badly beaten and had been taken to the hospital or they had run and hidden somewhere. There was nobody else to beat up. The stray Negroes whom they were picking up were not the Freedom Riders at all, the ones I saw. They were just any Negro who happened to pass by or be in the crowd.

Shortly after the Freedom Rider beatings, an amusing incident occurred. Judge Rives, who was going to hear these cases, was in the barber shop one day having his face shaved when two men came in. The men were bragging about the police chief, Sullivan. They said, "Sully kept his word. He said he'd give us half an hour to beat up those God-damned sons of bitches and he did." Well, the barber got in a perfect state, because he knew that they were talking in front of the federal judge. He began to gyrate around trying to tell them to hush. They didn't recognize Judge Rives because he was all covered up with lather, so they gave themselves away. In any case, that's exactly what happened. The city police had promised to give them time, and these Ku Kluxers or whoever they were had been waiting there all week for their opportunity.

I was terrified, the day of the Freedom Riders, that the white crowd would start up on a "nigger hunt," where any black man or woman was suspect and could be beaten up. But mostly I was scared for myself, if you want to know the honest-to-God truth. I just felt that I would live and die with people who could be absolute brutes, and how did I know they wouldn't turn on me? It was a terrifying sight. I still have nightmares about it sometimes. It was like seeing a friend you know change. It was just an ordinary Saturday morning crowd of ordinary white Montgomery people all of a sudden changing into a terrifying mob.

The crowd finally dispersed, and Decca and I decided there was nothing to do but to go on up to Pea Level where Cliff was. We got into the old Jeep and drove up. Decca drove because I was having a nervous tremor, the shakes.

When we got to Pea Level, I was still having shaking fits, and we told Cliff what had happened. He and Decca thought I should have a glass of iced tea or lemonade and lie down. So they gave me a glass of lemonade which was practically pure gin. They knocked me out completely. I didn't wake up till the next morning. Of course, when I woke up I didn't feel very well, but I was calm again. I wasn't shaking and I wasn't terrified.

Decca was absolutely thrilled. She was having the time of her life. Our reactions were diametrically opposite. She was onto a great story. She'd seen it with her own eyes. We didn't have a telephone at Pea Level at that time, so she couldn't wait to get back to town. She kept saying, "Let's go back to town. Let's go back to town." We finally persuaded her to wait till after lunch. She wanted to get in touch with the magazine and see if she couldn't sell the story. A professional writer is very different from an amateur. Her first idea was to get a contract.

We finally drove back into town. We didn't have a radio or a TV at Pea Level, but we had a radio in the Buick that Aubrey had given us. We heard that there was going to be a mass meeting that night, or late that afternoon, at the First Baptist Church, where Ralph Abernathy was minister. Martin Luther King had come over from Atlanta. They had planned a great rally to show support for the Freedom Riders. Decca said, "Oh, I've just got to go to that." We tried to dissuade her because we also heard that a mob was gathering in front of the church.

When we got back home, Decca was still hell-bent on going to that meeting. She was going, hell or high water. A young fellow from Antioch who was working for Aubrey came by. He was dying to go to the mass meeting, too. Cliff and I had no desire to go at all. We knew exactly what it was going to be like and we thought it was dangerous. We pled with them not to go, but they paid no attention at all. Of course, we knew they had to take one of our automobiles, our old Jeep or the Buick. They decided to take the Buick because it was such a heavy car and we felt that it couldn't be turned over. Decca kept saying, "Oh, Virginia, this is absurd—to be so scared."

Decca put on her Southern costume—a lovely sort of fluffy green hat with chiffon on it and pearls around her neck and white gloves and a green chiffon dress. She said, "Nobody would think of attacking me. I look like a perfect Southern lady." I said, "That's exactly why you might get attacked. What would a perfect Southern lady be doing going to this Freedom Rider meeting?" Well, she paid no attention whatever. The young boy from Antioch was in a great state of excitement, and they rode off together in the Buick.

We had urged Decca to park the car several blocks from the church. I tried to tell them how to get into the church through the back. The First Baptist Church has a big Negro housing project behind it. I told them to try to come up the back street and go in the back door.

We sat glued to the radio. People began to drop in. I don't remember who. Everybody was in a tremendous state of tension and excitement. Then we heard how the federal marshals began to throw tear gas at the crowd to keep them from storming the church. The mob would take the tear-gas bombs and throw them into the open windows of the church. Decca said later that was the most terrible thing you could imagine because it was crowded and hot as hell. She was afraid the whole place would be set on fire.

King and Abernathy and other preachers were taking turns preaching and praying and getting the people to sing. They finally closed all the windows, which of course made the place hotter than ever. Robert Kennedy told King over the telephone that he knew exactly what they were going through. He remembered that his grandfather had told him how mobs used to attack the nunneries in Boston. There had been a lot of anti-Catholic feeling in Boston and several nunneries were burned.

We heard that King and Kennedy were in conversation, and then we heard that the National Guard had been sent in. At that point, we felt great relief, but we heard that one of the marshal's cars had been turned over and burned. I think John Patterson was the one who called out the National Guard, and I think he did it to cut off the federal agents, to get the situation back under his control. I also think he did the right thing. John is my cousin and I disagree with him politically, but I don't think he is a brutal man. He's just a typical Alabama politician who wants to get votes. In fact, he told me that once. He said, "You know, cousin Virginia, I never have had the slightest prejudice against negras. It's just that you have to nigger to get elected. I'm a real liberal. I'm against the Alabama Power Company."

About two o'clock in the morning, Decca called from the basement of the church and said, "Virginia, I'm all right. It's the most terrifying evening of my life, but I'm all right. The National Guard is here and they will bring us all home." They escorted everybody out of the church area.

Decca came in about three o'clock with this young boy from Antioch. Of course they were quite stirred up. The first thing she said when she came in was, "Oh, Virginia, they burned your car. I'm so sorry." Instead of parking three or four blocks from the church, as we had advised them to do, they drove the car right in front of the church. When the mob saw this very handsome, well-dressed white woman get out and go into the church with this young white boy, they immediately grabbed hold of the car and turned it over. They put a match in the gas tank and it just burned up. There was nothing left but the frame. I saw it afterward, and it was absolutely burned down to the frame.

Decca was very upset. She had insurance. She gave us, I think, three hundred dollars for the car. We didn't collect anything from our insurance company, and after that we couldn't get insurance on any car we owned. We had to get insurance in Birmingham because the insurance people in Montgomery blamed us for letting our car be burned.

Decca's mind was gripped by the stories she had heard during World War II, stories of the Nazis locking people in churches and barns and burning them. Decca had been terrified. The church was all closed up. She was afraid they would start a fire. Of course, Dr. King must have been afraid of that, too, or he wouldn't have had the conversation with Robert Kennedy about the convents and nunneries being set afire in Boston.

Decca got up bright and early on Monday morning and began to call publishers. She got a contract with *Life* magazine to write the article. Then she pounded on the typewriter continuously until the article was finished. But it was never published because at that time the chaplain of Yale, William Sloane Coffin, came down and he also wrote an article that appeared in *Life*.

The only repercussions we felt from the incident came when the newspaper reported that our car was burned. Some people sympathized with us, but mostly we got a lot of heavy breathing telephone calls. The phone would ring all night long and all we would hear was heavy breathing.

Decca finally left. The original article she'd planned about the South finally came out in *Esquire*, but it was not as good as it would have been if she hadn't had the Freedom Rider experience. All the funny ways she can write were muted because she was so upset and disturbed by the riot. The article was rather good, but it was not terribly funny.

Then the trials began in the circuit court. The chaplain of Yale had come to Montgomery with a distinguished group of white professors and preachers, and they tried to drink coffee at the bus station with Abernathy and a group of blacks. They were all arrested, about thirteen of them. I remember going to their trial. Coffin was represented by Lou Pollak, who was dean of the Yale Law School and had been a friend of ours. Lucy and Sheldon Hackney, our daughter and son-in-law, were at Yale for four years while Sheldon was getting his Ph.D. under C. Vann Woodward, and we had renewed our acquaintance with Pollak.

Young Peter Taft was Judge Rives's law clerk at the time, and he introduced us to all the defendants. Peter's father was mayor of Cincinnati, and his uncle was Robert Taft. Peter was the handsomest young boy I've ever seen, and when he arrived in Montgomery, all the women and girls in town ran after him, trying to get him invited to parties. The same thing happened to young Bobby Kennedy, Jr., when he came to Montgomery a few summers ago. And he did exactly what young Kennedy did when he first got here—he took refuge with us, because we were no threat to him. We had no young girls that we were trying to marry off. Judge Rives was a friend of ours, so we saw a great deal of Peter and became extremely fond of him.

Peter introduced us to Coffin and the other defendants. Pollak remembered us, so we invited him and Coffin to have a drink with Peter Taft, the three of them. Peter had gone to Yale Law School. Lou Pollak consented, but Reverend Coffin said, "Mrs. Durr, I am very sorry. I cannot come unless you invite all the other defendants, all thirteen of them." Most of them were black, and this was when the town was like a bomb. Just the slightest match might have blown it sky-high. We lived on the corner of Felder and Court, one of the prominent corners in town. I just couldn't do it. I felt I just could not at five o'clock in the afternoon have thirteen defendants, black and white, to my house for a drink. I explained it to Reverend Coffin and he was very sweet about it, but he made me feel that I was one of the Southern segregationists. He wouldn't even stay in a hotel. He stayed with Mrs. West, who was one of the leaders in the black community. He also had his meals brought in to him from a black restaurant. He refused in any way to consent to segregation, and I was having a segregated party so he wouldn't attend. It made me rather angry. Cliff and I had been on the front line for about ten years, and this man was making us feel that we were just sorry Southern segregationists because we refused to have the black defendants to our house for a drink. We ran into that quite a bit with some of our Northern sympathizers, but they always got on the airplane to go back home, where they were perfectly safe. They thought we should do everything they were doing, and if we didn't we were pretty sorry folks.

21

White Southerners

THE SOUTHERN FEDERAL judges are the unsung heroes in the civil rights struggle. Frank Johnson is the reason integration in Alabama has gone as well as it has. The federal judges stood completely firm on obeying the law. Frank Johnson came here as a federal judge before the civil rights movement began. He was a Republican, but he was a Winston County Republican, which is something different from most Southern Republicans. Winston County is a mountainous area in the northwest part of the state. The pioneers who settled there were people who had come down to New Orleans from Tennessee to fight with Andrew Jackson against the British. They were a hardy lot. They voted for Andrew Jackson, of course, and at the time of the Civil War they stuck with the Union and even sent a company of soldiers to the Union Army.

Frank Johnson is a very tall, strong, handsome, dark-haired man. When I see him, I always feel as though he's looking at me down the barrel of a rifle. Occasionally he relaxes, but usually he's pretty tense. In court he's extremely strict. I was in his court one time when a policeman came in in uniform with his gun on. The commissioner of police was on the stand, and the policeman had come to bring a message to him. Frank Johnson stopped the proceedings and asked the policeman, "Is that a gun you have strapped to your waist?" The man said, "Yes, sir. I wear it all the time." He said, "You mean you dare to come in my courtroom with a gun strapped around your waist? Get out of this courtroom and don't ever come in here again with a gun on you or you'll be in jail. Court's adjourned for ten minutes." The policeman went out and everybody drew his breath because Frank was so mad. He was just furious at the idea of somebody coming into his court with a gun.

Frank Johnson had gone to the University of Alabama with George

Wallace. Both of them were poor country boys and had been friends. They were both nonfraternity because the fraternities favored the social boys from the big cities. They both started out as populists—all for the people against the establishment. But as time went on, they became enemies. Frank Johnson was standing like a rock enforcing integration because it was the law of the land, and George Wallace was doing everything he could to fight integration.

Frank Johnson's court decisions soon isolated him in Montgomery. The bus boycott decision was especially unpopular, and that was handed down by the three-man federal panel of Judge Rives, Judge Seybourne Lynne from Birmingham, and Judge Johnson. Judge Lynne dissented, so it was really Judge Rives and Frank Johnson who ruled that the segregated buses were unconstitutional.

Frank Johnson was raised in the Baptist church. His people believed in heaven and hell, and they believed in the United States Constitution. Judge Johnson and Hugo Black are very much alike. They came from hill people and rose out of poverty by their own brains and worth, by their own character. And they both believed in the law. The South had been lawless. It was essential to return the South to the law.

Since Judge Johnson came from Winston County, he was more or less a stranger in Montgomery. A cross was burned on his lawn, and his mother's house was bombed. He's very wary still and doesn't give his friendship easily. His wife, Ruth Johnson, went to the black college, Alabama State College, and now she teaches in a black school. She was the only white woman in many classes. She's very brave and principled. She and Judge Johnson have made friends in Montgomery now, and I think that they like Montgomery in a way. At least they're used to it. And Judge Johnson, of course, is protected by the power of the court.

Judge Richard Rives, who was born and raised here in Montgomery and was head of the bar and considered one of its leading lawyers, was faced not by strangers but by his intimate friends. When the State Bar Association met here, Cliff and I would go, really just to prove we were not scared. We knew we would be snubbed by a good many people, and we were. That's the reason I was so fond of Chuck Morgan—he was one of the first people who was willing to associate with us at those meetings. Chuck was a lawyer in Birmingham who later, in the sixties, left the state as a result of his outspoken support of Negro rights. At the bar association dinners, the members would spend the whole evening attacking Judge Rives and Hugo Black. They would say, "My former friend Richard Rives" and "Richard Rives who was raised in the South" and "Hugo Black who proved to be a traitor to his people."

There was a crazy columnist here with the *Montgomery Advertiser*, Bill Mahoney, who wrote a column saying that the way to dedicate a memorial

Cliff *(left)* and Judge Richard Rives shortly after the Montgomery bus boycott decision.

to Hugo Black was to find his birthplace and burn down the house and scatter salt over the ground where the house had been so there would always be a scar on the ground.

People in Montgomery respected Cliff, but we had very few friends. Cliff was never invited to join a luncheon club while he was here. John Kohn, the lawyer who defended me in New Orleans, was a friend of Cliff's. And Judge Rives, of course, was a great friend after he went on the bench. Drayton Hamilton, city attorney in Montgomery, was another friend, but we didn't see much of him. He wasn't afraid to associate with us, though.

Judge Rives and Cliff were very much alike in that they came from the same background. Judge Rives's family and Cliff's family settled Montgomery County before 1800. They were here in the 1790s. At one time both families were rich planting families with large plantations and slaves. They were members of the aristocracy, but both families lost everything in the Civil War. They may have been aristocratic, but they were poor. Judge Rives never went to law school except for a few months at Tulane. He studied law at Judge Hill's office. He was like Cliff, gentle but extremely firm. He didn't frighten people at all, because he was so mild mannered. But underneath that gentleness and mildness, he was extremely firm.

Because of their different backgrounds, Judge Johnson and Judge Rives came to the issue of race with different experiences and expectations. Judge

Johnson, like Hugo Black, was brought up in a county where they didn't have servants, so he hadn't been surrounded by black people. He never had that close connection with black people that Cliff and I had or Judge Rives had, where you depended on them, where they were part of the family. So Frank's and Hugo's feelings about black people were much less paternal.

How Judge Rives felt about black people personally, I don't know. He had always been surrounded by them, but I don't know that he ever had dinner with a black person. When I first knew him, and his wife was alive, they had a cook and they had a nurse. Mrs. Rives was ill for a long time. Georgia Brown, who sews for me, also sewed for Mrs. Rives, and she is as high class a lady as you'll ever meet, beautiful manners and soft and sweet and angelic, but Mrs. Rives never dreamed of eating at the table with her.

How much passion these judges had about the plight of the Negro, I couldn't say. I can only say that in Hugo's case, he had a passion for the poor. He had a passion for the helpless and the poor. And I think that is true of Johnson also. I think Judge Rives has a passion for the law and for justice. In his personal relations with blacks, he is extremely kind, but he is an aristocrat.

Cliff had a hard time getting over his aristocratic feelings, too. He, too, had a passion for justice. He was the one who took the police brutality cases and the loan shark cases, which brought him into such disrepute with his old friends, and it was because he had a passion for justice.

[I wasn't consciously bent on improving the lot of black people, although they were getting a bad deal. But I knew Rosa Parks well. She was a fine person. When she went to jail I found myself helping her instinctively. I never acted deliberately; I'm not basically an ideological person. But you move instinctively when you see somebody kicked around.

Sometimes the Negroes would come around and tell me how much they appreciated what I was doing for them. I said, "Look here, I'm not a damn bit interested in your legal and constitutional rights as Negroes, but I am interested in your legal and constitutional rights as people because I happen to be people myself. I know from long experience that our legal and constitutional safeguards are not selective. They've got to protect everybody or in time they won't protect any of us. It's a matter of fighting for my own rights along with yours."][1]

Cliff also had a great respect for many of the Negroes whom he knew, like Mr. Nixon and Mrs. Parks and Mrs. West and Fred Gray, but Cliff was an aristocrat, too. The thing that upset him most was not the plight of the

[1]"The Reminiscences of Clifford J. Durr," Columbia University Oral History Collection, New York, 1976, part 3, pp. 324–26.

Negro, although he felt it very strongly—he'd been raised by Negro women and Negro men and played with them as a boy. He had a great deal of passion about their oppression and their plight, but the most powerful feeling in him—and I think it was true of Judge Rives—was the shame he felt at the way the white man cheated and treated the Negro. Every time Cliff got one of these cases where a Negro had been cheated by an insurance company or secondhand automobile dealer, he felt a sense of shame, as a Southern white man, that anybody would treat helpless people that way.

So Judge Johnson and Judge Rives and Cliff came at the race issue from different angles, but their primary purpose was to uphold the law. The South had been lawless, and they were trying to make the South into a lawful community. Hugo became almost a high priest of the law. He would tell me over and over again, "For God's sake, tell your friends down there in Alabama, Martin Luther King and the rest of them that you know, to stop marching and to stop having all these demonstrations. That's just going to jeopardize their cause. They should leave it to the courts." He really believed in the courts. He thought that the marches and the young people coming to Mississippi were just hurting their cause.

Hugo believed that segregation was wrong and he was willing to take the blows he knew he would get from his fellow Southerners, but he was also protected by the fact that he lived in Washington and was on the Supreme Court and was making a handsome salary and had a chauffeur and a messenger and a beautiful house in Alexandria. In Washington he was a great hero. It was only when he came to Alabama that he got the full force of what we lived with all the time.

Hugo had lived all of his life in Alabama before he went to Washington. He was elected to the Senate twice by the people of Alabama. He was a man who was as deeply rooted as any man could be in Alabama. His people had come over here in the very early days and started farming in Clay County. It was a very poor county, and he was a poor man. He had a lot of sympathy for the poor white man of the South. He learned, in time, to have the same sympathy for the poor black man of the South, but he never gave up his faith in the poor white man of the South. Hugo came to have a great deal of feeling about the poor black man of the South, and the poor black woman, although he was never a woman's liberationist, I can assure you of that!

Hugo believed women should stay sweet and feminine and slim. He wanted to send his daughter to Sweet Briar because Sister had gone there. He wanted his daughter to be just like his wife—perfectly feminine and sweet. Of course, Sister had other things that she wanted to do than just be beautiful and charming all the time. She never did what she wanted to do until near the very end of her life, when she finally began to paint. She was a very good painter, and she finally made up her mind she was not going to any more luncheons and teas. She was not going to spend her life just being the wife of a Supreme Court justice and holding teas on Monday. She started to paint, which was what she really wanted to do, and she won a good many prizes. It gave her a great deal of pleasure, but it came awfully late in her life. She was well into her fifties before she painted at all. That's what she had wanted to do and never was able to do for so long. I think Hugo was perfectly willing for her to paint if he thought it gave her pleasure, but he didn't regard her painting as being of any great moment. It was just a hobby, nothing that was serious. It meant a great deal more than that to her.

Hugo was treated badly by the people of the South and by the people of Alabama in particular. Hugo's son, young Hugo, and his wife were living in Birmingham in the early sixties. They got a great deal of adverse criticism and comment just from his name, and they were very much snubbed in Birmingham. Hugo, Jr., was working for the AFL-CIO, which also was unpopular in Birmingham. They tolerated the ostracism until their boy, Hugo Black III, was going to start school. Then they just couldn't stand the idea that the little boy, six years old, would be going to school in Alabama with the name Hugo Black III and would be persecuted and made unhappy because of it, so they moved to Miami.

People don't like to remember any more, but a lot of Southerners were forced to leave their homes because of their views on race. I knew several in Montgomery. The Church of the Ascension had a young clergyman named Tom Thrasher who came from Mississippi originally and was married to a very pretty girl. He was rector of the Church of the Ascension and everybody adored him. He and Cliff became great friends. He was a lovely human being. He was well educated and, as they say in Montgomery, well born. His wife was also well born. They were extremely popular. Tom got an offer to go to Alexandria, Virginia, to St. Paul's, quite a famous old church. Usually the priests who go to St. Paul's go on to bigger and better things, the cathedral or a bishop's appointment. When Tom got the offer, his parishioners were so anxious for him to stay that they sent petitions around for people to sign to keep him in Montgomery. They finally persuaded him to stay.

Tom became president of the Council on Human Relations, the only integrated group in Montgomery. The Council on Human Relations made no waves at all. We'd meet once a month, usually at Alabama State Teachers' College, and we would discuss various things. They used the phrase "keeping the channels of communication open." We would talk to each other. Then Tom Thrasher began to preach sermons on the brotherhood of man, and he took the side of the blacks. Some of the people in his church were very much opposed to this. T. B. Hill, a conservative lawyer in town, was one, and the publisher of the *Alabama Journal*, one of two dailies in Montgomery, was another. There was quite a struggle within the church, in a very dignified way.

A black Episcopal clergyman came to Alabama State one summer to take some courses. There's a rule that if you're an Episcopal clergyman, you must take communion at least once a month. It's a rule of the church. There had been a black Episcopal church here, but the priest lost his mind during a racial incident, and the church disbanded after he left. So the young black clergyman who had come to take courses at Alabama State had nowhere to take communion but in a white church. He came to the Church of the Ascension one morning for early service, and he took communion at the altar. Well, all of the people who were against Tom Thrasher and against integration stirred up a tremendous storm and said that it was a frame-up.

Marjorie and Moreland Smith were great friends of Tom Thrasher, and they went to his church. It just so happened that that morning Marjorie was in charge of putting the flowers on the altar and arranging the communion table, so it was said there was a plot on the part of Tom Thrasher and Moreland Smith to let this Negro priest in to take communion. Several people walked out of the church.

The situation in the Church of the Ascension became extremely bitter. Some of the people in the church hired a policeman to stand at the door to see that no blacks came in. They did the same thing at the Presbyterian church. Tom objected to that very much, so finally the church convened a meeting and the bishop of Alabama came, Bishop C. C. Carpenter. Bishop Carpenter was about as reactionary as they come, and he decided that Tom was too liberal. Tom had to leave. He went to the University of North Carolina and was the chaplain there until his death.

A young Presbyterian minister was also forced to leave Montgomery. His name is Neil Segrest and he was from Tuskegee originally. His father was a leading lawyer in Tuskegee, and his mother was very prominent, too. He was kin to everybody in Macon County, everybody who was white. Many blacks had the same name, because they had been at the family plantation. He was a very dedicated young man and he had the church out in Oak Park, which is a working-class district. I never heard him preach, but I never saw a man so dedicated as a pastor. If anybody in the church got sick, he sat up with them. If anybody went to jail, which they sometimes did, he was down there in the jail with them. He did everything he could for his church members, and they all seemed to be just crazy about him.

Then the Southern Presbyterian Church had a meeting and they voted that the church would follow the open-door policy, which meant that blacks could come in the church and join the church. The church in Oak Park protested strongly against the open-door policy even though no blacks lived in the area and so none ever came in. The parishioners insisted that their pastor repudiate the policy and say that he would not allow any Negroes in the church. He wouldn't do it, so they stopped paying his salary. Mrs. Henry Collins, who was a woman with a great deal of standing and a lot of money, paid his salary for quite a while. But finally he had a nervous breakdown and had to leave.

Tom Thrasher's friends Moreland and Marjorie Smith were also forced to leave Montgomery because of their racial views. Moreland Smith's family had come to Montgomery about the turn of the century and had become wealthy. They had a chain of laundries. Moreland had become an architect and was head of a big architectural firm that designed a great number of public buildings—schools and hospitals and courthouses. He was on the Council of Human Relations and had been president of the country club, the Kiwanis Club, and the American Association of Architects.

Moreland had not wanted to get involved in the segregation struggle. After we became friends, he told us one night, "You know, I want to have my cake and eat it, too. I feel that segregation is wrong, but I don't want to lose my friends and I don't want to lose my business. I suppose I just want to have my cake and eat it, too."

When the state formed the Alabama Commission on Civil Rights, Moreland became its president. The first thing he did was to have a meeting on the segregation of the hospitals. I well remember going to that first meeting. Moreland was a handsome, dignified, white-haired fellow, very quiet. Like Cliff and Tom Thrasher, he was a perfect gentleman. He never got excited or lost his temper. The government had issued an order that the hospitals built with federal funds had to be integrated. Now, the hospitals in Montgomery were absolutely segregated. St. Jude's was the only hospital where blacks could be taken and have black doctors. The nuns from St. Margaret's, the Catholic hospital, were at the commission meeting that morning, and they got up and said that they had, as of that morning, opened their hospital to Negro doctors. They abolished all segregation in the hospital. These nuns were like a lot of hens, scared to death and quivering, but they had done everything that was required of them.

Shortly after this meeting, Moreland noticed that his firm wasn't getting any more work from the state, and he found out that George Wallace had passed the word that no state department could give any business to Moreland Smith. If you went against George, he took revenge, and he was taking revenge on Moreland. Moreland, who was head of the firm and who had been extremely successful, went to his partners and said, "Apparently I'm the cause of this order coming down from the governor and if you want me to, I will resign." He thought his partners would stick by him, but they didn't. They said yes, he was the cause of the order coming down and it would mean the business would be cut by half or more; so they bought him out. He felt terribly disillusioned.

Moreland set up a little office in his home, but he didn't get any business. The country club, of which he had been president at one time, refused to let him be a member any more. The reason given was that he'd bring blacks in and let them eat. The club still doesn't allow Jews or Negroes into its membership. When Moreland got an offer to go over to Atlanta and work with the Southern Regional Council on city planning, he took it.

I could give a lot more cases of people who left, but this is enough to show the pressures that were on people, and the pressures that were on us. These were brave Southerners, unsung heroes, but they were not typical. The South is often talked about as if all Southerners are alike, but the race issue, particularly, affected different Southerners differently. Even so-called liberals were not always in favor of integration. Two examples are Grover Hall, Jr., of the *Montgomery Advertiser*, and George Wallace. Both these men were liberals originally, but the pressures of the racial struggle here made them strangers to the liberal tradition.

Grover Hall, Jr., played a very strange part in Montgomery's troubles and in mine and Cliff's. His father, Grover Hall, Sr., was a great friend of ours. He'd been a friend and supporter of Hugo. Grover, Sr., got the Pulitzer Prize for his fight against the Ku Kluxers. He was an extremely attractive man. He was bright and witty and he wrote beautifully. When he was very young, he had married a woman who was a hardshell Baptist. They had one son, Grover Hall, Jr., and he was torn all his life between his mother and his father. His mother was a strict, narrow-minded, provincial, and bigoted woman, and a very strict Baptist. She thought to take a drink was a sin. Sex was sin.

I knew Mrs. Hall because my mother was at Hillcrest Sanatorium for a while when she was suffering from depression, and I met Mrs. Hall there. She was also a patient. I immediately told her how much I admired her husband, what a great writer I thought he was. I didn't know that they were at odds. She began to say terrible things about her husband. She criticized him every way you can think of. She not only didn't like him, she despised him.

Mr. Hall, Sr., was a genial man. He had a lot of friends. I wrote him a letter once. After news of Joe Gelders's beating came out in the La Follette hearings, an organization formed in Birmingham to keep outside agitators out of town, but there wasn't a word about it in the *Montgomery Advertiser* the next day. I wrote Grover Hall, who was editor of the paper, a very harsh letter and told him I thought it was dreadful—great liberal that he was supposed to be—that he hadn't even mentioned the fact that there'd been an organization of big businessmen in Birmingham who had determined to keep outside agitators out of town.

Mr. Hall wrote me back one of the most insulting letters that you could write: "So you think you're a liberal. . . ." It went on for two pages in his most vituperative prose. When I got the letter, I thought it was a masterpiece of vituperation. It was so beautifully written. When Cliff came home that night both he and I laughed and laughed over it because he thought it was an absolutely brilliant letter and so did I. When we came down to Montgomery the next time, we called Mr. Hall and he asked us to come and meet him for coffee about ten o'clock. We became fast friends. We carried on quite a correspondence for a number of years.

By the time we moved to Montgomery, in 1951, Grover Hall, Sr., had died, and Grover, Jr., had become editor of the paper. I met Grover, Jr., at a wedding reception. The first thing I said to him was, "We were great admirers of your father." Grover said, "Well, you must not have known him very well." That was a startling statement. He was just as cool as he could be. He didn't appreciate our claiming friendship with him because of our devotion to his father.

Grover and John Kohn were good friends, and when the Eastland hearing took place, in 1954, Grover sent a reporter to cover it. I think that the *Advertiser*'s coverage helped us a great deal. It certainly didn't put us in a bad light at all. It seemed as though we were being attacked by completely unprincipled, lying men. Grover even wrote an editorial about the hearing, and Allen Rankin wrote a column completely defending us. So the leading paper of the town, instead of accusing us and saying we were trying to overthrow the government by force and violence and all that crazy stuff, really supported us. We felt very grateful to Grover.

But when the *Brown* decision came down and the White Citizens' Council formed, Grover began to take a very hard stand about states' rights. He'd become a great friend of George Wallace. I don't think that Grover Hall formed a great affection and admiration for Wallace, but Grover believed in the exaltation of the South and the protection of the South through states' rights. It was the intellectual defense of segregation. He thought Southerners would have settled the problem themselves in a year or two or three. It was just intervention of the federal government that caused all the trouble. As time went on, his editorials became more and more bitter.

We never saw Grover during this time, but we had one very unfortunate episode with him. Nat Hentoff came down here from the *New Yorker*. He was the typical Greenwich Village type—he had sandals and a beard—but he was a very pleasant fellow, extremely nice. He'd been in Montgomery for a week interviewing people when one night he came to see us. He said he wanted to interview us, and we took him into our confidence. We said that we were having a terrible struggle making a living here and we didn't want to leave and we would talk to him but only off the record.

Cliff tried to explain to Mr. Hentoff the difficulty of a Southerner who loved the South and his home and family and who did not want to be cast in the guise of being critical, of being self-righteous. Cliff would always say, "I was exactly like them, like the Southerners who opposed integration. I just happened to have more opportunity to see the big world. If I'd stayed here in Montgomery, I'd probably still be thinking exactly like the rest of them." He was always trying to make it plain to the newspapermen that he wasn't criticizing the Southern people, that their beliefs were due to their background.

We trusted Hentoff. He asked us particularly about the preachers, the newspapermen, the businessmen, and the Jews, and we told him what we knew. His article came out in the next month's *New Yorker*. In it he said that he had been most interested in meeting a white civil rights lawyer who had a nervous, high-strung wife and a beautiful blonde daughter—that was Tilla, who was home then. He said the family was very close-knit and were like orphans in the storm, all huddled together. He didn't use our real names; he used pseudonyms. Hentoff quoted the white civil rights lawyer as saying that Grover Hall, Sr., had been a brilliant man and a man for whom we had much affection and respect. He told the funny tales about the letters, how Mr. Hall had skinned me alive. During the interview he had also asked about the son, and Cliff had said Grover, Jr., was a great disappointment because his father won the Pulitzer Prize for fighting the Ku Klux Klan and young Grover was opposing the ending of segregation in any way he could, but on a high intellectual level. He said, "He is certainly not the man his father was and it's been a disappointment to me because I was so devoted to his father and admired him so much."

Hentoff had asked about the preachers, and Cliff and I told him about the things that had happened to the preachers, how some of them had to leave town. When he asked about the Jewish community, I said that the Jewish community had reacted just like every other community in Montgomery. There were no differences. Some of them had taken the side of the blacks. In fact, a number of them had contributed money. Mr. Nixon was treasurer of the Montgomery Improvement Association, and he said a lot of the Jewish community was giving him money. He never would tell me who they were because he said they gave him the money on the promise that he wouldn't tell their names. They were scared like everybody else. People were terrified of economic reprisals and social reprisals.

On the day Hentoff's article appeared in the *New Yorker*, Cliff's nephew, Nesbitt Elmore, died. Cliff was at the house helping to arrange the funeral, and I was at the office. The phone rang and it was Grover Hall. I was so full of Nesbitt's death that I said, "Oh, thank you, Grover. I appreciate your calling so much. Nesbitt was a friend of yours, I know."

"I'm not calling about Nesbitt," he said.

"Well, what's the matter?" I asked.

"Have you seen that piece in the *New Yorker*?"

"Yes."

"I won't say anything now, but after the funeral's over I'm going to take this up with Cliff." So sure enough, he wrote a very bitter editorial.

That magazine article caused us more trouble than anything we ever did. People called from the churches to say that we had defamed their preachers. We got telephone calls in the night. One girl called me in the middle of the night and said, "If you don't like Montgomery, why don't you leave town?" Even though Hentoff had used fake names, it was clear who we were. There was no other white civil rights lawyer in Montgomery—certainly not one who had a high-strung wife! Hentoff's article just put the spotlight on us.

I wrote Mr. Hentoff an extremely angry letter, which I thought he deserved. Cliff thought I had been too sharp with him. Hentoff wrote the most puzzled reply, saying that he had done everything he could to protect us. He even changed our names. I think he called us the Williamses. But that article caused us to have more telephone calls and more opposition and hostility than anything we did. And it was the last episode we had with Grover Hall. We never had any personal communication with him after that.

Grover became an absolute Wallace devotee. After new management came in at the *Advertiser*, he went to Richmond, Virginia, and worked for James Kilpatrick, who was then editor of the *Richmond Times-Dispatch*. Then he organized support for Wallace in Virginia. Well, the people who owned the Richmond paper are very aristocratic Virginians, the very epitome. Grover organized a huge meeting for Wallace and all the ragtag, bobtail, poor white trash, common-as-pig-tracks people came to it. The owners of the *Times-Dispatch* did not like it. They didn't care at all for their paper to be associated with such a motley crew. They were typical upper-class, paternalistic Virginians. They believed in being kind and helping the underprivileged, but it never occurred to them that the world is not divided into those who ride and those who are the donkeys to be ridden. Grover got into difficulty about that meeting and left the paper. He went to Washington and started a syndicated column. But then he grew lonesome for Montgomery and was driving back here when he was arrested and put in jail in North Carolina. They said it was drunken driving, but they later found he had a brain tumor. He came back to Montgomery and died several months later.

In the crisis of our life, when Eastland was after us, Grover Hall helped us a great deal, so I have mixed feelings about him. When we needed him most, the paper and he were extremely supportive and took our side. But later on, as things changed, he changed. As the pressure got heavy, a lot of people changed, and he was one who did. He had a very sad life. Grover had great abilities and great promise, but his emotional life had been torn in two by the conflict between his narrow-minded, bigoted mother, and his broad-beamed, genial, liberal father.

George Wallace also changed with the pressure of the times. The first time I saw him I was quite impressed with him. I went to a dentist's office soon after we moved to Montgomery, and here was a young man with a pretty wife and two or three children. They were waiting for the dentist, too, so we fell into conversation. My father's family was named Foster and they came from Union Springs. George Wallace came from Eufaula in Barbour County, which is in the same part of the state. He said, "Why, yes indeed, I know who you are." And he did. He knew who the Fosters were and where Union Springs was. Of course, that's extremely flattering. I remember telling Cliff what a charming young man I had met in the dentist's office. Wallace was running for reelection to the legislature then.

Jim Folsom was ending his first term as governor when we came back to Alabama in 1951. He had already made a reputation for himself as a liberal. In fact, in 1949 he pledged equal justice for black people. He said as long as the Negroes were held down by deprivation and lack of opportunity, all other people would be held down alongside them. "Let's start talking fellowship and brotherly love and doing unto others as we would be done by." This was Jim Folsom's message, and young George Wallace became his lieutenant. In 1949, and in 1948 when he went to the convention in Philadelphia and did not walk out, Wallace had a reputation of being like Jim Folsom, a country boy who'd come up the hard way and made good and was a liberal.

Wallace first ran for governor in 1958. By that time he had built up a reputation of being a rabble rouser but also a populist. He had not said anything, that I recall, about blacks. He told a Folsom aide, "You've got to have the Negro vote from now on if you expect to run for anything, and I'm going to lay my groundwork right now." He became a member of the board of Tuskegee Institute.

My friend Mrs. Rutledge had met George Wallace when he first came back from the war. Wallace's mother was a practical nurse and was nursing someone who lived next door to Mrs. Rutledge. He stayed there with his mother for a while, and Mrs. Rutledge had a long talk with him. She thought, like I did, that he was an extremely attractive young man, very open and bright and pleasant. He always remembered her name and who she was. He told her that when he went into the war he had been like most Alabamians, he had been a racist and had thought Negroes were inferior and should be kept in their place. During the war he had had a complete change of heart because he'd had to fight beside Negroes and he had had to depend on them for his life, and they'd had to depend on him. He now believed that blacks were entitled to all the privileges and rights of white people.

When Wallace first ran for governor in 1958, I don't remember if I voted for him or not. I know I thought he was far more restrained than the race-baiting John Patterson. Folsom was ending his second term. The relationship between Folsom and Wallace was extremely close. There was almost a father-son or big brother relationship.

In his second administration Folsom had begun to drink a great deal. It was during this time that Folsom invited Adam Clayton Powell, the black congressman from New York, to the mansion and had a drink with him, which was a scandalous thing at that time. I knew Adam Clayton Powell fairly well because he was one of the people who supported the anti–poll tax fight. He always gave me the cold shivers, because I never thought I could trust him. He was extremely light and was terribly wounded by the fact that he was considered a black. He was not treated as an equal in Congress. All his life, I suppose, he had the same treatment. I felt that he was dangerous. Marcantonio was in charge of the poll tax bill at that time. He'd known Powell quite well in New York politics and he never trusted him. He thought Powell was terribly egotistical and would betray you in a minute. But on the other hand, his voting record was very good, and he could be very pleasant. He never treated me with anything but good manners. He looked more like an Italian or Puerto Rican. He had no black features at all, yet he was subjected to all the segregation there was in Washington at that time and was also treated to snubs and personal insults. He was an egocentric man, but I always felt that his egocentricity came from the fact that he was concealing a great hurt or rage.

In 1958 Adam Clayton Powell came to Montgomery to make a speech at Alabama State Teachers' College. Powell was well dressed, sophisticated, and extremely aggressive. As I understand the story, he called up Jim Folsom and said he would like to come by and see him before he made his speech. Jim Folsom not only said that would be splendid, but he sent the limousine for him. Powell was driven up to the mansion and then ushered into Jim Folsom's study. There they had a drink together. When he got up at Alabama State to make his speech he told about the visit with Folsom in great detail. He told how he had been met by the limousine and the liveried chauffeur Craig and taken to the mansion and invited into Folsom's private study. He praised Jim Folsom to the skies. He was trying to impress his audience with what a big man he was, but if he'd had any political sense at all, he would have known that in the present state of affairs he was going to hurt Folsom, who had been friendly to him. Even Teddy Roosevelt got into trouble when he had lunch with Booker T. Washington.

The Powell episode shows very clearly the state of mind of the people of Alabama in 1958, four years after the *Brown* decision. For a black man to be invited socially to the governor's mansion was considered a terrible, terrible breach of etiquette, and it hurt Jim Folsom a great deal.

Wallace ran for governor that year for the first time. My cousin, John Patterson, ran against him. John's father had been murdered while running for attorney general in 1954 by people who didn't want him to clean up

Phenix City, which he was threatening to do. John Kohn was the lawyer in that case, and he took young John under his political wing. Young Patterson was named to take his father's place as nominee for attorney general and he won. Then in 1958, John ran against Wallace for governor and won. You have never in your life heard as much niggering as was done by John Patterson. It was nigger, nigger, nigger all the time—just one long stream of racist insults, the danger of the black man and the black man taking over. Compared to John Patterson, Wallace was rather mild, but after the 1958 election was over and he'd been defeated, Wallace said he'd never be out-niggered again.

The next time Wallace ran was in 1962. He used the race issue as his chief claim to be elected. He promised that he would stand in the door and not let the University of Alabama be integrated. He did everything he possibly could to identify himself as the defender of the Southern way of life, which meant that he insulted the black people in every way possible.

By that time I'd become absolutely disgusted with George Wallace. I was beginning to be not only disgusted with him but fearful of him. He became the symbol of Southern resistance. He became a hero to a great many people, a great many white Southern people. I don't think it's possible to divorce Wallace from the Southern white people. He expressed what they felt at that time. And I think to explain it you have to go back to the aftermath of the Civil War. In fact, you have to go back to the settlers.

The people who settled in the South were people who had come from Europe because they were poor and run out. Nobody wanted them over there and they'd been treated very badly. They came to the South and they remained poor. They had very hard lives. Very few were in the planter class. Most people lived a very poor life.

A great many local historical societies have started looking into the lives of the pioneers. Of course, the great trouble with history is that the only people who wrote history are the people who could read and write. Most people were silent because they never could get it down in writing. It's just lately through the tape recorder that they've been able to express themselves.

I've read a lot of the material, which is mostly letters, in the Loacha-poka Historical Society. What is impressive is how simple the life was. The people had no slaves, but they seemed to have led a happy life. They raised everything they ate. They bought almost nothing. Their church was the center of social life. They had some sort of rough school that they all paid a little for. They had no public school. These people who lived in the up-lands, in the mountain districts or in what they called the Piney Woods, led a life which was rather satisfactory as far as they were concerned. It was the people who lived in close contact with the planting class and the deltas on the riverbanks and the black belt who began to feel that the Negroes were their enemies.

So actually, there have been two diverse strains in the South. One is the pioneer strain, people who have independence, pride, and a feeling that they can look after themselves. One of Hugo's ancestors named Black was such a pioneer. She came over here from Georgia with a lot of children and two or three other families. They were heading for a pioneer cabin where they were going to put up for the night. When they got there they found everybody in the cabin had been murdered and scalped by the Indians. Hugo's ancestor made the children stay outside and made the men draw water and bury the bodies, and she went in there with a broom and water and cleaned the place up so those children would have a place to stay that night. This is just one of the tales of the pioneers that has come down through Alabama history. There is in the South a strong strain of independent, proud, self-sufficient people. They are the people whom I count on as my allies, whether we vote together or not. They are the backbone of the South.

On the other hand, the South has a great lot of people who had a very bad time indeed, who didn't feel self-sufficient, who felt terribly oppressed and thought the Negroes were the ones who were keeping them from getting any land. They developed a morbid kind of hatred and self-pity that also runs through the Southern psyche.

George Wallace seemed to combine both strains. He was going to stand up in front of the federal government and tell them to go to hell, and he kept telling people how bad off they were, how the federal government took all their money. But while he was blasting the federal government for being the enemy, he was taking every dime he could get from the federal government. That was part of his demagoguery. The state of Alabama was getting two dollars for every one dollar we sent up in taxes. And the people of Alabama were just like Wallace—blaming the federal government for every ill and taking every federal dollar available. That has produced in Alabama a strange schizophrenia, which has made its politics unlike any other politics I've known.

George Wallace is extremely smart as a politician. In fact, I think he's got a quality of political genius, but anybody who can take the truth and twist it the way he has twisted it is a little off base. The way he has twisted it for the blacks now is amazing. He has convinced many blacks that he's the best friend they ever had, that they owe everything they've got to Wallace. How he can do that is an absolute miracle. The man is, I believe, a complete demagogue in the sense that he can take the truth and twist it completely around all the time he's gaining more and more power.

George Wallace has evolved his demagoguery or his twisting of the truth to the point that he has gained influence over a great many people in the entire country. His greatest influence in the country lies in the blue-collar workers. They work in a plant all day at monotonous jobs that they hate. They are paid pretty good wages now, but the workers don't think it's enough, and they certainly have a dirty, monotonous life. But Wallace has gotten those very people to believe that it's the United States government who's the enemy rather than the corporations. This seems to me to be a very dangerous thing, but it has made Wallace almost priceless as far as the industrialists and corporate giants are concerned because there's nothing in the country strong enough to curb their power except the United States government.

Wallace can even influence a county such as the one where we lived, a very poor county. The schools are falling in: the plaster's flaking off and the windows are broken and the toilets don't work. The people who live in this county are good people on a personal basis. They came up and saved my house when it was on fire. I thought they were the most marvelous people in the world because they were brave and kind and good. But these very same people, who live on food stamps or social security or unemployment insurance or veterans' benefits, just cheer and cheer when Wallace blames the government. The poor people of this state and the poor people of this county, particularly, are supported by the federal government, but George Wallace has been able to make them think the government is their greatest enemy.

The American people are ripe for Wallace's twisted message because their minds are confused. They don't understand the government or the system of economics of their own country.

In other countries you have the center and the right and the left, but in this country there is only a right and a center. The McCarthy years completely cut the left off. There is no left wing except for a few isolated groups who talk to each other. And there is no movement that people see as an alternative. Every other civilized country in the world has a left wing that believes in public ownership. There's no left wing in this country, and that's what makes it such a curious anomaly. Instead of looking to the government to help them out, the people look at the government as their great oppressor. In the meantime, the power of the corporations gets bigger and bigger and the multinationals get bigger and bigger. Yet according to Wallace the corporations are not the enemy; the government is the enemy. In other countries there are people who feel that way, but they're mostly the right-wingers who own stock in the corporations. Here we had the head of the labor movement, Meany, talking the same way. Even labor has subscribed to George Wallace's twisted message.

Although Wallace combines both the self-reliant pioneer spirit and the down-trodden poor white inferiority complex, it is the latter strain that he himself rose out of and now champions. He and Frank Johnson represent the two strains and exemplify the differences in them. Wallace and Johnson, both poor, both classmates at Alabama, came from different strains.

Frank Johnson lived in the northwestern part of the state in Winston County, in an almost classless society with very few blacks. Frank Johnson has a great deal of pride in himself and his father and his grandfather. He is a man of tremendous pride, just like Hugo Black, who came from Clay County. They were people you could admire. They worked hard. They were poor, but they were self-sufficient.

On the other hand, Wallace came from one of the oldest black-belt counties in the state, where there were great plantations and great white mansions. Eufaula had a society based on an aristocracy to which Wallace was never admitted. He was always made to feel inferior. His grandfather, Dr. Wallace, had been a man of some standing, but his father never succeeded. They were as poor as Job's turkey, and he was excluded. I don't think it hurt Frank Johnson one single bit not to be taken into a fraternity at the university. He didn't care. But I'm sure Wallace felt that he was again excluded.

The people who grew up in classless societies, where everybody was more or less on the same footing, had a rather pleasant life, a poor life but a pleasant one. But the people who grew up in a society like Eufaula, a river port with great mansions and beautiful ladies and beautiful horses—the people who grew up in that society but were not a part of it were looked down on. They were considered to be common or poor white trash. The major issue is not race or status but class. The very people who are looked down on, like poor whites, look down on the Negroes. That gives them some feeling of superiority because at least they're white, not black. But when the Negro is said to be as good as they are, they feel threatened.

It's that class difference, that economic difference, that still keeps the races apart. I don't think it's easier for white people and black people in the South to relate to each other. The history of the closeness of the two races, even though they were separate, just hasn't done that. After all, men and women have been very close to each other for several million years and women still don't have equal rights or equal opportunities. A man can be absolutely devoted to his wife and be a good husband and still not believe in equal rights for women because he doesn't think it's necessary. White people can be genuinely devoted to a black person, but I don't think you can form friendships and form connections except on an equal basis. And the Negro people in the South are not on an equal basis, by any means.

I find it difficult to relate to whites who've had absolutely no education, who are ignorant people. I feel sorry for them and yet I find it very difficult to relate to them. Cliff could do it much better than I could. I just run out of conversation. I don't believe you can relate to people on a personal basis unless there's equality. I don't think there can be real friendships and love relationships that are very deep unless it's on an equal basis. Beyond race, it's class. If you right every injustice and every discrimination against black people, there still would be a class difference. The same thing is true of women. Every law could be righted, but there'd still be a class difference, because men control the wealth of the country. Women may own wealth, but men are the ones who control it.

The great problem in this country, as it is all over the world, is the concentration of wealth and power in the hands of a few. Even in many socialist societies, while they've been able to give people a share of education or health, they certainly haven't been able to maintain a free and democratic society. Only a few people in the totalitarian socialist countries will struggle for free speech. Most simply accept the existing order because at least they're better off than they were before.

I find that true among the blacks. Issues of free speech have little appeal in the black community, because their minds are set on jobs. During the Vietnam War, I tried to get some of the blacks to protest against the war and with very little success, practically none. In fact, the black boys were joining up voluntarily, because they got paid and their dependents got money. Blacks in the South are not yet secure enough to feel there are other things more valuable than jobs.

There has always been a small number of people who have stood up and fought for what we consider to be basic democratic rights—free speech and elections. Most of the people who have done it have been people who have some kind of livelihood. When people are worried to death about where they're going to eat the next day they don't have much time to think about freedom of speech or freedom of religion. All of those freedoms were given to us by founding fathers who were pretty well off. The security you get from earning a decent living gives you time to think about other things.

I wish I could think this country was full of democratic spirit, but I saw it go through the cold war. I saw it go through McCarthyism. I saw it go through Dies and Jim Eastland. There were people who protested, but the great majority of people just took it. The protest of the Vietnam War was the biggest demonstration in recent years. I think that's because the young people didn't want to go off and die in a war they didn't believe in.

There were some young white Southerners who protested segregation, too, but not many. That wasn't a life-and-death matter for them. But there were a few brave white Southerners during the civil rights struggle, some federal judges, some preachers, and some businessmen who refused to be intimidated by George Wallace's demagoguery.

22

Getting the Next Thing Done

BETWEEN 1961 AND 1964 people from the Student Nonviolent Coordinating Committee, SNCC, began to come to our house. I met Jim Forman then. I never met Robert Moses, but I know that he's regarded as a living saint. Julian Bond's father, Dr. Horace Mann Bond, was a great friend of ours, and he said he thought Moses was the craziest guy he'd ever known. He thought he was a saintly figure who was trying to be crucified. Dr. Bond was a very practical man in most ways. He felt you had to deal with the situation as it was and he thought Bob Moses was trying to be like the biblical Moses leading people into the promised land—but not doing it very well.

During this period I belonged to the Women's International League for Peace and Freedom, which had a chapter in Atlanta. There were a few of us here, but very few. Mrs. Fletcher McLeod and I were the only white members in Montgomery. Many members from elsewhere came through Montgomery during the bus boycott, supporting the blacks. It was that old abolitionist strain. A lot of them were Quakers or Congregationalists. I went over to Atlanta for many of the meetings, and I became a great friend of Josephine Dibble, the head of the league. At one of these meetings she introduced me to Mrs. Horace Mann Bond. I said, "I don't know you, Mrs. Bond, but I have admired your husband ever since I read *Negro Education in Alabama*. I'm a great admirer of your husband." She asked me to come back and meet him and Julian, who was only sixteen then. They were trying to keep Julian in school, and he was determined to get out and get into SNCC.

I met Jim Forman on one of these trips to Atlanta through Dinkydonk, Decca's daughter, who had left Sarah Lawrence and was working in the movement in Atlanta in the SNCC office. Jim Forman was extremely pleasant, well mannered, and well dressed for those days. He was very anxious to get white support and he dealt with people, I thought, in a very diplomatic way. After I met him he began to send people to stay at our house, people like Tom Hayden, the fellow who ran for the Senate from California.

They were having a great deal of trouble in Albany, Georgia, in 1962. One night I got a telephone call from this young man who said his name was Tom Hayden. He said he had been arrested in Albany and had just gotten out of jail. He asked if he and a friend could spend the night with us. I don't know why our house was so full then, but it was. I said, "There's no place to sleep at all but on the floor. Literally, we don't have a bed vacant." He said, "Mrs. Durr, I've been sleeping on concrete for some time and a soft floor would do me." They got there late that night and they were the filthiest two boys I have ever seen. They smelled to high heaven. I had to hold my nose. They bathed and showered and we washed their clothes. Cliff provided them with pajamas. I don't think the fellows were lice-ridden, as some of the young people were, but they had been in jail for several weeks and were unbelievably dirty. And hungry—my God almighty! They ate as though they'd never seen food before. We couldn't fill them up. They only stayed a day or two.

Jim Forman would call me up from Atlanta and say somebody was going to Mississippi and wanted to spend the night in Montgomery and get to Mississippi in the daytime. I can't remember who all came through. I remember Tom Hayden because he became famous later on. These were young people whom I came to have a tremendous affection for because they were on the front line of the battle I was in. I found them to be delightful, warmhearted, good people. It was tremendous to have all these allies because we had so few in Montgomery. I was thrilled over that. Dinkydonk was like a daughter to me because she'd been born in my house and she would come over and bring a crowd to spend the night on the way to Mississippi. Dinkydonk was like her mother; she was determined to have her own way and wasn't scared of hell or high water.

During the sixties I saw a good deal of John Lewis, who became head of SNCC. He never stayed at our house, but I saw him in the courts. John Doar was in Montgomery at that time, too, trying a lot of cases, and he became a good friend. He was an assistant attorney general at the Justice Department. I would often listen to his cases. I became devoted to John Lewis, who was an Alabama boy, and to John Doar.

What bothered me the most was the growing disaffection with Martin Luther King among these young people. I had a great admiration for King. I liked him and I thought he was doing all that a man could do, but the young people by the time of the Selma march had grown dissatisfied. They thought his method of marches and nonviolence was too slow. Jim Forman, especially, was very critical of King. I spent a lot of time arguing with Jim about King and what he'd done, what a great man he was. A split was developing—a split between the young people in SNCC and the older church people who were following Martin Luther King.

I didn't go to Washington in 1963. I didn't have the money to go anywhere in those days, very much. Of course, I saw it on TV, and I kept up with it through the young people—people like Casey. Casey was from Texas and had been married to Tom Hayden. She came through and stayed with us quite a while, and I liked her very much. Through Casey and the other young civil rights workers coming through Montgomery, we kept up with what was going on.

Cliff and I were beginning to ease out of the Presbyterian Church by then. We hadn't broken entirely. Mainly we were going up to Pea Level every weekend. We were looking forward to moving there when Cliff retired. And he did retire in 1962. His law practice had gotten to the point where we were lending clients money rather than making any ourselves. We had an enormous number of clients, mostly black, but they never could pay us anything. We also had Negroes come in and say, "Mr. Durr, I used to cut grass for your sister, Miss Kate. And I'm in trouble." They never expected to pay a dime for Cliff's help because they thought the family should look after them. We lived such a split-level life. It's a wonder we were able to stay as sane as we did—or as solvent. We were living in the old South, with a lot of Negroes who depended on the Durr family as they had for years and years. They looked to us to get them out of jail or to get them in the hospital or lend them money. They were relics of the past, of slavery really.

Cliff never got bitter, but he did get disappointed and disillusioned. A lot of people who were cheating the Negroes on their insurance and on their loans and automobiles were members of the leading families of Montgomery. I went to a dinner one night and one of them sat by me. He turned to me and said, "Cliff thinks I'm just a loan shark, doesn't he?" Well, Cliff did think he was a loan shark, the lousiest loan shark in Montgomery. I said, "Oh, no. He thinks you're one of the fine young men." So it was a very strange kind of a double life that we lived. I look back on it now and wonder that we stayed sane. We had each other, and we had the children, although none of them was at home. And we did have support from friends in the North. Corliss Lamont occasionally sent us a thousand dollars, and others sent us money, too.

By the summer of 1965, at the time of the Selma march, we knew a lot of people all over the country who were concerned about race relations in the South. I was in Harrisburg, Pennsylvania, with my daughter Ann when the march started and the first incident happened. We saw on TV the first beatings at the bridge, where John Lewis was so beaten up and the marchers were pursued on horses with cattle prods. I was frightfully shocked at that. Then Dr. King put out a national call for people to come.

I came home and soon began to get telephone calls from people who were coming in to Selma. The first call was from C. Vann Woodward, the Sterling professor at Yale. He and Lou Pollak, dean of the Yale Law School, were coming down and they wanted to know if they could get a bed at our house. Tom Emerson's son, who was also a great friend of ours and a professor at Yale Law School, came down. Then John Beecher called from San Francisco. He was with a San Francisco paper that engaged him to cover the Selma march. Carl Braden came in with an Episcopal preacher, and then a group called the Brotherhood came down. The house was just full of people, absolutely full. I spent all my time making coffee and frying bacon and eggs for them. An injunction delayed the march for a week, and all these thousands of people who had gathered were rather at loose ends— the ones in Montgomery particularly.

This was when Forman and King finally had an open break. Forman wanted to march on the capitol and all of his followers were in Montgomery, with headquarters in Martin Luther King's church. They later went to another church. Jim at that time had thousands of followers and he had changed completely. He never wore anything but overalls and he'd grown a beard. He was entirely different from the young man I had first met. He was becoming a man of the people, so to speak. Jim was the inspiration for the marches in Montgomery—including the one with the famous episode at the capitol. The capitol police wouldn't let the marchers on anything that they controlled, which was the steps to the capitol and the sidewalks. And the Montgomery police wouldn't let them in the street. So they had a pee-in. Can you imagine anything more shocking? If they went to the capitol to go to the bathroom, they were arrested. If they went down the street to the Dexter Avenue Baptist Church, they were arrested. They were caught between the capitol police and the city police, so they gathered in a great ring with their backs turned to the populace and had a pee-in. This was an all-male performance. This was rather shocking to the people of Montgomery, and the followers of Martin Luther King thought all these young people were wild.

Then the Selma march finally began, and the writer Studs Terkel was here that day. He was taking down brief conversations. One of the funniest ones he had was with the society editor of the *Advertiser*, Madera Spencer. She's an extremely sweet, nice woman, but she's one of those lovely Southern types who just ignore things. Unpleasant things don't exist because she doesn't recognize them. As the black people were marching up Dexter Avenue and King was making his speech and they were all singing "We Shall Overcome," Studs interviewed Madera. She said to him that Montgomery was really the most social place in the South because they had more cocktail parties and more masked balls and more of the loveliest entertainment than any city in the South—even more, she thought, than New Orleans. All the time, you could hear "We Shall Overcome" and Martin Luther King in the background. Finally Terkel said, "Well, Miss Spencer, do you ever discuss the problem?" And she said, "No. We don't discuss problems like that. The people who go out in society in Montgomery are purely social."

Studs interviewed everybody who came to my house, too, and he played it all on a tape on his radio program in Chicago. He interviewed Polly Dobbs, who came all the way from California to the march. She had come from a very poor white family up in Jefferson County. She told about her life and what the march meant to her. She thought poor whites were treated just as badly as the blacks. Another friend of mine, a Jewish woman, was there helping me with coffee and helping me feed this vast lot of people. She talked to Studs, too, but she said, "Don't you ever use my name because I would be in bad with all my relatives and friends." That tape is nameless.

After the Selma march was over, after everyone had gone, we got the aftermath. Telephone calls started. It seems that John Beecher was regarded as the biggest hippy who had come. He arrived in a flowing cape with a beret and he rented a red Mustang, so he was rather outstanding.

The day the march ended we were sitting in our living room. With us were Lou Pollak, C. Vann Woodward, Carl Braden, who had been a labor agitator for I don't know how many years, an Episcopal preacher whom Braden had brought with him, and the members of the Brotherhood, who took up with us. We never did get all their names straight. Some of them were German and they were very religious and prayed a great deal. And we had a young couple—the boy had just gotten out of jail on a hunger strike and he was in very bad shape. They sort of clung together. He couldn't even drink milk, kept throwing it up because he'd been on this hunger strike so long. All these people were at our house the night that Mrs. Viola Liuzzo was killed. John Beecher got a call from someone on the *San Francisco Chronicle* who told him a white woman had been killed over near Lowndesboro. John got in his little red Mustang with a young English boy who was staying with us named Nicholas and drove lickety-split. Nicholas said they never went below ninety miles an hour. They got to Highway 80 in Lowndesboro, where she'd been killed. She had been ferrying back some of the marchers, and she was coming to get another load when she was killed. A carload of people pulled up beside the car she was driving and fired into the car and shot her.

After everybody cleared out and things began to settle down, the story got around all over Montgomery of the rapes that had taken place in Selma and on the trips from Selma to Montgomery—not only rapes but sexual orgies. The crazies put out pamphlets saying that nuns weren't nuns and priests weren't priests; they were just pimps and prostitutes who'd come down here. They said there'd been a wholesale rape at the black hotel in Montgomery. One girl had been raped forty-seven times. Mrs. Rutledge, who was living in Lillian, came up to Montgomery to a church meeting and all she heard about was these women and girls who had been raped—one of them forty-seven times. That's when she made the attractive remark, "Well, I think the poor dear would have done better if she'd screamed rather than counted."

I called up every police station. I called the sheriff's office. I called every hospital. And there was not one case of rape that was brought into the hospital. The stories were just ridiculous, but I met one dear old lady on Dexter Avenue who claimed otherwise.

"Virginia," she said, "I understand you had some of that scum staying at your house."

"Well, I hardly think that the dean of the Yale Law School and the Sterling Professor of History at Yale are exactly scum."

"They're scum to me." She explained, "I saw what other people just talked about. I saw it. I was right here on Dexter Avenue and I saw a black boy and a white girl licking the same ice cream cone."

The criticism went much farther than that. I went to a doctor whom I had a great respect for and really liked very much. I thought he was a brilliant man, yet he believed every word of this gossip. It was very odd. It changed our whole relationship. I couldn't feel the same way about him. He said, "Well, now, Mrs. Durr, I'm not going to argue because I know how you feel about it, but the goings on that went on. . . ."

What was so interesting to me—so terrifying—is that it always got down to sexual relations between a black man and a white woman. The fact was that the marchers slept on the ground, and the cold mud of Lowndes County is not very conducive to loving warmth, I wouldn't think. But people pictured the whole thing as a terrible sexual orgy.

Things began to level out after the Selma march. Lyndon Johnson's 1965 Voting Rights Act had the greatest effect in bringing an end to the violence and turbulence. Lyndon in my opinion was wrong on the Vietnam War and the Dominican Republic. Foreign policy was not Lyndon's strong point. But on the domestic scene I think Lyndon did a great deal of good. He got the Voting Rights Act through, which Kennedy hadn't been able to do. He was so proud of getting that act passed. When the blacks got the vote and began to vote in large numbers and had some power, then things began to quiet down.

The Voting Rights Act was passed in 1965. But the great dilemma now is that with the freedom to vote, look how people vote. I fought for all these years to get people the right to vote. It had been my life's work. Now women can vote and blacks can vote and poor people can vote. Even illiterates can vote. I feel that we won a great victory. At the same time I feel that the victory is hollow because it hasn't brought about—particularly for the blacks—the things they expected.

Cliff believed in the law. He believed that a lawful society where men knew what to expect was the answer. And of course Hugo was finally transmuted into almost a public prophet of the law. But I believed in politics. I felt that the vote and the people's participation in politics was the answer to our problems. Neither law nor politics proved to be the answer. The young whites and the young blacks are disillusioned with both.

We had a terrible experience over at Tuskegee that brought home to us this disenchantment of the young people. Dr. Gomillion, a professor at Tuskegee Institute, had been Cliff's and my dear friend for forty-five years. He started the voting movement among the blacks in Alabama there in Tuskegee. *Gomillion* v. *Lightfoot* is one of the classic cases in the Supreme Court, and books have been written about it. Dr. Gomillion is one of the gentlest, most dignified, most perfect Southern gentlemen.

Lewis Jones at Tuskegee, whom I'd known from the Highlander way back in the thirties, is one of the funniest people in the world. Both Dr. Gomillion and Lewis Jones had been great friends of Aubrey's, so we used to see them quite often at his house. They invited Cliff and me over to Tuskegee in the early seventies to speak to Lewis Jones's class in sociology. Cliff was to speak about the law, and I was to speak about politics and how people got the vote in Alabama, with particular reference to Tuskegee.

We drove over to Tuskegee and went into this rather large room with about twenty-five young blacks of both sexes sitting around. Lewis Jones introduced us, and I must say, he introduced us very favorably. He talked about his long knowledge of us and how we stood by in the fight and so on. Dr. Gomillion came and sat in on the class, too. Cliff, being the perfect Southern gentleman, said, "I'll let my wife speak first." As I began, I could feel a sense of hostility in the room, a sense of coldness, nonresponse, but I began anyway. I said, "I don't want to bore you young people with a two-hour seminar by telling you the things that you already know. I'd like to know how many people here have read and know about the case of *Gomillion* v. *Lightfoot*." Not one of them had ever read the case or ever heard of the book about that case. "My goodness, that's too bad because this is about Macon County and it's about the long struggle for the right to vote that Dr. Gomillion led." No response at all. "Have you ever read DuBois's book, *The Souls of Black Folks*? I think that is also one of the great classics that everybody should read." Nobody'd ever heard of it. "Have you read Dr. Horace Mann Bond's book, *Negro Education in Alabama*, which I also consider one of the great classics of Alabama history?" Nobody'd ever heard of that.

A young girl was sitting right behind me and all of a sudden she said, "You old lady, we don't want to hear you anyway. You just coming down here to take us down. 'Have we read this? Have we read that?' You just coming here to take us down. We know what kind of folks you are. We don't want to hear you." With that the whole class joined in: "No, we don't want to hear no white folks." I was shocked beyond words. I had never been treated that way in my life by black or white, with just open, insulting repudiation. I thought Lewis Jones would certainly bring them to order, but he didn't.

There was a girl in the back of the classroom who was flapping a book. She had gotten a great big book and she kept flapping the pages. I said, "I really can't say anything until the young lady over there stops making so much noise."

"I'll make all the noise I want to. I don't want to hear no white folks anyway."

Lewis did say, at that point, "Miss So-and-so, if you can't be quiet, you'll have to leave the room." So she got up and left the room. I thought everybody else would get up and leave the room, too.

Finally I said, "Now look, there are twenty-three people here. Each one of you has made it perfectly plain to me that you don't care one single thing about what I have to say." What I was so terrified of at that point was that Cliff might rise up and defend his wife and just blast them because I was being so insulted, so openly. I kept saying to him, "Please, please, don't say anything." Dr. Gomillion and Dr. Jones both looked as though they were in shock. I said to the students, "You've made it perfectly plain to me that you don't want to hear anything I have to say, but I am very eager to hear what you have to say. If you don't think we came to talk about the right to vote. . . ."

"That don't mean nothing!"

I asked, "Well, what does mean something? Mainly, I want to know why all of you hate me so much. You've never seen me before. I'm an old lady." I was sixty-nine or seventy then. "You never saw me before. You don't know anything about me. You're just expressing all this hatred for me because I'm white, which I can't help but be. Why do you hate me so much?"

I took each in turn and they told me why they hated white people. One of them was a veteran and something had happened to him in Vietnam and he hated white folks. The twenty-three black kids who were sitting there each told me in detail why they hated white folks. This took quite a while because they were extremely articulate about why they hated white folks.

I said, "You don't believe that politics is going to do you any good?" No. They said the big shots, the black leaders, in Tuskegee were just as bad as white folks any day. The black mayor and the black sheriff and the black people who'd been elected were no better than the whites before them. "What about Greene County?" I asked.

"They're a bunch of crooks, too. They're no good."

"You don't believe that politics is going to help your position at all?"

"No, not at all."

"Do any of you vote? Have you been registered?" None of them had even registered.

Cliff hadn't had a chance to speak on the law, but I did say, "Do you think that the law, the federal courts, have helped you any?"

"They don't amount to nothing either."

"Well, then you tell me what you think the solution is." And they gave me their solution—and this was unanimous.

"Eldridge Cleaver's coming back and we're going to take it away from the white folks. We're going to take what they got. We want what the white folks have got."

"In other words, you see the solution as economic?"

"We want what the white folks got."

The meeting ended on that note. They didn't give a damn about politics or about the right to vote or the right to sit down in a bus. It was like the time I asked young Donny, who worked for me on Saturdays, "Haven't you ever heard about the big struggle for desegregation of the buses?" "Huh, Mrs. Durr, who wants to ride on a bus? I want a car of my own."

They have absolutely no trust or faith in law or politics. They want a car. They want a good house. They want a job. They want opportunity to rise in the world. Eldridge Cleaver was coming back and he was going to have a revolution. Cleaver had married a girl from Tuskegee whose father was on the faculty and at that time he was in Algeria. Of course, Eldridge Cleaver has come back, but he's a totally different man. That class in Tuskegee was, in a way, the most painful moment of my life, because I felt that they didn't give a damn about all I'd worked so hard for.

We went to dinner with Dr. Gomillion and Dr. Jones afterward. I was quite upset by the rudeness, and they were, too. But you know what they told me? They said, "Virginia, we have the same experience in class ourselves all the time." Dr. Gomillion, who had been the pioneer of the struggle for the right to vote, said they had no respect for him at all, for what he'd done. He said, "I was surprised they didn't all get up and walk out when you asked that girl to stop flapping the pages of her book." Lewis Jones said the same thing: "I was surprised they didn't walk out. I have the same problem. It's become a class struggle now, not a race struggle, for these young blacks."

I don't know about the young whites so much, how they feel, but those young blacks hated the big shots, as they called them, in the black community as much as they hated the ones in the white community. The race issue had become a class issue. They didn't seem to have any strategy, but they knew what they wanted. They wanted what white folks had. They wanted all the good things of life that well-off white people had.

Yet there has been a great change in Alabama since the early 1960s. The change has come so fast really. Despite all the rioting and all the Klan and White Citizens' Council activity, Southerners accepted integration once it finally happened. I remember going to Morrison's Cafeteria the first day it was integrated, and nobody paid the slightest attention to the black people eating there. The South has reacted to integration far better than I expected. The South went through a terrible struggle, but Southern people accepted it remarkably well in the end.

It's interesting, too, how one effort relates to another. I believe that the struggle of the blacks against segregation led to the women's movement. The women who took part in that struggle for black emancipation began to realize that they weren't very well emancipated either. When your husband disassociates himself from you because you have been to a prayer meeting, you're not very free to go to those meetings.

We used to go to meetings over at Mrs. Tilly's in Atlanta. These sweet church women, black and white, were scared to death of their husbands. The white women were always terrified. Sometimes they would lie and wouldn't let their husbands know where they were going, because their husbands were afraid their wives' going to such meetings would hurt their business. The women began to realize that they weren't emancipated either—that they were pretty well held down. If you go to any of the Southern women's movement meetings, you would be surprised at the amount of passion that comes forth. They really feel held down and they are trying to break loose.

There has been a tremendous change in the South. Just the fact of integration has changed everything. You see blacks in restaurants and hotels and the movies and on the buses. If they can pay for it, they can go any place they want to. That is a tremendous change. It's hard to imagine that a black person couldn't even get a book out of the library. It has been a tremendous change to see blacks able to go anywhere they want to if they can pay for it.

But now that integration is accomplished, the young black people want economic equality. The whole struggle has entered an entirely new stage, of which I'm not really a part. The things that I believe in, the law and the vote, have not brought about the change the young people are demanding. I don't know how to bring about those changes. I certainly don't believe in revolution. I don't think the people know what they want. The idea of public ownership is anathema because people no longer trust their own government.

I believe the saddest thing that's happened to this country is that young people have never had a feeling of belief and trust in their own government—the feeling that your government is on your side. That is the great loss in the country to me, the fact that people have lost faith in their own

Virginia with Rosa Parks at the fiftieth anniversary of the Highlander Folk School, Tennessee, October 1982. (Photograph by Tom Gardner, Montgomery, Alabama)

government. And what can you tell people? The corporations control the government and the people don't seem to have any control over the government at all. I don't know what's going to be the end of it.

Cliff didn't know what the end of it was going to be. He believed in change by political means. He finally came to believe that the government had to control the corporations. He didn't go as far as I did in wanting the government to take them over. He never became a socialist, but he thought the corporations all ought to be licensed under a federal license.

But I don't believe the corporations can be controlled. I think they're bigger than the government. I think the difference in Cliff's attitude and mine is that I grew up in Birmingham where the Tennessee Coal, Iron and Railroad Company completely controlled the town. We were prosperous when they were, and we were poor when they shut down. They were able to elect anybody they wanted to. They controlled the legislature. I grew up knowing that a corporation controlled by a foreign, absentee landlord could control a whole city and everybody in it, financially and politically.

But Cliff grew up in Montgomery, which was entirely different. There were a lot of little businesses. He never had that feeling that the corporation could take control. He was upset about the multinational corporations, the ones that were extending all over the world, but he never did quite arrive at the point of believing in socialism, because he thought it concentrated too much power. He read *Khrushchev Remembers* and he was terrified of dictatorships and tyranny and loss of democratic rights. He didn't know what the solution was going to be, and neither do I.

I won't live long enough to see the resolution of it. From now on out, it's going to be just one hell of a struggle. And it's going to be waged on a different plane. I think we're in very great danger of having a corporate state, which I hope won't develop into a police or fascist state.

I'm glad I did what I did, and I think what I did was right. I think what Cliff did was right. I think our efforts brought the South forward to a degree. I think the terrible segregation and the setting aside of the blacks is over with. But the blacks themselves are so dissatisfied, the young blacks. Over in Atlanta when I was there, I asked the young blacks what they thought about Maynard Jackson. "Just a big shot." It's so strange.

The women's movement hasn't gotten to be economic at all. They want to be free and they want to get equal justice, but they don't want to change anything. They just want to be equally represented. I haven't been in any women's group that believes in change in the economic system.

I wish I could be more cheerful and end on an upbeat note and say, "We're all going into the land of Canaan now. We've been through the desert and we've crossed the . . ." But I'm like Moses. I glimpsed the promised land, but I never got there, and I never will. It's sad, because I would like very much to live long enough to see a change come about, a really fundamental change. I don't think I ever will, because I think it's going to take an awfully long time. And I'm afraid before any fundamental change takes place we're going to have a dictatorial, corporate state.

I have seen a process of change developing. I have seen the Negroes waking up and beginning to protest against their lot. I've seen women waking up and beginning to protest against their lot. I saw the labor movement rise up and begin to protest against labor's lot. To me that was the most thrilling thing of all, but look at labor today. Now what the unions believe in is more military spending so they can get more jobs for the people. On many issues, labor is one of the most reactionary forces in the country.

Life has a strange irony. You fight for something—like the right to vote in the South. Give the Negroes and the poor folks the right to vote. And you win. And then they elect George Wallace. You fight for the right of women to get representation and they elect Lurleen Wallace. I've seen all of the things that I fought for turn out not to be the answer—certainly not the final answer.

In Birmingham not too long ago I ran into Roland Cooper. He's dead now. He was from Wilcox County and he was such a segregationist. He got a book removed from the library, a little children's book about a black rabbit and a white rabbit that played together and finally produced black and white rabbits. He was so shocked by the idea of a black rabbit having sexual relations with a white rabbit that he had the book removed from the shelves. Just by chance at a Democratic party meeting in Birmingham I was walking across to the big hall with him. He didn't know me, and I didn't know him. We were both saying, "Where do we go? Which door do we go in? This whole thing's so big." Finally I said, "I'm Mrs. Durr. What is your name?"

"My name is Cooper, Roland Cooper from Wilcox County." He was then probate judge.

"Good God," I said, "you know you've been one of the worst enemies I've ever had. I've been fighting you ever since I've been in Alabama."

He was very nice; he said, "I know who you are. You're Hugo Black's sister-in-law and Cliff Durr's wife. Well, Mrs. Durr, you know, you-all won."

That was a satisfactory note to end on, to say we won. What we won was, we got the vote and we got segregation abolished, but now there's a whole new fight to fight. The only thing I regret is I won't be here to fight it.

We have to have another economic system. There's no doubt about that. The economic system we have now is insane. What I want is a just economic system but a democratic system, which of course may be asking for the world with a ring around it. I get horrified at the things the Russians do. I get horrified at the things the Chinese do, although they're the ones we consider to be so wonderful these days. The idea of living in a society in which I couldn't say what I wanted to, I couldn't print what I wanted to, and I couldn't buy magazines, and I couldn't hear things—to my mind that would be a horrible society. Even if I did have food and housing and education and hospitalization, it would be a horrible system.

I've been a very fortunate person. In spite of the hard times we've had, I've always felt that I've been in the group that ran the country. It's very difficult to explain without sounding snobbish, but I've always felt I belonged to the ruling class. But I don't feel any more that that group is leading the country in the right way.

It's up to the young people to change things. There are certain things you can't change. One of them is, you can't change your sex. A few people do, but that's very odd. You can't change your color. And you certainly can't change getting old. You can fight against it all you please, but you get old just the same. You have to learn to accept old age and you have to learn to accept death. It's the hardest thing in the world to learn to do. In the end, we're all going to die. The young people who come on are the only hope we have. The only life, I believe, after death is what you have been able to leave with the generations that come after you.

I think Cliff has left a great deal. I'd say I have left a little, but Cliff has left a great deal. It's a terrible, hard thing to learn, and you never think about it when you're young. Death never crossed my mind until I got to be about seventy. Literally, I never thought about dying. I never thought about Cliff's dying. I just thought we were going on forever and a day. Young people never think about dying. That's why it seems so stupid, all the killing and fighting and blowing people up and massacring people and burning them up in ovens, when they're going to die anyway, eventually.

I don't know that the human race will ever learn that. They've given in on segregation and they've given in on a good many things—like old age pensions and medicaid and medicare. But when it comes to taking their property, this is where they're going to fight. Think about the South fighting for slavery. There were so few slaveowners and yet the whole South went to war to fight for these few, because they were made to feel it was their struggle. And that's what you see today. The corporations get bigger and bigger and more and more powerful, yet they persuade people that they represent free enterprise, that they're what you've got to fight for. All I can say is, to be young and alive is the greatest thing in the world.

As difficult as life was for us in Alabama at times, it was never dull because we were so busy—busy just trying to make ends meet and busy fighting for things we believed in. Two or three times Cliff had offers from universities to come north and I would beg him to take them, but he wouldn't. He would never even think about it. I am sure I made his life miserable trying to get him to leave. I had been raised wanting everybody to love me and admire me like all of the Southern girls, so I found it much harder to take the ostracism than he did. And it was particularly hard on the children. They got scholarships to schools in the North, but they were so miserable. I minded that terribly. But Cliff would wake up every morning and say, "Thank God I am back in Alabama." I used to say to him, "What in the world do you say that for every morning?" He would make the same reply every morning. It got to be a joke. He said, "Well, in Alabama I know who the s.o.b.s are. When you go up North, you don't know who they are. They'll hit you from every side. You don't know who they are. But back here in Alabama I know who they are and I can more or less protect myself." He loved it. It was his. He felt that he owned Alabama. It was his. The South was his. He didn't regard the Southern people as his enemy or the South as his enemy. It was his, and if they did wrong, well, that was his fault, too.

Now, I'm Presbyterian. I knew that the things we were working for were right. When times get bad, you only have one thing to fall back on— that you believe in what you are doing. I knew that Cliff was right and I knew that I was right. To have an atomic war against Russia—what could

Virginia Foster Durr, still exuberant and still cheerful.

be worse than that? To go against the American Constitution and the Bill of Rights and haul people up in secret meetings—what could be worse than that? To deny people the right to vote? How could that be right?

My children, as they reached young adulthood, would sometimes say they wished I had stayed at home and baked brownies as other mothers did. But what good were brownies in a society that tolerated poverty and denied people the education to enable them to get out of poverty? What good were brownies in a society that denied people the right to vote?

When things get rough, if you don't believe in what you are doing, then you might as well give up. That's the one thing that keeps you going. People would say, "How do you know you are right? Why do you think that you have the wisdom of the ages?" Well, if you don't believe in what you are doing, why do you do it? You don't get anything out of it. You certainly don't get fame or glory or money or high position. You just do it because you believe it is right.

I was so busy all the time that I never had much time to think about any role I played in anything that happened. In the first place, we had very little money. All these civil rights cases that Cliff took didn't bring him much income, so we had a very small income. I was his secretary, and I had the house to run. I had three children to educate, and I had to work in my husband's office from 8:30 in the morning till late at night. I did have a young woman who would come in and do the ironing, and the children helped, but I still had lots of housework to do. I never even thought about what role I was playing. I was just trying to get the next thing done, whether it meant getting out a brief or getting the next meal on, just trying to get through the next thing that had to be done.

INDEX